# Online and Distance Education
for a Connected World

# Online and Distance Education for a Connected World

Edited by
Linda Amrane-Cooper,
David Baume, Stephen Brown,
Stylianos Hatzipanagos, Philip Powell,
Sarah Sherman and Alan Tait

**⁂UCL**PRESS

First published in 2023 by
UCL Press
University College London
Gower Street
London WC1E 6BT

Available to download free: www.uclpress.co.uk

Collection © Editors, 2023
Text © Contributors, 2023
Images © Contributors and copyright holders named in captions, 2023

The editors and contributors have asserted their rights under the Copyright, Designs and Patents Act 1988 to be identified as the authors of this work.

A CIP catalogue record for this book is available from The British Library

Any third-party material in this book is not covered by the book's Creative Commons licence. Details of the copyright ownership and permitted use of third-party material is given in the image (or extract) credit lines. If you would like to reuse any third-party material not covered by the book's Creative Commons licence, you will need to obtain permission directly from the copyright owner.

This book is published under a Creative Commons Attribution-Non-Commercial 4.0 International licence (CC BY-NC 4.0), https://creativecommons.org/licenses/by-nc/4.0/. This licence allows you to share and adapt the work for non-commercial use providing attribution is made to the author and publisher (but not in any way that suggests that they endorse you or your use of the work) and any changes are indicated. Attribution should include the following information:

Amrane-Cooper, L., Baume, D., Brown, S., Hatzipanagos, S., Powell, P., Sherman, S. and Tait, A. (eds.) 2023. *Online and Distance Education for a Connected World*. London: UCL Press. https://doi.org/10.14324/111.9781800084797

Further details about Creative Commons licences are available at http://creativecommons.org/licenses/

ISBN: 978-1-80008-481-0 (Hbk.)
ISBN: 978-1-80008-480-3 (Pbk.)
ISBN: 978-1-80008-479-7 (PDF)
ISBN: 978-1-80008-482-7 (epub)
DOI: https://doi.org/10.14324/111.9781800084797

# Contents

| | |
|---|---|
| *List of figures* | ix |
| *List of tables* | xi |
| *Notes on editors and contributors* | xiii |
| *Preface: learning from over 150 years of distance education*<br>*Mary Stiasny and Michael Davis* | xxiii |
| *Centre for Online and Distance Education*<br>*Linda Amrane-Cooper* | xxxi |
| 1 Online, distance, blended. It's all just education<br>*Stephen Brown* | 1 |
| **Section 1** Planning distance education | 13 |
| Introduction to Section 1<br>*Stephen Brown* | 15 |
| 2 The student voice<br>*Pete Cannell and Julie Voce* | 19 |
| 3 Exploring digital learning<br>*J. Simon Rofe* | 35 |
| 4 Marketing digital education for an inclusive learning society<br>*Endrit Kromidha and Benedetta Cappellini* | 49 |
| 5 Supporting employability<br>*David Winter* | 64 |
| 6 Strategic models for distance education<br>*Philip Powell, Mary Stiasny and Michael Davis* | 95 |
| 7 Open and distance learning in Nigeria: a case study<br>*Stephen Brown and David Baume* | 118 |

**Section 2** Doing distance education         131

    Introduction to Section 2         133
    *Stephen Brown*

8  Course design, pedagogy and staff development         139
   *David Baume and Matthew Philpott*

9  Interactive social learning and fostering learning communities         167
   *Ayona Silva-Fletcher and Christine Thuranira-McKeever*

10  The Icarus simulation tool: a case study         187
    *Lynsie Chew and Alan Parkinson*

11  Digitally supported assessment         195
    *Leo Havemann, Simon Katan, Edward Anstead,*
    *Marco Gillies, Joanna Stroud and Sarah Sherman*

12  Taking assessment online – systems, issues and practices:
    a case study         211
    *Linda Amrane-Cooper, David Baume, Stylianos Hatzipanagos,*
    *Gwyneth Hughes and Alan Tait*

13  Inclusive practice         227
    *Shoshi Ish-Horowicz, Diana Maniati, Nicholas Charlton,*
    *Danielle Johnstone, Beatrice Hyams, Sarah Sherman*
    *and Sarah Gonnet*

14  Retention and success: approaches and tools for making a
    difference         253
    *Gwyneth Hughes and Joanne Harris*

15  MOOCs for public health: a case study         277
    *Sally Parsley and Daksha Patel*

16  Practising open education         293
    *Daksha Patel, Sally Parsley, Pete Cannell and Leo Havemann*

17  Building the online library         320
    *Matthew Philpott, Sandra Tury and Shoshi Ish-Horowicz*

**Section 3** Researching and evaluating distance education 353

    Introduction to Section 3 355
    *Stephen Brown*

18  Academic development, research and practice in online and distance education 357
    *David Baume*

19  Monitoring and evaluating online and distance education 383
    *David Baume*

20  Designing the future 407
    *Stephen Brown*

*Index* 434

# List of figures

5.1 The Advance HE framework for embedding employability within HE 65
6.1 Stakeholder salience model 104
12.1 Focus of project evaluation Source: Authors. 214
15.1 Quality evaluated throughout the MOOC production cycle 280

# List of tables

| | | |
|---|---|---|
| 5.1 | Distance students' intended career transitions and employability needs | 75 |
| 6.1 | Is e-learning strategic? | 101 |
| 8.1 | Bloom's taxonomy | 152 |
| 9.1 | Key features to maximise learner participation in an asynchronous online discussion forum | 172 |
| 10.1 | Questions/focus areas in purposive sampling survey and responses | 192 |
| 12.1 | Findings and implications: student behaviours | 215 |
| 12.2 | Findings and implications: student sentiment from survey and interviews | 216 |
| 12.3 | Findings and implications: academic integrity | 221 |
| 12.4 | Findings and implications: academic sentiment (from programme director interviews) | 222 |
| 12.5 | Findings and implications: academic sentiment (from examiner survey) | 224 |
| 14.1 | Breakdown of high achievers' engagement in discussion forum and peer review (n=15) | 259 |
| 14.2 | Breakdown of moderate achievers' engagement in discussion forum and peer review (n=18) | 259 |
| 14.3 | Breakdown of low achievers' engagement in discussion forum and peer review (n=19) | 260 |
| 15.1 | Global Blindness user types: target learners and key stakeholders | 281 |
| 15.2 | Three examples of Global Blindness users' goals and needs | 281 |
| 19.1 | Goals for 11 stages of engagement | 389 |

# Notes on editors and contributors

**Linda Amrane-Cooper** is Director of the University of London's (UoL's) Centre for Online and Distance Education (CODE) and Director of Academic Practice in Distance Education at the university. She leads the PG Learning and Teaching in HE programme. Prior to joining UoL, Linda was Dean and Head of Glasgow Caledonian University's London campus and Dean of the Royal Docks Business School at the University of East London. She moved into the business discipline after a long career in education and social science, where roles included Associate Dean of Education and International Lead and Head of Initial Teacher Training.

**Edward Anstead** is a lecturer in Computer Science at Goldsmiths, UoL. His research specialism is in human computer interaction with a particular focus on group practices, interaction with video and photographic media and learning technologies. He has developed several modules for both online and on campus settings, including Sleuth, a film noir-themed platform for teaching rudiments of code. With deployments on the Coursera platform and in use as a campus teaching tool, it has reached over 25,000 players to date and provided a platform for understanding the impact of gamified learning on programming students.

**David Baume** was founding chair of the UK Staff and Educational Development Association (SEDA); co-founder of the UK Heads of Educational Development Group; a founding council member of the International Consortium for Educational Development; and founding editor of the *International Journal for Academic Development*. Since 2001 he has been an independent international higher education researcher, evaluator, consultant, staff and educational developer and writer. He is a member of the Executive Committee of SEDA. David was previously Director of the Centre for Higher Education Practice at the UK Open University. He has been a CODE fellow since 2010.

**Stephen Brown** is Emeritus Professor of Learning Technologies at De Montfort University, a CODE fellow at UoL and Director of the learning media design consultancy Hyperworks Ltd. His career includes Head of the School of Media and Communication at De Montfort University, Senior Technology Adviser for Jisc, Head of Distance Learning at BT, Royal Academy of Engineering Visiting Professor in Engineering Design at Queen's University Belfast and the University of Ulster and President of the Association for Learning Technology. His research interests span distance learning, learning technologies, media design and digital humanities.

**Pete Cannell** is a freelance educational researcher and Associate Lecturer in Mathematics with the Open University (OU). Based in Scotland, he has worked in the field of open and distance education for 35 years. He was Depute Director (Learning, Teaching and Curriculum) at the OU in Scotland from 2005 to 2014. From 2014 to 2017 he was co-director of the Scottish Funding Council's Scotland-wide Opening Educational Practice in Scotland project (OEPS) and he is currently the chair of SCAPP (Scotland's Community of Access and Participation Practitioners). He has particular interests in widening participation, open educational practice and distance learning.

**Benedetta Cappellini** is Professor of Marketing at the University of Durham and director of the Executive MBA. She is a qualitative researcher and has published extensively on consumer culture, food consumption and gender. She is an associate editor of the *Journal of Marketing Management* and a member of the editorial board of *Marketing Theory*. She is interested in distance education and has been a fellow of the Centre for Online and Distance Education, UoL.

**Nicholas Charlton** has a background spanning education, learning technology, science and conservation. He previously worked at UoL as a Learning Technologist and, as part of their Inclusive Practice Panel for three years, helped to progress the accessibility of online learning agenda. He currently resides in Auckland, New Zealand, working within conservation education.

**Lynsie Chew** is Associate Professor in Accounting Education at UCL School of Management (SoM), a UoL CODE fellow and Programme Director of the MSc Professional Accountancy, a UoL-UCL online programme aimed at qualified accountants around the world. She regularly contributes to the design and delivery of executive education and CPD. She is co-editor/co-author of over five textbooks and actively engages in international accounting and education scholarship activities. She is a key member of the team that developed an innovative and unique business simulation, Icarus, which won Gold Award for Best Learning Simulation at the 2017 UK National Learning Technology Awards.

**Michael Davis** has worked at UoL for around 20 years in various management roles relating to Teaching Centres liaison and support, the Undergraduate Laws Programme and policy analysis and development. His professional interests relate primarily to trends in recognition of open and online distance learning qualifications, quality assurance in transnational education and collaborative provision.

**Marco Gillies** is Reader in Computing at Goldsmiths, UoL, and a CODE fellow. He was one of the founders of the BSc Creative Computing programme which pioneered a new view of computing as a creative discipline aligned with the arts. Marco has worked on massive open online courses (MOOCs) in responsive web development and design and virtual reality. Since September 2016, Marco has been Academic Director: Distance Learning at Goldsmiths. Marco's interest in learning with technology overlaps with his research interests in human-centred approaches to computing. He has a long history of work on virtual reality, including educational applications.

**Sarah Gonnet** is an artist and independent scholar from the North-East of England. She has published academic articles in the *Journal of Creative Writing Research* and arts journalism pieces in *The Guardian* and *Little White Lies* among others. She has given talks at conferences for UoL, the National Association of Writers in Education and the NHS. She is the author of the novel *MaTilda* and the poetry collection *Voices*. She is an associate artist at Greyscale Theatre Company, and is on the board of directors of The Writing Squad, which mentors young writers. Her interests are in mental health, intersectional feminism and autodidactism.

**Joanne Harris** is a chartered manager who has worked for UoL since the mid-1990s in a number of roles, notably heading up the Student Advisory Services Department and managing the UoL website and intranet before moving on to her role as Associate Director, Student Experience, in November 2015. Her mission is to provide an excellent and distinctive student experience to students, irrespective of where they live and study, and to produce graduates distinguished by their intellectual capabilities, employability, leadership qualities and ability to contribute to society from the experience and learning they receive.

**Stylianos Hatzipanagos** is CODE fellow and Executive Co-lead for Research and Dissemination. He has held university leadership roles in blended learning and distance learning contexts. His research and scholarship portfolio includes: learning design and effectiveness of online learning environments, formative and technology-enhanced assessment, ICT-supported collaborative work, flexible and distance education, digital literacies, social media and social networks in an educational context. He has led and participated in research projects at an international level (EU-digital competences and social inclusion, lifelong learning, e-learning professional training, Minerva programmes) and nationally (HEA, Jisc).

**Leo Havemann** graduated from the University of Waikato in New Zealand, and went on to teach in higher education both there and in Australia, before working in the UK in industry and then in further education as a librarian and learning technologist, prior to joining UCL as a Digital Education Advisor in 2018. He is currently a Programme Development Advisor in the UCL Arena Education and Practice Development team, a CODE fellow at UoL and also a part-time PhD researcher at the Open University, investigating institutional strategies and policies to enable open and digital educational practices.

**Gwyneth Hughes** is Reader in Higher Education at the Institute of Education (IOE), UCL's Faculty of Education and Society, where she was programme leader for the Masters in Teaching and Learning in Higher and Professional Education. She is also a UoL CODE fellow. As a UCL Connected Curriculum fellow, she has worked on assessment and feedback guidelines and staff development. She is also a consultant for the UoL online Postgraduate Certificate in Learning and Teaching in Higher Education. She has published widely on learning and teaching in higher education and her book *Ipsative Assessment: Motivation through marking progress* was published by Palgrave Macmillan in 2014.

**Beatrice Hyams** has worked, over the past 20 years, in a number of capacities for UoL, the last six years for the online learning arm of the organisation. Her role there included assuring the quality of the academic provision and reviewing the quality of the student experience. She took an active role in enhancing the university's approach to inclusion and to ensuring the diversity of the student body was reflected within their learning artefacts. She has now left the world of academia behind and is focusing on developing creative skills which can support sustainability and a more planet-friendly lifestyle.

**Shoshi Ish-Horowicz** is Head of Innovation and Learning at Queen Mary UoL. She has an MSc in digital education and is a CODE fellow. Shoshi began her career as a classroom teacher in an inner-city comprehensive school, and has since worked in vocational, university and executive education, driving forward change and improving student experiences and outcomes. She is an assessor for Certified Membership of the Association for Learning Technology and sits on the editorial board of *Advances in Online Education: A Peer-Reviewed Journal* and her interests include accessibility, inclusion and technology-enhanced learning (TEL).

**Danielle Johnstone** is Instructional Technology Manager at King's Online. She leads work on accessibility and sustainable approaches to technology, and product manages the development of content production tools and customisation of the virtual learning environment (VLE) platform. Danielle's research interests centre around the inclusive design of learning and critical digital pedagogy. She is a certified member of the Association for Learning Technology (CMALT) and sits on the steering committee for ALT's regional M25 Learning Technology Group as well as co-leading a community of practice for Moodle users. Danielle received her MA in Education and Technology from the UCL Institute of Education.

**Simon Katan** is a creative technologist and educator interested in relationships between people and how technology mediates them. His expertise covers audio-visual performance, interactive installation and full stack web development. He completed a PhD in audio-visual composition at Brunel University and won a Prix Ars Electronica Honorary Mention for his work. Simon lectures in creative coding at Goldsmiths University. His project Sleuth, a film noir-themed learn-to-code detective game, has been running since 2018, reaching over 20,000 learners on the Coursera platform. More recently he founded Handl Education Ltd to apply his knowledge in game design to the problem of online social learning in higher education.

**Endrit Kromidha** is Associate Professor in Entrepreneurship and Innovation at the University of Birmingham, the Vice President for Policy and Practice at the Institute for Small Business and Entrepreneurship, a certified Project Management Professional by the Project Management Institute and a fellow of the British Higher Education Academy. He has industry experience in banking and finance, is the Director of the MBA Singapore at the University of Birmingham, and has extensive experience with international programmes in Singapore and Hong Kong. A former UoL CODE fellow, his research interests include digital platforms for entrepreneurship, collaborative innovation, project management and information technologies for development.

**Diana Maniati** is a disability practitioner with a particular focus on inclusion. With over 20 years in higher and further education, she has experience in helping institutions to shape inclusive practice policies, implementing inclusion procedures and advising on accessibility matters as well as providing ongoing support to disabled students. She also has extensive experience in inclusive practices for distance learning and has worked as a dyslexia and maths tutor. Diana holds a BSc in Mathematics and a Masters in Special Needs.

**Alan Parkinson** is Professor of Financial Education at UCL where he is School Deputy Director (Education) in UCL SoM, and Lead of the Finance, Accounting and Economics Teaching Team. He is a qualified accountant, with a Doctorate in Education, Deputy Director of UoL's online MSc Professional Accountancy, co-lead of the development team of UoL's online MSc Accounting and Financial Management and a fellow of UoL's CODE. Alan's scholarship and research interests focus on curriculum evaluation, performance measurement in accounting education, historical perspectives on business and technology applications within education.

**Sally Parsley** was the Digital Education Manager at the Disability and Eye Health Group, London School of Hygiene & Tropical Medicine until 2021. A major part of her role was as the design and production lead for the Open Education for Eye Health initiative open online courses. During the COVID pandemic she supported faculty to adapt modules for online delivery, sharing her experience, tools and approaches to design, create and deliver teaching and learning centred on the learner experience. Since 2021 Sally has been working as a Senior Learning Designer at the World Health Organization Academy, supporting lifelong learning in priority public health topics around the world.

**Daksha Patel** is an ophthalmologist and Associate Professor with specialisation in public health for eye care. She has been involved with postgraduate educational programmes in public health at the International Centre for Eye Health (ICEH) and at the London School of Hygiene & Tropical Medicine (LSHTM). As the e-learning Director for ICEH, she was involved in developing open education for eye health. She led the digitisation of the MSc programme in eye health at LSHTM during the COVID-19 pandemic. Daksha is a fellow of CODE at UoL and has been a UNESCO mentor to support open education.

**Matthew Philpott** is an independent writer, educator and historian with over a decade of experience with digital teaching practices. Originally trained as a historian, he is now an expert in managing, designing and delivering online, face-to-face and blended training solutions in both higher education and commercial sectors. Until 2021, Matthew was Digital Projects Manager at the School of Advanced Study (SAS) and Senate House Library, UoL. His work there focused on learning technologies, research skills training and open access. He is a fellow of CODE and the HE Academy and a certified member of ALT.

**Philip Powell** is Director of the Business School for the Creative Industries at the University for the Creative Arts and has held senior positions at the universities of Hull, Bath and Birkbeck, UoL. Philip's research into management, information systems, operations and higher education management has led to more than 360 published outputs. He is a fellow of the British Computer Society, the Academy of Social Sciences, the Higher Education Academy and CODE at UoL. He is a Senior Scholar of the Association of Information Systems and is a former president of the UK Academy for Information Systems.

**J. Simon Rofe** is Reader/Associate Professor of International Politics at the University of Leeds where he is responsible as subject lead for the Curriculum Redefined project; and Deputy Director of CODE at UoL. Simon previously headed the Knowledge Exchange and Enterprise portfolio and was Academic Head of Digital Learning at SOAS University of London. He has designed, developed and delivered numerous online learning programmes at a variety of HEIs, NGOs and other organisations; he led reviews of digital learning at a number of institutions, developed MOOCs in the first wave of their deployment, and has been at the forefront of digital learning for over a decade.

**Sarah Sherman** began her career working as a primary school teacher and educational researcher. She has since worked in the field of digital learning for over 20 years and has headed up the Bloomsbury Learning Exchange (BLE) since 2007. Sarah is responsible for managing the coordination, implementation and development of shared digital education activity across the BLE partners, helping to support institutional digital learning strategies and practices. Sarah is a senior fellow of the Higher Education Academy, a fellow of UoL's CODE, a former trustee of the Association for Learning Technology and coordinates several regional and national digital education user groups in the UK.

**Ayona Silva-Fletcher** is Professor in Veterinary Education at the Royal Veterinary College, UoL, and a fellow of UoL's CODE. Ayona has been working to optimise the cross-disciplinary training/education within social, cultural and political dimensions of the veterinary sector for over 20 years. She is involved in several international projects that include collaborations with Bangladesh, Sri Lanka, India, Vietnam, Thailand and Jordan. In 2012, Ayona was awarded the National Teaching Fellowship (UK) for her contributions to advance veterinary education and, in 2018, the Principal Fellowship of the UK Higher Education Academy for her strategic influence in the field of veterinary education.

**Mary Stiasny** is Pro-Vice Chancellor (International and Education) at UoL and is the CEO of University of London Worldwide, the distance learning arm of the university. Previously Mary was Pro-Director (International, Learning and Teaching) at IOE, Director of Education and Training for the British Council, Head of the School of Education and Training at the University of Greenwich, Deputy Head of the School of Education at Oxford Brookes University and Deputy Head of the Department of Education Studies at Goldsmiths College. Mary started her career as a teacher of social studies at Holland Park School. She was appointed OBE in 2013.

**Joanna Stroud** is Head of Online Learning at UCL, and has worked at a number of research-intensive and teaching institutions in the UK, including the London School of Hygiene & Tropical Medicine, London School of Economics (LSE) and Sheffield Hallam University. At UCL she leads the design and development of online courses, providing guidance relating to online pedagogies and learning design and course production management processes. She also works on developing the public-facing learning platform, UCL Extend and managing UCL's relationship with online course provider, FutureLearn. Joanna coordinated the strategic, pedagogic and developmental components of UCL's move to online teaching as part of its COVID-19 response. Joanna is a fellow of the HEA.

**Alan Tait** is Emeritus Professor of Distance Education and Development at the Open University UK, Visiting Senior Online Consultant at the Open University of China and a CODE fellow at UoL. Previously Alan was Pro-Vice Chancellor (Academic) at the Open University and he has been Visiting Professor at several major universities; transformation advisor for the Commonwealth of Learning at Botswana Open University; President of the European Distance and E-Learning Network; Special Advisor to the International Council for Open and Distance Education and editor of journals in the field of open and distance learning. He has recently worked on the establishment of open universities in Kazakhstan and Myanmar.

**Christine Thuranira-McKeever** is Director of Distance Learning Programmes at the Royal Veterinary College and a CODE fellow at UoL. With an academic background in agricultural economics, Christine spent the early part of her career in international development, a field in which she maintains an active interest. Her education research is mainly in design for science-based courses, learning communities and enhancing the student experience, particularly in tools to support student engagement. She also has a keen interest in institutional partnerships and capacity building, and has been involved in a number of projects with international partners developing distance and online training.

**Sandra Tury** is Associate Director – Online Library Services at UoL, where she has worked since 2005. She is responsible for developing and managing the university's completely 'digital' library service, which supports over 50,000 students and faculty from over 180 countries of the world. She is also a dissertation tutor on two distance-learning Masters programmes. Sandra holds a Doctorate in Information Science (Information-Seeking Behaviour in Distance Learning) from City University of London, an MSc in Information Technology and a Bachelor of Library and Information Studies from Loughborough University.

**Julie Voce** is Head of Digital Education and Senior Lecturer in Educational Development at City University, UoL, having previously held positions at Imperial College London, UCL and the University of Manchester Institute of Science and Technology. She is also a UoL CODE fellow. As Head of Digital Education, Julie is responsible for overseeing key institutional projects in the areas of learning spaces, lecture capture, digital accessibility, digital literacies and learning analytics. Julie teaches on City's MA Academic Practice on modules related to digital education, digital literacies and open practice. Julie completed her PhD at Lancaster University on the topic of institutional support models for TEL within UK higher education.

**David Winter** has worked in higher education careers services for over 25 years. In 2003, he developed an innovative online careers education tool, 'sort-it', and was a leading proponent of using webinars within the Careers Group. In 2014, with colleague Laura Brammar, he developed the first ever careers and employability MOOC for UoL, materials from which are still in use within the university's online courses. One of the focuses of his current role within the Careers Group and as Learning Director in the Association of Graduate Careers Advisory Services Experts, is equipping careers professionals to deliver high-quality online career development support and education.

# Preface: learning from over 150 years of distance education

Mary Stiasny and Michael Davis

This book focuses on distance education, but it also considers the rapid growth in the adoption of technologies that blur the distinction between traditional and distance education. The book has been produced by the Centre for Online and Distance Education (CODE) at the University of London (UoL). CODE has recently (early 2022) added 'online' to its name, acknowledging the growing overlap between online and distance education. It is informed both by the experiences of the UoL Federation and by CODE's broad fellowship, which brings expertise from UoL and other online and distance learning institutions (see the 'Centre for Online and Distance Education' section in this book).

UoL holds a keen interest in distance education and is one of the very earliest players in distance learning. From 1865, UoL students were able to undertake their entire degree (including assessment) without visiting London. It is also a modern-day provider of distance education to around 50,000 students in more than 180 countries around the world.

With a base of evidence, UoL describes itself as a market leader in distance education. However, due to its complex and peculiar history, and in particular the historical dichotomy between teaching and examination, London's focus was the administration and the assessment of distance learning for most of its history. Both administration and assessment remain essential to effective distance education. However, education per se at a distance had to await the birth of the Open University (OU), whose pioneering approach was subsequently adopted and then adapted by UoL, first at postgraduate study level and, more recently, and increasingly online, at undergraduate level.

Many people cannot now imagine life without smartphones, tablets or computers. Distance education is no exception. A book on distance education practice in a digitally connected world is not an obvious forum for a history of UoL. However, UoL's experience of working in more than 180 countries may offer context and better understanding of the transition that many universities around the world are making, from the 'dark ages' (of just a few years ago) to where we are now and where we are headed, and better insight into how education and technology and organisations evolve, why history matters and what we may risk leaving behind as we advance.

UoL has an unusual history. The Council for External Students claimed in 1910:

> The far-reaching and Imperial character of the work ... conducted by the External side of the University ... constitute it [as] a national necessity which cannot be replaced by any other educational system. (Quoted in Bell and Tight, 1993: 92)

Furthermore, UoL's work as an examination body, and then as a wartime university supporting prisoners of war and refugees (Kenyon-Jones and Letters, 2008), continues to reflect the capacity of distance education to transform lives despite difficult circumstances, and to adapt itself to address changing needs and opportunities.

UoL was founded in 1836 as a purely examining and degree-awarding body to which approved institutions could submit students for examination. Although its famous separation of teaching and assessment would give rise to controversy, this early decision ensured that cooperation and collaboration would be central to its future operations. Under UoL's Supplemental Charter of 1849, it first became possible for an institution situated 'anywhere in the Empire or Territories of the East India Company' to be recognised for the purpose of admission of students to examinations. Within a decade, the list of institutions recognised ranged from the University of Toronto, Canada, to the Bishop's Stortford Collegiate School, UK. By 1858, when UoL started offering degrees by distance, the intention was not, either then or now, to avoid rigour, undermine quality or simply provide a quick, cut-price alternative for the 'wandering British' as they 'set up and served their Empire' (Tait, 2004). UoL received its new charter from Queen Victoria, dispensing with the requirement of attendance at an approved institution and accepting as candidates anyone passing the London Matriculation Examination, wherever they were registered. The ultimate impact was to diversify UoL student population forever. Students could have access to higher education (HE) regardless of their gender, race or religion. By 1865, as London exams became available remotely,

HE was freed from the constraints of location. Students could complete assessment processes without physical attendance in London. The pattern for future education at a distance was established.

Over UoL's first 185 years or so, distance learning has evolved away from being a system for 'degrees by examination' that was, in reality, a very basic correspondence course. It provided no teaching, only a cursory framework syllabus. Students sourced readings, evidence and learning for themselves in preparation for summative assessments. These assessments were completed locally and shipped back to London for marking under central academic boards that oversaw all UoL awards. However, until the establishment of the Council for National Academic Awards (CNAA, 1969) in 1964 and OU five years later, UoL offered the only pathway, anywhere in the world, to obtaining a degree without attending a university.

Post war, its 'special relations in the vanguard of educational decolonisation' (Kenyon-Jones and Letters, 2008; Pattison, 1984) between 1947 and 1970 assisted eight institutions in Africa and the Caribbean to become universities. These partner institutions were autonomous, but their teachers enjoyed the same rights as teachers within the UoL Federation, were appointed examiners and could propose amendments to syllabuses. Through London, newly independent states gained around 7,000 graduates, educated in their own countries with internationally recognised qualifications.

Despite its important role in the vanguard of decolonisation, UoL's place in the modern HE system came increasingly into question from the 1970s. Existential soul-searching stemmed from internal resource burdens, education reforms, the birth and subsequent demise of the CNAA, new offerings by the OU that boasted the latest in high technology and, later, from seismic upheavals around funding and changes to the UoL Federation. Indeed, between 1977 and 1984, having spent years trying to direct overseas registrations to other institutions, UoL closed overseas registrations completely due to unsustainable costs. However, popular demand ensured their early resurrection. Overseas nations sought to provide sufficient HE but were wary of the opening up of education to 'foreign' providers. They found in UoL a known and trusted entity and growth in the external programmes resulted.

UoL's capacity-building and access work remained prominent amid a greatly enlarged global HE sector. In many overseas markets, UoL retains the greatest market share of any UK provider of transnational and distance learning to this day. UoL's contemporary identities came to reflect the trans-governmental character of its work with non-governmental organisations and other civil society actors.

Throughout, myriad changes were needed: to enhance UoL's provision worldwide, to better accommodate learner and market needs and to ensure that perceptions of value and relevance continued to be strong and true. From sparse beginnings, as just a syllabus initially, successive generations of guidance and resources from UoL have included detailed course specifications of the Independent Guided Study Scheme in the 1970s and 1980s, then sending students their large boxes of course books, including purpose-written course guides, in the late 1980s and 1990s. By contrast, today's students access advanced, innovative and interactive online pedagogical platforms, systems for flexible and blended delivery through a network of over 120 recognised teaching centres (RTCs), as well as individualised online teaching and learning, built on an online library that now accommodates over 100 million items.

Its standing, however, continues to derive, not just from the quality both of the content and the pedagogy of its courses, but, more broadly, from managerial and administrative expertise, as well as brand associations as an enabler of access, broadcaster of standards and nexus for connection, forged in most regions of the world throughout a long and often difficult history, as summarised, perhaps a little harshly, by H. G. Wells (1986: 351–2) thus:

> At that early stage in the popularisation of education and the enlargement of the educational field, it is hard to see how the stimulus and rough direction of these far-flung ... London University examinations could have been dispensed with. It was the only way of getting any rapid diffusion of learning at all. Quality had to come later. It was a phase of great improvisation in the face of much prejudice and resistance.

Such terrain is entirely alien now. Transnational education (TNE) opportunities are abundant, advanced, perceived generally as a global good and subject to sophisticated and rigorous quality assurance. Capacity for significant improvisation remains, as UoL's response to the COVID-19 pandemic, described in Chapter 12, attests. However, in an era of growing regulation and control, shortcuts can lead to missteps and difficulty. Yet the familiarity of UoL's template for connection and capacity still allows access even into the least permissive environments. UoL's blend of analogue (in person in RTCs) and digital (online) education still ensures that it remains well suited to broadcast educational opportunity across differences of time, culture, infrastructure and development in an increasingly digital, connected world.

The perspectives and motivations of federation members to draw upon UoL's managerial, reputational and networked strengths as a platform for development remains key to perceptions of UoL abroad. The internal approach to cross subsidy between qualifications follows UoL's mission to provide access and opportunity to study for its awards. To ensure access alongside sustainability it seeks to identify new programmes that cater to common sets of core needs across a number of markets, rather than specific to a single market. Tailoring to local circumstances and tastes remains, and is largely left to, independent third parties.

Cross subsidy still permits the maximum financial benefit to accrue, equitably, to all participating federation members. To do otherwise risks negating goodwill established through an access mission that still informs vital relationships worldwide. Access has been central to maintaining local governmental and regulatory goodwill, shielding UoL from accusations of exploitation and indirectly proving a major marketing asset. Surpluses are generated where there is a defined capacity need, typically via blended programmes involving local tuition. These are balanced with a diverse portfolio of small, specialist postgraduate distance education offerings, promoting modernisation, social and cultural development, core administrative competencies, capacity building and international accord.

Thus, for nearly two centuries (and through partnership, innovation and sustained commitment to universal rights to enable suitably qualified applicants to access education), UoL has provided a platform for building capacity across HE. It still strives to disrupt modes of delivery in HE and remains little understood at home or abroad. But UoL's contribution to educational development and connection in the UK and across the world is unique. Its early platform addressed capacity needs but was also notable for providing no instruction on how to think. This protean template proved attractive and adaptable in many markets historically. However, the template has needed huge updates to address the modern environment, which no longer prioritises capacity in education over pedagogical competence and that advances quality in education beyond a simple calculus of standards. In spite of this, while distance education becomes increasingly accepted in global job markets, its authenticity and legitimacy as a mode of HE continues to be challenged, especially in the face of mounting expectations around learner experience and disruptive technologies.

Disruptive technologies, and intense and increasing competition for overseas students, are just the beginning. Quality assurance issues and complexities have increased as education has become ever more borderless and global. Challenges appear in regulatory changes around local HE, as policy reforms expand or restrict opportunities for 'non-traditional' modes of delivery or affect admission to professional bodies. (Calling distance education 'non-traditional' feels odd to a university that has been doing forms of distance education for over 150 years.) Meanwhile, declining market share and increasing competition has reduced returns. This reduction applies pressure on UoL's capacity to maintain diverse, specialist elements of its portfolio in areas that generate less surplus but are invaluable loss-leaders in terms of their ultimate diplomatic soft power and reputational returns.

As the global educational environment evolves, UoL is forging vital new connections and dialogues to provide the foundations for future growth and diversity, both blended and online. This requires more careful management than ever to ensure that it supports rather than impedes the development of local infrastructure, whether in terms of educational institutions or the regulatory and societal conditions under which students still choose to undertake a degree at a distance.

Distance education has suffered reputational damage by being lumped with some very low-quality commercial correspondence courses. Some audiences still lack confidence in its methodology. Some perspectives on this may have changed due to the exigencies of the COVID-19 pandemic, but equally other concerns have been reinforced.

Over many years, UoL has had to work hard to build and protect its reputation and has taken myriad steps to ensure that confidence in its awards and methods is upheld, that recognition for the quality and rigour of its qualifications is maintained and that the value of its offer to students and their future employers is high. Its machinery, established over the years, requires multiple and continuing upgrades to accommodate digital ways of working. Advances in technology have long since overtaken some of the traditional administrative benefits of centralised approaches to reach global audiences. Nonetheless, by virtue of global dispersion, distance education still requires a very different administrative approach to that of the traditional university. Technology's perpetual dividend notwithstanding, deadlines still remain relatively short and, as errors cannot always be rectified easily, there is a disproportionate impact on the resources required for delivery. Distance education has always been resource intensive, so centralised approaches that permit significant economies of scale and efficiency savings remain attractive.

Caution has always been required in ensuring that legal requirements for providers of overseas courses are met and requisite permissions obtained. Personal contacts built up over a number of years are another important consideration in many cultures, where changes in personnel can be viewed with suspicion and relationships can take several years to re-establish. As regulation of globalised TNE becomes more sophisticated, an ever-growing panoply of (occasionally burdensome) local procedures have been undertaken to register programmes with local agencies.

Successful online and distance education does not require 150 years of history but, to be successful, distance education has to take very seriously the provision of and access to high-quality content and pedagogy. It cannot simply carry out face-to-face education online. To be effective, distance education has to develop a complex set of relationships and interactions; address a concern for, and perhaps some redefinition of, quality; ensure reliable and responsive student support (as described in Chapter 14); provide meticulous, robust and agile management and administration; use what is learned from research about student learning in general and more particularly about online and distance learning; and take a long-term and strategic approach to online and distance education that is much more than just a way of dealing with bumps in the road such as the COVID-19 pandemic.

This book offers information, advice and expertise, much of it hard gained. However, it cannot provide the sustained commitment that is essential for successful distance education. As the long history of distance education at UoL may suggest, that sustained commitment has to come from the students and their institutions.

## References

Bell, R. and Tight, M. (1993) *Open Universities: A British tradition?* Buckingham: Open University Press.
CNAA (Council for National Academic Awards) (1969) 'The Council for National Academic Awards'. *International Journal of Electrical Engineering & Education*, 7 (3–4), 467–2. Accessed 27 June 2022. https://doi.org/10.1177/002072096900703-424.
Kenyon-Jones, C. and Letters, S. (2008) *The People's University: 150 years of the University of London and its external students*. London: University of London External System.
Pattison, B. (1984) *Special Relations: The University of London and new universities overseas, 1947–1970*. London: University of London.
Tait, A. (2004) 'On institutional models and concepts of student support services: The case of the Open University, UK', 3rd EDEN Research Workshop. Accessed 27 June 2022. http://www.c3l.uni-oldenburg.de/cde/support/fa04/Vol.%209%20chapters/KeynoteTait.pdf.
Wells, H. G. (1986) *Experiment in Autobiography*. London: Faber.

# Centre for Online and Distance Education

Linda Amrane-Cooper

This book has been produced by the Centre for Online and Distance Education (CODE) at the University of London (UoL).[1] CODE is an international community of fellows, associates and visiting scholars, drawn from across UoL member institutions and more widely. The book is informed both by the experiences of the UoL Federation and by CODE's broad fellowship, bringing together expertise from UoL and other online and distance learning institutions.

The foundations of CODE were created in 2000 when UoL established a Distance Education Resource Centre. Its original aims were to support capacity building for teaching and learning across the federal university; to improve the quality of educational provision within the External System, as the home for UoL's distance learning work was then called; and systematically to embrace the educational opportunities presented by new technologies. A Virtual Campus Project was launched in the same year to develop a shared, networked service delivery system to support online teaching and learning in the External System and to provide virtual campus services to other areas of the university.

In 2004, UoL made a bid to the Higher Education Funding Council for England (HEFCE) to become one of the new Centres for Excellence in Teaching and Learning, building on the foundations of the Distance Education Resource Centre. The HEFCE bid was unsuccessful but further discussion within the university concluded that the overall concept retained considerable merit and potential benefits for the External System and the university more widely. Consequently, internal funding was authorised to establish the Centre for Distance Education (CDE) in 2005 as an infrastructure for a networked community of practice, comprising three key elements:

- a network of Distance Education fellows in the UoL Federation member institutions
- a Teaching and Research Awards scheme
- an online resource centre.

However, the university funded the newly reformed CDE to provide advice, information and support for programme and policy development and build a community for the exchange of information and good practice, with CDE fellows from the UoL member institutions and beyond.

An important strand of CDE's work was, and remains, the Teaching and Research Awards, which are intended to provide a research basis on which proposed enhancements to practice can be developed. A 2006 review of these awards said:

> The Teaching and Research Awards proposals, which were selected for funding all appeared to ask legitimate academic questions which are worthy of study.

There were some shifts in priority over the years between development and research, but CDE's primary focus on supporting the development of distance learning across the university continues.

In 2022, CDE was renamed the Centre for Online and Distance Education (CODE), in recognition of the wider shift to online learning in recent years and the corresponding expertise of the centre.

There are currently 42 CODE fellows, drawn from across UoL member institutions and from thought leaders in distance and open education in the UK and internationally. CODE fellows' roles include teachers, course leaders, senior managers, researchers, educational technologists, academic developers, learning designers and policy advisers.

The core function of CODE is to support UoL and member institutions by promoting scholarly best practice in online and distance education. Activities include:

- an annual programme of conferences including the Research in Distance Education conference, workshops and webinars
- resources, projects, news, blogs and awards
- UoL's own Postgraduate Certificate in Learning and Teaching Higher Education.

UoL's research output and conferences reach international audiences. Its programmes of training, consultancy, research and activity have worked with international partners, including the Open University of China, the Nigerian National Universities Commission and the Friends of Birzeit University in Palestine. This work shows the university's commitment to building both quality and trust in open and distance education and supporting a community of professional, scholarly and research-informed practice in online and distance education.

This book is but one small output of UoL's work. In sponsoring and writing this book, fellows and associates of CODE thank UoL and the member institutions for their ongoing support and engagement.

## Note

1   Further information about CODE and its work and resources can be found at https://london.ac.uk/centre-online-distance-education.

# 1
# Online, distance, blended. It's all just education

Stephen Brown

This is a book about online and distance higher education (HE). For some in HE that sentence may be a bit off-putting. In some quarters, distance education has long been regarded as a poor substitute for the 'real thing'; that is, in-person learning (Daniel, 2012). Until recently, most universities did not practise distance education. Arguably, the COVID-induced 'Great Leap Online' of 2020 and 2021 changed that. No book on distance education can be published now without reference to the COVID-19 pandemic that swept across the world in 2019, excluding about 1.37 billion learners, as well as about 60.2 million teachers, from schools and classrooms (UNESCO, 2020).

Virtually overnight, traditional on-campus universities almost everywhere found themselves obliged to adopt some form of online distance learning as their primary modus operandi in the face of national lockdowns.

However, changes were already happening before the pandemic. Distance education used to be a highly specialised field, serviced by a small number of dedicated organisations around the world, including the University of London (UoL). But in recent years, growth in the adoption of technology to enhance on-campus learning through online learning resources and activities, so-called blended learning (Gulc, 2006), has blurred the distinction between 'traditional' and 'distance' learning, enhancing the relevance of effective distance education strategy and practice for universities more generally. On-campus students have increasingly been able to watch recorded lectures from their study bedrooms, read course materials online, test themselves with online self-assessment questions, talk to their tutors and peers online and download and submit assessments and receive feedback via the learning management system or virtual learning environment. Some commentators even suggested that it is no longer useful to talk about 'distance education' as such, because it is all just 'education' (Hurst, 2001).[1]

However, despite the blurring of differences between on-campus and distance education, some important distinctions remain, inasmuch as traditional mainstream universities have tended to use distance education to supplement the on-campus experience rather than replace it. By the end of 2019 these trends seemed set to continue into the foreseeable future. Distance education appeared destined to become just one of many currents running through the mainstream of HE. Then COVID-19 happened.

Some of the distinctive advantages of distance education, including both spatial and temporal flexibility for students and teachers and combinations of synchronous and asynchronous working, were highlighted by the pivot to online learning in the wake of the COVID-19 pandemic. According to the Jisc 2020/1 staff digital experience insights survey, HE staff reported a wide range of positive effects. Respondents felt that they were able to respond more quickly to students and that there were more ways to engage with them and stay in touch using chat forums and video calls (Jisc, 2021). They also reported an improved work–life balance because they were not spending time commuting and there were fewer distractions working from home. Some reported increased student engagement online and improved access to learning and to resources compared with on campus. They also observed that the flexibility for learners to participate at a time and in a way that suited them made a positive difference. The chapters in this book describe and explore this more positive account of distance education as it applies to contemporary online provision, while acknowledging and addressing the particular difficulties posed by online and distance education.

Although references to COVID-19 will be found throughout the chapters, this is not a book about its impact on HE. Many such have already been written and doubtless more will be, seeking to learn from the hard-won experiences of staff, students and governments as they strove in a few short months to adjust to dramatically changed circumstances. Important lessons have been learned; some of them about distance education and possibly more about adaptation and managing change in a crisis. This book is not about those crisis management and emergency measures. Instead, it draws on a deeper well of knowledge and experience developed painstakingly over decades of distance education practice and research as theories, technologies, markets, government policies and societies themselves have evolved more gradually.

The chapters here have been written by individuals from a broad range of backgrounds and represent a spectrum of interests reflecting different experiences in a variety of organisations and roles. In particular, the book encompasses the collective experiences and insights of fellows and associates of the UoL's Centre for Online and Distance Education (CODE).[2] UoL has over 150 years of experience of delivering education at a distance. What is taught and how it is taught has changed considerably over the last century and a half, but the university currently delivers distance education to over 50,000 students studying in over 180 countries, supported by over 100 recognised teaching centres worldwide, and has developed substantial experience in its provision. This book seeks to make that experience available to a variety of stakeholders in HE and more widely, as many of the challenges and solutions are similar in other sectors. These stakeholders include governments and their agencies charged with delivering education, people holding a variety of roles in educational institutions, including leaders, academics, learning developers, administrators, technologists and researchers, those supporting students and, not least, students themselves.

If some convergence of on-campus and distance education practices was already evident before COVID-19, its acceleration by the pandemic makes this book even more relevant to traditional HE institutions than it would have been before. As CODE fellow Alan Tait, retired Professor of Distance Education and Development and Pro-Vice Chancellor (Academic) at the UK Open University (OU), observed at the 2021 UoL Research in Distance Education conference: 'there will be no return to 2019 in 2022 – or, almost certainly, at any time after that'. Tait was talking about the COVID-induced switch to online assessment, but his remark applies to the deployment of distance education throughout HE more widely.

In this book, we explain and illustrate our view that this COVID-induced change is a potentially positive opportunity. We say 'potentially' because some of the early and necessarily very rapid implementations of distance education in the Great Leap Online of 2020 and 2021 were, entirely understandably, not of the highest quality. However, these rapid innovations are now being reviewed, lessons learned and more considered implementations of distance learning undertaken. This book is intended to support and inform those who wish to develop a more considered implementation of distance education.

## What we mean by 'distance education'

As this is a book about distance education and its latest manifestation, online, an obvious place to start is with an account of the key features of distance education, as contrasted with in-person or conventional classroom-based or 'face-to-face' education. Definitions of distance education abound (Keegan, 1980: 13). We start with this older but still useful account:

> Distance teaching may be defined as the family of instructional methods in which the teaching behaviours are executed apart from the learning behaviours, including those that in a contiguous situation would be performed in the learner's presence, so that communication between the teacher and the learner must be facilitated by print, electronic, mechanical or other devices. (Moore, 1973: 664)

This definition is useful as it captures three key elements:

- distance or separation between the teacher and the learner (this could be temporal as well as physical distance)
- technology, such as print or electronic devices that are used to bridge that gap
- pedagogy or 'instructional methods' that are deployed via the technology to facilitate learning.

Certainly, separation between the teacher and the learner is present to some degree in any learning or teaching situation. For example, students are commonly set activities to do out of class and away from the gaze of the teacher, such as essay writing, reading and library research. But Moore's concept of 'Transactional Distance' (Moore, 1973: 664) aptly identifies the crucial difference between traditional on-campus or 'in-person' teaching and learning contexts and distance education. On campus, at least until recently, most of the important transactions between teacher and learner took place largely face to face. In distance education, by contrast, those key transactions are conducted at a distance, mediated by one or more technologies. Transactional distance creates unique challenges for learners and teachers, quite apart from the obvious difficulties of running practical sessions such as laboratory, clinical or workshop activities. If a learner cannot hear the teacher's tone of voice, can they be sure they have captured the nuances of the information? If they cannot interrupt to ask a question or to seek clarification, how can they check their understanding? Equally, if a teacher cannot see how their students are reacting to a learning activity, how can they fine-tune and personalise their teaching to ensure that each individual learner receives the best possible support?

Technology can go some way to overcoming these problems, depending on its affordances (Glaver, 1991). According to Kirschner (2002), educational affordances can be defined as the relationships between the properties of an educational intervention and the characteristics of the learner that enable certain kinds of learning to take place. Different technologies have different properties that allow, enable or afford certain kinds of transactions to take place between the people using those technologies. Laurillard (2002), in her seminal work on rethinking university learning and teaching, provides a helpful classification of technologies used in education, mapped to different types of learning and teaching activities and the affordances they offer. For example, she suggests that radio and broadcast television are 'narrative' media, similar to a lecture, that allow the teacher to transmit an essentially linear narrative about a topic and the learner to 'receive' that narrative in a relatively passive way by listening or watching. Learners can engage more actively by making notes throughout, but it is not usually possible to put a live lecture or a broadcast on pause, so the opportunities for note taking and other forms of more active learning, such as questioning and discussing, are limited.

New technologies often bring new affordances. The widespread availability of domestic VHS recording and playback machines in the late 1970s allowed the OU to supplement its educational television broadcasts via a video cassette loan service, through which students could watch the programmes at a time most convenient to them instead of the broadcast time. However, transposing the content into a new technology created new affordances for students who realised that not only could they watch the programmes whenever they liked, they could also watch them as often as they liked, pause and replay segments, fast forward and rewind between different parts and watch multiple programmes together. The new affordances created new, more active, learning opportunities (Brown, 1984).

A lot of teaching now takes place online. In the early days of the internet, content was mostly conveyed via one-way publications, broadcasts if you like, from one person or organisation (usually with advanced technical skills and facilities) to many, so the opportunities for interaction were highly constrained. The emergence of the so-called Web 2.0 as a suite of applications that required much lower levels of technical capability to engage in publication of video, audio, photographs, stories (blogs) and real-time commentary, opened up a wide range of potential educational affordances for interaction via discussion, debate, collaboration, exploration, aggregation, synthesis, repurposing, repackaging and so on, along the synchronous/asynchronous spectrum. Therefore, while the internet can be (and still is) used by educators for distributing content to learners, it can be (and is) used to support more active engagement by learners with content, in line with contemporary theories of learning.

This is not the place to rehearse well-established notions about constructivism and knowledge creation through active learning and social interaction. Suffice it to say that a recent meta-review of the conditions for good student learning (Baume and Scanlon, 2018) describes, among these conditions, students collaborating closely and receiving and making use of feedback on their work, as well as learners being sustainedly active in their pursuit of high standards of work and attainment. All of these conditions can be met just as well in online and distance education as in-person education, as is explored in this book in Chapter 8.

To summarise, the term 'distance education' in this book refers to pedagogical practices that exploit the affordances of available technologies and our understanding of how students learn, to facilitate key transactions taking place at a physical and/or temporal distance between learners, teachers and learning and assessment activities. This definition applies as much to the online teaching and learning activities of mainstream HE institutions as it does to those of specialist, niche, distance education universities. It encompasses online learning, blended learning and a range of technologies, including printed resources delivered to students by post or by other means (Carlsen et al., 2016). In the following chapters we shall refer to these various forms as simply 'distance education'.

## How effective is it?

As already noted, distance education has long been regarded by some as a poor substitute for the 'real thing'; that is, in-person learning (Daniel, 2012). This, notwithstanding the 150-year history of successful distance education at UoL (as described in the Preface), over 50 years of acclaimed success of the OU and the spread of this model around the world through many prestigious institutions, including Athabasca University (Canada), the Indira Gandhi National Open University (India), the Open University of the Netherlands, Universitat Oberta de Catalunya (Spain), FernUniversität (Germany), Sukhothai Thammathirat Open University (Thailand), Open University of Malaysia, the National Open University of Nigeria and the Open University of China.

This is not the place for in-depth analysis into why such negative attitudes persist. To be fair, they are not always due to distrust of the unknown, of technology or sheer ignorance of what distance education is and how it works. Sometimes there are good reasons why online learning is not the right strategy for an institution or its stakeholders (Brown, 1998), but the idea that online, technology-enhanced distance education is inherently less effective than traditional, classroom-based face-to-face education is not one of them. A multitude of research studies illustrate that both approaches work just as well, or just as badly, depending on the competence of their implementation. For example, Thomas Russell's seminal work on the relative effectiveness of different teaching delivery modes and media demonstrates through a meta-analysis of over 350 individual published research studies that there is no significant difference in student outcomes between alternate modes of education delivery (and only a few cases where there are differences) (Russell, 2001).[3]

Meanwhile, during the Great Leap Online in the pandemic, institutions steeped in traditional face-to-face teaching methods sought to rapidly find ways of achieving the same results at a distance from their students, while students had to quickly change their study habits to become effective distance learners. As discussed in Chapter 20, the results of these emergency measures were neither uniformly successful nor unanimously welcomed, but institutions where staff and systems already had some experience and hence understanding of distance education practice tended to respond more effectively (Lederman, 2020).

However, one important difference that transcends the delivery competency issue is the equity of access to educational opportunity. Barriers to access might include lack of availability of places, as described in Chapter 7, or an inability to attend the campus where teaching takes place, for example, because it is too far away or dangerous to travel to, because of personal disabilities, or because of discriminatory practices predicated on gender, religion or ethnicity. Consideration of access and equity leads to the notion of 'openness'.

The terms 'open' and 'distance' are often bracketed, as in 'open and distance learning', and sometimes used interchangeably. Although closely related, they are not the same thing, as illustrated in Chapter 16. Lewis and Spencer (1986: 9) define open learning as:

> A term used to describe courses flexibly designed to meet individual requirements. It is often applied to provision which tries to remove barriers that prevent attendances at more traditional courses.

Until the establishment of the UK Council for National Academic Awards in 1964 and the OU five years later, UoL offered the only pathway, anywhere in the world, to obtaining a degree without physically attending a university and thus could claim a degree of openness. The OU took this one step further by setting out not just to remove the physical barriers to studying on campus, but aiming to be as open as possible to potential learners by dispensing with the requirement for entrance qualifications and by offering courses at extremely low cost (Perry, 1976). Distance learning was a means to that end.

Since the early days of open and distance learning, there have been many attempts to refine our understanding of what we mean by these terms, with varying degrees of emphasis on different pedagogical, technological, administrative and regulatory aspects: flexible learning, technology-enhanced learning, computer-supported collaborative learning, mobile learning, distributed learning, online learning, blended learning and, more recently, 'hybrid' and 'high-flex' learning. The authors of this book agree with Derek Rowntree (retired Professor of Educational Development in the Institute of Educational Technology at the OU) that the label used is less important than a shared understanding of the concept.

> Open learning? Distance learning? Flexible learning? Which are you concerned with? Maybe some combination of the three, or perhaps your form of learning goes under another name. No matter. (Rowntree, 1994: 2)

Our accounts of 'online and distance education' throughout this book are intended to encompass these various nuances and interpretations, including emerging practices in traditional face-to-face teaching institutions.

## Pathways through this book

The aim of this book is to guide, support and inform those responsible for the development and implementation of online and distance learning anywhere in the world, at all levels from policy and strategy to practice, across the many roles required to plan and operate successful distance education in HE institutions. Elements of distance education, in particular the use of online learning, have featured more and more across mainstream education over the last decade or so. The chapters in this book offer a practical, practice, research- and theory-informed approach to the development of institutional policy and practice in planning and running high-quality distance education, including within universities that have moved quickly and recently to distance education. They also provide a practical, practice-, research- and theory-informed account of the current and likely future state of online and distance education in HE and offer guidance to current and future leaders and practitioners of online and distance education.

This book is aimed at people from a variety of professional backgrounds including government, education agencies and policy makers; institution heads and leaders such as vice chancellors, pro-vice chancellors, deans; heads of distance education, academic development and learning technology functions; academic developers, learning designers and learning technologists; academics, variously as distance learning course leaders and managers, designers and tutors and those moving their face-to-face teaching online; programme administrators, student support, student unions; university quality assurance functions; researchers into distance education.

Notwithstanding this long list, the range of interests held by the majority of readers can probably be encompassed by the following three key roles:

- policy makers and managers, including government, education agency and senior university staffing
- practitioners, including academics, learning designers and technologists, programme administrators and student/academic support
- researchers into distance education.

The book is organised into three overlapping sections: 'Planning distance education', 'Doing distance education' and 'Researching and evaluating distance education', which reflect these main target audiences, while this introduction and a concluding chapter consider possible futures. Each section investigates a different aspect of distance education. Thus, Section 1 of the book considers high-level planning issues most likely to interest policy makers and managers. Section 2 is focused more on the interests of practitioners and researchers, addressing the practicalities of design and delivery of distance education. Section 3 targets researchers with a review of the relations between development, research and practice and a discussion of how we define and measure success.

The final chapter of the book returns to the macro level to consider how the ideas and experiences presented here might be combined to build a better future and what we might mean by that. It begins by reviewing the trajectory of distance education, from its mid-nineteenth-century origins to the present day, identifying significant trends – in summary, steadily increasing demand for, and increasing mainstreaming of, distance learning, some blurring between online and in-person HE and the huge possibilities opened up by the internet. Building on these trends and recent events, it proposes some conjectural scenarios to explore how different kinds of institutions may evolve and what that might mean for the people who engage with them as learners, teachers, support staff and managers. These scenarios are not forecasts, but tools to help you consider for yourself what you know, or strongly expect, will change in your discipline and in your institution's educational provision over the next few years and how you will adapt your distance education practice to meet these changes. The chapter concludes by considering what we have learned from the recent pivot to online and distance learning and how we can use it to inform our choices about the future in such uncertain times – times which are likely to continue to be uncertain.

One way to read the book would be to focus on chapters from the sections that most closely align with your own role. However, while the three sections map broadly onto different interest groups, the issues discussed would benefit from cross-reading between sections. High-level policy and strategy need to be informed by understanding of practice and practical challenges. Equally, designers and practitioners need to understand the policy and strategy context within which they are working. Policy and practice both require firm foundations in research-based evidence, while researchers need close connections with practitioners to remain grounded and equally close connections with policy makers and senior managers if they hope to influence change. We therefore encourage readers to select relevant chapters from across the different sections, following their own path through the book. For those wishing for some guidance we provide a summary of the contents of and links between the chapters at the start of each section and we have included a variety of case studies, both as fully developed chapters and as shorter, in-chapter, examples that readers may find useful to see how the ideas discussed in the book have been implemented in practice.

## Notes

1. The UoL Centre for Distance Education has recently changed its name to the Centre for Online and Distance Education (CODE) to reflect these changes.
2. https://london.ac.uk/centre-online-distance-education.
3. See also the accompanying online database: https://detaresearch.org/research-support/no-significant-difference/.

## References

Baume, D. and Scanlon, E. (2018) 'What the research says about how and why learning happens'. In R. Luckin (ed.), *Enhancing Learning and Teaching with Technology: What the research says* (1st edn). London: UCL IoE Press, 2–13.

Brown, S. (1984) 'Videocassettes'. In A. W. Bates (ed.), *The Role of Technology in Distance Education*. London: Croom Helm, 43–56.

Brown, S. (1998) 'Re-inventing the university'. *ALT-J Association for Learning Technology Journal*, 6 (3), 30–7. Accessed 27 June 2022. http://repository.alt.ac.uk/281/1/ALT_J_Vol6_No3_1998_Reinventing%20the%20university.pdf.

Carlsen, A., Holmberg, C., Neghina, C. and Owusu-Boampong, A. (2016) *Closing the Gap: Opportunities for distance education to benefit adult learners in higher education*. Hamburg: UNESCO Institute for Lifelong Learning (UIL). Accessed 28 June 2022. https://unesdoc.unesco.org/ark:/48223/pf0000243264.

Daniel, J. (2012) 'Dual-mode universities in higher education: Way station or final destination?' *Open Learning: The Journal of Open, Distance and E-Learning*, 27 (1), 89–95.

Glaver, G. W. (1991) 'Technology affordances'. In S. Robertson, M. Olson and J. Olson (eds), *CHI '91: Proceedings of the SIGCHI Conference on Human Factors in Computing Systems*. New York: Association for Computing Machinery, 79–84. Accessed 15 January 2022. https://dl.acm.org/doi/proceedings/10.1145/1978942.

Gulc, E. (2006) 'Using blended learning to accommodate different learning styles', Higher Education Academy. Accessed 27 December 2021. https://s3.eu-west-2.amazonaws.com/assets.creode.advancehe-document-manager/documents/hea/private/2917_1568036925.pdf.

Hurst, F. (2001) 'The death of distance learning'. *Educause Quarterly*, 3, 58–60. Accessed 18 January 2022. https://er.educause.edu/-/media/files/articles/2001/9/eqm0138.pdf?la=en&hash=AEC66239713D92568FA1F1517785C88A1BD365D1.

Jisc (2021) 'Teaching staff digital experience insights survey 2020/21: UK higher education (HE) survey findings', report, November. Accessed 17 December 2021. https://repository.jisc.ac.uk/8568/1/DEI-HE-teaching-report-2021.pdf.

Keegan, J. (1980) 'On defining distance education'. *Distance Education*, 1 (1), 13–36.

Kirschner, P. A. (2002) 'Can we support CSCL? Educational, social and technological affordances for learning'. In P. A. Kirschner (ed.), *Three Worlds of CSCL: Can we support CSCL?* Heerlen: Open University of the Netherlands, 7–47.

Laurillard, D. (2002) *Rethinking University Teaching: A conversational framework for the effective use of learning technologies*. London: Routledge Falmer.

Lederman, D. (2020) 'How teaching changed in the (forced) shift to remote', *Inside Higher Education*, 22 April. Accessed 17 December 2021. https://www.insidehighered.com/digital-learning/article/2020/04/22/how-professors-changed-their-teaching-springs-shift-remote?utm_source=Inside+Higher+Ed&utm_campaign=be8f8da570-DNU_2019_COPY_02&utm_medium=email&utm_term=0_1fcbc04421-be8f8da570-198221877&mc_cid=be8f8da570&mc_eid=8dbe0024a7.

Lewis, R. and Spencer, D. (1986) *What Is Open Learning?* London: Council for Educational Technology.

Moore, M. G. (1973) 'Towards a theory of independent learning and teaching'. *Journal of Higher Education*, 44 (9), 661–79.

Perry, W. (1976) *Open University: A personal account by the first vice-chancellor*. Buckingham: Open University Press.

Rowntree, D. (1994) *Preparing Materials for Open, Distance and Flexible Learning*. London: Kogan Page.
Russell, T. L. (2001) *The No Significant Difference Phenomenon* (5th edn). N.p.: IDECC.
UNESCO (United Nations Educational, Scientific and Cultural Organization) (2020) '1.37 billion students now home as COVID-19 school closures expand, ministers scale up multimedia approaches to ensure learning continuity', UNESCO press release, 24 March. Accessed 28 June 2022. https://en.unesco.org/news/137-billion-students-now-home-covid-19-school-closures-expand-ministers-scale-multimedia.

# Section 1
# Planning distance education

# Introduction to Section 1

Stephen Brown

We begin Section 1 with Chapter 2, asking who distance education is for and what we know about learners' motivations, their needs and what they think of distance learning. Building a successful online and distance education operation, or university, obviously depends on understanding the primary target audience, the learners and how the methods used affect key factors such as inclusion and learner retention and progression.

There is not simply one student perspective – distance learning students are diverse and experience distance education in multiple ways. Their experience is affected by factors such as socioeconomic background, prior learning, language, sociocultural perspectives, disability and gender. Moreover, because distance learning opens up study options to individuals who would not be able to study in campus mode, there is a complex interrelationship between who studies, their life circumstances and their study experience. The chapter identifies and explores four issues that have been found to be particularly important for the quality of the distance learning student experience:

- **Assessment for learning.** Recent research suggests that designing assessment for learning as opposed to assessment of learning contributes to retention and success.
- **Peer support.** Peer support has been shown to have a positive impact on retention but there is a need for more research into effective ways of implementing this in ways that retain flexibility for distance learners.
- **Learning analytics.** While the use of analytics is growing rapidly, there are dangers in basing pedagogical innovation on analytic data alone. It may be that learning analytics are best combined with systematic, contextualised qualitative research.

- **Transitions.** One of the strengths of retention practice aimed at widening participation has been the recognition that learning journeys include critical points of transition.

The conclusion, 'New developments in pedagogy and in sensitive learning design that build on well-researched insights into student needs are needed to meet the challenges of the twenty-first century', anticipates the discussion in Chapter 8 (Section 2) and Chapter 18 (Section 3).

Chapter 3 explores the relationship between digital learning and distance education. By exploring the nature of the challenges for digital learning and distance education, the chapter aims to provide educators with (a) insight on, and context to, the relationship; and (b) advice on how to meaningfully engage with both dimensions of twenty-first-century education to the benefit of themselves, their students, their institutions and the sector as a whole. It picks up the theme of the digital divide between those with ready access to technology infrastructure and those without and asks 'if there is anything in contemporary education that does not have some aspect of digital?' The chapter considers the appropriate use of the digital in contributing to the digital learning experience and argues that the successful application of digital learning is about tailoring the use of the digital rather than wholly distinct practices. It outlines the potential for students, academics, educational designers and institutions, as a multiple stakeholders' team of practitioners engaged in digital and distance education, to contribute to innovation and further development of education as part of a global society, foreshadowing the discussion in Chapters 8 and 17.

Chapter 4 further develops a key theme introduced in Chapter 2: understanding the target audience in order to use that understanding, not just for recruitment, but also for keeping students engaged in the post-sale learning environment, motivating them to participate, to succeed and, ultimately, to graduate and become part of an active alumni community for the university. Thus, this chapter aims to assist new distance education programmes to develop a vision that goes beyond current job market trends. Inspiring and nurturing learning skills of enquiry, critical analysis, curiosity, creativity, persistence, discipline and vision should happen alongside the knowledge transfer within the courses. A deeper student involvement in distance education programmes will influence behaviours in the classroom and also develop active ambassadors of the programmes. Finally, the chapter argues that learning should be an enjoyable experience powered by digital innovations offering quality, flexibility and diversity in distance education courses for an inclusive and progressive society.

Chapter 5 returns once again to the theme of building courses around an understanding of learners' motivations for studying, while taking account of the distinctive characteristics and opportunities of distance learning. This chapter argues the importance of embedding careers and employability learning within the curriculum or core student experience for distance learning courses. It further argues that this learning should be provided in a way that helps less experienced students to develop core employability skills and helps those currently in employment to value and build on their capabilities. Addressing these topics, it describes a range of models of employability and discusses their relevance to distance education. It further offers an understanding of the ways in which employability learning can be incorporated into a distance learning context, differentiating between curricular, co-curricular and extracurricular approaches and discussing their resource implications, key principles underpinning employability provision in higher education (HE) and the importance of student awareness, acceptance and engagement with employability learning. The chapter discusses ways of measuring and evaluating employability impact that go beyond the obvious measure of employment itself and makes recommendations for ways of embedding careers and employability learning within the curriculum. It stresses the importance of senior management commitment and wide stakeholder engagement, which are themes that are illustrated in the case study in Chapter 7 and discussed in the concluding chapter, Chapter 20.

As this book demonstrates, distance education entails virtually all aspects of an HE institution (HEI), including pedagogy, student support, marketing, technology and remuneration. In addition, most HEIs were not born digital, which means that they will need to manage a significant organisational change programme to deliver online distance education successfully. Chapter 6 offers guidelines for assessing the extent to which distance education may be a strategic imperative for institutions. The decisions an institution needs to consider in relation to distance education revolve around a number of factors, including its strategic relationship to the core mission; how what is provided online relates to other educational provision; the needs and expectations of distance learning and other institutional stakeholders; who provides the different resources and how they are bundled together; and how online provision is funded or monetised. For some institutions, and for some educational systems, distance learning will be strategic – often because there is no viable alternative mechanism to deliver education at scale or over distances. For other institutions, the decision to invest in distance education is more problematic and more complex. The chapter discusses how complexity arises from a variety of possible business models and the number of actors within the distance education value chain, creating a spectrum of possibilities as to who best does what in distance education. Here, many external actors can come into play – content providers, technology suppliers, online pedagogists, accreditors and others.

The arguments developed in this section around the strategic aspects of online and distance education provision, the views of stakeholders and the student voice, as well as how distance education courses are marketed successfully, are explored in the context of the final chapter in the section, Chapter 7. This case study investigates how the National Universities Commission of Nigeria worked with the University of London's Centre for Online and Distance Education to develop distance education as a solution to the problems of a rapidly growing young population within a developing country. It describes how learner needs are driving a large-scale pivot to distance education, what barriers, such as the digital divide, need to be overcome and how the development of communities of practice involving a wide range of stakeholders is helping to build growing acceptance of, and capability and capacity for, distance learning.

# 2
# The student voice

Pete Cannell and Julie Voce

In this chapter we look at the student experience of distance learning. There is not simply one student perspective – distance learning students are diverse and experience distance education in multiple ways. Their experience is affected by factors such as socioeconomic background, prior learning, language, sociocultural perspectives, disability and gender. Moreover, distance learning opens up study options to individuals who would not be able to study in campus mode. There is a complex interrelationship between who studies, their life circumstances and their study experience. We argue that distance learning educators need to understand the distinctive voice, context and experience of distance learners and that incorporating this understanding in module and programme design is critical to ensure student engagement and retention.

The chapter begins by contextualising student experience in the historical development of distance education and the ways in which it has contributed to opening up access to higher education (HE). Throughout the chapter, widening access runs as a theme that structures an analysis of who distance students are and how they experience HE. We suggest that despite a diversity of backgrounds and motivation and despite some convergence in the use of technology between distance and campus-based HE, there are important distinguishing characteristics of the distance learner experience. In the conclusion, we reflect on the way in which campus-based students around the world suddenly became 'distance learners' as the global pandemic forced institutions to move teaching online.

Until the nineteenth century, access to HE was only possible for a small number of individuals who could access universities, libraries and other places of learning. The development of efficient national and international postal services opened the door to participation from a distance by means of correspondence tuition. By the latter half of the century, students studying by correspondence could sit University of London (UoL) examinations from locations around the world (Peters, 2001). For nearly a century this system provided opportunities for colonial administrators throughout the British Empire to obtain UoL degrees. Later, it also provided a degree pathway for a cohort of individuals growing up under colonial rule. Many of the graduates went on to play prominent roles in movements for independence and in the governments of newly independent states. Other campus universities that were based in countries such as Canada, the USA and Australia, and served large geographical areas with dispersed populations, adopted the 'external degree' model pioneered at UoL. Daniel (2012) notes, however, that degree study by correspondence was often viewed as second best to classroom provision and remained largely outside the mainstream. This model of combining face-to-face with distance provision is often referred to as a 'dual mode'.

## Opening up access

Until the 1960s, distance education by correspondence played an important but limited contribution to widening access to HE. However, in 1969, the establishment of the UK Open University (OU) sparked step changes in scale and opportunities to access HE via distance study. The demographic profile of the new distance students was more diverse than previous instances of distance education but was shaped by very specific national circumstances. The OU was formed at a critical juncture in the development of HE in the UK. In the 1950s, only 4 per cent of school leavers went on to study at university (Boliver, 2011). The 1960s saw a sharp increase to above 10 per cent of school leavers, but university entrance remained highly skewed by socioeconomic background, gender and age. A rapid expansion in the number of universities and polytechnics marked the beginning of a shift towards a mass HE system. Yet, while opportunities for school leavers expanded rapidly, there remained a large pool of adults in professional and semi-professional occupations who had not had the opportunity to obtain a degree when they left school. These people made up a significant proportion of the early recruits to the OU (Rumble, 2001: 37). The new university's aim was to provide opportunities for adults and open up access to undergraduate degrees. From the outset the system was open entry. Although this was controversial at first, student numbers rose rapidly, reaching 70,000 a year by 1979 (OU Library, 2019).

The OU model of a specialist distance teaching institution had an international impact. Open universities were set up around the world (Mugridge, 1997). The new institutions shared an ethos defined by distance education pedagogy, administrative systems that could support large-scale recruitment and an emphasis on widening access. However, just as in the UK, national circumstances and policy priorities meant that methods, institutional mission and demographics of student populations varied. In the global south, open universities often formed part of national strategies to develop primary and secondary education – sometimes directly and sometimes through increasing the numbers of trained teachers.

Many of the new open universities grew to have very large-scale enrolments – often in the millions. Daniels (1996) coined the term 'mega university' for those with more than one hundred thousand students. Typically, most of these students were resident in the national territory of the particular institution.

From the 1990s onwards, however, both specialist distance institutions and campus universities began to make use of the capabilities of the internet and digital communication technologies. For the latter, distance and online often became conflated, although in practice online spans a spectrum, from provision that is simply complementary to face-to-face teaching, through variations on blended teaching to wholly online teaching (Graham et al., 2013). As this process evolved, some private providers adopted elements of the delivery at large scale typical of the specialist open universities, but more typically distance provision by campus institutions was smaller scale and often at postgraduate level. There was a further change in the character of distance learning provision from 2013, when campus universities around the world took up the massive open online course (MOOC) model (Lambert et al., 2018; Shapiro et al., 2017). These courses use web technology to support large numbers of enrolled students. Building on their success, there are a range of initiatives aimed at using the technology to provide scaffolding for new forms of online degrees. One example is the OERu, an international consortium of universities that seeks to develop a collaborative and cost-effective international model of curriculum development based on free openly licensed education resources (OER). The explicit aim of the OERu is to provide opportunities for the many millions of qualified individuals worldwide who currently cannot find places at university.

## The students

Given the complex evolution of university-level distance learning, is it possible to identify characteristics of distance learners and their experience that set them apart from their campus-based colleagues? Who studies at a distance in any given location is influenced by multiple factors and yet distance learning students share some important common characteristics (OECD, 2019; Peters, 2001). Because face-to-face study remains the dominant paradigm and to study at a distance is choosing to do something different, the choice is always contextual, driven and constrained by circumstance. Most often, students opt for distance learning because conventional campus-based HE is not an option. Full-time, campus-based study may be too expensive or involve too much travel, or campus institutions may be unable to meet demand for places. If there are places, campus-based provision may lack the flexibility to offer the necessary support for certain kinds of disability, or to accommodate other demands on the potential student's time; for example, to work full or part time, act in a caring role or fulfil other family responsibilities. Some of these issues are reflected in the example that follows this section.

Some authors have suggested that new forms of learning technology have brought distance learning and campus study closer together (Tait and Mills, 1999). Certainly, technological developments have had a significant impact and this is considered in more detail later in this chapter. However, student experience is intimately connected to the reasons that influenced their choice of study mode. Distance learning students are more likely to be older than their campus-based colleagues, to be part time, to be in paid employment and to have caring responsibilities (Poskitt et al., 2011). On campus, an individual's 'student' identity tends to dominate, yet distance learning students are frequently studying in the context of the other aspects of their life. Other identities may well dominate: employee, parent, carer and so on. Peters (2001) notes that distance students often have much more life experience and that their study is encompassed by life plans and lifecycles in a different way than is the case for campus-based students.

The study experience of distance learning students arises from a reciprocal relationship between personal factors such as socioeconomic background, prior learning, language, disability and gender, and the pedagogical approach and support structures of the institution that they choose to study with. For all students the first year of a new phase of study represents an important challenge. The concept of 'first year' may be less relevant to distance learning students who are often studying part time;

nevertheless, 'getting started' remains a critical point of transition (Simons et al., 2018; Simpson, 2003).

Self-evidently distance implies physical separation from tutors and other students. So, not only are students juggling multiple life commitments, but they may find that their experience of study is dominated by a sense of isolation. Their prior experience of learning and their sociocultural assumptions about HE may also mean that they have expectations that are at odds with those of their course. The excitement and anxiety associated with becoming a distance student is captured in a study carried out with students enrolled at one Australian and one New Zealand university (Brown et al., 2015). Brown and his co-authors note that the first year of study is one in which expectations and understanding of what it is to be a distance student, and what learning at a distance involves, are challenged and modified. At the same time, priorities of work, childcare and other aspects of everyday life intrude in expected and unanticipated ways. Study is an emotional rollercoaster for many students, whether on campus or at a distance. Kahu et al. (2015) explore this aspect of the student learning journey in depth; their research suggests that student emotions affect, and are affected by, progress and learning and that both emotion and effective learning are a result of a complex interplay between pedagogy, support, motivation and background. These factors have a particular resonance for distance students.

### Example

**Student perspective – Dr Julie Voce**

I have studied at a distance on several occasions, both at undergraduate and postgraduate levels. At undergraduate level I studied for interest mainly, as I already had an undergraduate degree. I studied natural sciences, with a focus on physics and astronomy, with the OU and it was interesting to see the transition from when I first started to when I finished. My initial courses used printed books and CDs and relied on face-to-face tutorial sessions in the evenings or full days at the weekend. With a young child this was manageable but could be difficult. Part of the degree programme included a week-long residential course, which sounded exciting, but I felt it would be difficult for me to attend due to work and childcare commitments. I was pleased when the OU started moving more things online and revamped the practical module so that a residential wasn't a mandatory part. The changes meant that I was able to choose activities that could be from the comfort of my home. One of the astronomy activities involved taking pictures of star clusters using a telescope in Mallorca and I worked as part of a group to use the telescope remotely using exactly the same interface as those in Mallorca. Another activity involved undertaking an experiment as part of a paired activity controlling a real system based at the OU. Webcams enabled us to see exactly what was happening when we used the software to control the parts of the apparatus. As the OU moved its content online, I used both e-books and content directly in the virtual learning environment. The content was structured on a weekly basis, which was helpful in planning my work. If I knew I had a busy week coming up, I would often try and get ahead. The courses were supported by the tutors via online forums, but there were also more informal Facebook groups set up where students discussed aspects of the course outside of the main tutor forums. The face-to-face tutorials moved to online webinars and these were just as useful, but if I could not attend one I knew I could watch the recording back.

At postgraduate level, I studied for a professional doctorate at Lancaster University, which included two years of taught modules followed by my own research. This structure helped me to study for my PhD while working and the programme team fully understood the demands of professionals studying at the same time as working. It also served as a good introduction to research and the mini projects for each module meant I could explore different methodologies and topics. The modules involved peer review as a key element and this helped to refine the draft papers before submission and provide a similar experience to submitting to a journal. I decided to try submitting one of my module papers to a journal and was pleased when it was accepted and later published. I studied as part of a cohort of initially around 25 and the course and the two residentials helped me to develop relationships with others doing the programme. This helped avoid feelings of isolation during both the taught part and during the thesis stage. Developing a relationship with my supervisor was a key part of the experience and we used web-conferencing tools like Skype and Zoom for our regular meetings. This worked well and when I went to Lancaster for my viva I met my supervisor in person for the first time, yet it didn't feel strange as we had developed a good rapport.

> The challenges in both experiences have been around the group work aspects, as you are often reliant on your group members logging into the virtual learning environment to communicate. Different working patterns meant that some people would complete tasks early in the week while others completed them at the weekend. This could be problematic when you had to respond to something others had written as sometimes others hadn't completed the work yet. This was a less of a problem for the doctorate as I worked with the same cohort throughout, whereas with the OU you could be with different people for each module and rarely work with the same people more than once.
>
> The main benefit of distance learning for me has been enabling me to continue my studies while working and fit around other commitments. I have found a week-by-week structure to be really helpful and I benefited from having access to active course forums with tutor support.

## Motivation for study

A study undertaken in 2010 by Caddell and Cannell (2011) surveyed the motivations of more than a thousand Scottish distance learners enrolled as undergraduate students with the OU. While an interest in course content was the strongest single motivating factor, the other five reasons in the top six were all employment related. Most students wanted to improve their ability to progress within an existing job, move to a new job or to simply obtain a job. Milligan and Littlejohn (2014) found that students on professional MOOCs reported a similar range of motivations. Importantly, however, Caddell and Cannell found that concern with career progression was intimately connected to a range of other life factors. Motivation was 'mediated by a complex range of other factors, including missed opportunities, family and personal satisfaction and enjoyment' (Caddell and Cannell, 2011: 6). These factors were often dominant in making the decision to undertake a distance learning course. Students valued recognition by their peers and rated recognition by employers more highly than financial support for their studies. The study also noted that whereas campus students typically experience a linear journey from school through to university, distance learners often traverse complex and non-linear learning journeys. These journeys are best understood as learning pathways that are interspersed with personal and practical transitions.

## The impact of technology

The story of how distance education has developed is entwined with developments in educational technology. Writing in 1998, Peters (2001) identified three generations of learning technology: correspondence, teleconferencing (radio and television) and personal computing. Two decades later, the availability of mobile digital devices on a mass scale has added a further dimension. Ownership of mobile digital devices has grown rapidly. In the advanced economies, 72 per cent of people owned a smartphone in 2017, while in the global south the proportion was 42 per cent, with the highest growth rates in Africa (Poushter et al., 2018).

Technology enables distance education and opens up new possibilities for access and participation. However, extending access and widening participation do not follow automatically from the affordances of new technologies. Indeed, each new development has features that may help in overcoming barriers to access and participation while also offering the potential to reshape and reinforce existing barriers. For example, smart mobile devices are now part of the lived experience of perhaps half the people on our planet. Using these devices to search for information and communicate with friends in groups defined by social interest is routine. For many people, the internet is an integral part of how they experience and learn informally from the world around them. As a result, students now encounter formal distance learning in HE with existing skills and assumptions about the digital world that are potentially helpful but not sufficient to be a competent learner in a digital environment.

Students' perception and use of technology is a key area for distance learning (Wild et al., 2013). For many an advantage of distance learning is that asynchronous interaction, with tutors or fellow students, is compatible with self-regulation of the time and pace of their engagement with learning resources (Watts, 2016; and see reflections in the example). Some forms of social media open up the possibility of pedagogical approaches that include synchronous interaction. From a student perspective this may be undesirable both because it reduces flexibility and presents a new challenge since social interaction in the context of HE learning may expose a lack of confidence.

The digital world presents real challenges for course designers. Research suggests that students rank assimilative activities such as reading text and watching video more highly than activities that involve communication or collaboration with peers (Rienties and Toetenel, 2016). Moreover, Clifton (2017) notes activities such as online forums that are designed to encourage active learning tend to be unpopular with students. This research also found that 'learner satisfaction and academic retention were not even mildly related to each other' and that student-centred 'learning design activities that had a negative effect on learner experience had a neutral to even positive effect on academic retention' (Clifton, 2017: 281). This is a real challenge for course designers, since what students rank highly in evaluations tends not to correlate well with student learning and successful outcomes.

While social media engages huge numbers of individuals around the world, institutions have struggled to incorporate it effectively in formal course designs in ways that engage distance learning students. In the boxed example, Julie explains how students on her course were encouraged to make use of Facebook, a familiar medium for social interaction. However, there are indications that distance learners are using social media to find and communicate with others on their course, whether or not it is suggested by tutors. Much of the evidence to date is anecdotal because researching this phenomenon is a challenge. By definition, these are initiatives that are below the radar, by students, for students and beyond the formal boundaries of the institution. Biddix et al. (2015) note in a study of the use of student-initiated social media groups in a campus setting that this challenges conventional approaches to the design of distance learning environments. Similar conclusions are drawn in a review of the use of short, openly licensed online courses to support widening participation (Cannell et al., 2015), which was part of a Scotland-wide project that provided evidence that the recognition of student context and opportunities for social learning can have a positive impact on student satisfaction, retention and success.

MOOCs have added another dimension to the distance learning landscape. Large-scale and online delivery has a longer pedigree linked to specialist distance teaching universities. However, MOOCs represent a move by campus-based institutions to offer courses that make use of the internet and the widespread availability of mobile devices. Most participants are distance learners, although some are campus based and study MOOCs alongside more conventional face-to-face and blended courses. MOOCs illustrate the contention that technology, access and participation are not synonymous. They were heralded as opening up HE to anyone who had internet access (Laurillard and Kennedy, 2017). The reality has been somewhat different, and most participants already have HE qualifications.

Perhaps unhelpfully, the term MOOC is often applied to any large-scale online course. This tends to oversimplify a landscape that is more diverse – including the provision of (online) courses by long-standing distance learning universities and a burgeoning set of free open online courses developed as OERs, and often specifically designed from the perspective of widening participation. The OpenLearn and OpenLearnCreate sites administered by the OU are currently the largest of these resources, while the Commonwealth of Learning also has a range of related initiatives focused on student audiences in the global south.

## Focusing on distance learning and widening participation

The demand for HE around the world is anticipated to more than double by 2030 (Atherton et al., 2016). Most of this new demand is located in the global south and the prospects of meeting this additional demand through campus-based provision are poor. Indeed, in many countries, demand for HE places already outstrips supply. National governments, private providers and international consortia are looking to distance education as the only way of responding effectively at scale.

In contrast, developed economies have evolved systems of mass HE that provide access to significant proportions of their populations. However, large-scale access is not synonymous with equity and often goes hand in hand with inequality (OECD, 2019). In the UK, part-time distance learning has been one way in which disadvantaged adults have been able to obtain access to further and higher education. Although this success has sometimes been marginalised in terms of government policy and confined to a limited number of institutions, there has been a resurgence of interest in England. Guidance from the Government's Office for Students (2018) notes that part-time and distance education provides an important route into HE for students from disadvantaged backgrounds and tasks all institutions to consider developing appropriate provision.

There is a real danger that the challenges of extending access in the global south and widening participation in the global north are seen as primarily an issue of exploiting technology. The experience of MOOCs to date provides a warning. Briefly hailed as a way in which good-quality education could be made accessible to anyone with an internet connection, they have largely provided another option for those who have already had access to HE.

The problem of access has often been characterised as digital divide – separating those with the technology from those who either cannot afford it or lack the skills to use it. This divide still exists. In the developed economies and in the global south there remain significant numbers who cannot access distance provision via the internet. Conole (2012: 132) argues that 'the technological divide might be narrower, but it is deeper – those not connected or not using these new technologies are being left behind at an alarming rate'.

The barriers to widening participation through distance education are complex and multilayered. The issues are not just about access to devices or software. Brown et al. (2016) argue strongly against the assumption that we are in a simple transition, in which a new generation of digital natives takes the place of their less digitally literate forbears. They argue that the ability to learn in digital environments is not a function of age, rather a new net generation is maturing to replace an older analogue generation and the digital divide in South Africa is enhanced not as a function of age but of access and opportunity.

Sadly, there has been relatively little dialogue between practitioners and researchers involved in online and distance learning and their counterparts in widening participation. The latter have developed substantial literature outlining the social, cultural and material barriers to participation in HE (Fuller and Paton, 2008). However, in the digital age these barriers intersect and interact with new challenges that are specific to the digital environment. Cannell and Macintyre (2017) note that:

> Individuals making educational transitions do so in a world where digital technology has become ubiquitous. For some, a prerequisite of engaging with education is the acquisition of basic skills for digital participation.

Other authors, such as Lea and Jones (2011), have argued that distance students have a diversity of prior experience and sociocultural practice that makes it essential to include the development of digital literacy skills in the core curriculum for new entrants to HE. Cannell and Macintyre (2017) conclude that good practice in supporting transition into formal education needs to understand and value existing digital skills. Success and retention in formal education needs long-term support for the development of appropriate digital literacy skills. None of this is unique to distance education, but it is critical for distance education because of the way in which it is always mediated by technology.

The digital environment also has the potential for amplifying barriers that are familiar in face-to-face contexts where students may lack confidence and familiarity with academic practice. Kop et al. (2011) note in the case of MOOCs that even though designers may be concerned to create a 'learner-centred' learning environment, students may still find the scale of the online community disorientating.

## Retention and success

Dropout from distance learning courses is high compared with campus-based education. This is true of more traditional distance learning courses and of MOOCs, which typically have high enrolments yet only a small percentage of students complete them. However, as noted, the motivation for study, personal definitions of success and life circumstances of distance learning students mean that student retention is highly contextual. It is contingent on institutional and student aims, their expectations and their conceptions of how 'success' is defined (Cannell et al., 2019).

There is extensive literature on student retention, but relatively little of it is concerned with distance learning. Good practice models designed for face-to-face teaching do not translate easily to distance learning where student demographics and the challenges faced by students are different (Gaytan, 2015). It is also important to note that precisely because retention is contextual it is necessary to continually reassess and rethink strategies as circumstances change:

> If attrition is to be meaningfully understood and purposefully managed, then the institution needs to implement their student success strategies, policies, and actions with specific social, cultural and organizational context in mind. (Huang et al., 2019: 218)

For 50 years, open universities tended to design for retention and success with variants of a pedagogical model that essentially separated academic tuition from student support (understood as infrastructure and support services). Tait (2014) claims that in the digital age this model is less appropriate and argues for the integration of academic and student support in a student-centred online environment. He suggests that learning design is the critical factor influencing student retention in digital distance and e-learning and enables student support to be integrated with teaching and assessment. Street (2010) takes a similar view:

> A student's decision whether to drop-out or persist in an online environment influences and is influenced by personal factors such as self-efficacy, self-determination, autonomy, and time management. A student's decision whether to drop-out or persist in an online environment also influences and is influenced by environmental factors such as family support, organizational support, and technical support. A third, unique factor can be added

for online attrition. Course factors of relevance and design influence a learner's decision to persist or drop an online course.

With a new interest in online and distance retention from MOOC providers it is important to bring this new experience together with insights and experience from open and distance learning and the rich history of campus-based retention practice. Stone (2017) provides a useful synthesis of the latest Australian work on retention, while Weller (2018) provides a set of principles for good practice in learning design to support student retention. In an overview report, Cannell et al. (2019) conclude that within an overall frame of improving learning design for retention there are four areas for research and for developing practice that are particularly pertinent:

- **Assessment for learning:** recent research suggests that designing assessment for learning as opposed to assessment of learning contributes to retention and success (Admiraal et al., 2015; Perrotta and Whitelock, 2017).
- **Peer support:** peer support has been shown to have a positive impact on retention but there is a need for more research into effective ways of implementing this in ways that retain flexibility for distance learners.
- **Learning analytics:** while the use of analytics is growing rapidly, there are dangers in basing pedagogical innovation on analytic data alone. Zawacki-Richter and Anderson (2014) suggest that learning analytics are best combined with systematic, contextualised qualitative research.
- **Transitions:** one of the strengths of retention practice aimed at widening participation has been the recognition that learning journeys include critical points of transition. Developing these insights in the context of learning design for distance learning would be of great value.

## Conclusion

Distance education is in flux. After more than 40 years of growth and success, traditional open and distance learning providers face a triple challenge: to adapt to the possibilities of the new digital world, to competition from private providers and to unhelpful national educational policy frameworks. At the same time, the rise of the MOOC has turned out to be less disruptive to conventional universities than the initial hype suggested. While many more institutions are now offering distance courses in MOOC format, the target demographic has turned out to be much narrower than expected and the most successful developments are tending to be in relatively niche areas of the curriculum.

Unequal access remains a problem in the developed economies and there is huge and growing demand for HE in the global south. Over the next decade a new generation of students will be ready for, and deserve, good-quality HE and there is a strong argument to suggest that distance education has a critical part to play in achieving the increase in participation required. Digital technology can help make this possible. The speed with which mobile digital devices have become mass consumer items across the world has created an environment and infrastructure with potential for widening and deepening access. However, this potential remains largely untapped and institutional practices often lag behind student expectations and needs. While technology is necessary it is not sufficient. Moving distance education into the mainstream requires rethinking student support (Tait, 2014) so that it is integrated into the learning environment and speaks to the needs of distance learners. Simply digitizing campus systems and approaches is not enough (King, 2012). New developments in pedagogy and in sensitive learning design that builds on well-researched insights into student needs are needed to meet the challenges of the twenty-first century.

## References

Admiraal, W., Huisman, B. and Pilli, O. (2015) 'Assessment in massive open online courses'. *Electronic Journal of e-Learning*, 13 (4), 207–16.

Atherton, G., Dumangane, C. and Whitty, G. (2016) *Charting Equity in Higher Education: Drawing the global access map*. London: Pearson. Accessed 5 August 2019. https://www.pearson.com/content/dam/one-dot-com/one-dot-com/global/Files/about-pearson/innovation/Charting-Equity_WEB.pdf.

Biddix, J. P., Chung, C. J. and Park, H. W. (2015) 'The hybrid shift: Evidencing a student-driven restructuring of the college classroom'. *Computers & Education*, 80, 162–75.

Boliver, V. (2011) 'Expansion, differentiation, and the persistence of social class inequalities in British higher education'. *Higher Education*, 61 (3), 229–42.

Brown, C., Czerniewicz, L. and Noakes, T. (2016) 'Online content creation: Looking at students' social media practices through a connected learning lens'. *Learning, Media and Technology*, 41 (1), 140–59.

Brown, M., Hughes, H., Keppell, M., Hard, N. and Smith, L. (2015) 'Stories from students in their first semester of distance learning'. *International Review of Research in Open and Distributed Learning*, 16 (4), 1–17.

Caddell, M. and Cannell, P. (2011) 'Rethinking graduate attributes: Understanding the learning journeys of part-time students in the Open University in Scotland'. In B. Jones and S. Oosthuizen (eds), *Part-Time Study: The new paradigm for higher education?* Stirling: UALL.

Cannell, P. and Macintyre, R. (2017) 'Are open and online reconfiguring learner journeys?' Paper presented at the 2017 Scottish Enhancement Themes Conference. Accessed 5 August 2019. https://www.open.edu/openlearncreate/mod/page/view.php?id=130951.

Cannell, P., Macintyre, R. and Hewitt, L. (2015) 'Widening access and OER: Developing new practice'. *Widening Participation and Lifelong Learning*, 17 (1), 64–72.

Cannell, P., Patel, D. and Tait, A. (2019) 'Supporting progression and completion: Final report'. University of London Centre for Online and Distance Education. Accessed 5 August 2019. https://london.ac.uk/centre-distance-education/cde-activities/cde-projects#supporting-progression-and-completion.

Clifton, G. (2017) 'An evaluation of the impact of "learning design" on the distance learning and teaching experience'. *International Review of Research in Open and Distributed Learning*, 18 (5). Accessed 5 August 2019. https://doi.org/10.19173/irrodl.v18i5.2960.

Conole, G. (2012) 'Fostering social inclusion through open educational resources (OER)'. *Distance Education*, 33 (2), 131–4.

Daniel, J. (1996) *Mega-Universities and Knowledge Media, Technology Strategies for Higher Education*. London: Kogan Page.

Daniel, J. (2012) 'Dual-mode universities in higher education: Way station or final destination?' *Open Learning: The Journal of Open, Distance and e-Learning*, 27 (1), 89–95. Accessed 7 July 2022. https://doi.org/10.1080/02680513.2012.640791.

Fuller, A. and Paton, K. (2008) '"Barriers" to participation in higher education? Depends who you ask and how'. *Widening Participation and Lifelong Learning*, 10 (2), 6–17.

Gaytan, J. (2015) 'Comparing faculty and student perceptions regarding factors that affect student retention in online education'. *American Journal of Distance Education*, 29 (1), 56–66.

Graham, C. R., Woodfield, W. and Harrison, J. B. (2013) 'A framework for institutional adoption and implementation of blended learning in higher education'. *Internet and Higher Education*, 18 (3), 4–14.

Huang, Q., Nathawitharana, N., Ong, K. L., Keller, S. and Alahakoon, D. (2019) 'Mind the Gap: From analytics to action in student retention'. In Shah J. Miah and William Yeoh (eds), *Applying Business Intelligence Initiatives in Healthcare and Organizational Settings*. Hershey, PA: IGI Global, 218–36.

Kahu, E., Stephens, C., Leach, L. and Zepke, N. (2015) 'Linking academic emotions and student engagement: Mature-aged distance students' transition to university'. *Journal of Further and Higher Education*, 39 (4), 481–97.

King, B. (2012) 'Distance education and dual-mode universities: An Australian perspective'. *Open Learning: The Journal of Open, Distance and E-Learning*, 27 (1), 9–22.

Kop, R., Fournier, H. and Mak, J. S. F. (2011) 'A pedagogy of abundance or a pedagogy to support human beings? Participant support on massive open online courses'. *International Review of Research in Open and Distance Learning*, 12 (7) 74–93. Accessed 5 August 2019. https://www.irrodl.org/index.php/irrodl/article/view/1041.

Lambert, L. A. and Hassan, H. (2018) 'MOOCs and international capacity building in a UN framework: Potential and challenges'. In W. L. Filho, M. Mifsud and P. Pace (eds), *Handbook of Lifelong Learning for Sustainable Development*. Cham: Springer, 155–64.

Laurillard, D. and Kennedy, E. (2017) 'The potential of MOOCs for learning at scale in the Global South', Centre for Global Higher Education working paper no. 31, December. Accessed 5 August 2019. https://www.researchcghe.org/perch/resources/publications/wp31.pdf.

Lea, M. R. and Jones, S. (2011) 'Digital literacies in higher education: Exploring textual and technological practice'. *Studies in Higher Education*, 36 (4), 377–93.

Milligan, C. and Littlejohn, A. (2014) 'Supporting professional learning in a massive open online course'. *International Review of Research in Open and Distributed Learning*, 15 (5), 197–213.

Mugridge, I. (1997) *Founding the Open Universities*. New Delhi: Sterling Publishers.

OECD (Organisation for Economic Co-operation and Development) (2019) 'How does socio-economic status influence entry into tertiary education?' Education Indicators in Focus brief, no. 69. Accessed 5 August 2019. https://doi.org/10.1787/b541bfcd-en.

Office for Students (2018) 'Regulatory advice 6: Good practice advice on the preparation of access and participation plans for 2019–20'. Accessed 5 August 2019. https://www.officeforstudents.org.uk/media/1105/ofs2018_06.pdf.

OU (Open University) Library (2019) 'The first 10 years 1969–1979'. Accessed 5 August 2019. https://www.open.ac.uk/library/digital-archive/exhibition/53/theme/2/page/5.

Perrotta, C. and Whitelock, D. (2017) 'Assessment for learning'. In E. Duval, M. Sharples and R. Sutherland (eds), *Technology Enhanced Learning: Research themes*. Berlin: Springer International Publishing, 127–35. Accessed 5 August 2019. https://www.researchgate.net/

profile/Carlo_Perrotta2/publication/317173877_Assessment_for_Learning/links/59f847a0458515547c24effd/Assessment-for-Learning.pdf.

Peters, O. (2001) *Learning and Teaching in Distance Education*. London: Kogan Page.

Poskitt, J., Rees, M. and Suddaby, G. (2011) 'Engaging with university at a distance: The differences in levels of student engagement among extramural and campus-based students'. In A. Radolf (ed.), *Student Engagement in New Zealand's Universities*. Melbourne: Australian Council for Educational Research (ACER), 70–6.

Poushter, J., Bishop, C. and Chwe, H. (2018) 'Social media use continues to rise in developing countries but plateaus across developed ones'. Pew Research Center, 19 June. Accessed 5 August 2019. http://medienorge.uib.no/files/Eksterne_pub/Pew-Research-Center_Global-Tech-Social-Media-Use_2018.06.19.pdf.

Rienties, B. and Toetenel, L. (2016) 'The impact of learning design on student behaviour, satisfaction and performance: A cross-institutional comparison across 151 modules'. *Computers in Human Behavior*, 60, 333–41.

Rumble, G. (2001) 'Re-inventing distance education'. *International Journal of Lifelong Education*, 20 (1–2), 31–43.

Shapiro, H. B., Lee, C. H., Roth, N. E. W., Li, K., Çetinkaya-Rundel, M. and Canelas, D. A. (2017) 'Understanding the massive open online course (MOOC) student experience: An examination of attitudes, motivations, and barriers'. *Computers & Education*, 110, 35–50.

Simons, J., Beaumont, K. and Holland, L. (2018) 'What factors promote student resilience on a level 1 distance learning module?' *Open Learning: The Journal of Open, Distance and e-Learning*, 33 (1), 4–17. Accessed 10 September 2018. https://www.tandfonline.com/doi/abs/10.1080/02680513.2017.1415140.

Simpson, O. (2003) *Student Retention in Online, Open and Distance Learning*. Oxford: Routledge.

Stone, C. (2017) *Opportunity through Online Learning: Improving student access, participation and success in higher education*. National Centre for Student Equity in Higher Education (NCSEHE) final report. Accessed 5 August 2019. https://www.ncsehe.edu.au/publications/opportunity-online-learning-improving-student-access-participation-success-higher-education/.

Street, H. (2010) 'Factors influencing a learner's decision to drop-out or persist in higher education distance learning'. *Online Journal of Distance Learning Administration* 13 (4). Accessed 5 August 2019. https://pdfs.semanticscholar.org/5993/10d5e8334a5864b019d457e717b19fe5c8ab.pdf.

Tait, A. (2014) 'From place to virtual space: Reconfiguring student support for distance and e-learning in the digital age'. *Open Praxis*, 6 (1), 5–16. Accessed 5 October 2019. https://www.learntechlib.org/p/130684/.

Tait, A. and Mills, R. (eds) (1999) *The Convergence of Distance and Conventional Education: Patterns of flexibility for the individual learner*. London: Routledge.

Watts, L. (2016) 'Synchronous and asynchronous communication in distance learning: A review of the literature'. *Quarterly Review of Distance Education*, 17 (1), 23.

Weller, M., van Ameijde, J. and Cross, S. (2018) 'Learning design for student retention'. *Journal of Perspectives in Applied Academic Practice*, 6 (2). Accessed 7 July 2022. https://doi.org/10.14297/jpaap.v6i2.318.

Wild, J., Cant, M. C. and Nell, C. (2013) 'Open distance learning students' perception of the use of social media networking systems as an educational tool'. *International Business & Economics Research Journal*, 12 (8), 867–82.

Zawacki-Richter, O. and Anderson, T. (eds) (2014) *Online Distance Education: Towards a research agenda*. Athabasca, AB: Athabasca University Press.

# 3
# Exploring digital learning
## J. Simon Rofe

This chapter explores some of the challenging relationships between digital, online and distance education. These are often global in scope and localised in effect. The United Nations' Sustainable Development Goals for 2030 recognise the challenge and the opportunity 'that digital technologies provide for humanity, and the great potential that the spread of information and communications technology (ICT) and global interconnectedness have in accelerating human progress, bridging the digital divide and developing knowledge societies' (United Nations, 2015: 5). Exploring the challenges and opportunities for digital, online and distance education allows us to provide insights into, and context for, the relationships between these different modes and advice on how to meaningfully engage with both dimensions of twenty-first-century education, to the benefit of educators, their students, their institutions and the sector as a whole.

This chapter provides context to the use of digital methods in distance education. It offers the reader assistance in their own practice by providing handholds to the ongoing and evolving discussion, unpicking some key facets of the language involved and offering points of advice. The chapter then considers the skills and status of those engaged in digital learning and distance education, recognising that best practice in education needs multifaceted design teams with flexible, adaptable skills operating in a consistently changing environment. The chapter then explores approaches and models and thereby shares practice.

Not all digital or online learning is at a distance and not all distance education is digital. High-quality (and indeed low-quality) digital education can take place on campus; some forms of distance learning involve no digital component, being analogue in their content and/or mode of operation – for example, via print, post or telephone.

That said, the two are usually closely related, with considerable overlap, including some tensions that affect the relationship. It is to that relationship between digital and distance education that we now turn, while recognising that the goal of quality learning is as relevant in the digital space as it has been throughout the ages in physical learning environments.

## What is digital learning?

One of the most evident tensions that exists here is over what constitutes digital learning. Definitions can be, and are, offered: a cursory scan of hashtags such as #digitallearning #edtech #onlinelearning #learning reveals a rich, vibrant and evolving debate among a wide range of actors globally. Equally, there is a tension between digital learning and the physical spaces that are used in its presentation and delivery. Gourlay (2021) explores this in considering what she terms the 'Materiality of Digital Education'. Digital learning, in contrast to a default notion that it is something other, beyond the physical, intrinsically links digital affordances with analogue in-person education. Digital does not mean unreal.

Digital learning challenges a spatial account of education. It also poses questions about the temporal dimension. This is a significant challenge to a campus-based, timetabled orthodoxy because it is not constrained by the need for a classroom. As Gannon (2019) notes, using the digital space 'creates the space for intentionally deliberate discourse to unfold over time. The result: students' conversations – with both the course material and with one another – are richer and more reflective than in person.' The discourse is over the employment of synchronous (where all learners dedicate the same period of time to learning and conversing) and asynchronous learning (where learning takes place across a range of times). For the purposes of this chapter, its relevance stems from the opportunities to use time flexibly in digital learning and distance education that the campus-based orthodoxy mostly denies.

A further tension here exists in the wider society in which higher education (HE) sits and which HE shapes. The digital world appears to be everywhere, all the time: those who live 'off the grid' are increasingly rare and what functions of society are now solely analogue? Digital infrastructure and interfaces support, to varying degrees, finance, healthcare, relationships *and* education. These literal interpretations (beyond the literal meaning of the words) show that we should be mindful of how differentiated interpretations indicate the precision needed in the use of language. They also show that we must take seriously the values attached to such language. In other words, there are multiple ways of seeking to understand the relationship between digital learning and distance education.

The discussion that follows touches on topics within online and digital education, such as learning design, technological advances and career professional development. Each of these topics have related aspects but employ their own discourses and literatures. This speaks to the complex network of issues that digital learning and distance education touch upon.

## Contemporary education environment: context

Society is facing an unprecedented rise in automation, machine learning and other technologies, which has been framed as the Fourth Industrial Revolution (Schwab, 2016). In this chapter we look into our understanding of the contemporary environment for HE and the challenge of melding educational practice with advances in technology. The opportunity to meld educational practice and advances in technology is at the heart of this chapter's challenge.

Perhaps the most significant learning tool available to learners is the mobile phone (Shuler et al., 2013). Its evolution technologically and its current near ubiquity – perhaps 80 per cent of the world's population – achieved within a generation, are remarkable. What is equally clear is that individuals and groups using this particular piece of technology have a gateway into mobile learning that was denied to previous generations. A swathe of research suggests that HE institutions have not successfully engaged with this dimension of twenty-first-century learning on a sector-wide basis (see, for example, Ahmad, 2019; Cook et al., 2015; Mohammadi et al., 2020; Santos, 2013, 2017). In 2019, '68% of internet traffic was via mobile devices; more of the world has a mobile device than a telephone or a desktop' (Silver, 2019). Importantly when considering distance education, the statistics for internet usage on mobile devices continue to rise 'and the percentages [are] shifting rapidly towards mobility, especially in Asia and Africa' (Silver, 2019). The latter are traditionally sites of distance education in the global south provided by indigenous and external providers from the global north – Europe and North America. Despite the colonial antecedents of such arrangements, the opportunities for meaningful partnerships and initiatives from the global south may be the catalysts to meeting the challenges faced here. A recent study from one Ugandan institution,

Makerere University, recommends: 'The university should revise its strategies for extensive use of mobile phones in supporting ODL [online distance learning] students, since students are already using mobile phones to support their own study' (Mayanja et al., 2019: 184). The latter dimension, learners already using their mobile devices, is significant, not just in this particular case but across the world. This is because the different capabilities of different devices (for example, download speed and storage space) in turn shape the opportunities, affordances and limitations of digital learning and distance education. Salmon (2019) suggests that there is a 'major rethink about the insistence of "going to university" and the dominance of location-based universities' with the implication being that this 'could lead to increased access to, and participation in, higher education.' Salmon's thinking, in a pre-COVID-19 age, speaks to the tension that has played out between technological innovation and status quo thinking. Think of the Gutenberg printing press in the fifteenth century. The advent of digital has the potential to be similarly disruptive.

Perhaps the most fundamental challenge has been the de-centring of what the UK's 1963 Robbins Report concluded was the purpose of HE as being 'the imaginative acquisition of knowledge' (Robbins, 1963). Instead, the generational shift of the twenty-first century suggests that HE's purpose now means we can add to the Robbins Report's mantra: 'The imaginative acquisition *and facilitation* of knowledge, *and the skills to effectively interpret, analyse and relay said knowledge*' (Robbins, 1963, emphasis added). This reflects the massification and omnipresence of knowledge and the evolving, multidimensional and networked nature of global society that digital learning affords.

The context of the twenty-first century for digital learning shapes the environment for HE in three important ways. Firstly, most of those engaging in HE in whatever form have increased awareness of, and facility in, the use of digital technologies than previous generations. Their initial experience with HE is likely to be digital in so far as it will be through a webpage and an application process that are both digital experiences. However, there is debate over the extent to which they may be accurately termed 'digital natives' (Bennett et al., 2008; Palfrey and Gasser, 2008; Prensky, 2001) – the term attributed to those who have grown up with digital technology as part of their daily lives and the emergence of a 'digital divide' between those who have access to the digital world and those who do not and suffer from a form of digital poverty. The distance between different cohorts across the digital landscape is important to recognise in the application of digital learning.

The discrepancies, themselves evolving, reflect different skills and accessibility and therefore the ability to participate in, and contribute to, an increasingly digitised society. These discrepancies are seen most starkly in societies at local and national levels that are already socioeconomically differentiated.

The second dimension in the way a digital society shapes the space for HE is that many countries' national education policies place, or at least aspire to place, considerable emphasis on developing digital skills. These policies blend political aspiration from primary and indeed nursery-level education, with digital technologies as a key part of the learning experience. Secondary and further education follow suit, which means that students engaging with HE, whether on campus or at a distance, have had prior exposure to a degree of digital learning.

A third element here is the relevance of lifelong learning and flexible learning to the digital domain. With the former, lifelong learning can entail providing the opportunity to backfill digital skills for those to whom the digital realm is new. Allied to this is the recognition that, as digital technologies develop, maintaining mastery of them is an ongoing enterprise for us all. With the latter, and with universities concerned about their place in provision, Universities UK stressed the economic benefits of flexible learning in HE (UUK, 2019). This was followed up with a joint statement from the UK Confederation of British Industry stressing the synergy of flexible learning with individual and society benefits:

> There is a strong economic imperative to improve flexible learning opportunities to improve the life chances and employment outcomes of those wishing to change or improve their careers, as well as increasing productivity of businesses by addressing skills shortages and upskilling existing employees. (UUK/CBI, 2019)

Those engaging in distance education can have a considerable range of digital learning experiences and capabilities.

Therefore, as educators seeking to enhance the learning experience, how do we make sense of this environment to decipher what matters? To show the challenge, Educause Learning Initiative has annually captured the leading issues in teaching and learning by surveying educators and producing an infographic that illustrates what is important to those surveyed (see Educause, 2018, 2019). Mapping the rise and fall of issues offers an insight into the evolving nature of what matters to practitioners. Comparing the 2018 and 2019 versions, we see a significant increase in digital learning issues – Digital & Information Literacy, Online & Blended

Learning, Instructional & Learning Experience Design, Learning Analytics, Evaluating Instructional & Learning Innovations – underpinned by a relationship with, and application of, emerging technology. While these five issues emerge as the most prominent of the 15, digital learning is evident across the other key issues. We might reasonably ask if there is anything in contemporary education that doesn't have some aspect of 'digital'?

Such infographics outline what is important each year. Over time, they show a series of evolving elements in the mysterious alchemy of digital learning and distance education. In such a complex, evolving and disrupted environment – and in endeavouring to explain it to colleagues in HE – what do we mean by 'digital learning' and 'distance education'.

## Digital learning

Digital learning is a piece of vernacular whose meaning has evolved and will continue to do so. It has emerged – for now at least – as a term that encompasses a range of educational practices and approaches, underpinned by the use of digital technologies, cultures and affordances. In essence, it refers to learning that takes place mediated by digital means supported by digital technologies. What matters is the 'learning'; the digital dimension, as we have seen, can exist without 'learning'.

An alternative definition is provided by Davis (2019), the editor of *EdTech*, for whom digital learning 'includes blended learning, flipped learning, personalized learning, and other strategies that rely on digital tools to a small or large degree'. In positivist tones Davis (2019) suggests that digital learning 'can enhance learning experiences, save teachers time, enable teachers to better tailor learning to student needs, aid in tracking student progress, provide transparency into the learning process for all stakeholders, and much more'. It can also be overwhelming because of this scope – and it is in this respect that this chapter seeks to provide handholds to help understand digital learning as a contested term. Illustrating the challenge succinctly, the University of Southampton (n.d.) asks the question: 'Digital learning: What is it'?

The term digital learning has antecedents in other terms: e-learning; online learning; blended learning – the balanced blend of digital and face-to-face pedagogies in addressing student learning; technology-enhanced learning; adaptive learning – the tailoring of the learning experience through computer algorithms; artificial intelligence (AI);

open learning – including the use of open educational resources, which make learning freely available through digital means, as explored in Chapter 16; social learning – the use of forms of social media (itself much debated) to address and facilitate learning as considered in Chapter 9 (see also Anderson, 2019). These different pieces of terminology are often used interchangeably, leading to an 'alphabet soup' of terms and can be disorientating to many. Borrowing from another field in cultural diplomacy, the plethora of terms can be framed as a 'semantic constellation' (Ang et al., 2015: 361, 385). Further, and to demonstrate again that the societal context matters in our reflections on our practice, the use of the term 'digital learning' is not restricted to its use in HE to facilitate student–teacher interactions. Professional development within HE is delivered increasingly through digital learning and draws on sources from outside the sector in the breadth of approaches.

'Digital learning covers many formal and informal learning techniques and should be seen as one element in an organisation's learning strategy …', according to the Chartered Institute of Personnel and Development, 'often enhanced by being linked to other learning methods such as face-to-face sessions, coaching and mentoring' (CIPD, 2021). In light of this, it is therefore little surprise to learn that what constitutes digital learning can mean different things to different people: its meaning is not agreed.

## Distance education

Distance education is similarly contested. Distance education has a longer history and pre-dates the emergence of the digital age of the latter half of the twentieth century that has become synonymous with digital learning (see the Preface to this book). Distance learners are usually remote from their academic institution. In the nineteenth century, when the University of London (UoL) became the world's first form of HE to award degrees to students at a distance through its external programmes (chartered in 1858), the embryonic international postal service was used to send materials to students overseas. The provision predated the Universal Postal Union, which was itself formed in 1874 by the Treaty of Bern, so distance education was at the cutting edge of available technology. Distance education has often been known therefore as 'correspondence education'. Since then, telegram, radio and television – the latter a keystone in the founding of the Open University in the UK in 1969 – have all been utilised to aid student learning in distance education. The digital epoch has given the opportunity for HE to once more embrace new technology, although not without facing challenges.

These developments have been led by institutions in what international relations scholars would call the West, more recently the global north: the UK, Europe and the USA. Their endeavours have been marketed – sometimes aggressively – to those from the global south. The implication here for those contemplating the enterprise is that there is a debate about the extent to which distance education has reinforced – often through access to particular technologies – prevailing power structures or has the capacity to challenge them through education's capacity for social mobility. UoL distance learning graduate Nelson Mandela would probably have suggested the latter. As so often, we should probably replace 'or' here with 'and' so the twin foci of this chapter are relevant to the discourse of decolonisation of HE (Mwaanga, 2022).

It is important to also note that the word 'distance' precedes 'education' rather than 'teaching'. The edifice of the physical university, the configuration of many lecture theatres and the default thinking of many practitioners and students has prejudiced academics' teaching over students' learning in HE. While this touches upon broader debates about the very purpose of HE in considering 'distance' and 'digital' as academic practitioners, it is not about *their* teaching, as much as it is about *our* learning.

## Into practice: approaches

### Translation

To provide practical assistance to the reader in addressing the evolution of distance education and digital learning, let us consider the design, development and delivery of courseware. Essentially, the task is one of translation; that is, to translate what is often familiar, based on years of research, into something comprehensible and useable via distance and digital means. Scholars of translation recognise that using certain grammatical 'rules' enhances understanding and guides the development of vocabulary. In following these 'rules', through comprehension exercises, protagonists are obliged to use their developing knowledge and understanding. The 'practice' underpins the 'practise' of a language. There are demonstrable parallels between the act of translation and the deployment of digital learning in distance education in taking what is known, enhancing it through practice, and with appropriate skills and understanding, with a view to enhancing comprehension.

*Working together helps*

One dimension of this that is particularly noteworthy is the communal effort involved in enhancing comprehension. In other words, digital learning in distance education is a team effort. The make-up of the team is a blend, incorporating a number of stakeholders, with the 'teacher' and the 'student' often considered as key members of the starting line-up. However, here again the affordances of digital learning in distance education challenge the orthodoxy of a binary teacher–student relationship. Distance education suggests that there is a greater distance between teacher and student than within a classroom and into that space others can helpfully be part of the learning experience, making up a community of practice to assist educational practice.

The endeavour is therefore a 'team effort'. Mosley (2020) argues that the COVID-19 global pandemic must strengthen the bonds between lecturers and education specialists: 'Forget lone lecturers – the pandemic shows teaching must be a team sport.' It is also a team that it is itself evolving, with the capacity to embrace new players and practices. So, who are those individuals making up the community of practice to enable digital learning in distance education? They typically include a tutor and student cohort but are augmented by a growing and evolving number of stakeholders. The parlance can vary from institution to institution (and indeed within institutions) and thus add potential for confusion, but the point is that they can involve a range of 'players': those known as educational designers, learning technologists, digital education advisors and perhaps traditionally *librarians*. What matters is that these individuals all contribute to the design, development and delivery of learning. This range of team members exposes potential tension between their contribution and what is seen as 'front-of-house teaching' typically delivered by an academic. Fawns et al. (2019: 295) argue it is 'more crucial than ever' to see beyond the front of house to recognise that 'what goes as the visible, synchronous dimension of learning does not tell the whole story'. In short, to effectively engage is a digital education in distance education is a team enterprise.

## Advice and 'know-how'

To readers of this book, it will be of little surprise that different approaches can be employed to address digital learning and distance education. This chapter ends with brief descriptions of three approaches. The ones to be considered are: Laurillard's (2002) *Conversational Framework*; Fung's

(2017) *Connected Curriculum*; and the *IR Model of Intellectual Reflection* (Rofe, 2011a).

Laurillard's Conversational Framework rests upon several learning types that have been developed and proven robust for almost two decades in enabling high levels of academic engagement and professional learning. The six types Laurillard identifies are acquisition (read/watch/listen), investigation, practice, discussion, collaboration and production. Consideration of these produces the opportunity for 'educational design thinking'. Importantly for the framework's success and demonstrating its applicability, a 'quick', 'base'-level introduction learning design toolkit entitled ABC (illustrating its simplicity) was developed and has been widely available through the ABC Learning Design website (www.abc-ld.org). What impresses most in the ABC approach is the adaptability of Laurillard's thinking to different education contexts, giving rise to widespread acclaim and support from educational practitioners (Holmberg, 2017).

The flexibility is an enabler in enhancing and maintaining a community of practice – something that has seen versions of the ABC approach adapted to the circumstances of the global COVID-19 pandemic.

Fung's *Connected Curriculum* is a wholesale examination of the institutional approach to curriculum and learning. It is a holistic approach that engages with the full complement of issues facing HE, from research-led teaching and accessibility to employability and decolonisation of curricula. The flower image that adorns the cover of Fung's book is integral to the analysis within its pages, as the petals represent different dimensions to 'learning through research and enquiry'. The six-fold petals address: (1) students' connections with researchers and their institutions' research; (2) the evidence of that research in programme provision; (3) students making connections across programmes and outside of HE; (4) students connecting learning from different parts of their lives: as students, as workers and as citizens; (5) students directing their learning to producing outcomes – whatever they are; (6) students making connections with other students and communities. It is the connections and the networks that they encourage that provide the opportunity to consider digital technologies and distance education. In keeping with this thinking, Fung's book was made available as an open access volume (https://www.uclpress.co.uk/products/86213), with many thousands of downloads and views since its 2017 publication. Integral to the *Connected Curriculum* is the role of learners: education happens *with* students not *to* them.

The IR (international relations) Model's approach is to emphasis a comprehensive approach in designing, developing and delivering digital learning (Rofe, 2011a). Its antecedents come from a constructivist tradition and the model builds out from Gilly Salmon's formative work in identifying 'e-tivities' in providing structure to different learning objects (Rofe, 2011b). Its particular application in distance education stems from the familiarity of process – purpose, task, respond, outcome – that enables the focus on learning the subject at hand in the absence of space for clarification that face-to-face learning typically affords (Salmon, 2002). Clear evidence of learning can be measured in any manner of assessment tasks over the course of a class, study session or programme against Salmon's Five-Stage Model.[1] The latter demonstrates the facilitation of learning through individuals and technologies towards achieving high-level learning outcomes from low-cost engagement and socialisation.

Each of these three models of learning has been influenced and shaped by their relationship with digital learning and distance education. What characterises all three is their flexibility and ability to adapt to their environment – a readiness to be applied by engaged educators.

## Conclusions

Everyone is a learner in the twenty-first century and learning is an ongoing process that does not stop at the doors of a lecture hall or a graduation ceremony. Distance education is an established feature of the HE landscape; it has often been at the vanguard of embracing technological change in the sector. In this regard, the employment of digital learning has its antecedents in the use of the international postal service, the telegraph and the telephone. All of these advances needed technological revolution and challenged appreciations of location and space with the idea of the world getting 'smaller' and more connected. The challenge for HE is whether learning via digital is more than just the next evolution and the extent to which it challenges the foundations of education ontologically.

The advent of AI, accelerating processing speeds, portable digital technologies and the networks that support these technologies have provided the education sector with opportunity and challenge in equal measure. Some will point to the Orwellian quality of the digital world that never 'switches off'; for example, Moore's law – where computing speeds double every 18–24 months – means that the unimaginable becomes imaginable. With 38.6 billion smart devices collecting, analysing and sharing data by 2025 (Golave, 2021) there has never been a greater scope for learning. Yet with such scope comes the challenge of understanding and the role for HE remains enhanced, translating the known and the familiar into the workable and practicable. As such, digital learning is a welcome reflection, a back-eddy to the fundamental principles of education.

The chapter has considered the *appropriate* use of the digital in contributing to the digital learning experience, where many educators – and learners – start from a familiarity with face-to-face learning. It acknowledged the relationship between a campus-based face-to-face orthodoxy and distance education and argued that the successful application of digital learning is about tailoring the use of digital opportunities rather than something that is wholly distinct. Finally, it has outlined the potential opportunities for students, academics, educational designers and institutions as a multiple stakeholders' team of practitioners engaged in digital and distance education, to contribute to innovation and further development of education more broadly as part of a global society.

## Note

1   See https://www.gillysalmon.com/five-stage-model.html.

## References

Ahmad, T. (2019) 'Students' perceptions on using cell phones as learning tools: Implications for mobile technology usage in Caribbean higher education institutions'. *PSU Research Review: An International Journal*, 4 (1), 25–43.

Anderson, T. (2019) 'Challenges and opportunities for use of social media in higher education'. *Journal of Learning for Development*, 6 (1), 6–19.

Ang, I., Isar, Y. R. and Mar, P. (2015) 'Cultural diplomacy: Beyond the national interest?' *International Journal of Cultural Policy*, 21 (4), 365–81. Accessed 30 June 2022. https://www.tandfonline.com/doi/full/10.1080/10286632.2015.1042474.

Bennett, S., Maton, K. and Kervin, L. (2008) 'The "digital natives" debate: A critical review of the evidence'. *British Journal of Educational Technology*, 39, 775–86. Accessed 30 June 2022. https://bera-journals.onlinelibrary.wiley.com/doi/10.1111/j.1467-8535.2007.00793.x.

CIPD (Chartered Institute of Personnel and Development) (2021) 'Digital learning', Chartered Institute of Personnel and Development factsheet. Accessed 30 June 2022. https://www.cipd.co.uk/knowledge/fundamentals/people/development/digital-learning-factsheet#15763.

Cook, J., Mor, Y. and Santos, P. (2015) 'Ideas in mobile learning'. *Journal of Interactive Media in Education*, 1 (18). Accessed 30 June 2022. http://doi.org/10.5334/jime.aw.

Davis, L. (ed.) (2019) 'Digital learning: What to know in 2019'. Accessed 30 June 2022. https://www.edtechuk.org/.

Educause (2018) 'Key issues in teaching and learning'. Accessed 20 July 2019. https://www.educause.edu/eli/initiatives/key-issues-in-teaching-and-learning-2018.

Educause (2019) 'Key issues in teaching and learning'. Accessed 20 July 2019. https://www.educause.edu/eli/initiatives/key-issues-in-teaching-and-learning.

Fawns, T., Aitken G. and Jones, D. (2019) 'Online learning as embodied, socially meaningful experience'. *Postdigital Science and Education*, 1, 293–7. Accessed 30 June 2022. https://doi.org/10.1007/s42438-019-00048-9.

Fung, D. (2017) *Connected Curriculum*. London: UCL Press.

Gannon, K. (2019) 'Teaching online will make you a better teacher in any setting'. *The Chronicle of Higher Education*, 2 September. Accessed 30 June 2022. https://www.chronicle.com/article/teaching-online-will-make-you-a-better-teacher-in-any-setting/.

Golave, N. (2021) 'How fast is technology growing: Can Moore's law explain the progress still?' Web Tribunal blog. Accessed 24 January 2021. https://hostingtribunal.com/blog/how-fast-is-technology-growing/#gref.

Gourlay, L. (2021) 'There is no "virtual learning": The materiality of digital education'. *Journal of New Approaches in Educational Research*, 10 (1), 57–66. Accessed 30 June 2022. https://doi.org/10.7821/naer.2021.1.649.

Holmberg, J. (2017) 'Applying a conceptual design framework to study teachers' use of educational technology'. *Education and Information Technologies*, 22 (5), 2333–49.

Laurillard, D. (2002) *Rethinking University Teaching: A conversational framework for the effective use of learning technologies*. London: Routledge.

Mayanja, J., Tibaingana, A. and Birevu, P. M. (2019) 'Promoting student support in open and distance learning using information and communication technologies'. *Journal of Learning for Development*, 6 (2), 177–86.

Mohammadi, M., Sarvestani, M. S. and Nouroozi, S. (2020) 'Mobile phone use in education and learning by faculty members of technical-engineering groups: Concurrent mixed methods design'. *Frontiers in Education*, 5 (16). Accessed 30 June 2022. https://doi.org/10.3389/feduc.2020.00016.

Mosley, N. (2020). 'An online course creates the space for intentionally deliberate discourse to unfold over time', Twitter, 27 October. https://twitter.com/neilmosley5/status/1320983622460022784.

Mwaanga, O. (2022) *Decolonisation of the University of London Worldwide Distance Learning Curricula and Pedagogies: Recommendations for practice and research*. Centre for Online and Distance Education: University of London. Accessed 30 October 2022. https://www.london.ac.uk/centre-online-distance-education.

Palfrey, J. and Gasser, U. (2008) *Born Digital: Understanding the first generation of digital natives*. New York: Basic Books.

Prensky, M. (2001) 'Digital natives, digital immigrants part 1'. *On the Horizon*, 9 (5), 1–6. Accessed 30 June 2022. https://doi.org/10.1108/10748120110424816.

Robbins, L. (1963) 'Higher education: Report of the committee appointed by the prime minister under the chairmanship of Lord Robbins 1961–63'. Cmnd. 2154. London: HMSO.

Rofe, J. S. (2011a) 'The IR Model: A schema for pedagogic design and development in international relations distance learning programmes'. *European Political Science*, 10 (1), 103–17.

Rofe, J. S. (2011b) 'The IR Model and e-moderating'. In G. Salmon (ed.), *E-Moderating: The key to teaching and learning online* (3rd edn). London: Routledge Falmer.

Salmon, G. (2002) *E-tivities: The key to active online learning*. New York and London: Routledge Falmer.

Salmon, G. (2019) 'How the UK and Australia could collaborate to compete in digital transformation'. Wonkhe blog, 8 August. Accessed 20 August 2019. https://wonkhe.com/blogs/how-the-uk-and-australia-could-collaborate-to-compete-in-digital-transformation/.

Santos, I. M. (2013) 'Integrating personal mobile devices in teaching: The impact on student learning and institutional support'. *Learning and Teaching in Higher Education: Gulf Perspectives*, 10 (2), 43–63.

Santos, I. M. (2017) 'Using students' personal mobile devices in higher education'. In L. Menano and P. Fidalgo (eds), *Art and Technology*. Rotterdam: Sense Publishers, 59–75. Accessed 30 June 2022. https://doi.org/10.1007/978-94-6300-863-1_4.

Schwab, K. (2016) *The Fourth Industrial Revolution*. Geneva: World Economic Forum.

Shuler, C., Winters N. and West, M. (2013) 'The future of mobile learning: Implications for policy makers and planners'. UNESCO. Accessed 26 July 2022. https://unesdoc.unesco.org/ark:/48223/pf0000219637.

Silver, L. (2019) 'Smartphone ownership is growing rapidly around the world, but not always equally', Pew Research Center report, 5 February. Accessed 28 July 2022. https://www.pewresearch.org/global/2019/02/05/smartphone-ownership-is-growing-rapidly-around-the-world-but-not-always-equally/.

United Nations (2015) 'Transforming our world: The 2030 Agenda for Sustainable Development'. Accessed 26 July 2022. https://sdgs.un.org/2030agenda.

University of Southampton (n.d.) 'What is digital learning?' Accessed 30 June 2022. https://www.southampton.ac.uk/digital-learning/what-is-it/index.page.

UUK (Universities UK) (2019) 'The economic case for flexible learning', 9 January. Accessed 30 June 2022. https://www.uall.ac.uk/resources/policies/the-economic-case-for-flexible-learning.

UUK/CBI (Universities UK/Cognitive Behavior Institute) (2019) 'The economic case for flexible learning: Joint statement by the CBI and Universities UK', States News Service, 26 October. Accessed 30 June 2022. https://go.gale.com/ps/i.do?id=GALE%7CA559824283&sid=sitemap&v=2.1&it=r&p=AONE&sw=w&userGroupName=anon%7E4c6cb922.

# 4
# Marketing digital education for an inclusive learning society

Endrit Kromidha and Benedetta Cappellini

Digital innovations have transformed education and how we learn, making it more flexible and accessible but also more complex to manage (Collis and Moonen, 2012). Technology has allowed many institutions to scale up their educational offer globally (Daniel, 1998). With increased competition and market saturation, higher education institutions (HEIs) are focusing more on aggressive digital marketing strategies to gain visibility (Blumenstyk, 1999). As a result, balancing educational and marketing goals for an inclusive society with fair access to quality lifelong education is becoming increasingly challenging.

The globalisation of higher education (HE) and technology advancements have increased the number of potential students, but also their expectations in distance HE (Rovai and Downey, 2010). As a result, since around 2010, there have been an increasing number of distance education courses and programmes offered by colleges, universities and other providers. Research shows that the change in the landscape of distance enrolments is characterised by relatively few institutions having large gains or large losses and most other institutions showing only modest changes in either direction (Allen and Seaman, 2017). Some speculate that failing in the distance learning education market is due to poor marketing management, but the situation is more complex.

This chapter reviews current marketing trends in distance education programmes, reflecting on how new technologies, devices and ways of interaction are changing the current system towards an inclusive learning society. In an increasingly competitive market, quality translates into value, which is essential to stay ahead of others. To really understand the value proposition of distance education offers in the digital age, we must look at the core of its system: the team and the technology. In many education institutions they are taken for granted as an extension of the digital system, but their very existence remains fundamentally human and essential to connect infrastructure, content and people.

This chapter looks at the value proposition of distance education courses. Exploring why students want them and how to best address their needs is done by looking at the challenges of being visible in a competitive distance education market. It has become increasingly important not only to find the 'right' students but also to be discoverable, by understanding their expectations, commitment and behaviour. The social and business dimensions of distance learning need to be seen in the context of career choices. For this, we look at how lifelong learning relationships between distance education institutions and students could replace the current transactional marketing model depending on agents, sales and commissions. Marketing distance education programmes in a digital space swamped with catchy advertisements can only stand out if done with a sense of responsible inclusivity. For that, students have to be respected as customers, but also be more involved in engaging learning activities and listened to when creating the educational experience.

The aim of this chapter is to help distance education programmes with a vision that goes beyond current job market trends. Inspiring and nurturing learning skills of enquiry, critical analysis, curiosity, creativity, persistence, discipline and vision should happen alongside the knowledge transfer within the courses. We believe in deeper student involvement in distance education programmes not only in the classroom but also as active ambassadors of the programmes. Finally, we argue that learning should be an enjoyable experience, powered by digital innovations that offer quality, flexibility and diversity in distance education courses for an inclusive and progressive society.

## Redefining marketing for distance learning programmes

To understand the role of marketing in distance education it is important to revisit its definition. The value proposition of HE is considered to be the provision of high skills, knowledge and certifications that will enable individuals to access social prestige and income earning (Marginson, 2006). This is called a positional good (Hirsch, 1976) that can be the subject of marketing. Marketing management has been defined as 'the process of planning and executing programs designed to influence the behaviour of target audiences by creating and maintaining beneficial exchanges for the purpose of satisfying individual and organizational objectives' (Andreasen et al., 2003: 39). While the definition addresses all the aspects of planning and executing a new programme, here we are interested in the promotional aspect, which relates to the interaction with the audience (students). One of the central points of this definition is the focus on meeting the needs of students (bottom-line goal), as well as the needs of the other stakeholders involved. As the needs and expectations of students are not static and monolithic, a constant monitoring of the market segment is necessary. This is particularly relevant for institutions operating on a global scale whose student population is heterogeneous in terms of demographics but also, and crucially, in terms of lifestyle and culture.

The delivery and promotion of distance education programmes have progressed from product mindset to sales mindset, to the current customer mindset (Shah et al., 2006). The first mindset is driven by the institution providing the programme. Courses are built around the existing expertise of faculty and the available technological resources. This mindset limits the potential market since the aims of the programme and the implemented technology do not necessarily meet the needs of distance learning students. The approach is particularly problematic in a global learning environment where courses developed in a specific context are then exported with little adaptation. Promoting such programmes becomes difficult since the needs of potential students are not considered when planning the programme. At the very best, they are built around existing students and existing scholarly expertise.

The sales mindset is certainly more market driven, as it is focused on persuading students to enrol in the programme. As the efforts are concentrated mainly on marketing a programme (via traditional promotional activities, student fairs, as well as social media), there is a risk that the programme will not meet the needs of students. According to this mindset, students' needs are understood only in a simplistic and reactive way since they are acknowledged only via marketing activities and not anticipated in the pedagogical planning of the programme. As such, learning activities are also reactive and short term, responding to current demands with little planning for the future. The costs of promotional activities can be very high and might jeopardise the revenue of the programme and the possibility of investing resources in developing learning activities.

The customer mindset is driven by anticipating, channelling and satisfying the needs of students, as well as determining students' access to technology and their technological abilities. At the heart of the planning of the programme there is a careful and constant monitoring of potential markets and identification of potential students. Operating in a global environment makes this approach particularly challenging but also rewarding, since it aspires to proactively anticipate students' demands and to accommodate the pedagogical offer to local contexts. Considering this 'back and forth' between the analysis of the market and the pedagogical planning of the programme, it is not surprising that the promotion of the programme is not seen as a final and distinct phase of the delivery. On the contrary, marketing efforts are incorporated into the various stages of planning of the programme, since a market-oriented perspective can provide a constant account of the students' needs, as well as the evolution of the market (including competitors' initiatives and new regulations in the sector). Such an integrated approach does not mean that the planning of a programme is driven solely by the analysis of the market and by the needs of potential students. It means that the students' needs are a crucial part of the values of the academic institution and, as such, the planning of the curriculum and the use of the technology are context driven. This also means that programmes are not done once and for all, but have to be agile and readapt themselves to the changes in the marketplace, including technology, competitors' initiatives, the job market, pedagogical innovation, discipline innovation, students' needs and institutional changes.

To achieve flexibility in distance education implies creating and nurturing a synergy between academics and marketing departments. A constant monitoring of the market is undertaken to adapt the programme to current and future challenges and opportunities. Consequently, promotional activities do not occur in isolation and at the end of the implementation process. Promotion happens organically as the programme is readapted and reshaped while also considering the changes of the market. Promotional initiatives typical of this mindset include webinars, tester lectures and virtual open days. These initiatives are customer focused since they allow students to gain an understanding of the structure, support, content and teaching style of the programme.

The conversion rates in distance education marketing vary and they depend on the degree students perceive the selected programme to meet their needs. They are also valuable sources of feedback for the institution since interactions with potential customers provide ad hoc responses from students. Among initiatives for promoting courses there are also massive open online courses (MOOCs), which can provide students with a more in-depth understanding of the overall learning experience (including content, teaching style, learning material and assessments). Certainly,

MOOCs are not simply promotional initiatives, since their role is much more complex than 'selling' a programme, but they can provide valuable feedback to the marketing and academic teams. For example, the low rate of completion of a MOOC could stimulate reflections on how to improve the pedagogical approach to a discipline, how to rethink a course and, consequently, how to reposition an entire programme in the market.

Institutions like the University of London (UoL) operate within the customer mindset and its current structure – which links together colleges of UoL and partner institutions across the world – making the overall marketing and promotional activities very complex. For example, promotional activities are designed and implemented by partner institutions and UoL. Arguably, promotional initiatives by partner institutions are tailored for specific geographical and cultural contexts and are more in tune with the specific needs of the local market. They can also provide in-depth feedback on local markets and students' needs. While promoting programmes via partner institutions is a good way of responding to customers' needs, it is important that the brand values of partner institutions are aligned with those of UoL. A misalignment of brand values might cause customer dissatisfaction and overall reputational damage. In this context, regardless of the current advancements in marketing tools and techniques that have intensified the efforts of many distance education institutions, the challenge of finding and matching the right students to the programme offers remains the same.

## Finding the right students and being easy to find

Being easy to find as students' preferred choice is a key objective for distance education programmes. From virtual campuses to open days and university recruitment events, one can be sure that distance education courses attract many who already work and require flexible learning arrangements. Many often fail to consider how much has happened before those encounters on open days. The university programmes have managed to penetrate the dense web of digital distractions to grasp the attention of both prospective students and parents. Perhaps the information was filtered down from a friend or relative. The reputation and rating of the university together with affordable fees are attractors, along with career prospects and life earnings. It could also simply be the convenience of working from home or taking classes nearby that made the choice easy. And let's not forget, distance education programmes are called this for a reason, so information has to travel some way to reach the students. However, thanks to Google and a plethora of digital agents, information about programmes to choose from is closer at hand than ever. The complexity of variables through which students find distance education programmes has increased tremendously beyond what a book chapter can cover, but acknowledging it is only half of the story.

How distance education programmes find the right students is equally important. The history of distance learning that started in the 1700s with the correspondence school model suggests that programmes did not have to look for students in the early days (Harting and Erthal, 2005). To select the right students the system relied on three pillars that remained unchanged for decades, perhaps centuries: previous study results, references from third parties and personal statements. Recent trends have shown that distance education is struggling to preserve its core educational values in an era of corporate globalisation (Sumner, 2000). As a result, it was not surprising to see increasing competition, especially among world-leading UK/US universities, fuelled by the networked open information environment (Marginson, 2006). This situation creates the need for advertising to reach out to potential students. While for full-time programmes reaching out can often happen in high-school sites or university fairs, in the case of distance education a lot of digital marketing searching, filtering and matching is carried out virtually. At the same time, little credit goes to recruitment teams that have realised it is necessary to look in the best places to get the best candidates.

Currently, many universities are looking at artificial intelligence (AI) with hope that it will help them match the right students with their offer, while also reducing costs and increasing efficiency, but such changes do not come without challenges. An article published in the *Wall Street Journal* in January 2019 with the provocative title: 'Colleges mine data on their applicants' (Belkin, 2019) investigated how some universities use complex analytics to identify candidates with potential interest tracked through their digital interactions with websites and social media. This practice could clearly create marketing opportunities for distance education programmes, but not without a few ethical implications related to the privacy of candidates and the right of universities to influence their choices. More importantly, when such practices become the norm, a number of structural and technical changes are expected to happen in every HEI, so the apparent competitive advantage will not be sustainable with something not only scalable but also self-adaptable in the way AI is supposed to be.

The human aspects of learning, even after intensified human–computer marketing interactions, remain essentially the same in both distance education and traditional classrooms. Therefore, advancements in technology should not be the ultimate answer or solution. The immediate challenge might be how to use the advantages that AI can provide without diminishing the cultural and contextual perspectives that traditional marketing tools can offer to institutions. In other words, the challenge is how to integrate two different understandings and applications of marketing and adapt them in the complex scenarios of distance education.

## Discussing a peer-to-peer model of marketing and learning

Could students act as marketing agents? This might sound like a provocative question, but it is a useful way to reflect on the role and direction of HE and distance learning programmes. From a consumer perspective, selecting and enrolling in a programme is a once-in-lifetime purchase and, as such, consumers have zero-repurchase intention (Yang et al., 2020). This means that students might have gone through an extensive decision-making process consisting of extensive information searching and evaluation of alternatives. While we know that some students are influenced by word of mouth (Yang et al., 2020), the possibility of developing a more systematic promotion using customer-to-customer initiatives is something we know little about. Alumni initiatives are often limited to 'networking' events and mentoring schemes for graduates, which do not use the full potential of promoting a programme via alumni communities. Certainly, there are ethical considerations to be made since alumni and current students are not sales agents and do not have any formal contract with the institution as sales representatives. However, the enthusiasm of alumni and current students can still be channelled and developed ethically.

A lesson to be learned from brand communities, for example, is that their members can help a brand remain alive via a series of online and offline events organised by consumers and for consumers (Laroche et al., 2012). These initiatives are not finalised for purchasing items (in our case, enrolling in the programme), but they are focused on keeping the brand values alive and strengthening the network of consumers. As these initiatives are not developed by the brand but often supported by it, a close relationship is crucial for retaining some control over the community. Brand communities tend to have a hierarchical structure in which some members (leaders) have more control over the ethos of the group, the social activities and the cultural norms. As such, institutions can work closely with such members to exercise some form of control without jeopardising the spirit of communities and members' enthusiasm.

The idea of using intermediaries and paid referrals is well established in sharing economy marketing (Weber and Zheng, 2007). We know that peer-to-peer marketing and advancements in digital platforms that allow better monetisation opportunities for socially connected users remain underused in online distance education marketing. Online businesses are increasingly making use of paid referrals whereby existing customers are offered payments or rewards for bringing in new customers. For example, Airbnb in the UK offers any existing registered traveller £15 for every new member they refer to register with Airbnb when they complete a qualifying stay and the new member will receive up to £34 off their first trip. However, it is hard to imagine a university operating in a similar way, offering referral compensation to their alumni, to students or even to members of staff for bringing in more students and discounts aimed at new students. While we understand that financial remuneration might sound problematic, we need to remind ourselves about the role of the agents. Distance education programmes are products and commission to agents is around 10 per cent (Paton, 2013). In global markets a similar fee is paid to the international company to secure this agent's exclusive service (Hulme et al., 2014). If creating a monetised referral system for alumni, current students and employees is ethically problematic, what about other forms of collaboration and rewards? Learning from brand communities, in which members do not obtain any direct financial remuneration from brands, institutions can activate forms of collaboration in which alumni are 'ranked' depending on their commitment and engagement.

Institutions can facilitate a more active role of certain alumni who can become ambassadors of the institutions, or 'endorsers' in marketing terms. Being an ambassador might involve the creation of a brand community around the branding values of the institutions. As such, being an ambassador would go above and beyond the organisation of onsite networking events. It would mean supporting the local community of alumni, applicants, current and future students by creating a distinct collective identity within the group around the values of the institution. While there is no financial compensation for the creation and maintenance of such communities, institutions can financially support communities and reward ambassadors and active members with symbolic recognition. Certainly, this way of thinking about alumni and current students might require a rethinking of the role of past, current and future students. It might also require investment in online and onsite activities that do not directly recruit students but are more a long-term investment in localised brand communities operating independently from the institution but in connection with the marketing department.

A balanced relationship between communities and marketing departments needs to be in place, as we do know that communities can cause trouble for the brand when they do not align with the values of it. This could be a way of linking together peer marketing activities and online learning relationships, which are two spheres operating far from each other. Peer-to-peer learning in the classroom has generally been considered a positive strategic move to deal with large numbers of distance education classes, especially MOOCs, where tutors are unable to provide feedback for thousands of students (Suen, 2014). Social networks have complemented this process by making the most of the social capital for enhancing peer mentoring and learning beyond the classroom and sometimes for creating a sense of community in digital learning spaces (Cho et al., 2007). However, it is important not to forget that the business model of online social platforms is based around online advertisement. It is currently the programmes and universities themselves that pay for advertisements on such platforms.

Online distance education courses are among the first that could, and should, make use of online communities and innovative digital platforms used by companies operating within a sharing economy framework. This would strengthen the existing traditional marketing activities, which are based on agents, in-house marketing capabilities and traditional advertising.

## The team and the technology behind the process

'User-friendly' and 'intuitive' have become the synonyms of quality in any human–computer interaction (Bullinger et al., 2002), including online distance education, yet we often forget the people and the technology behind the screens and devices that make it all happen. The typical distance education team consists of academics, administrative staff and information technology support, which, at best, have good communication flows, both internally and externally to prospective students, yet department silos and procedures are not uncommon. The challenge is balancing communication and interaction across various information technology systems and moving from a silo-based approach to an integrated approach, where the marketing, academic and administrative work seamlessly.

While investigating the creation of the learning content is not the aim of this chapter, it is still relevant to addressing this issue. As previously mentioned, the delivery and promotion of a programme via a customer mindset implies that the planning of the learning material is created in tune with students' needs, but also a broader understanding of the job market and indeed the evolution of the disciplines constitute the bases of the programme.

HE programmes differ from vocational programmes (Powell et al., 2012) as they are not focused on equipping students with specific and ad hoc sets of technical skills that are tailored to a specific profession, although recently they have started to converge. HE programmes equip students with theoretical foundations of disciplines and professions as well as more focused technical skills. While the latter are relevant in the immediate job market, the first ones remain crucial to surviving the changes in the job market. Indeed, theoretical and practical skills of disciplines and professions are key elements of an impactful curriculum of programmes that can remain relevant for the current and future job market. Adopting such a ponderation between various skills in designing and managing a programme seems particularly relevant for institutions operating on a global scale whose students are not restrained by a specific geographical area. Ponderation is also challenging for institutions operating in different contexts, in which localised job markets might require specific technical skills and knowledge. It is again the role of partner institutions to support the delivery of an impactful curriculum since they can integrate context-based learning material with the broader ones offered by UoL. Considering that the partner institutions have such a relevant role, their feedback on the planning and delivery of the programme is central to the implementation of impactful learning content.

The role of technology also needs to be addressed. While distance education programmes are attempting to update legacy and outdated information technology systems, we agree with Chaney and colleagues that the most appropriate medium of delivering instruction to students via distance learning does not necessarily mean the newest, most expensive technology available; there are several factors to consider, such as learner autonomy, types of interaction, access and cost of the media (Chaney et al., 2007). As the students' needs need to be considered in designing a learning experience, assessing students' access to specific technology is crucial for distance learning programmes. Students' needs – including their current and future skills, learning styles and study–life balance – should drive the technological choices to be made at the planning stage of the programme. Since some of these choices might impact on the delivery of the content (as well as the delivery of partner institutions) and the overall learning experience, it is important to understand the technology available to future students.

UoL is one of the biggest providers of distance education globally, although the programmes are offered and marketed individually by the respective UoL colleges. This presents a unique set of challenges for the distance education team, especially across intercollegial programmes. The strategic approach in this case has been moving towards a more centralised system, starting with a unified, simple-to-use yet intuitive mobile-first web portal. This is complemented by an interactive, user-centric virtual learning environment for the students, the colleges, the partner institutions in other countries and all the respective support teams. UoL's role in this case is changing from a repository of learning materials to be focused on communication flows rather than on structure – the links rather than the nodes. The marketing efforts in this case are facilitated by a centralised use of online social media where diversity and sharing become the main strengths of this multimodal system.

The Centre for Online and Distance Education supports the UoL International Programmes as a community of practice, promoting collaboration and knowledge sharing with a focus on the development of high-quality teaching and research in open and distance learning throughout all institutions. In its advisory and consulting role, meeting the needs of central systems or individual programmes by translating research expertise into practical advice and applicable solutions, it aims to set an example of excellence for open innovation in distance education teams led by shared expertise and knowledge rather than by operational obligations.

## Concluding remarks: marketing and learning integration avenues for the future

HEIs have evolved beyond learning and discipline centres to become polycentric hubs of green space and high-tech incubators, entrepreneurship labs and theatres, debate groups, numerous societies, counselling services and much more. These additions have turned university campuses into ecosystems where thinking, imagination and intellectual talent is nurtured and encouraged, adding value to the traditional learning experience. As a result, it is not surprising that such additions to the learning experience have increasingly become an essential part of competitive marketing strategies in HEIs. But how can distance education programmes compare and compete with traditional face-to-face HE in this regard? The answer comes from a technology-enhanced student experience from the first moment of contact with an agent to post-graduation relationships.

What about the future? How will education simulations or immersive learning experiences powered by technology transform distance education? While we do not know the definite answers to these questions, companies like CampusBird and Third Wave Digital pride themselves in creating virtual 3D campus maps as immersive marketing experiences for prospective students.[1] In a new future, we would expect to see more of such experiences making their way into the digital distance education classroom, blurring the difference between a physical experience on campus and a digital one powered by virtual reality.

We know that distance education differs from traditional full-time HE, not only in terms of format, higher flexibility and independence in learning but also in the way they are perceived (Hannay and Newvine, 2006). Comparative data from UoL and its colleges offering face-to-face education in the UK consistently show that student retention in distance education is lower than in face-to-face programmes.

The real marketing challenge for distance education programmes is not reaching out to students for recruitment purposes worldwide. This has been solved by technology and recruitment events. The challenge is keeping students engaged in the post-sale learning environment and motivating them to participate, submit their assignments to pass and ultimately graduate and become part of an honourable alumni community for the university. Some of the reasons for lapsing are not entirely related to motivation but include the ability to pay fees and being able to find the time to study, given that many online students are combining study with work and family commitments.

In a more realistic future and considering the differences in distance education between developed and developing countries, 'mobile-first' is a must considering the scale of mobile penetration worldwide (ITU, 2018). For UoL 'mobile-first' is the default approach of communicating with prospective and current students, starting with mobile-friendly websites and continuing with an increasing number of mobile apps. The number of virtual and physical campus apps has increased exponentially, from maps to schedule management, from social media to work groups, from project collaboration to plagiarism and proofreading. The mobile-first approach not only offers a practical and literally hands-on experience to marketing distance education and maintaining relationships with students, but also extends access socially, economically and geographically. An International Telecommunication Union report on information and communications technology facts and figures shows that among young people aged 15–24 in developing countries, 67 per cent are connected to the internet, increasingly through mobile devices, compared to 94 per cent in developed countries (ITU, 2018). Therefore, the mobile-first approach is particularly relevant to tap into new markets in developing countries.

Gamification, however, is gaining ground in marketing and corporate management and even wellness initiatives in business are slowly penetrating the distance classroom for an enhanced student experience (Dicheva et al., 2015). Research shows that gamification can help students' motivation to learn by offering an experiential and more immersive experience (Buckley and Doyle, 2016). Yet the two worlds – that of gamification for business marketing and gamification for education – seem to be far apart in the way distance education programmes operate. The opportunity, best practices and tools are all there, but ultimately it is a matter of strategic choice, vision and ambition to bring the two worlds together in a collegial and sustainable way.

Big data analytics and AI are the growing trends revolutionising content systems, including distance education (Prinsloo et al., 2015; Wei, 2013). Big data analytics is turning into a corporate strategy for delivering customers' dreams by understanding them and Netflix's use of it to determine casting and storytelling is a good example, among many (Mazzei and Noble, 2017). While there are some dangers in targeting the learning offering to suit customer needs rather than social and economic needs that are harder to capture, universities and distance education programmes can certainly consider the potential of this approach. Education institutions often sit on a lot of data, but it is unusual for is the value of such data to be acknowledged or used to its full potential. For learning, there is rarely any resource to dive into learning analytics. For marketing, over-reliance on external agents and traditional advertisement in terms of stakeholder relationships builds a symbiotic relationship with agents and adverts rather than with the post-enrolment data. The first step to see any improvement in this direction is for marketing teams to take a deeper interest in learning analytics, student profiles and career prospects. If marketing experiences and teaching experiences can be better related in a way that both marketers and teachers can observe how their individual actions influence the whole system, these individuals could take better steps for improvements.

To conclude, let us not forget that public relation managers in politics (Brader, 2005) and brand managers in marketing (Ding and Tseng, 2015) already know that appealing to people's emotions is easier than appealing to their rationality. After all, a degree does not only offer knowledge but also recognition, a network and a social dimension. Acknowledging this should lead to important transformations in the way we perceive the relationship between marketing and education functions in universities. After all, knowledge is shared and so are many marketing activities in the sharing economy. Before learning how to learn, acquire and share knowledge it is important to find the best way to engage with students. While learning sometimes hurts, as any training usually does, the intellectual and personal strengths it is supposed to equip everyone with are key motivations for pushing everyone to excel. And right there, between the discipline and creativity of learning and marketing, lies a fine line between success and failure.

## Note

1   https://tracxn.com/d/companies/campusbird.com; https://www.thirdwavedigital.com/.

## References

Allen, I. E. and Seaman, J. (2017) 'Digital Compass Learning: Distance education enrollment report 2017', Babson Survey Research Group report, May. Accessed 7 July 2022. https://files.eric.ed.gov/fulltext/ED580868.pdf.
Andreasen, A. R., Kotler, P. and Parker, D. (2003) *Strategic Marketing for Nonprofit Organizations* (6th edn). Upper Saddle River, NJ: Pearson/Prentice Hall.
Belkin, D. (2019) 'Colleges mine data on their applicants'. *The Wall Street Journal*, 26 January. Accessed 17 October 2022. https://www.wsj.com/articles/the-data-colleges-collect-on-applicants-11548507602.
Blumenstyk, G. (1999) 'The marketing intensifies in distance learning'. *Chronicle of Higher Education*, 45 (31), 27–8.
Brader, T. (2005) 'Striking a responsive chord: How political ads motivate and persuade voters by appealing to emotions'. *American Journal of Political Science*, 49 (2), 388–405.
Buckley, P. and Doyle, E. (2016) 'Gamification and student motivation'. *Interactive Learning Environments*, 24 (6), 1162–75.
Bullinger, H., Ziegler, J. and Bauer, W. (2002) 'Intuitive human–computer interaction–toward a user-friendly information society'. *International Journal of Human–Computer Interaction*, 14 (1), 1–23.
Chaney, B. H., Eddy, J. M., Dorman, S. M., Glessner, L., Green, B. L. and Lara-Alecio, R. (2007) 'Development of an instrument to assess student opinions of the quality of distance education courses'. *American Journal of Distance Education*, 21 (3), 145–64.
Cho, H., Gay, G., Davidson, B. and Ingraffea, A. (2007) 'Social networks, communication styles, and learning performance in a CSCL community'. *Computers & Education*, 49 (2), 309–29.
Collis, B. and Moonen, J. (2012) *Flexible Learning in a Digital World: Experiences and expectations*. London: Routledge.
Daniel, J. (1998) 'Knowledge media for mega-universities: Scaling up new technology at the Open University'. *Continuing Higher Education Review*, 62, 16–27.
Dicheva, D., Dichev, C., Agre, G. and Angelova, G. (2015) 'Gamification in education: A systematic mapping study'. *Educational Technology & Society*, 18 (3), 75–88.
Ding, C. G. and Tseng, T. H. (2015) 'On the relationships among brand experience, hedonic emotions, and brand equity'. *European Journal of Marketing*, 49 (7–8). Accessed 1 July 2022. https://www.emerald.com/insight/content/doi/10.1108/EJM-04-2013-0200/full/html.
Hannay, M. and Newvine, T. (2006) 'Perceptions of distance learning: A comparison of online and traditional learning'. *Journal of Online Learning and Teaching*, 2 (1), 1–11.

Harting, K. and Erthal, M. J. (2005) 'History of distance learning'. *Information Technology, Learning, and Performance Journal*, 23 (1), 35–44.

Hirsch, F. (1976) *Social Limits to Growth*. Cambridge, MA: Harvard University Press.

Hulme, M., Thomson, A., Hulme, R. and Doughty, G. (2014) 'Trading places: The role of agents in international student recruitment from Africa'. *Journal of Further and Higher Education*, 38 (5), 674–89.

ITU (International Telecommunication Union) (2018) *ICT Facts and Figures 2017*. Geneva: International Telecommunication Union.

Laroche, M., Habibi, M. R., Richard, M. and Sankaranarayanan, R. (2012) 'The effects of social media-based brand communities on brand community markers, value creation practices, brand trust and brand loyalty'. *Computers in Human Behavior*, 28 (5), 1755–67.

Marginson, S. (2006) 'Dynamics of national and global competition in higher education'. *Higher Education*, 52 (1), 1–39.

Mazzei, M. J. and Noble, D. (2017) 'Big data dreams: A framework for corporate strategy'. *Business Horizons*, 60 (3), 405–14.

Paton, G. (2013) 'Foreign recruitment agents "paid £120m" by universities', *The Telegraph*, 29 July. Accessed 1 July 2022. https://www.telegraph.co.uk/education/educationnews/10207365/Foreign-recruitment-agents-paid-120m-by-universities.html.

Powell, J. J., Graf, L., Bernhard, N., Coutrot, L. and Kieffer, A. (2012) 'The shifting relationship between vocational and higher education in France and Germany: Towards convergence?' *European Journal of Education*, 47 (3), 405–23.

Prinsloo, P., Archer, E., Barnes, G., Chetty, Y. and Van Zyl, D. (2015) 'Big(ger) data as better data in open distance learning'. *International Review of Research in Open and Distributed Learning*, 16 (1), 284–306.

Rovai, A. P. and Downey, J. R. (2010) 'Why some distance education programs fail while others succeed in a global environment'. *The Internet and Higher Education*, 13 (3), 141–7.

Shah, D., Rust, R. T., Parasuraman, A., Staelin, R. and Day, G. S. (2006) 'The path to customer centricity'. *Journal of Service Research*, 9 (2), 113–24.

Suen, H. K. (2014) 'Peer assessment for massive open online courses (MOOCs)'. *International Review of Research in Open and Distributed Learning*, 15 (3), 312–27.

Sumner, J. (2000) 'Serving the system: A critical history of distance education'. *Open Learning: The Journal of Open, Distance and e-Learning*, 15 (3), 267–85.

Weber, T. A. and Zheng, Z. (2007) 'A model of search intermediaries and paid referrals'. *Information Systems Research*, 18 (4), 414–36.

Wei, S. (2013) 'Learning analytics: Mining the value of education data under the big data era'. *Modern Educational Technology*, 23, 5–11.

Yang, H. P., Yen, D. and Balmer, J. M. T. (2020) 'Higher education: A once-in-a-lifetime purchase'. *Qualitative Market Research*, 23 (4), 865–90. Accessed 1 July 2022. https://dx.doi.org/10.1108/QMR-12-2017-0169.

# 5
# Supporting employability
David Winter

This chapter explores developments in the thinking and practice of institutional student employability development and attempts to highlight issues of particular relevance to distance education.

In the UK, a comprehensive framework for embedding employability within higher education (HE, see Figure 5.1) has been produced by Advance HE (formerly the Higher Education Academy (HEA)). This includes a recommended process consisting of four stages (HEA, 2016):

- Stage 1 – agreeing a definition of employability with all stakeholders.
- Stage 2 – auditing and mapping existing provision against the agreed definition.
- Stage 3 – prioritising actions to address gaps, share good practice and identify measurable outcomes.
- Stage 4 – measuring the impact of actions to inform future priorities.

This chapter will broadly mirror this process. The first section, 'Understanding employability', examines a number of conceptualisations of employability, exploring their implications and examining their relevance to distance education. The second section, 'Approaches to employability development in HE', describes some possible approaches to employability development and a range of common activities and interventions undertaken by institutions in order to provide employability learning for students. We then consider a number of factors that might determine the most appropriate strategies for a distance education provider and help them to prioritise the mix of employability development activities provided. The third section, 'Measuring and evaluating employability impact', highlights some possible approaches to the evaluation of employability

**Figure 5.1** The Advance HE framework for embedding employability within HE. Reproduced by permission of Advance HE.

development provision. The final section, 'Conclusions and recommendations', draws together a number of conclusions and key recommendations for implementing employability development within distance education.

## Understanding employability

There are numerous definitions of employability and multiple frameworks that attempt to articulate factors thought to contribute to the employability of graduates (Pegg et al., 2012; Small et al., 2018). Such models can provide a consistent framework with which to audit existing levels of employability development within specific courses or across whole institutions and guide the design of future employability development strategies. It is important to identify a definition and a model of employability that is appropriate for the particular needs and characteristics of an institution and its students.

The definition of employability proposed by Oliver (2015: 59), based on an earlier definition by Yorke (2006), seems particularly appropriate to distance education, as it emphasises employability as an aspect of lifelong learning within a constantly changing labour market:

> Employability means that students and graduates can discern, acquire, adapt and continually enhance the skills, understandings and personal attributes that make them more likely to find and create meaningful paid and unpaid work that benefits themselves, the workforce, the community and the economy. (Oliver, 2015: 59)

As well as setting out a process for embedding employability, the HEA (2016) framework identifies a comprehensive array of factors that have been linked to graduate employability development over the years:

- specialist, technical and transferable skills
- knowledge and application
- behaviours, qualities and values
- enterprise and entrepreneurship
- career guidance and management
- self-, social and cultural awareness
- reflection and articulation
- confidence, resilience and adaptability
- experience and networks
- attributes and capabilities.

Although the full HEA framework has been used to audit and design employability development in several institutions, a number of simpler models have been used in practice to underpin an employability strategy. Such models can be grouped into three main categories, characterised by Holmes (2013) as being primarily 'possessive', 'positioning' or 'processual', depending on the particular factors emphasised within the model.

### 'Possessive' models: the acquisition of in-demand skills

In these models, emphasis is placed on the skills acquired by students while learning that are desired by employers because they lead to effective performance in the workplace. Many of these are catalogued in the reviews of employability literature by Artess et al. (2017) and Dalrymple et al. (2021). These workplace skills can be divided into specialist technical skills required to perform specific job roles and generic or transferable skills that are considered to be common across a wide range of roles.

Specific technical skills and knowledge are usually of concern to highly vocationally oriented courses: for example, accredited qualifications for professions such as engineering or accountancy. For such courses, there is often close collaboration with relevant industry and professional bodies to define the required skills and understand the contexts in which they will be used in order to determine how they can be developed as integral learning outcomes.

Great effort has been put into defining sets of generic or transferable skills, identifying how these are developed within the learning experience, proposing ways of enhancing their development and equipping students to recognise and articulate these skills to recruiters. In Australia, there have been extensive national efforts to articulate a core set of such transferable skills (termed 'graduate attributes') that should be developed by learners within HE (Oliver and Jorre de St Jorre, 2018). The Council of the European Union has adopted a recommended set of eight key competencies for lifelong learning (European Commission, 2019) intended as a tool for education and training providers to facilitate the personal fulfilment, healthy lifestyle, employability, citizenship and social inclusion of EU citizens within an increasingly mobile global economy. The key competencies are:

- literacy competence
- multilingual competence
- mathematical competence and competence in science, technology and engineering
- digital competence
- personal, social and learning-to-learn competence
- citizenship competence
- entrepreneurship competence
- cultural awareness and expression competence.

In the UK, the Open University (OU) originally had an approach to employability that utilised a framework of core employability skills identified by the Confederation of British Industry (CBI, 2011). Following a review by the HEA, they have broadened their approach to a framework that includes core skills (problem solving, communication, collaboration, numeracy and digital and information literacy), personal attributes and behaviours (initiative, self-management and resilience and self-awareness) and external awareness (commercial/sector awareness and global citizenship) (Tunnah and Peeran, 2019). They have found that OU students undertaking distance learning while juggling other life commitments are predictably strong in the area of self-management and resilience but need development in the areas of self-awareness and sector awareness so that they are able to recognise these as qualities that are worth promoting to prospective employers. In their auditing of academic programmes using the framework, they discovered numerous examples of these skills and attributes being developed but found that the challenge was making this skills development more explicit to students and enabling students to articulate their strengths. The challenge of making students aware of the skills they are developing as part of their learning has also been identified in the context of Australian graduate attributes (Oliver and Jorre de St Jorre, 2018).

There are, however, a number of other challenges inherent in an approach to employability that focuses on marketable skills, especially for non-vocational disciplines with no specific market sector as a primary destination for graduates. The proliferation of these lists of skills indicates that there is no universally agreed set of core transferable skills for graduates. Even when the same skills appear in different lists, there is disagreement about what constitutes competence in that skill (Messum et al., 2017), as it may vary from one context to another. There is no guarantee that the high-level communication skills developed to suit the needs of an academic context would be similarly effective in the workplace. This might explain why attempts to teach these skills at university may have less impact on successful graduate outcomes than developing them through work-integrated learning (WIL) or through employer involvement in course design (Cranmer, 2006; Mason et al., 2009).

An additional problem is the fact that the set of key skills demanded by employers is subject to continual change. Although some skills remain perennially popular, others go in and out of favour as the demands of the workplace alter. Any skills-based approach to employability needs to be future focused. Some education providers have attempted to address this ever-changing demand for skills by developing micro-credentials – certified, modular, short-term learning experiences – which learners can take individually or accumulate towards a formal qualification (Resei et al., 2019; Selvaratnam and Sankey, 2021). These micro-credentials potentially offer learners the flexibility to choose the combination of learning most suited to their career development and employability needs in a rapidly changing workplace. For example, the University of Maine offers a suite of

'21st Century Skill Badges', including 'Creative Problem Solving', 'Empathy', 'Intercultural Fluency' and 'Resilience', which are available free to its students and to residents of Maine. Students can combine these badges into a personalised 'Career Prepared Learning Pathway'. However, lack of standardisation, inconsistent quality assurance, resistance to the transfer of micro-credentials between institutions and limited recognition by employers present ongoing challenges to the usefulness of such an approach. In addition, skills taught in this atomised way may suffer even more from the issue of de-contextualisation that limits skills learning incorporated into the curriculum.

Of growing importance is rapid technological change leading to the increasing digitisation and automation of roles across all employment sectors. According to the Pearson Global Learner Survey (Pearson, 2019: 24), 20 per cent of learners undertook further learning as a result of part of their job being automated and 36 per cent because they were required to use new technology or software. This was particularly pronounced in India and China. There are calls for educational institutions to focus on the development of students' digital capabilities irrespective of the academic discipline or intended employment area (Orlik, 2018). Although the specific technical skills that constitute digital capabilities are constantly changing, a number of overarching frameworks attempt to capture the underlying competencies (Biggins et al., 2017). Providers of distance education are well placed to help students develop confidence in their ability to acquire new technological skills by focusing on the reflective use of a mix of learning technologies as an end in itself rather than just as a means to an end in delivering traditional teaching (Chatterton and Rebbeck, 2015; Ferrell et al., 2018).

Another approach to the development of future-proof employability skills is to focus on workplace skills that are less likely to be supplanted by developments in artificial intelligence (AI) in the near future. In a worldwide survey of employers, 67 per cent believed that AI would provide a more cost-effective alternative to highly skilled jobs by 2030, with quantitative, technical, problem-solving and language skills alongside depth of subject knowledge being the areas where AI might most likely outperform humans (QS, 2019). The skills thought least likely to be replaceable were creativity, resilience, interpersonal, leadership and negotiation. The list below shows the top ten trending skills predicted for 2022 by the World Economic Forum (WEF, 2018).

- analytical thinking and innovation
- active learning and learning strategies

- creativity, originality and initiative
- technology design and programming
- critical thinking and analysis
- complex problem solving
- leadership and social influence
- emotional intelligence
- reasoning, problem solving and ideation
- systems analysis and evaluation.

Prominent in this list is 'active learning and learning strategies', which includes the ability of the individual learner to select and use instructional methods appropriate for the situation. Although many distance learners may have chosen this method of study for practical rather than pedagogical reasons, the capacity for self-directed learning is an important success factor whose link to future employability could be emphasised. Learners in most countries believe that universities and colleges must do more to build human skills, such as complex problem solving, critical thinking and collaboration, in order to equip people for the future job market (Pearson, 2019: 27).

Yet another important trend in the labour market is the growth of crowd-sourced work via the 'gig economy'. There may be a case for focusing on the development of students' entrepreneurial skills in order to prepare them for the likelihood that some form of self-employment may be part of their future career development (Barnes et al., 2015; Clinkard, 2018; QAA, 2018; Rae, 2007). Again, many of the characteristics listed as necessary for entrepreneurship are also important for students successfully undertaking distance learning.

## 'Positioning' models: the development of individual capital

Other models of employability extend beyond a focus on skills in order to identify the ways in which education helps to develop various forms of 'capital' – conceptualised as resources that confer benefits to individuals in relation to access to, and acceptance within, particular employment contexts. The Solent Capital Compass Model (Whistance and Campbell, 2018) highlights three types of capital: human, social and psychological. This has been used to develop an Employability Self-Evaluation (ESE) tool to help students identify their career development needs and to measure learning gain from employability interventions. The ESE focuses seven factors of student self-evaluation:

- My Career – the clarity of students' career ambitions.
- My Experience – students' acquisition of career-relevant skills and experience.
- My Opportunities – students' awareness of labour market information and opportunity sources.
- My Network – the range and usefulness of students' social connections.
- My Creativity – students' problem-solving abilities.
- My Attitude – students' optimism and resilience.
- My Communication – students' confidence in self-presentation.

Another similar model (Tomlinson, 2017) articulates five types of graduate capital: human, social, cultural, identity and psychological. This model has been adapted by the University of Southampton Careers and Employability Service to inform the development of learning outcomes and the measurement of learning gain for employability input to the curriculum, to support mentoring and placement preparation and to inform career discussions within tutorials (Careers and Employability Service, n.d.; McCafferty, 2016; Tomlinson et al., 2017). Anglia Ruskin University has made Tomlinson's model a core element of its employability strategy and its attempt to develop an active inclusive curriculum framework (Anglia Ruskin University, 2018).

This approach to employability seems to be particularly applicable to a strategic aim of addressing inequalities in graduate outcomes linked to socioeconomic differences (Britton et al., 2016; Mountford-Zimdars et al., 2015). As distance learning plays an important part in widening access to HE for non-traditional students, the development of individual capital could be a major consideration for employability in this context. There is some evidence that distance learners from lower socioeconomic backgrounds may need support in order to build confidence in their future professional identity (Delaney and Farren, 2016).

The prominence of cultural capital in Tomlinson's model also lends itself to considering the employability of transnational students, where the cultural norms of local job markets may differ considerably from those in the West or where individuals may aspire to move from one cultural context to another.

The development of social and cultural capital places an emphasis on encouraging and equipping students to develop and extend their social networks. This could involve promoting extensive student interaction with peers, alumni and employers, which may present a challenge for some distance learners and may require significant incentivisation and support from the institution. The 'Enhance Your Career and Employability Skills' massive open online course (MOOC) by the University of London (UoL) was designed to encourage high levels of student–student interaction through peer assessment and the heavy promotion and monitoring of discussion forums (Brammar and Winter, 2015). Discussion forum activity was higher than many other courses on the same platform and there were a large number of meaningful peer exchanges. However, only approximately 16 per cent of active participants engaged in this interactive learning.

### 'Processual' models: the development of individual agency and professional identity

Other models focus on developing the characteristic attitudes and behaviours that increase students' chances of making successful career transitions and continuing to develop themselves throughout their working lives by undertaking self-directed career management (Bridgstock, 2009). An example of such a model is CareerEDGE, originally developed at the University of Central Lancashire (Dacre Pool and Sewell, 2007) and subsequently used by a number of institutions (Howard, 2019; Robertson, 2019; Winfield, 2019) as a basis for developing employability strategies and programmes. This model includes degree-specific knowledge and skills as well as generic skills, but places them alongside career development learning, experience acquisition and emotional intelligence. This is typical of models developed and promoted by HE careers services in its strong emphasis on career decision making, goal setting and the development of a professional identity as key components in employability (Fugate et al., 2004; Holmes, 2015). Often, this aspect of employability is based on the earlier DOTS Model (Law, 1999; Law and Watts, 2003), which incorporates elements of **D**ecision learning, **O**pportunity awareness, **T**ransition learning and **S**elf-awareness. The prominence of career decision making is supported by research showing that better career planning and reflection are significant predictors of short- and long-term positive graduate outcomes (Praskova et al., 2015; Purcell et al., 2013; Shury et al., 2017; Taylor and Hooley, 2014; Tuononen et al., 2019). However, the idea of career direction being primarily a matter of personal choice is a characteristic of Western individualistic world views and may not be as applicable to transnational students from collectivist cultures, where the needs of family and wider society may predominate. Additionally, Arulmani (2011) argues that programme effectiveness is enhanced when fundamental career concepts are adapted in order to connect them to cultural ideas that are already familiar to the participants.

Employability models of this kind would appear to be particularly useful for non-vocational academic disciplines with no strong link to specific employment sectors and where students might be expected to engage in career decision making and career planning at some point in their university journey. However, as most of these models were developed to prepare traditional HE students for their first entry into the graduate workplace, it is not clear whether they are equally applicable to mature students undertaking part-time and distance learning as a way of bringing about career advancement or career change. In this case, models specifically developed in relation to the transformation or reinvention of professional identities of individuals already in employment may be more appropriate (Arthur et al., 1995; Ibarra, 2002; Walker, 2019). These career transformation models focus on acquiring novel experiences and new social connections in order to reinterpret past experiences and build new career identities, which may align with the motivations of many mature students undertaking distance education to reinvent themselves.

The Career Planning Micro-Module developed by the UoL Careers Service helps flexible and distance learners at UoL to develop career self-management skills through a self-directed and structured series of career learning activities. The aim is to help students to articulate an adaptable career plan within a changing global labour market. The four core topics of the module are:

- 'Global employment trends and opportunities'
- 'Career planning and decision making'
- 'Developing future-facing graduate competencies'
- 'Effective self-presentation and career narratives'.

Launched in March 2020, the Career Planning Micro-Module is open to 42,000 UoL distance learning students across 180 countries. In the first five months of delivery, there were 18,600 views, 5,600 posts and 33 per cent in sustained engagement, despite the fact that the model includes no in-course tutor moderation or assessment. This may partly reflect the incentivisation of an optional Career Future certification on the students' degree transcript.

## Which model of employability is most appropriate for distance education?

Part-time and transnational students undertaking distance education have a more complex range of employment-related motivations than traditional undergraduate students (Butcher and Rose-Adams, 2015; Caddell and Cannell, 2011; Mellors-Bourne et al., 2015). This makes it unlikely that a one-size-fits-all approach to employability development will be universally effective and emphasises the need to gain a nuanced understanding of the needs and aspirations of distance learners. Caddell and Cannell (2011) highlight the role of education in facilitating key career-related transitions for individuals. Table 5.1 attempts to elaborate on their categories of transition in order to identify the possible employability development needs for various types of distance student career aspirations.

It seems likely that any distance education provider offering a range of vocational and non-vocational courses would need to have a holistic model of employability that encompasses the development of skills, capitals and career self-management capabilities, or would need to offer a range of approaches to employability development in order to meet the varied needs and aspirations of distance learners. For example, the UoL Careers Service has further developed a range of extracurricular careers and employability learning activities tailored and differentially marketed to the specific needs of three categories of flexible and distance learning students: 'career starters', 'career developers' and 'career changers'.

## Approaches to employability development in HE

Having considered possible definitions of employability most relevant to the needs of distance learners, the next task is to consider how support for employability development could be implemented within the distance education context. Historically, careers and employability development have been incorporated into the HE experience in a variety of ways, which can be grouped, according to Hooley and Grant (2017), as:

- curricular – employability development is integrated into the formal curriculum through teaching and assessment
- co-curricular – employability development opportunities related to the subject of study are provided or supported outside the curriculum
- extracurricular – generic careers and employability learning opportunities not directly related to a specific degree discipline are provided or supported within the institution.

A mixed approach to integration has evolved in most UK HE institutions although, in recent years, this has moved in the direction of embedded

Table 5.1 Distance students' intended career transitions and employability needs. Adapted from Caddell and Cannell (2011).

| Transition type | Employability priority |
| --- | --- |
| Career entry – students seeking to enter the graduate job market for the first time | Likely to need career decision-making support, depending on amount of prior career planning and decision making.<br>Likely to need awareness and development of core skills or graduate attributes plus confidence in articulating these skills.<br>May also need development of social, cultural, identity and psychological capital. |
| Career transformation – students seeking to change their career or lifestyle | Likely to need development of individual capital (especially social, cultural and identity capital).<br>May also require support in career decision making, individual agency and resilience depending on maturity and realism of career transition plans. |
| Career re-entry – students seeking to return to the workplace after a break | Likely to be seeking to update skills for re-entry to a specific sector (especially technological skills).<br>May need development of psychological capital and self-confidence.<br>May require support in career decision making if they are re-evaluating their career direction. |
| Career progression – students seeking promotion or advancement in their existing career area | Likely to be seeking to develop skills relevant to higher-level roles in specific sectors.<br>May require additional support in developing social and cultural capital.<br>May also require support in career decision making and resilience, depending on how well informed they are on the realistic chances of progression via education. |
| Personal development – students undertaking study for intrinsic personal enjoyment or challenge | May not need employability support but may benefit from a re-evaluation of identity linked to career transitions such as retirement.<br>May benefit from an emphasis on employability attributes that are also attributes of successful distance learners. |

curricular and co-curricular approaches. The importance of this move to embedding is highlighted by the adoption of academic alignment as one of four key topics identified in the strategy for the UK Association of Graduate Careers Advisory Services (AGCAS, 2019).

It is possible to categorise curricular employability development activities into different types:

- Optional standalone – credit-bearing careers and employability modules, projects or placements that can be chosen by the student as an option within their academic programme.
- Compulsory standalone – credit-bearing careers and employability modules, projects or placements that form part of the core curriculum for all students.
- Extracted embedded – existing curriculum is audited and learning relevant to employability is emphasised and articulated without necessarily changing teaching content or methods significantly.
- Transformational embedded – teaching and assessment outcomes, content and methods are reconfigured to increase the application of learning to employability (and vice versa).

In general, standalone provision tends to be delivered by careers and employability professionals with teaching and learning expertise, whereas embedded provision is often the result of collaboration between subject academics and employability professionals or employers. In some cases, embedding extends to academic programme approval being dependent on consultation with careers and employability professionals (Daubney, 2019). The approach taken varies from institution to institution across HE and may vary from department to department within a single institution. Often the approach within an institution is determined by the commitment of senior institutional leaders to establishing employability as a key strategic priority and by the willingness of academic departments to engage with employability development. It could be argued that a requirement to provide employability benefits to all students is more likely to be met by a compulsory or embedded approach. However, compulsory employability modules may suffer from limited student engagement, especially from those who are undertaking distance education for personal enrichment and who may not see employability development as being relevant to their needs. Embedded approaches require greater commitment from busy academic staff but do offer potential benefits of increased student engagement and enhanced learning of the subject matter through real-world application.

Whatever approach is chosen, employability development can be delivered through a wide range of specific activities. As well as the practical and financial implications of such activities, it is important to consider strategic priorities and stakeholder engagement when considering an approach to delivering careers and employability development remotely.

## Typical activities

HE institutions have engaged in a wide range of activities in order to develop student employability. These include:

- provision of information on occupations, labour markets and employers
- curation and publication of vacancies and volunteering opportunities
- coaching and advice on job hunting, applications and interviews (individual and group)
- coaching and guidance on career choice and goal setting (individual and group)
- formal teaching and assessment on careers and employability topics
- interaction with employers through careers fairs, panels, presentations and employer involvement in other activities
- work-integrated or 'real-world'-integrated learning, such as work shadowing, projects or placements
- skills development auditing through activities such as skills awards, personal development portfolios and achievement records
- peer, alumni and employer mentoring
- enterprise and entrepreneurship development and support
- support for extracurricular and co-curricular activities, such as student clubs and societies
- psychometric and other self-evaluation tools for developing self-awareness and identifying options.

The most appropriate mix of activities will depend largely on student needs. For example, students who fit distance education around work or family constraints may need access to effective careers and employability development that is available round the clock, such as on-demand online learning resources or access to asynchronous communication with employability professionals rather than live communication only available at certain times. Students who access distance learning for reasons of geographical remoteness may benefit from support in developing an online peer community through activities such as structured mentoring programmes.

## Remote delivery of activities

It is possible to deliver the majority of the above activities remotely to varying degrees. The online provision of information, vacancies and self-evaluation tools (Gati and Asulin-Peretz, 2011) is a long-standing practice. E-portfolios have also been used extensively for recording the development of skills from students' experiences, although they tend to be most effective in professional areas where portfolios are regularly used for demonstrating achievements to recruiters or where their use is thoroughly integrated into learning and assessment (Andrade, 2019; Bryant and Chittum, 2013).

The availability of online learning platforms and synchronous online audio and video communication tools has increased the ability of institutions to provide remotely delivered careers and employability teaching, coaching and mentoring. Large-scale examples of online career development learning include the 'Enhance Your Career & Employability Skills' MOOC developed by UoL (Brammar and Winter, 2015) and the 'EMPLOY101x' MOOC developed at the University of Queensland (Reid and Richards, 2016). AI systems using natural language processing are increasingly able to provide some of the simpler aspects of personalised advice and coaching, such as CV/résumé feedback (Cronje and Ade-Ibijola, 2018).

There is a burgeoning industry of virtual careers fairs (McIlveen et al., 2009) alongside online professional networking platforms that provide contact with potential employers. In 2018, the OU started running virtual careers fairs using the iVent platform (Laws and Hawkins, 2020). These have garnered growing engagement from students and employers. The OU Online Talent Connect event saw employer attendance grow from 38 to 69 and student attendance grow from 3,339 to 4,353 between 2018 and 2019. They have also used the platform to host fairs focusing on the charity and law sectors, as well as a diversity and inclusion fair. In January 2020, they also used the platform to conduct a virtual employer site visit.

The provision of WIL within distance education has most commonly been used in vocational qualifications and the ongoing professional development of individuals already in a particular occupation. As well as remote support and monitoring of physical placements, there have been some efforts to develop truly virtual placements (Vriens et al., 2010) and internships (Herrero de Egaña et al., 2012), which have grown as support for remote working continues to increase among employers following the COVID-19 pandemic. The development of innovative models of WIL, such as micro-placements, hackathons and student-led consultancy and start-ups, also offers the potential for more flexible opportunities to gain valuable experiential learning (Kay et al., 2019). Virtual WIL models also offer unparalleled opportunities for trans-disciplinary, trans-institutional and transnational collaborative projects. For example, students from the University of Birmingham in the UK and Swinburne University in Australia collaborated on a ten-week project working with Ecoexist, a social enterprise based in Pune, India, to reduce the use of plastic bags in the region. However, a barrier to this type of activity, as well as the uptake of other extracurricular activities within distance education, will continue to be the number of students undertaking study alongside existing employment or caring responsibilities. Even if the opportunities for field-based WIL remain limited, there are still possibilities for increasing the amount of real-world content in teaching through case studies, guest lecturing, the use of industry tools and gamification (Gellerstedt and Arvemo, 2014; Moffat et al., 2015).

In 2020, the COVID-19 pandemic forced universities and employers throughout the UK to explore how to engage remotely with students and graduates. Careers services have rapidly developed increased confidence and competence in the delivery of remote one-to-one appointments, webinars, virtual fairs, digital internships and other online resources to replace traditional face-to-face activities (UUK, 2020). The increased opportunities have widened the range of students able to engage with careers activities provided by this move to remote delivery. The long-term effect of this expansion into distance provision across the HE sector is likely to be a continued interest in developing tools and methods to ensure that remote delivery is not perceived as a poor alternative to face-to-face delivery. Similarly, the wide-scale move to remote working as the norm across various employment sectors is likely to increase the demand for digital self-management skills from graduates and may lead to increased provision of digital employability opportunities, such as virtual internships.

## Resource considerations

There is no doubt that a commitment to employability involves a commitment of resources. The ideal number and type of staff needed to support employability development will depend on the strategic priorities identified (see the section 'Measuring and evaluating employability impact'), the resulting mix of activities undertaken and the resources available. Since around 2010, UK HE careers services have seen a great diversification in roles (Neary and Hanson, 2018), driven by the introduction of student fees and the increasing emphasis on the employment outcomes of graduates. Many of the activities listed above have individuals or teams of staff dedicated to them. The Enhanced Employability and Career Progression programme within the OU has raised the profile of employability as a strategic priority for the university. As a result, the Careers and Employability Service has almost doubled in size in less than three years (Tunnah and Peeran, 2019). Much of this staff increase is in response to a rise in student demand and to support employability professionals working alongside academics to embed employability development within the curriculum.

A key consideration when assessing the resources needed for providing employability development is scalability. The increasing emphasis on proactive outreach by careers services and the embedding of employability within the curriculum has often led to increased student demand for tailored individual coaching and advice, which many institutions have struggled to provide. A range of approaches has been taken to manage this demand. Some institutions have introduced triage systems to prioritise student need, directing those with more complex careers issues to individual support and those with more common concerns to group or online support. Many institutions have created 'employability adviser' roles to handle the bulk of lower-level enquiries, such as CV review or job-hunting advice. Often seasonally employed to cope with periods of peak demand, these roles are sometimes filled by specially trained senior students and thus also provide skill development opportunities for these individuals. Another approach is to ration these labour-intensive activities to students who have paid higher fees, students from disadvantaged backgrounds or students identified as having particular employability needs through the use of career readiness surveys, although this could be seen as contradicting the strategic principle of inclusivity.

The development of AI systems to review CVs may indicate the future possibility of providing computerised careers guidance in the same way that online cognitive behavioural therapy is increasingly being provided as an effective treatment for depression. However, as mentioned, part-time and distance learners are likely to have more complex employability needs, which implies that the management of demand for tailored individual support is likely to continue to be an important consideration for any distance learning provider for the foreseeable future. However, the high numbers of experienced mature students undertaking distance learning means that there is also the potential for encouraging peer support as long as this is carefully considered in course design (Brammar and Winter, 2015).

Many of the information, teaching and coaching activities can be delivered through existing learning technologies but there may be additional ongoing costs for licensed third-party resources, such as global careers information databases, psychometric tools and virtual event platforms. A significant amount of co-curricular and extracurricular activity may require investment in specific systems to manage such things as appointments, vacancies, events, employer or alumni contacts, placements or e-portfolios. A number of dedicated careers service management systems exist to handle these activities but they vary in cost, functionality and capacity for integration with existing learning and student registration systems.

The costs of content production for employability resources for distance education will be similar to that of academic content, but the rapidly changing nature of the job market may mean that some of the content needs to be updated more frequently. In addition, the desire of students for tailored employability support (Donald et al., 2018) and the diverse needs of distance students mean that it may not be advisable to engage in wholesale duplication of employability content across all courses.

## Principles and strategic priorities

The HEA framework identifies three key principles underpinning employability provision in HE:

- Inclusivity – ensuring equitable access to employability-enhancing opportunities for all students.
- Collaboration – involving all relevant stakeholders (academics, careers professionals, employers, students and senior decision makers) in the efforts to develop students' employability.
- Engagement – ensuring that communication around employability is based on a mutual understanding of the needs and motivations of the stakeholders involved.

Similarly, Blackmore et al. (2016) describe a holistic or 'ecosystem' approach to employability taken by many institutions, which requires the commitment of senior leadership and the involvement of academics and employers. The analysis of employability literature by Artess et al. (2017) further emphasises the importance of:

- embedding employability in the curriculum
- providing a range of co-curricular and extracurricular activities
- building links with the labour market

- developing student self-confidence
- encouraging reflection and students' ability to articulate their learning
- encouraging student mobility and a global perspective
- working with institutional careers and employability services to coordinate employability strategies.

As indicated in the section on employability models, priorities in employability provision may also be influenced by the structure and mission of the institution, by the mix of vocational and non-vocational courses and by the characteristics and motivations of the student population.

## Acceptance and engagement

Essential to the success of any employability strategy is the level of engagement of students in the activities and opportunities provided. Although students regularly report career development and progression as important motivations for undertaking HE, this is often accompanied by an admission that they do not take advantage of available employability support opportunities during their time at university (Donald et al., 2018; Jorre de St Jorre and Oliver, 2018; Mellors-Bourne et al., 2015; Tymon, 2013). This may be particularly true of students from more deprived socioeconomic backgrounds (Doyle, 2011). Employees, including graduates, are using various forms of distance education to maintain their employability in a changing job market (Pearson, 2019) or to acquire employer-desired skills not developed by traditional HE courses (Calonge and Shah, 2016). However, Butcher and Rose-Adams (2015) point out that many part-time and distance students have chosen this method of learning because it is the only option available to them that is compatible with work or family commitments. So, although distance learning students may be strongly motivated to use their studies to facilitate their personal career development goals, they may be limited in their capacity to engage in extracurricular and co-curricular activities aimed at developing aspects of employability.

Donald et al. (2018) elicited student recommendations for careers services to enhance their provisions. The fact that many of the suggestions related to activities and support are typically already available from careers services indicates that the real problems may be student awareness, student proactivity and the communication or marketing of services by the institution. A common recommendation from such studies on student expectations is for greater embedding of employability within the curriculum to make it unavoidable. However, care needs to be taken. Jorre de St Jorre and Oliver (2018) point out that even the development of institution-wide learning outcomes linked to graduate attributes can suffer from lack of engagement by students who perceive them as too generic to be meaningful. They recommend that employability outcomes are clearly contextualised, linked to assessment and endorsed by academics and employers. It may be fruitful to make student engagement a primary consideration when designing employability development activities by utilising approaches such as motivational design (Keller, 2009; Mohamad et al., 2016), especially where such activities are optional.

Another factor that emerged from studying students' engagement with employability was the importance of the attitudes and involvement of academics. Despite increasing emphasis on the importance of employability as a key outcome of HE, the receptiveness of academics to greater employability content within the curriculum is highly varied (Sin et al., 2019; Speight et al., 2013). Reasons for academic resistance range from philosophical concerns about the purpose of education and a perceived dilution of intellectual rigour to more practical considerations of timetabling, workload and academics' lack of confidence in their knowledge of labour markets. Speight et al. (2013) argue that much of the resistance stems from a limited understanding of employability by many academics, who often see it as merely concerning the acquisition and articulation of specific skills demanded by employers, as emphasised by more simplistic 'possessive' models. There may be more potential for finding common ground in multidimensional, holistic approaches to employability, which emphasise the development of students' capability for life-wide and lifelong learning. Many of the attributes emphasised in 'processual' employability models, such as self-awareness, self-directedness and open-mindedness, are also likely to be important characteristics of high-performing students. In addition, self-efficacy in career decision making and the development of career goals are linked to the academic performance and persistence of students (Hull-Blanks et al., 2005; Peterson and Delmas, 2001). This focus on boosting students' self-efficacy and perceptions of degree utility may be of particular importance for distance education, where the social engagement and belonging factors that influence persistence in on-campus education are weaker and where many students come from non-traditional backgrounds (Glazer and Murphy, 2015; Rovai and Downey, 2010).

Even when academic staff and students see the value of incorporating the development of employability skills within teaching, it is important to ensure that there is a common understanding of the skills that are required and how they are developed within the learning experience. In a study at Universidade Aberta (a distance education provider in Portugal), teachers and students only agreed on 40 per cent of the top ten skills that are most important for employability (Silva et al., 2013).

Both students and employability professionals see employer involvement in the development of employability in HE as highly important. Such involvement takes a variety of forms, from the provision of opportunities for work-related learning and networking to involvement in the design and delivery of teaching (Blackmore et al., 2016; Kettle, 2013; Stanbury et al., 2009). Within distance education it is also important to consider the indirect involvement of employers through their support for employee learners (Mason, 2014; Stewart, 2018). Mason (2014) recommends gathering information from part-time students about their employers and looking for ways to develop more direct engagement, but caution should be exercised as many students may be undertaking study in order to leave their current employer or sector.

## Measuring and evaluating employability impact

The literature reviews by Artess et al. (2017) and Dalrymple et al. (2021) catalogue various attempts to measure and evaluate the impact of employability learning initiatives.

### Extracurricular and co-curricular methods

An obvious way to evaluate the employability of graduates is to measure their success in obtaining appropriate jobs on graduation. However, this involves using a measure of employment as a proxy for measuring employability. Employment outcomes are influenced by a wide range of individual and market factors alongside institutional efforts to develop student employability (Britton et al., 2016). When using employment outcomes as a measure of employability development it is important to be clear about what constitutes a successful outcome. Is it merely having a sufficient percentage of graduates in employment or further study? Is it the proportion of graduates achieving an appropriate level of graduate employment as defined by occupational classification or salary? Is it the extent to which employment outcomes match student expectations for career progression or transformation? Should it be based on what happens immediately after graduation or on longer-term career outcomes? All of these questions, alongside the challenge of collecting the data, mean that graduate employment outcomes cannot be relied upon as the sole measure for success of an employability development strategy. The more complex circumstances of distance learners, where many are in permanent employment throughout their studies, present further difficulties in the use of outcome data alone in the evaluation of employability development (Shale and Gomes, 2007).

In Australia, as well as recording employment outcomes of graduates, the annual International Graduate Outcomes Survey (Social Research Centre, 2022b) asks graduates to identify whether their education developed specific graduate attributes. A similar Employer Satisfaction Survey (Social Research Centre, 2022a) asks graduates' line managers to assess the graduates' levels of competence in a similar set of attributes. A Student Experience Survey (Social Research Centre, 2021) asks current commencing and later year students to undertake a similar assessment of the skills they are developing as part of their learning. All of these measures are included in a nationally reported assessment of the quality of learning and teaching. This emphasis on measuring skills development has primarily driven the Australian HE sector in the direction of possessive models of employability over other approaches.

Where an institution has a vacancy and application management system, it may be possible to record patterns of student applications and interviews and link these to employability development activities. Such outcomes would be similarly dependent on factors not directly related to employability development efforts, such as student motivation and practical constraints. Although collecting information on proactive student job hunting outside such systems may provide a better indication of potential employability, this would be considerably more complicated.

Another common approach to evaluating effectiveness of employability development activities is through the collection of feedback from students. This could be direct feedback related to particular interventions or indirect feedback via wider student satisfaction surveys or focus groups. The usefulness of such measures is often limited by issues of self-selection of respondents, the subjective nature of the data and the extent to which students are aware of, and understand, the existing provision. Within distance education, the regular collection of such feedback could be easily incorporated into learning systems, but there is always the danger of creating 'survey fatigue' if students are not clear about how such information is used to support them.

Measuring levels of participation or involvement in activities through attendance data, page read counts, assignment completion rates and other learning analytics is yet another commonly used method of evaluation. While student engagement was highlighted above as a vital factor in the success of an institutional employability approach, it is worth considering that participation and engagement are not the same thing. Merely undertaking headcounts may produce a measure of popularity and marketing success but is not a true measure of learning gain.

Methods of assessing the usefulness of careers and employability interventions often focus on attempts to evaluate development in characteristics linked to success, such as confidence, self-efficacy and adaptability through self-report questionnaires. Validated psychometric tools of this kind are time-consuming to administer and suffer from diminishing response rates. Another approach growing in usage is the inclusion of a simplified set of career readiness-related questions in compulsory student registration questionnaires to facilitate year-by-year tracking of student career development (Cobb, 2019). It is hard to correlate this annual 'careers registration' data with specific interventions but it can be used to identify groups of students in particular need of support or to help students select the activities most appropriate to their employability development needs. Other approaches attempt to use frameworks to articulate specific careers and employability learning outcomes for each activity and capture student self-evaluations of attainment of these outcomes. The growing availability of data and the attention given to demonstrating the effectiveness of employability development has led to an increasing emphasis for careers and employability professionals to engage with more structured research and evaluation (Winter, 2018).

At a macro level, a number of standards and frameworks also exist to assess the quality and value for money of whole service provision rather than to evaluate the impact of individual interventions (AGCAS, 2018; AMOSSHE, 2011; The Growth Company, 2020; Holman, 2014). Using such frameworks to identify an appropriate balance of meaningful performance indicators is an important part of a strategic approach to employability development.

## Curricular methods

If career and employability development is embedded in the curriculum, then existing course approval and teaching quality assurance processes can be used to evaluate the design and implementation of these activities. It is also possible to use academic assessment as a tool for measuring the impact of such activities as well as a tool for promoting learning and engagement. Existing approaches to the assessment of curricular employability learning can be grouped into three main categories (self-presentation, skill performance and career self-management) based on the point at which the learning will be applied in practice.

Self-presentation approaches assess the students' ability to articulate their skills and achievements to potential employers in attempts to secure employment. Methods used in these approaches tend to resemble selection practices of recruiters, such as CV reviews, mock job interviews, assessment centres and business pitches. In some cases, employers may be involved in the design and the delivery of the assessment process.

Skill performance approaches attempt to assess skills in ways consistent with how an employee's performance might be evaluated on the job. This often involves the development of behavioural competency frameworks or standards as rubrics to assess performance on particular tasks or the completion of portfolios to record skills developed from various activities and achievements. In the assessment of work-based learning through placements, actual structured appraisals by workplace managers may be included. Osborne et al. (2013) argue that such assessment tasks should mirror the conditions under which performance evaluation happens in the workplace through the use of real-world problems, distributed assessment timings, collaborative activities, explicit self or peer review, light structure and the inclusion of specific audience viewpoints in the evaluation.

Career self-management approaches attempt to assess the extent to which individuals are able to engage in activities that they will undertake throughout their lives in order to develop their careers. This often involves the completion of career investigation or skills development activities coupled with some form of assessed reflective activity, which may also include some element of goal setting or planning. This type of assessment is compatible with approaches to assessment aimed at promoting lifelong learning (Nguyen and Walker, 2016). It may also be coupled with ipsative assessment using some self-report measure of career readiness or employability capital in order to evaluate learning gain.

A comprehensive and robust assessment of employability learning may need to use a mixture of approaches, specifically combining quantitative measures of engagement with qualitative measures of impact and subjective measures of usefulness with objective measures of progress. Within distance education, one important limiting factor may be the capability of the learning platform to encompass a sufficiently wide range of assessment and evaluation techniques.

## Conclusions and recommendations

When designing employability development support for distance learners it is vitally important to gain an understanding of students' motivations for studying and how these link to their long-term career aspirations. Combining this understanding with a sufficiently sophisticated model of employability should produce a more in-depth assessment of students' employability development needs than merely asking students what they want. In turn, combining this needs analysis with an understanding of students' reasons for choosing distance education, prior employability learning, practical constraints, cultural contexts and the affordances of institutional systems, resources and structures, should help to prioritise the particular approach and mix of activities that can be used to address those needs. This is more likely to produce an approach to employability that is specifically suited to the distinctive characteristics and opportunities of distance learning than attempting to replicate a version of on-campus employability development approaches.

The centrality of learning technologies within distance education, the demands of distance learning and the nature and circumstances of many distance students point towards approaches that include an emphasis on the development of future-focused digital capabilities, lifelong learning skills and entrepreneurial attributes alongside efforts to promote student self-awareness and self-confidence.

Institutional employability strategies need to be driven by both top-down and bottom-up forces. Senior leadership commitment is necessary to secure the level of collaboration and resource allocation necessary to have a genuine impact. Wide stakeholder involvement and buy-in are essential to ensure that the strategy becomes more than just a well-meaning statement of intent. A coherent and consistent institution-wide approach to employability development will facilitate the communication necessary to encourage engagement from students, academics, employability professionals and employers at all stages in the development and implementation of an employability strategy. It will also help to promote and audit equity of provision for all students. However, any institution-wide employability framework should be sufficiently contextualised to be meaningful to different student groups on different types of course in order to avoid being perceived as too generic to be useful.

To be effective and to address the constraints of distance learners, employability development should be embedded as much as possible into the core student experience rather than being presented as an optional extra. If some form of assessed curricular embedding is not possible, then it is important to engage in clear, early and regular messaging to students about employability development from trusted advocates, such as academics, employers, fellow students and alumni. It would also be beneficial to make strong links between employability-enhancing characteristics and the qualities needed for academic success as a distance learner.

# References

AGCAS (Association of Graduate Careers Advisory Services) (2018) 'AGCAS Membership Quality Standard'. Accessed 3 July 2022. https://www.agcas.org.uk/write/MediaUploads/Resources/Quality/AGCAS_Membership_Quality_Standard.pdf.

AGCAS (Association of Graduate Careers Advisory Services) (2019) 'AGCAS strategy – 2016/17 to 2018/19 – update'. Accessed 3 July 2022. https://www.agcas.org.uk/write/MediaUploads/Resources/AGCAS-Strategy_updated_January_2019.docx.

AMOSSHE (Association of Managers of Student Services in Higher Education) (2011) 'Value and impact toolkit: Assessing the value and impact of services that support students', May. Centre for Higher Education and Research and Information. Accessed 3 July 2022. https://www.amosshe.org.uk/resources/Documents/ValueandImpactToolkitJune2011.pdf.

Andrade, M. (2019) 'E-portfolios and online learning: Applying concepts of organizational behavior'. *International Journal of E-Learning & Distance Education/La revue internationale de l'apprentissage en ligne et de l'enseignement à distance*, 34 (1). Accessed 3 July 2022. http://www.ijede.ca/index.php/jde/article/view/1096.

Anglia Ruskin University (2018) 'Anglia Ruskin employability strategy 2018–2023'. Accessed 3 July 2022. https://aru.ac.uk/anglia-learning-and-teaching/about-us/our-strategy.

Artess, J., Mellors-Bourne, R. and Hooley, T. (2017) *Employability: A review of the literature 2012–2016*. York: Higher Education Academy.

Arthur, M. B., Claman, P. H. and DeFillippi, R. J. (1995) 'Intelligent enterprise, intelligent careers'. *Academy of Management Perspectives*, 9 (4), 7–20.

Arulmani, G. (2011) 'Striking the right note: The cultural preparedness approach to developing resonant career guidance programmes'. *International Journal for Educational and Vocational Guidance*, 11 (2), 79–93. Accessed 3 July 2022. https://doi.org/10.1007/s10775-011-9199-y.

Barnes, S. A., Green, A. and de Hoyos, M. (2015) 'Crowdsourcing and work: Individual factors and circumstances influencing employability'. *New Technology, Work and Employment*, 30 (1), 16–31.

Biggins, D., Holley, D., Evangelinos, G. and Zezulkova, M. (2017) 'Digital competence and capability frameworks in the context of learning, self-development and HE pedagogy'. In G. Vincenti, A. Bucciero, M. Helfert and M. Glowatz (eds), *E-Learning, E-Education, and Online Training*. Cham: Springer International, 46–53.

Blackmore, P., Bulaitis, Z., Jackman, A. and Tan, E. (2016) *Employability in Higher Education: A review of practice and strategies around the world*. London: Pearson Education.

Brammar, L. and Winter, D. (2015) '"I've been astounded by some of the insights gleaned from this course": Lessons learnt from the world's first careers and employability MOOC by both instructors and participants'. *Journal of the National Institute for Career Education and Counselling*, 34 (1), 22–31.

Bridgstock, R. (2009) 'The graduate attributes we've overlooked: Enhancing graduate employability through career management skills'. *Higher Education Research & Development*, 28 (1), 31–44. Accessed 3 July 2022. https://doi.org/10.1080/07294360802444347.

Britton, J., Dearden, L., Shephard, N. and Vignoles, A. (2016) 'How English domiciled graduate earnings vary with gender, institution attended, subject and socioeconomic background'. Institute for Fiscal Studies working paper no. W16/06.

Bryant, L. H. and Chittum, J. R. (2013) 'ePortfolio effectiveness: A(n ill-fated) search for empirical support'. *International Journal of ePortfolio*, 3 (2), 189–98.

Butcher, J. and Rose-Adams, J. (2015) 'Part-time learners in open and distance learning: Revisiting the critical importance of choice, flexibility and employability'. *Open Learning: The Journal of Open, Distance and E-Learning*, 30 (2), 127–37. Accessed 3 July 2022. https://doi.org/10.1080/02680513.2015.1055719.

Caddell, M. and Cannell, P. (2011) 'Rethinking graduate attributes: Understanding the learning journeys of part-time students in the Open University in Scotland'. In B. Jones and S. Oosthuizen (eds), *Part-Time Study: The new paradigm for higher education?* Stirling: UALL. Accessed 3 July 2022. http://oro.open.ac.uk/46147/.

Calonge, D. S. and Shah, M.A. (2016) 'MOOCs, graduate skills gaps, and employability: A qualitative systematic review of the literature'. *International Review of Research in Open and Distributed Learning*, 17 (5). Accessed 3 July 2022. https://doi.org/10.19173/irrodl.v17i5.2675.

Careers and Employability Service (n.d.) 'Graduate Capital Model', University of Southampton. Accessed 17 June 2019. https://www.southampton.ac.uk/careers/staff/employability-exchange/graduate-capital-model.page.

CBI (Confederation of British Industry) (2011) *Building for Growth: Business priorities for education and skills: Education and Skills Survey 2011*. London: CBI.

Chatterton, P. and Rebbeck, G. (2015) *Technology for Employability: Study into the role of technology in developing student employability*. Bristol: Jisc.

Clinkard, K. (2018) 'Are employability and entrepreneurial measures for higher education relevant? Introducing AGILE reflection'. *Industry and Higher Education*, 32 (6), 375–90.

Cobb, F. (2019) '"There's no going back": The transformation of HE careers services using big data'. *Journal of the National Institute for Career Education and Counselling*, 42 (1), 18–25. Accessed 3 July 2022. https://doi.org/10.20856/jnicec.4204.

Cranmer, S. (2006) 'Enhancing graduate employability: Best intentions and mixed outcomes'. *Studies in Higher Education*, 31 (2), 169–84. Accessed 3 July 2022. https://doi.org/10.1080/03075070600572041.

Cronje, M. and Ade-Ibijola, A. (2018) 'Automatic slicing and comprehension of CVs'. In *2018 5th International Conference on Soft Computing Machine Intelligence (ISCMI), Nairobi, Kenya*. New York: IEEE, 99–103. Accessed 3 July 2022. https://doi.org/10.1109/ISCMI.2018.8703234.

Dacre Pool, L. and Sewell, P. (2007) 'The key to employability: Developing a practical model of graduate employability'. *Education + Training*, 49 (4), 277–89. Accessed 3 July 2022. https://doi.org/10.1108/00400910710754435.

Dalrymple, R., Macrae, A., Pal, A. and Shipman, S. (2021) *Employability: A review of the literature 2016–2021*. York: Advance HE. Accessed 3 July 2022. https://www.advance-he.ac.uk/knowledge-hub/employability-review-literature-2016-2021.

Daubney, K. (2019) 'Extracting employability from the curriculum: Embedding without invasion'. Paper presented at the AGCAS Heads of Service Conference, Edinburgh, 10 January.

Delaney, L. and Farren, M. (2016) 'No "self" left behind? Part-time distance learning university graduates: Social class, graduate identity and employability'. *Open Learning: The Journal of Open, Distance and E-Learning*, 31 (3), 194–208. Accessed 3 July 2022. https://doi.org/10.1080/02680513.2016.1208553.

Donald, W. E., Ashleigh, M. J. and Baruch, Y. (2018) 'Students' perceptions of education and employability: Facilitating career transition from higher education into the labor market'. *Career Development International*, 23 (5), 513–40. Accessed 3 July 2022. https://doi.org/10.1108/CDI-09-2017-0171.

Doyle, E. (2011) 'Career development needs of low socio-economic status university students'. *Australian Journal of Career Development*, 20 (3), 56–65. Accessed 3 July 2022. https://doi.org/10.1177/103841621102000309.

European Commission (2019) *Key Competencies for Lifelong Learning*. Luxembourg: European Union.

Ferrell, G., Smith, R. and Knight, S. (2018) 'Designing learning and assessment in a digital age', Jisc, 26 January. Accessed 3 July 2022. https://www.jisc.ac.uk/guides/designing-learning-and-assessment-in-a-digital-age.

Fugate, M., Kinicki, A. J. and Ashforth, B. E. (2004) 'Employability: A psycho-social construct, its dimensions, and applications'. *Journal of Vocational Behavior*, 65 (1), 14–38.

Gati, I. and Asulin-Peretz, L. (2011) 'Internet-based self-help career assessments and interventions: Challenges and implications for evidence-based career counseling'. *Journal of Career Assessment*, 19 (3), 259–73. Accessed 3 July 2022. https://doi.org/10.1177/1069072710395533.

Gellerstedt, M. and Arvemo, T. (2014) *Work-Integrated Learning with Work-Integrated Learners*. New Tapei City, Taiwan: International Association for Development of the Information Society. Accessed 3 July 2022. https://www.learntechlib.org/p/158353/.

Glazer, H. R. and Murphy, J. A. (2015) 'Optimizing success: A model for persistence in online education'. *American Journal of Distance Education*, 29 (2), 135–44. Accessed 3 July 2022. https://doi.org/10.1080/08923647.2015.1023093.

The Growth Company (2020) *Matrix Quality Standard for Information Advice and Guidance Services: Guidance for organisations*. Manchester: The Growth Company.

HEA (Higher Education Academy) (2016) *Framework for Embedding Employability in Higher Education*. York: Higher Education Academy.

Herrero de Egaña, A., Bravo, C. S. and Cabanes, A. M. (2012) 'Models and practices of virtual internships outside Europe'. *IJAME*, 1 (6), 141–8.

Holman, J. (2014) *Good Career Guidance*. London: Gatsby Charitable Foundation.

Holmes, L. (2013) 'Competing perspectives on graduate employability: Possession, position or process?' *Studies in Higher Education*, 38 (4), 538–54. Accessed 3 July 2022. https://doi.org/10.1080/03075079.2011.587140.

Holmes, L. (2015) 'Becoming a graduate: The warranting of an emergent identity'. *Education + Training*, 57 (2), 219–38. Accessed 3 July 2022. https://doi.org/10.1108/ET-08-2013-0100.

Hooley, T. and Grant, K. (2017) 'Graduate career handbook: A supplementary guide to the Handbook for Providing Career Support and Employability Programmes'. Bath: Crimson Publishing. Accessed 3 July 2022. https://indigo.careers/wp-content/uploads/2019/08/YH-Graduate-Career-Handbook-Supplementary-Booklet.pdf.

Howard, M. (2019) 'Forging strategic partnerships to develop future global leaders'. *Phoenix*, 157 (June), 30–1.

Hull-Blanks, E., Robinson Kurpius, S. E., Befort, C., Sollenberger, S., Foley Nicpon, M. and Huser, L. (2005) 'Career goals and retention-related factors among college freshmen'. *Journal of Career Development*, 32 (1), 16–30. Accessed 3 July 2022. https://doi.org/10.1177/0894845305277037.

Ibarra, H. (2002) 'How to stay stuck in the wrong career'. *Harvard Business Review*, 80 (12), 40–7. https://hbr.org/2002/12/how-to-stay-stuck-in-the-wrong-career

Jorre de St Jorre, T. and Oliver, B. (2018) 'Want students to engage? Contextualise graduate learning outcomes and assess for employability'. *Higher Education Research & Development*, 37 (1), 44–57. Accessed 3 July 2022. https://doi.org/10.1080/07294360.2017.1339183.

Kay, J., Ferns, S., Russell, L., Smith, J. and Winchester-Seeto, T. (2019) 'The emerging future: Innovative models of work-integrated learning'. *International Journal of Work-Integrated Learning*, 20 (4), 401–13.

Keller, J. M. (2009) *Motivational Design for Learning and Performance: The ARCS Model approach*. Berlin and Heidelberg: Springer Science & Business Media.

Kettle, J. (2013) *Flexible Pedagogies: Employer engagement and work-based learning*. York: Higher Education Academy.

Law, B. (1999) 'Career-learning space: New-dots thinking for careers education'. *British Journal of Guidance & Counselling*, 27 (1), 35–54. Accessed 3 July 2022. https://doi.org/10.1080/03069889908259714.

Law, B. and Watts, A. G. (2003) 'The DOTS analysis', National Institute for Careers Education and Counselling, the Career-Learning Network. Accessed 3 July 2022. http://www.hihohiho.com/memory/cafdots.pdf.

Laws, E. and Hawkins, G. (2020) 'OU TalentConnect: Our online careers fair to reach a large diverse student body'. Case study presented at the AGCAS webinar, 'Virtual Careers Fairs – What Are They and Are They Right for You?' 29 May.

McCafferty, H. (2016) 'Capitals and career readiness'. *Phoenix*, 148 (June), 20–1.

McIlveen, P., Hoare, P. N., McKeown, L. and Vagg, K. (2009) 'Internet career fairs in Australian higher education'. *Career Planning and Adult Development Journal*, 25 (3), 59–70.

Mason, G. (2014) 'Part-time higher education: Employer engagement under threat?' *Higher Education Quarterly*, 68 (3), 305–27. Accessed 3 July 2022. https://doi.org/10.1111/hequ.12053.

Mason, G., Williams, G. and Cranmer, S. (2009) 'Employability skills initiatives in higher education: What effects do they have on graduate labour market outcomes?' *Education Economics*, 17 (1), 1–30. Accessed 3 July 2022. https://doi.org/10.1080/09645290802028315.

Mellors-Bourne, R., Jones, E. and Woodfield, S. (2015) *Transnational Education and Employability Development*. York: Higher Education Academy.

Messum, D., Wilkes, L., Peters, K. and Jackson, D. (2017) 'Content analysis of vacancy advertisements for employability skills: Challenges and opportunities for informing curriculum development'. *Journal of Teaching and Learning for Graduate Employability*, 7 (1), 72–86. Accessed 3 July 2022. https://doi.org/10.21153/jtlge2016vol7no1art582.

Moffat, D., Farrell, D., Gardiner, B., McCulloch, A. and Fairlie, F. (2015) 'A serious game to give students careers advice, awareness and action'. In A. Jefferies and M. Cubric (eds), *ECEL 2015: Proceedings of the 14th European Conference on e-Learning*. Hatfield: Academic Conferences and Publishing Limited, 396.

Mohamad, S. N. A., Embi, M. and Nordin, N. M. (2016) 'Designing e-portfolio with ARCS motivational design strategies to enhance self-directed learning'. *Higher Education Studies*, 6 (November), 138. Accessed 3 July 2022. https://doi.org/10.5539/hes.v6n4p138.

Mountford-Zimdars, A., Sabri, D., Moore, J., Sanders, J., Jones, S. and Higham, L. (2015) 'Causes of differences in student outcomes', HEFCE report. Accessed 3 July 2022. https://doi.org/10.13140/RG.2.2.34621.36326.

Neary, S. and Hanson, J. (2018) 'A new career in higher education careers work'. In C. Burke and F. Christie (eds), *Graduate Careers in Context: Research, policy and practice* (1st edn). London: Routledge, 140–52. Accessed 3 July 2022. https://doi.org/10.4324/9780203732281.

Nguyen, T. T. H. and Walker, M. (2016) 'Sustainable assessment for lifelong learning'. *Assessment & Evaluation in Higher Education*, 41 (1), 97–111. Accessed 3 July 2022. https://doi.org/10.1080/02602938.2014.985632.

Oliver, B. (2015) 'Redefining graduate employability and work-integrated learning: Proposals for effective higher education in disrupted economies'. *Journal of Teaching and Learning for Graduate Employability*, 6 (1), 56–65. Accessed 3 July 2022. https://doi.org/10.21153/jtlge2015vol6no1art573.

Oliver, B. and Jorre de St Jorre, T. (2018) 'Graduate attributes for 2020 and beyond: Recommendations for Australian higher education providers'. *Higher Education Research & Development*, 37 (4), 821–36. Accessed 3 July 2022. https://doi.org/10.1080/07294360.2018.1446415.

Orlik, J. (2018) 'Delivering digital skills: A guide to preparing the workforce for an inclusive digital economy', NESTA. Accessed 3 July 2022. https://www.nesta.org.uk/documents/680/Readie_Digital_Skills_booklet_online.pdf.

Osborne, R., Dunne, E. and Farrand, P. (2013) 'Integrating technologies into "authentic" assessment design: An affordances approach'. *Research in Learning Technology*, 21 (September). Accessed 3 July 2022. https://doi.org/10.3402/rlt.v21i0.21986.

Pearson (2019) 'The Global Learner Survey: September 2019'. Accessed 3 July 2022. https://www.pearson.com/content/dam/one-dot-com/one-dot-com/global/Files/news/gls/Pearson_Global_Learner_Survey_2019.pdf.

Pegg, A., Waldock, J., Hendy-Isaac, S. and Lawton, R. (2012) 'Pedagogy for employability', Higher Education Academy. Accessed 3 July 2022. https://www.advance-he.ac.uk/knowledge-hub/pedagogy-employability.

Peterson, S. L. and Delmas, R. C. (2001) 'Effects of career decision-making self-efficacy and degree utility on student persistence: A path analytic study'. *Journal of College Student Retention: Research, Theory & Practice*, 3 (3), 285–99. Accessed 3 July 2022. https://doi.org/10.2190/4D9V-DFW1-VDLX-K7GF.

Praskova, A., Creed, P. A. and Hood, M. (2015) 'Career identity and the complex mediating relationships between career preparatory actions and career progress markers'. *Journal of Vocational Behavior*, 87 (April), 145–53. Accessed 3 July 2022. https://doi.org/10.1016/j.jvb.2015.01.001.

Purcell, K., Elias, P., Atfield, G., Behle, H., Ellison, R. and Luchinskaya, D. (2013) *Futuretrack Stage 4: Transitions into employment, further study and other outcomes*. Warwick: HECSU and IER, University of Warwick.

QAA (Quality Assurance Agency) (2018) 'Enterprise and entrepreneurship education: Guidance for UK higher education providers', The Quality Assurance Agency for Higher Education, QAA2042, January. Accessed 3 July 2022. https://www.qaa.ac.uk/docs/qaas/enhancement-and-development/enterprise-and-entrpreneurship-education-2018.pdf.

QS (Quacquarelli Symonds) (2019) *How Artificial Intelligence Is Influencing Graduate Employability and the Global Higher Education Sector: Analyzing the ripple effects of technological change on higher education*. London: QS Quacquarelli Symonds.

Rae, D. (2007) 'Connecting enterprise and graduate employability: Challenges to the higher education culture and curriculum?' *Education + Training*, 49 (8–9), 605–19. https://doi.org/10.1108/00400910710834049.

Reid, A. and Richards, A. (2016) 'EMPLOY101x: Embedding employability into the curriculum', The 2016 National Conference of the Australian Collaborative Education Network (ACEN), Sydney, Australia, 28–30 September.

Resei, C., Friedl, C., Staubitz, T. and Rohloff, T. (2019) 'CORSHIP result 1.1c. Micro-credentials in EU and global'. Accessed 3 July 2022. https://www.corship.eu/wp-content/uploads/2019/07/Corship-R1.1c_micro-credentials.pdf.

Robertson, B. (2019) 'From resistance to innovation: Mapping embedded employability'. *Phoenix*, 157 (June), 28–9.

Rovai, A. P. and Downey, J. R. (2010) 'Why some distance education programs fail while others succeed in a global environment'. *The Internet and Higher Education*, 13 (3), 141–7. Accessed 3 July 2022. https://doi.org/10.1016/j.iheduc.2009.07.001.

Selvaratnam, R. M. and Sankey, M. D. (2021) 'An integrative literature review of the implementation of micro-credentials in higher education: Implications for practice in Australasia'. *Journal of Teaching and Learning for Graduate Employability*, 12 (1), 1–17.

Shale, D. and Gomes, J. (2007) 'Performance indicators and university distance education providers'. *International Journal of E-Learning & Distance Education/Revue Internationale du E-Learning et la Formation à Distance*, 13 (1), 1–20.

Shury, J., Vivian, D., Turner, C. and Downing, C. (2017) *Planning for Success: Graduates' career planning and its effect on graduate outcomes*. London: UK Department for Education.

Silva, A. P., Lourtie, P. and Aires, L. (2013) 'Employability in online higher education: A case study'. *International Review of Research in Open and Distributed Learning*, 14 (1), 106–25. Accessed 3 July 2022. https://doi.org/10.19173/irrodl.v14i1.1262.

Sin, C., Tavares, O. and Amaral, A. (2019) 'Accepting employability as a purpose of higher education? Academics' perceptions and practices'. *Studies in Higher Education*, 44 (6), 920–31. Accessed 3 July 2022. https://doi.org/10.1080/03075079.2017.1402174.

Small, L., Shacklock, K. and Marchant, T. (2018) 'Employability: A contemporary review for higher education stakeholders'. *Journal of Vocational Education & Training*, 70 (1), 148–66. Accessed 3 July 2022. https://doi.org/10.1080/13636820.2017.1394355.

Social Research Centre (2021) '2020 Student Experience Survey: National report', Melbourne, Australia. Accessed 3 July 2022. https://www.qilt.edu.au/docs/default-source/default-document-library/2020-ses-national-report.pdf.

Social Research Centre (2022a) '2021 Employer Satisfaction Survey: National report', Melbourne, Australia. Accessed 3 July 2022. https://www.qilt.edu.au/docs/default-source/default-document-library/2021-ess-national-report.pdf.

Social Research Centre (2022b) '2021 International Graduate Outcomes Survey: National report', Melbourne, Australia. Accessed 3 July 2022. https://www.qilt.edu.au/docs/default-source/default-document-library/2021-gos-international-reportb5ff0a7af7a54ca2a1ebc620f2570151.pdf.

Speight, S., Lackovic N. and Cooker, L. (2013) 'The contested curriculum: Academic learning and employability in higher education'. *Tertiary Education and Management*, 19 (2), 112–26. Accessed 3 July 2022. https://doi.org/10.1080/13583883.2012.756058.

Stanbury, D., Williams, H. and Rees, J. (2009) *Engaging Employers to Enhance Teaching and Learning: Ideas and approaches for work-related and placement learning*. Reading: Centre for Career Management Skills, University of Reading.

Stewart, E. J. (2018) 'Employer-supported higher education: Challenges and opportunities'. PhD thesis, School of Education, Deakin University, Geelong, Australia. Accessed 3 July 2022. http://hdl.handle.net/10536/DRO/DU:30110899.

Taylor, A. R. and Hooley, T. (2014) 'Evaluating the impact of career management skills module and internship programme within a university business school'. *British Journal of Guidance & Counselling*, 42 (5), 487–99. Accessed 3 July 2022. https://doi.org/10.1080/03069885.2014.918934.

Tomlinson, M. (2017) 'Forms of graduate capital and their relationship to graduate employability'. *Education + Training*, 59 (4), 338–52. Accessed 3 July 2022. https://doi.org/10.1108/ET-05-2016-0090.

Tomlinson, M., McCafferty, H., Fuge, H. and Wood, K. (2017) 'Resources and readiness: The graduate capital perspective as a new approach to graduate employability'. *Journal of the National Institute for Career Education and Counselling*, 38 (1), 28–35. Accessed 3 July 2022. https://doi.org/10.20856/jnicec.3805.

Tunnah, E. and Peeran, A. (2019) 'A joint approach to curriculum design and development'. *Phoenix*, 157 (June), 12–13.

Tuononen, T., Parpala, A. and Lindblom-Ylänne, S. (2019) 'Graduates' evaluations of usefulness of university education, and early career success: A longitudinal study of the transition to working life'. *Assessment & Evaluation in Higher Education*, 44 (4), 581–95. Accessed 3 July 2022. https://doi.org/10.1080/02602938.2018.1524000.

Tymon, A. (2013) 'The student perspective on employability'. *Studies in Higher Education*, 38 (6), 841–56. Accessed 3 July 2022. https://doi.org/10.1080/03075079.2011.604408.

UUK (Universities UK) (2020) 'How universities are supporting graduates in a COVID-19 economy', case study. Accessed 3 July 2022. https://www.universitiesuk.ac.uk/policy-and-analysis/reports/Documents/2020/graduate-support-case-studies.pdf.

Vriens, M., Op de Beeck, I., De Gruyter, J. and Van Petegem, W. (2010) 'Virtual placements: Improving the international work experience of students'. In L. G. Chova, D. M. Belenguer and I. C. Torres (eds), *EduLearn 10: International conference on education and new learning technologies*, 1175–83.

Walker, L. (2019) 'Coaching during late career reinvention: The Discovering Model'. *International Journal of Evidence Based Coaching & Mentoring*, 13, 63–75. Accessed 3 July 2022. https://doi.org/10.24384/8s09-x110.

WEF (World Economic Forum) (2018) 'The future of jobs report 2018', Centre for the New Economy and Society, Geneva.

Whistance, D. and Campbell, S. (2018) 'Seven ESE factors for career-ready students', Solent University/HECSU, November. Accessed 3 July 2022. https://luminate.prospects.ac.uk/media/c89d1842-909c-451a-9019-3bbe5ad32f7c/hecsu-research-seven-ese-factors-for-career-ready-students.pdf.

Winfield, F. (2019) 'Establishing a coordinated approach to employability at school level'. *Phoenix*, 157 (June), 22–3.

Winter, D. (2018) 'The rise of the practitioner-researcher: How big data and evidence-based practice requires practitioners with a research mindset'. In C. Burke and F. Christie (eds), *Graduate Careers in Context: Research, policy and practice* (1st edn). Abingdon: Routledge, 167–78. Accessed 3 July 2022. https://doi.org/10.4324/9780203732281.

Yorke, M. (2006) *Employability in Higher Education: What it is – what it is not*. York: Higher Education Academy.

# 6
# Strategic models for distance education

Philip Powell, with example materials and analysis from Mary Stiasny and Michael Davis

The role of online and distance education in any higher education institution (HEI) may be central – that is, distance education is vital to the mission of that organisation, as in the case of the University of London (UoL) – or it can complement the organisation's current activities, going hand in hand with face-to-face provision. Alternatively, it can be a substitute, whereby all physical, in-person interaction is replaced by virtual engagement. The decisions around all of these possibilities could be strategic – or they may be a tactical response to a challenge or opportunity, as the emergency response of many institutions to the COVID-19 pandemic demonstrated.

The COVID-19 pandemic pushed many institutions to venture into distance education in 2020. They recognised that face-to-face, in-person education was neither safe nor viable and so rapidly switched, en masse, to distance education. However, there is a difference between a crisis response and a strategic shift to online education. The COVID-19 experience will probably result in greater moves to blended delivery (as discussed in Chapter 20), but any decision to abandon face-to-face education or to run online education in parallel is likely to be a strategic one.

This chapter sets out a range of factors that help determine the extent to which online and distance education is likely to be a strategic imperative for HEIs and the decisions an institution needs to consider. These factors are:

- the strategic importance of distance learning to the institution
- how what is provided online relates to other educational provision
- the needs and expectations of distance learning and other institutional stakeholders
- who provides the different resources and how they are bundled together
- how the online provision is funded or monetised.

## Strategic importance of distance learning to the institution

For some HEIs, and for some higher educational systems, distance learning will be a strategic necessity – because there is no viable alternative mechanism to provide education at scale or over distances. This is clearly a driver in the case study of the Nigerian higher education (HE) system described in Chapter 7. However, for other institutions, the decision to invest in distance education is more problematic and more complex. The complexity arises from the variety of business models that are possible and the number of actors within the distance education value chain. When the decision to engage in distance learning is taken, then this strategy is enacted through business models. There are a variety of ways in which distance learning can be resourced. This chapter will outline and model these aspects of online educational provision.

Distance education, like much of contemporary education, is now facilitated through the use of online digital technologies. Of course, education at a distance has been provided around the world for decades without the use of digital technologies (see the Preface), but any HEI currently contemplating it is likely to be employing digital means for the bulk of its provision, unless it is operating in a particularly challenging environment; for example, where digital networks and electricity supplies are unreliable.

> Distance learning presents an opportunity, and a threat, to HEIs. Many stakeholders are active participants, or worried on-lookers, in assessing the changing role of technology in educational provision. (Barber et al., 2013: 62)

The two key drivers underlying the institutional adoption of distance learning are the need to quickly and affordably upskill national populations to meet the challenges of the knowledge society and the need for accessible and flexible access to tertiary education to meet the changing nature of society and the lifelong learning agenda (Anderson et al., 2006; House of Commons, 2016). Individual HEIs will engage in online learning for a variety of reasons (Schiffman et al., 2007), though many of these reasons may not be mutually exclusive. These reasons include the desire to:

- reach new students
- contribute to educational extension efforts
- assist in on-campus student retention
- provide pedagogic improvements
- increase student diversity
- generate a financial return to the institution
- increase students' speed to graduation
- reduce or contain costs.

HEIs engage in distance education in the hope of reaping benefits – for their students and/or for themselves. In general, the benefits of online distance learning are similar to those of digital learning technologies more generally (Cook and Triola, 2014; Singh and Hardaker, 2014). These include the ability to access global markets and to do so at lower costs. Distance education has the potential to deliver cost reductions for the provider and for the student, though the costs of providing quality online provision are often underestimated.

Given its digital underpinning, distance education has the potential to enhance and deliver more flexible learning. The digital aspect of distance education means that provision and use generate substantial quantities of data that can be mined to better understand how students learn and to create an evidence base to improve educational provisions and student outcomes. Students are typically looking for a prestigious qualification that will help them secure a job or promotion that carries professional certification and accreditation. They therefore need a course that will be flexible, provide value, be recognised for credit transfer and attract subvention on fees. As well as those in the developed world who cannot attend an institution due to location or personal commitment, capacity challenges continue throughout much of the developing world. In some regions and communities distance education remains the only viable opportunity for education at all.

### Example

**Stiasny and Davis analysis: institutional drivers**

- Cost reduction may be one driver for the development of online and distance education, but UoL uses cross subsidy between qualifications as its mission to provide access and opportunity to study for its degree. Cross subsidy reinforces an overseas aspect that is academically motivated rather than driven by other reasons. Access has been central to maintaining local governmental and regulatory goodwill, shielding UoL from accusations of exploitation and indirectly proving a major marketing asset. UoL employs a model that generates surplus where there is a defined capacity needed at undergraduate level, in balance with a diverse portfolio of small, specialist postgraduate offerings of a wider developmental benefit. Although it is a successful global business, it is a social business with a diverse portfolio, promoting modernisation, social and cultural development, core administrative competencies, capacity building and international accord in specialist areas of global concern such as climate change, food security, epidemics, refugees and migration, poverty reduction, human rights or social justice.
- One of the goals of much online activity is to provide 'mass customisation'; that is, to enable a personalised experience, but to provide this at scale. For distance education, this means that the provision is adaptivity to respond to individual students. Digital provision may allow new assessment methods that could be continuous, although, as Chapters 11 and 12 demonstrate, online assessment is not straightforward. The same digitisation should enhance the institution's agility to implement new curricula faster. Finally, control should be improved so that educators can judge course quality and content and re-sequence learning as required. Otherwise, common characteristics in the majority of markets where the UoL has a significant presence comprise a one-time or continuing capacity need and the availability of third-party tuition. The fact that 80 per cent of UoL undergraduate learners seek to mediate their studies with conventional classroom-based learning indicates that, although undergraduates have embraced the merits of distance education, they continue to seek a conventional experience where possible.

However, unless the development of distance education is carefully thought through, then the benefits may reside with some participants and not with others. For example, the development of massive open online courses (MOOCs) has been an imperative, or even a fad, over the last few years. MOOCs were propounded by many as the 'next big thing' in education. Organisations, private and public, have invested heavily in developing many MOOCs. Some are exceptional products, but very few are revenue generating, fewer still profit generating. There may be other strategic reasons for developing MOOCs. Chapter 15 explores the role of MOOCs in world health developments. Some MOOCs may act as loss-leaders, driving students to programmes in the institution that developed the MOOC, but fewer have had the impact that many commentators, and investors, had predicted.

The value of the benefits of distance education will need to be assessed in relation to the costs of distance education. Many benefits, such as quality, will be subjective and difficult to quantify. Further, with many actors and stakeholders in the distance education value chain, the costs may fall disproportionately upon some while the benefits are accrued by others. For example, many MOOCs were very expensive to develop and they proved harder for many developers to monetise, but those who use the MOOC to educate themselves often had a tremendous learning experience, essentially for free. However, in an evolving market, the role and value of MOOCs will change. These issues, and others, are explored more deeply in Chapter 19. However, many researchers (for example, Cook and Triola, 2014; Salmon, 2005; Singh and Hardaker, 2014) argue that most of the outcomes of investment in distance education so far have been poor and the adoption of distance learning in HEIs has been slow and disappointing in many instances. There are clearly exceptions to this. UoL has successfully delivered distance education for over 150 years (see Preface), and there are Open Universities (OUs) around the world that are thriving. However, moves online by others have often proved less successful.

The realisation of a vision of ubiquitous and lifelong access to HE requires a distance learning strategy at an institutional level, and probably at a national system level as well, that is transformative of traditional HEIs (MacKeogh and Fox, 2008). Such a transformation requires that universities have strategies and policies that 'implement flexible academic frameworks, innovative pedagogical approaches, new forms of assessments, cross-institutional accreditation and credit transfer agreements, institutional collaboration in development and delivery and, most crucially, commitment to equivalence of access for students on and off campus' (MacKeogh and Fox, 2008: 1). As this book demonstrates, there is much more to distance education than the digitisation of face-to-face provision.

## Relationship to other educational provision

Distance education now typically involves the electronic delivery and support of teaching and learning activities. As such, it comprises a wide range of applications. Distance education may involve new technologies for HEIs and new skills in online pedagogy and digital media for teaching and learning. It may also enable HEIs to enhance learning and teaching, to deliver new services and to enter new markets. Some of the most successful distance education institutions predate digital delivery, so it is worth bearing in mind that non-digital or mixed or blended provision may be appropriate in some circumstances. UoL's programmes are supported by teaching centres in many global locations. Up to 80 per cent of UoL undergraduates have some face-to-face provision in this way. This demonstrates the potential transnational aspects of distance education.

Distance learning embraces a wide range of technologies that differ in the way they affect the institution. Some applications will have a marginal effect on pedagogy and on organisational structures, while others require a new pedagogy and complex uses can engender intended or unintended organisational change. At the simpler end of the continuum, the use of distance learning technology is little different from traditional teaching methods. However, at some point, distance learning requires a new or re-visioned pedagogy in order to fully exploit the teaching, learning and assessment opportunities. If HEIs are to manage distance education effectively, they need to consider its strategic and transformation opportunities and the implications, rather than viewing it simply as a pedagogical initiative.

Studies that have identified criteria associated with success, or failure, of distance education initiatives have been synthesised by Singh and Hardaker (2014). They argue that successful adoption depends on the ability of management to create a culture of trust, creativity and collaboration built upon a supportive administrative and technical infrastructure. Many of these criteria are evident throughout this book.

One way of assessing the extent to which distance learning is strategic for an HEI has been developed by Sims et al. (2017). They use Ansoff's (1965) growth vector matrix and adapt it to assess whether distance education is strategic (see Table 6.1).

The matrix involves distance education 'products' that are teaching programmes and the mission is defined as strategic or not. In the first

**Table 6.1** Is e-learning strategic? Sims et al. (2017) adapted from Ansoff (1965).

|  |  | Programmes | |
|---|---|---|---|
|  |  | Present | New |
| Strategic | No | Acquire more students | Develop current programmes |
|  | Yes | New markets | Develop new programmes |

inner cell of the matrix a current programme and non-strategic use of distance education is essentially about 'acquiring more students': there is no product development, no new types of students, merely growth within existing programmes. With this level of use, distance learning becomes just another tool for providing existing teaching and learning and is not strategic.

In the new programmes/non-strategic cell, 'Develop current programmes', distance education is used to enhance and develop existing programmes. There are still no new products or markets, merely improvements to existing products and, again, distance education cannot be judged as strategic for the HEI.

In the strategic/present programmes cell, distance education is used to enter new markets with existing programmes and, thus, becomes strategic.

In the strategic/new programmes cell, distance education is used to develop new programmes and consequently is strategic. Such a model can be useful in 'normal' times, but crisis responses to global events such as the COVID-19 pandemic may override such considerations. Then, as with the post-COVID case, HEIs have a wealth of educational material that they have moved online (though not necessarily of the highest quality), which may open up new opportunities for distance education.

Sims et al. (2017) identify two categories of distance learning organisations. First are organisations where individual academics are free to experiment with e-learning tools. These are termed as 'experimental implementers'. The design of distance learning in these organisations is intentional and experimental and strategy here tends to be emergent. Organisations in which there is a strategic planning objective in using distance learning, where strategy is top-down and designed, are seen as 'strategic design implementers'.

In the case of the 'experimental implementers', individual academics tend to experiment with distance learning tools, using them to build distance education into their teaching. The HEI provides software, platforms, servers and support, including administration and educational technologists. Experimental exploitation here is a bottom-up process, led by those who choose to develop distance learning. Those who choose to develop distance learning materials are enthusiastic, inquisitive, form links with other enthusiasts and tend to experiment.

'Strategic design implementers', however, plan for distance education. They differ from 'experimental implementers' in that they adopt policies to encourage or pressure distance education use, overcome inertia, regulate e-learning activity and develop distance education initiatives as a top-down strategic approach. The principal driver for 'strategic design implementers' is a perceived business opportunity. However, it is worth reiterating here that successful adoption depends on the ability of management to create a culture of trust, creativity and collaboration, and, as argued in the final chapter of this book (Chapter 20), this cannot be achieved without active participation in goal setting and solution generation by stakeholders.

Chapter 7 shows a composite approach, working both downwards from national and institutional strategy and upwards from the capabilities and enthusiasms of particular universities and staff, together with practical steps to ensure that these two directions of travel meet in the middle.

Distance learning delivers new products and services. One set of these is in the form of re-engineered, interactive, on-campus and distance teaching and learning. Another new product is communications available outside the geographic and chronological boundaries that restrict conventional campus and distance communications and that enable virtual communities of students, synchronous and asynchronous student–tutor communication and online assessment for distant students. Distance education enables the HEI to enter new markets. Students who would otherwise be unable to attend on-campus HEI study due to geographic or time constraints can attend campus-based courses supported by e-learning, while continuing with work or with caring commitments.

Strategy can be developed at the institutional level or at the product level. UoL launched a series of new 'flagship' programmes, informed directly by focused intelligence on market need and demand. These include an MSc in professional accountancy in partnership with the Association of Chartered Certified Accountants (ACCA), an MSc in supply chain management (the only online programme to be accredited by the Chartered Institute of Logistics and Transport and the Chartered Institute of Procurement and Supply) and an upgraded BSc in computer science, in partnership with Coursera.

For HEIs, it is important for senior managers to understand the need to support academics and technologists as they experiment with distance learning and develop new innovative ways of teaching and learning and to plan for the changes that experimentation brings. Pedagogies and course design for distance education are explored in Chapter 8. Senior managers need to consider the different strategies available to their organisation.

Those involved in the decisions about distance education – the developers, the funders, the academic and technical staff, the support services and the students – all have stakes in the outcome and need to be considered in any decision to invest heavily in distance education. However, not all stakeholders are equal, and the HEI will need to balance the needs, desires and requirements of many parties. One way of doing so is discussed next.

## Needs and expectations of distance learning stakeholders

Distance education involves many stakeholders. These stakeholders will have different perspectives on what they want to be achieved by distance education. Many of these wants will be somewhat, or perhaps even completely, incompatible. Some of the stakeholders may be local but others may be national or global regulatory bodies. No institution will be able to satisfy all their stakeholders. Hence, the institution needs to have a mechanism for balancing how they respond to stakeholders. The need to understand and manage stakeholders is then illustrated by the experiences of UoL. One useful tool to assist stakeholder management is stakeholder salience theory.

Stakeholder salience theory (Mitchell et al., 1997) identifies that the most important stakeholder groups possess one or more of three relationship attributes: power, legitimacy and urgency.

- Mitchell et al. (1997) defined any group or party in a relationship as having power to the extent it has access to coercive, utilitarian or normative means for imposing its will in the relationship.
- Legitimacy is seen as a desirable social good – it is more overarching than individual self-perception and is recognised by groups, communities or cultures.
- Urgency is based on time sensitivity and criticality – the importance of the claim or the relationship to the stakeholder.

Combining these attributes generates seven types of stakeholder: dormant, discretionary, demanding, dominant, dangerous, dependent and definitive. In addition, there is an eighth group, which are the non-stakeholders. These eight groupings are mapped in Figure 6.1.

Unpacking Figure 6.1 identifies the following:

1. Dormant stakeholders possess the power to impose their will but, by not having a legitimate relationship or an urgent claim, their power remains underutilised.
2. Discretionary stakeholders possess legitimacy yet have no power to influence issues and they have no urgent claims. There is no pressure to engage in a relationship with such a stakeholder.
3. Demanding stakeholders exist where the sole stakeholder relationship attribute is urgency. Such stakeholders have urgent claims while possessing neither legitimacy nor power.
4. Dominant stakeholders are powerful and legitimate. Their influence in the relationship is assured, since by possessing power and legitimacy they form the dominant coalition.
5. Dependent stakeholders are characterised by a lack of power, though they have urgent and legitimate claims. These stakeholders

Classification of stakeholders: Salience model

1. Dormant stakeholder
2. Discretionary stakeholder
3. Demanding stakeholder
4. Dominant stakeholder
5. Dangerous stakeholder
6. Dependent stakeholder
7. Definitive stakeholder
8. Non-stakeholders

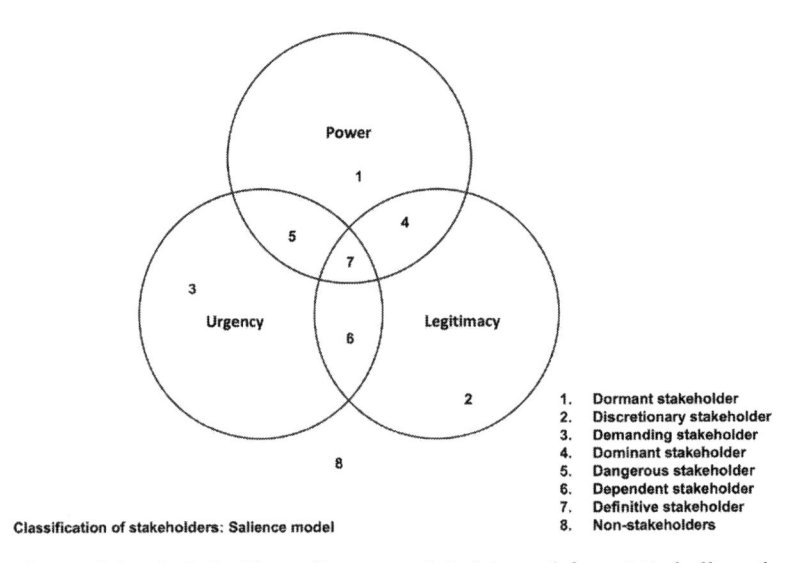

**Figure 6.1** Stakeholder salience model. Adapted from Mitchell et al. (1997).

must depend on others to carry out their will. Any influence that dependent stakeholders gain is advocated through the values of others.
6. Dangerous stakeholders possess urgency and power but not legitimacy. They may therefore be coercive or dangerous. The use of coercive power often accompanies socially illegitimate status.
7. Definitive stakeholders possess power, legitimacy and urgency. Any stakeholder can become definitive by acquiring the missing attribute(s) or by having the missing attributes thrust upon them.
8. Non-stakeholders possess none of the attributes and, thus, do not have any type of relationship with the issue.

The key role of such a tool is to remind those developing distance education that they need to consider these and that, in failing to do so, they may face insurmountable obstacles in their developmental journey.

The stakeholder salience model has been used in a variety of contexts, from understanding changes in HE (Powell and Walsh, 2017), the automotive industry supply chain (Howard et al., 2003), public health (Page, 2002) and business and educational policy (McDaniel and Miskel, 2002) to social and environmental policy (Zyglidopoulos, 2002). The stakeholder saliency model recognises that stakeholders can move from one category to another and are not confined to any particular situation in an ongoing dynamic. For example, Stiasny and Davis comment on how UoL has long benefited from graduates in influential positions worldwide acting as informal ambassadors for its consistent application of standards, demonstrating the role of informal stakeholders.

Institutions developing distance education may use the stakeholder salience model to identify and assess their stakeholders. These will vary by context. For example, in a state-funded directive HE model, the state, education ministry or funding council will be dominant or even definitive. These bodies can direct how distance education is enacted, the quality and the price. Institutions may have autonomy, but within a regulated system. Alternatively, HEIs may be able to offer distance education for profit in certain segments (continuing professional development, for instance) but not be able to change fees for certificated undergraduate education. Adaptations to achieve compliance with evolving professional and regulatory requirements have been a consistent hallmark across UoL's history of working overseas, stimulating various regional adjustments. Regulatory priorities, however, vary by country, imposing challenges to UoL's historically uniform and 'distant' approach.

> **Example**
>
> **Stiasny and Davis analysis: the role of regulation**
>
> Regulation is not only the province of governments. In line with UoL's growing portfolio and market-oriented adaptations, professional accreditations appear more regularly attached to UoL awards. From 2010, for example, articulations with a number of professional bodies, beginning with ACCA, were put in place for programmes in economics, management, finance and the social sciences. Accreditations soon followed with the Institute of Financial Services, the Institute of Chartered Accountants, the Chartered Institute of Management Accountants, CPA Australia, the Institute of Singapore Chartered Accountants and others. In 2007, a new MBA was launched with accreditation from the Association of MBAs, which, in turn, hinged upon regional plenary sessions at specially designated centres. Obtaining and maintaining professional accreditation is leading UoL to establish new collaborations designed to better mediate the learning experience or address new markets. Most overseas governments' regulatory concerns have focused on twinning, transfer and joint programmes, rather than the 'external' model of supplementary tuition for an overseas qualification. This is true not only of the UoL approach but also that of various professional bodies.
>
> In a global context, there may be multiple stakeholders of the same type. HEIs may need to conform to the regulations of their home nation, the regulations of the countries they operate in, as well as the requirements of any professional bodies from which accreditation is sought. UoL's belated participation in the UK quality regime and its subsequent verdict(s) of confidence provided vital ballast to overseas dialogues. Regulation depends partly upon the subject area but, in general, overseas agencies typically considered the corporate fitness of the provider, what it provides, for whom and how it operated locally. This was carried out against parameters established locally, but also in collaboration with other international agencies, such as the Quality Assurance Agency (and increasingly transnational quality assurance (QA) networks, including the Quality Beyond Boundaries Group). Criteria for local approval always included compliance with national policy and consideration of national labour market needs.

Today, they increasingly scrutinise the activities underpinning providers' perceptions of what is relevant and valuable locally.

For instance, quality frameworks domestically and abroad unquestionably aided UoL to address markets better where old approaches had created unnecessary difficulties for regulators. UoL's experience, policy, networks and internal resources accumulated throughout the preceding evolutions have positioned it to contemplate a fresh alignment with the needs of regulators and authorities around the world, especially those markets where its model has travelled less well historically, and where adaptation has generally been to little avail.

The growing complexity of globalised international HE has ensured that resources have expanded to service the growing network of connections, the increasing range and complexity of delivery and changing levels of regulation and control. Regulation covering collaborations with public and private institutions has provided a particularly complex challenge for UoL, not least because it can touch upon complex debates around the role of private colleges in relation to the national system, and the regulatory controls established as a result, whether in relation to quality or, more recently, permanent establishment and tax liability. The patterns of these changes fall into the three broad attitudes: systematic changes to the degree parchment (and the introduction of diploma supplements), qualitative changes in descriptions of quality and standards and relationships with third parties.

UoL has worked continuously to establish a network of over 650 examination centres that maximise flexibility of location and underpin the integrity of assessment. In particular jurisdictions or regions, written agreements are required with specific government agencies. Such organisations have sometimes grown to represent important lobbies in overseas government structures and have lent crucial support to UoL's model at various points. They play a vital role in maintaining the integrity of the award and, at a practical logistical level, benefit from a single point of contact in coordinating examinations.

In another aspect of stakeholder relations, UoL cooperates with other institutions either by recognising their courses or by providing syllabuses of its own. Under such arrangements, it has provided an academic qualification with its 'core' learning materials while the collaborating institution provides the teaching support. Relationships with teaching centres are dependent upon regular ongoing contact and liaison with UoL, which in turn liaises with appropriate government ministries overseas that monitor local involvement in provision.

Caution is required in ensuring that legal requirements for providers of overseas courses are met and requisite permissions obtained. Specific permissions have been granted that require continuous personal contact with relevant officials. As regulation of globalised transnational education (TNE) becomes more sophisticated, an ever-growing panoply of local procedures will be undertaken to register programmes with local agencies. Personal contacts are an important consideration in many cultures.

Access has been central to maintaining local governmental and regulatory goodwill, shielding UoL from accusations of exploitation and indirectly proving a major marketing asset. Whereas individual institutions might be assumed to focus on qualifications that generate surplus or promote reputation, perceptions of UoL perhaps take deeper root.

As regulatory approval of TNE has become more widespread and sophisticated, various potential barriers to operation have been created. In such a crowded and confusing global market for education, with contentious claims and questionable accreditors, this can only be seen as an aid to students seeking to identify an offer in which they can have confidence. Regulatory priorities differ by country, imposing challenges to UoL's historically uniform and 'distant' approach, which was enthusiastically adopted in many markets for a variety of reasons, ranging from the proven capabilities of a protean template for development to a simple absence of alternatives.

UoL increased attention to the guidance and support offered to teaching centres mediating undergraduate studies and the level of academic visits. Although this would inevitably draw UoL more closely into overseas systems of regulation and control, it yielded growth as institutions globally sought to develop their reputations and revenue through teaching to UoL qualifications.

In line with its growing portfolio and market-oriented adaptations, professional accreditations appear more regularly attached to UoL awards. Obtaining and maintaining professional accreditation is leading UoL to establish new collaborations designed to better mediate the learning experience or address new markets.

Regulation can pose other problems. Over the course of several decades, changes in governance, organisation, statute and ordinance have improved the clarity of these arrangements and their alignment with stakeholder expectations, ensuring that global esteem continue to be accorded to UoL awards, irrespective of mode or place of study.

The patterns of these changes fall under three broad headings:

- systematic changes to the degree parchment (and the introduction of diploma supplements)
- qualitative changes in descriptions of quality and standards
- relationships with third parties.

Perceptions of value and relevance around UoL qualifications are often dependent upon the availability of tuition support and local centres have played a prominent role in advancing the programme, ensuring recognition and relevance of qualifications earned at a distance from London, leveraging local relationships and championing the benefits of its model.

It remains vital to successful management of stakeholder perspectives that UoL's impetus is education led. Global regulation of delivery of overseas degree programmes is naturally tremendously diverse, but complexity usually accompanies private sector involvement. In tandem with more sophisticated systems for recognition, development and monitoring of centres, and also local QA measures, teaching approaches are policed more closely and the balance of recognition agreements is starting to shift noticeably from private tutorial arrangements towards parallel degree articulations with public institutions.

For UoL, developments around branding, resource and internal organisation effected significant change in policy, language, process and locus of responsibility. These improved local clarity, compliance and dialogue, helped explain UoL's work in less mythical ways and better managed stakeholder perspectives through a closer mesh with foreign and domestic quality assurance frameworks and channels for local representation. This positioned UoL's present-day distance education provision to effectively address emerging trends in overseas regulation, the challenges in maintaining equilibrium between activities that are commercially and academically led and the paramount importance of ensuring that the 'local needs' being addressed are identified collaboratively with local stakeholders rather than imposed by London.

> A further set of stakeholders may be the press and media. For example, in an age of greater regulation and control, trends around increasing reliance on league tables to determine such 'top' universities as permitted to operate locally present particular challenges, as UoL does not even appear in league tables. In contrast, in an HE market, students will be much more central, as they can decide from whom to purchase their education. However, even in these extremes, there will be other stakeholders whose needs require addressing, such as staff. It is important to remember that stakeholder saliency is not static. Changes to regulations, to funding systems and to political priorities may see different stakeholders' urgency, legitimacy and power alter.

Having considered stakeholders, there are many ways in which distance education can be delivered, so the HEI will need to make choices. Considering the educational value chains – who is involved in producing and consuming the end product and how is it produced and consumed – and the business models that underlie the choices is vital, and these are considered next.

## Who provides the different resources and decides how they are bundled together?

Once an institution has decided that it will engage in distance learning, and has considered its stakeholders, it needs to consider how it will deliver the distance education. The strategy will be delivered through a business model. Timmers (1998) defines a business model as architecture for the product, service and information flows, including the actors and their roles, the potential benefits for the actors and the sources of revenue. He proposes 11 types of digitally based business models, while Rappa (2004) identifies nine: brokerage, advertising, information intermediary, merchant, manufacturer direct, affiliate, community, subscription and utility. Distance learning can exhibit characteristics of many of these business models, depending on who does what and how revenue is derived. By virtue of global dispersion, distance education is resource intensive, so centralised approaches that permit significant economies of scale and efficiency savings are attractive.

Software products, such as distance learning products that are delivered digitally, have specific features that distinguish them from other products. For instance, software can be reproduced at low marginal cost with very low variable costs. Also, software, including courseware, can be reproduced repeatedly without any loss of quality. Software products are more easily modified than physical products – which means that the markets for software have a tendency to become more unstable as technology changes disrupt them. However, software markets feature strong internationalisation and there are advantages in the network effects gained from scale and market domination.

For an HEI developing distance education, an understanding of business models is helped by identifying value chain elements and assessing how the value chain can be deconstructed and reconstructed. Porter and Millar (1985) distinguish a number of value chain elements – inbound logistics, operations, outbound logistics, marketing/sales and service – and the support activities, technology development, procurement, human resource management and corporate infrastructure. Any, some or all of these elements can be supplied by one or more actors. HEIs will have many of these elements for their face-to-face provision, although not necessarily all labelled with these terms. The key question to ask here is – are these suitable for distance educational development? As is discussed elsewhere in the book, there are specialists in distance education, including digital pedagogists, content developers and technologists. An HEI may seek to buy in these resources or to partner with others. Many of the major distance education providers, such as Coursera, edX, Udacity and FutureLearn, offer education from a variety of providers. These organisations offer platforms, technology and developers, but the content is often devised by HEIs. As well as being a major provider in its own right, UoL also partners with Coursera in some of its offerings, as does the UK OU with FutureLearn.

Many organisations combine some of these models to achieve competitive advantage in distance education provision. Content providers offer predetermined distance learning content. This content can be standardised or individualised. Application providers offer distance learning applications, such as virtual learning environments or learning management systems. The hardware that HEIs need is typically not specific to distance education but will need to provide the functionalities required. Further along the value chain, service providers can provide student recruitment, market research, course design, technology platforms and training or employment placements. Finally, full-service providers offer complete solutions. Most HEIs will have some of the value chain elements in-house, or will wish to develop them internally, such as tutoring and assessment (see Chapters 11 and 12), but other services, such as examination proctoring, may need to be procured through partnerships or, more likely, through transactions.

## How online provision is funded or monetised

Distance education, enacted online, is a form of electronic business. There are a variety of e-business models. Many of these have currency in planning distance education. While e-auctions have little role in distance education, many other e-business models do.

Distance education may be thought of as a form of e-shop. Students need to be able to access materials and services, choose to buy them and have a payment mechanism. Alternatively, distance education may be delivered as part of an online community, in which the focus is on the added value of communication between members of the community. This will need technologies that support such interactions. Many distance education courses will require students to work collaboratively and, again, a variety of tools will be needed to enable this. The HEI may need to work with value chain service providers that support elements of the value chain such as logistics or payments, or with value chain integrators who integrate multiple steps in the value chain. They may need to collaborate with platform providers or place their educational offerings on an e-marketplace. HEIs will probably use e-procurement systems to source and tie together their courses. Finally, information brokers may provide services such as trust, business information services and consultancy.

In each of these models there are several ways in which revenue may be generated by the various actors in the value chain. In the distance education market, there are actors in each of these spaces. The HEI needs to decide where its expertise lies, which elements it will do for itself and for which it will partner with external providers – and the form of that partnership.

Distance education needs to be resourced. It may be that the provision is funded by the state, in which case revenue comes from general taxation. Alternatively, for example, there are a number of charities that also make some distance learning materials available free. However, in most cases, the value chain actors will be seeking remuneration of some sort.

A major business difference between online and distance education and conventional face-to-face education is the balance between upfront investment and operating costs. In face-to-face education, the concept of investment in the production of a new course is unfamiliar – rarely is a distinction made between the costs of course production and course operation. By contrast, the cost of producing a major distance learning programme can run into millions of pounds. Assinder et al. (2010) consider course design as in part an economic activity, a decision based on the allocation of resources, on investment and then, over the life of the course, on return on that investment. The increasingly rapid turnover of essential course content means that the balance of investment is now shifting away from initial course production and towards more frequent course updating. In the business world of distance education, little, if anything, is constant.

There are many ways in which distance learning can be paid for. This is not unique to distance education. In most HE contexts, institutions have a variety of funding sources – government grants, tuition fees, research income, sponsorship and consultancy, among others. All these are still relevant to an institution developing distance education, but the digital context enables new ways of gaining revenue.

Eight 'atomic business models', each representing a different way of conducting business electronically, have been identified (Weill and Vitale, 2001). E-business initiatives can be pure atomic business models or can be a combination of them. Alternatively, Applegate (2001) identifies six e-business models: focused distributors, portals, producers, infrastructure distributors, infrastructure portals and infrastructure producers. The different ways of monetising distance education can be summarised as:

- commission-based models in which services are provided for a fee
- advertising-based models in which content is provided and click-through advertising generates income
- mark-up-based models that resell content via branding or reputation
- production-based models that use an online presence to lower marketing costs and make direct contact with end users
- referral-based models that are used to steer customers to a supplier for a fee
- subscription-based models that involve users paying a flat fee for providing a service or content
- fee-for-service-based models that provide services that are based on usage.

All these models have been used in distance education provision. They are not mutually exclusive. A subscription-based model may also carry advertising, for example, or rebranded content may be offered based on usage. HEIs need to iron out these issues before they launch into distance education development.

## Conclusions

This chapter considers how far distance learning is strategic for HEIs. More precisely, it suggests that each HEI that is contemplating moving into or extending its position in distance education needs to answer this question for itself. It has demonstrated that the simplest business model for an HEI looking to engage in distance learning would involve an institution going it alone. Here, they would develop, design, launch, support, market and quality assure all the programmes offered. Such a model retains maximum control for the institution. However, it is unlikely that many have all the resources and skills needed internally. To buy in staff with all the expertise necessary, or to develop the necessary capabilities in existing staff, as well as obtain the necessary technologies, might well be expensive. At the other extreme, an institution might consider doing nothing other than license its brand to an online educational provider in return for a revenue share. Aside from contract monitoring, the institution would have minimal involvement in any distance delivery.

In between these two ends of a spectrum lie many possibilities as to who best does what in distance education. Here, many external actors can come into play – content providers, technology suppliers, online pedagogists, accreditors and others.

Beyond the delivery models lie decisions about purpose, audience and funding.

---

**Example**

**Stiasny and Davis analysis: distance learning provision**

In an educational system in which HE is funded by the state, the decision about the provision of distance learning will rest on factors such as the ability to reach students that are poorly served by face-to-face provision and cannibalisation or replacement of existing provision. Among most younger communities of school leavers, online and distance education has rarely been a first choice of study mode. However, this is changing. Some students opting for distance education may have failed to gain admittance to first-choice universities on grounds of quotas, cost or other factors. Others may simply be saving money for later studies abroad at postgraduate level. Price may, for example, be an important factor in underscoring

> UoL's access mission and profile, but it is often less relevant than such factors as the availability of local tuition support across the world. For undergraduate qualifications, UoL prices are generally kept low in order to enable students to seek additional teaching support from independent providers, should they so wish. Also, flexibility provides significant value, both for students and crucially for the local education economy. At postgraduate level, both the student profile and the greater provision of educational support typically obviate the need for third parties in teaching, but also require a higher price point that reduces access and distribution.

Distance learning provision may be all-encompassing – that is, all aspects of education are included – or the educational package can be disintermediated. Disintermediation involves some elements of the package being provided, probably online, by UoL and some by other media or by partners. For example, the institution could develop its own bespoke content but use a commercial platform for delivery; it could outsource student support while setting and marking its own exams.

There is clearly a relationship between the disintermediation of the pedagogic package and its provision. The more elements are disaggregated, the more the institution can seek the best providers for individual elements, albeit at an increased cost of ensuring coherence. A key issue here is whether the institution develops a partnership or it subcontracts. An arm's-length contract of provision in exchange for money will differ from a partnership where joint brands may have much more value than individual ones. Formal joint ventures may be established.

A final decision arises around the funding of, or the monetising of, the educational provision. Again, this is tied into the actors in the value chain. Each actor will seek reward from its activity and, while some actors will be only playing in one value chain, most will have feet in more. Some will seek scale, as what they provide is only viable when the fixed costs such as the development costs are covered by many users, as discussed earlier. Others might seek exclusivity in order to protect their brand. It is unlikely that all the value chain actors will have the same cost-resource structures or the same motivations for participating. Any resolution of these may depend on negotiation and regulation. Of course, all actors are working somewhat in the dark – or the twilight – as data, for example, on enrolments, completions, fee levels and actions of competitors will affect outcomes, but these are probably mostly unknown and unknowable during the negotiations. The darkness can be illuminated most effectively by market insights or by the actions of competitors.

A distance education platform supplier would seek to sell its platform to multiple users. A content provider might license its content to more than one provider but may seek exclusivity, or at least non-competing clients. Online developers may be freelance, so might work for a variety of providers.

The form of monetisation may range from a free model, whereby all or some aspects of the online provision are provided to students at no cost to them. In the case of blended educational provision, the online element may be bundled into annual fees. Other models would involve paying a subscription, an access fee, a fee for 'premium' aspects of provision such as individual feedback or study support, a fee for assessment or a fee for a credential.

HEIs must assess distance learning provision strategically and then decide whether and how it is to be delivered. The market for distance education is constantly changing as new players and new technologies disrupt it. Hence, an HEI will need to have a strategy for updating and evolving its distance learning programmes.

The world of distance education continues to evolve rapidly. While digital support for face-to-face delivery can be achieved quickly and with few resources, many institutions mistake this for authentic distance education. As this book demonstrates, successful distance education affects virtually all aspects of an HEI. The pedagogy, student support, marketing, technology, remuneration and many other aspects will need to be rethought. In addition, most HEIs were not born digital, which means that they will need to manage a major organisational change programme to deliver distance education.

## References

Anderson, W., Brown, M., Murray, F., Simpson, M. and Mentis, M. (2006) *Global Picture, Local Lessons*. New Zealand: Ministry of Education.

Ansoff, I. (1965) *Corporate Strategy*. New York: McGraw-Hill.

Assinder, S., Baume, D. and Bates, I. (2010) 'Focusing on student learning to guide the use of staff time'. *Innovations in Education and Teaching International*, 47 (4), 357–67.

Applegate, L. M. (2001) *Emerging e-Business Models: Lessons from the field*. HBS No. 9-801-172. Boston: Harvard Business School.

Barber, M., Donnely, K. and Rizvi, S. (2013) *An Avalanche is Coming*. London: Institute for Public Policy Research.

Cook, D. A. and Triola, M. M. (2014) 'What is the role of e-learning? Looking past the hype'. *Medical Education*, 48, 930–7. Accessed 3 July 2022. https://doi.org/10.1111/medu.12484.

House of Commons (2016) 'Digital skills crisis: Second report of session 2016–17', Science and Technology Committee, HC 270, 13 June. Accessed 3 July 2022. https://publications.parliament.uk/pa/cm201617/cmselect/cmsctech/270/270.pdf.

Howard, M., Vidgen, R. and Powell, P. (2003) 'Overcoming stakeholder barriers in the automotive industry: Building to order with extra-organisational systems'. *Journal of Information Technology*, 18, 27–43.

MacKeogh, K. and Fox, S. (2008) 'Strategies for embedding elearning in traditional universities: Drivers and barriers'. Proceedings of 7th European Conference on e-Learning, 6–7 November, Cyprus.

McDaniel, J. E. and Miskel, C. G. (2002) 'The nature of influence in national reading policymaking: The role of beliefs and the importance of collaboration'. Paper presented at the annual meeting of the National Reading Conference, San Antonio, TX.

Mitchell, R. K., Agle, B. R. and Wood, D. J. (1997) 'Toward a theory of stakeholder identification and salience: Defining the principle of who and what really counts'. *Academy of Management Review*, 22 (4), 853–86.

Page, C. (2002) 'The determination of organization stakeholder salience in public health'. *Journal of Public Health Management & Practice*, 8 (5), 76–84.

Porter, M. and Millar, V. (1985) 'How information gives you competitive advantage'. *Harvard Business Review*, 63 (4), 149–60.

Powell, P. and Walsh, A. (2017) 'Whose curriculum is it anyway? Stakeholder salience in the context of degree apprenticeships'. *Higher Education Quarterly*, 72 (2), 90–106. Accessed 3 July 2022. https://doi.org/10.1111/hequ.12149.

Rappa, M. (2004) 'The utility business model and the future of computing service'. *IBM Journal*, 43, 32–42.

Salmon, G. (2005) 'Flying not flapping: A strategic framework for e-learning and pedagogical innovation in higher education institutions'. *ALT-J: Research in Learning Technology*, 13 (3), 201–18.

Schiffman, S., Vignare, K. and Geith, B. (2007) 'Why do higher-education institutions pursue online education?' *Journal of Asynchronous Learning Networks*, 11 (2), 61–71.

Sims, J., Powell, P. and Vidgen, R. (2017) 'Mediating role of inertia in organisational transformation: E-learning in higher education'. *Higher Education Review*, 50 (1), 35–62.

Singh, G. and Hardaker, G. (2014) 'Barriers and enablers to adoption and diffusion of elearning: A systematic review of the literature – a need for an integrative approach'. *Education + Training*, 56 (2–3) 105–21. Accessed 3 July 2022. https://doi.org/10.1108/ET-11-2012-0123.

Timmers, P. (1998) 'Business models for electronic markets'. *Electronic Markets*, 8, 3–8.

Weill, P. and Vitale, M. (2001) *Place to Space: Migrating to e-business models*. Boston: Harvard Business Press.

Zyglidopoulos, S. C. (2002) 'The social and environmental responsibilities of multinationals: Evidence from the Brent Spar case'. *Journal of Business Ethics*, 36, 141–51.

# 7
# Open and distance learning in Nigeria: a case study

Stephen Brown and David Baume

In the wake of the COVID-19 pandemic, universities worldwide had little choice other than to move their teaching, learning and assessment online wholesale. The pivot to online was a tactical emergency response, not a strategic plan. The outcomes were mixed. More time to plan, a clearer picture of learning and its facilitation, better understanding of the challenges involved in moving education online and greater capacity to effect change would all have helped institutions to make the pivot more successfully.

Pre-COVID, the national context for higher education (HE) in Nigeria – in summary, demand for HE massively outstripping supply – was already driving a government-led strategy to build national capacity for open and distance learning (ODL).

Effective development work requires close alignment between, on the one hand, policy and strategy and, on the other hand, front-line operational capabilities, resourcing and practice. For maximum effect, policy and strategy should exist at a number of levels – national, perhaps regional, institutional and at department, faculty or school level. Policy and strategy at these various levels should of course be coherent, all pulling in the same broad direction towards the same overall goals. In the example considered in this case study, that direction is towards a substantial expansion of the capacity of Nigerian HE through greatly increased use of ODL.

However, a policy or strategy without front-line operational capabilities, resourcing and practice remains just a document, an idea, possibly a hope. Nothing much may happen. And practice uninformed and unsupported by policy and strategy is unlikely to have a long-term effect, or indeed much effect at all, beyond the immediate and the local.

Policy and strategy need not always precede practice. Working with skilled local enthusiasts before a policy is in place can generate the kind of enthusiasm that may lead to, or encourage, the development of policy and strategy as well as practice. Those who write the policy and strategy will be cheered to see local enthusiasm, which increases the chances of success.

These interactions between national and institutional policy and practice are visible in the Centre for Online and Distance Education's (CODE's) work with the Nigerian National Universities Commission (NUC), in support of expansion of Nigerian HE through the use of ODL.

This work is ongoing, so the account in this case study is incomplete. However, in our description and analysis of plans, activities and achievements to date, we hope to give you a rich picture of an ambitious capacity-building programme at the various levels at which it is being undertaken.

## Nigeria and the demand for education

Nigeria is the largest country in Africa by population, currently around 200 million and growing by about 2.7 per cent annually. Population is expected to double by 2066. Nigeria is also a young country, with over 120 million people under the age of 25 as of 2022. This may rise to over 200 million in 50 years (Jegede, 2016). This is creating an enormous demand for education, but access to educational opportunities is restricted by limited numbers of places at all educational levels and also by affordability. Despite significant oil reserves, Nigeria is not a wealthy country at the level of individual households.

### Nigerian HE aspirations

The Nigerian Federal Ministry of Education and its Tertiary Education Department are responsible for the National Policy on Education (NPE), first published in 1997 and currently in its sixth edition. The Federal Ministry of Education is supported by the NUC, which provides policy advice regarding universities, assures the quality of HE in Nigeria and regulates the establishment of new HE institutions (HEIs). The NUC recently published a five-year plan for improving the Nigerian HE system, known as the 'Rasheed Revitalisation Plan', after Professor Abdulrasheed Abubakar, Executive Secretary of the NUC, who helped to develop it. Its recommendations reflected the enormous challenges faced by Nigerian HE (The PIE News, 2018):

- By 2018, the curriculum of Nigerian universities should be rated among the best three in Africa in terms of its relevance to producing nationally and regionally relevant graduates.
- By 2020, a sustainable funding model should have been approved at all levels and implemented via appropriate instruments of federal and state governments.
- By 2023, at least 30 per cent of facilities for teaching, learning and research should have been upgraded to meet international standards.
- By 2023, the gap in the number of teachers needed in the Nigerian university system and those in post should have been reduced from 30 per cent to 20 per cent.
- By 2023, access to university education should have increased by a factor of 20 per cent over 2018 figures.

## Challenges faced by Nigerian HE: capacity, stability, quality and relevance

There are not enough places in Nigerian HE to meet demand. Between 2010 and 2015, only 26 per cent of the 10 million applicants to Nigerian tertiary institutions gained admission. Many of those who failed to obtain a place had passed the necessary examinations. In 2018 there were around 750,000 tertiary education places, but more than 2 million applicants for these places. Many of those who failed to obtain a place had met the entry requirements (The PIE News, 2018). After the 2017 Joint Admissions and Matriculation Board examinations, the NUC stated that, due to limited slots for admission, Nigerian universities could only accommodate about 30 per cent of the 1.7 million candidates who took the examination (Abutu, 2018). Speaking in April 2018 at the annual conference of the UK's Quality Assurance Agency, Abdulrasheed Abubakar said, 'This is a very serious situation. One million students do not get access to university, not because they have failed their exams, but because the capacity is not there' (The PIE News, 2018). In 2018, the situation improved, but only slightly: the total number of university places available was 695,449, some 44 per cent of the total applications of 1,592,305 (Jegede, 2016). Evidently, the system cannot accommodate the numbers of students who apply each year. If population forecasts prove correct, then, without radical intervention of some kind, it will become even more difficult for huge numbers of young people to secure a university place in Nigeria.

Those university places that are available are not reliably accessible. In recent years some Nigerian universities have shut down for months at a time because of strike action (The PIE News, 2018). Parts of the country have been disturbed by civil unrest and terrorist activity, causing closures and making travel difficult and dangerous. Nigeria's militant Islamist group Boko Haram and, more recently, Islamic State West Africa are fighting to overthrow the government and create an Islamic state (*The Guardian*, 2021). The name 'Boko Haram' is often translated as 'Western education is forbidden' and schools, further education colleges and universities are all regular targets in Nigeria (UK Government, n.d.). Most recently, as in many countries around the world, universities were closed in 2020 as a measure to help limit the spread of the COVID-19 virus (Abutu, 2020).

Implementation of the NPE has hitherto been hampered by the difficulty of meeting all the educational needs of a country with a large and rapidly growing population from within the limited resources of the government. Federal and state-owned universities that draw their budgetary allocations from the government have responded to financial constraints by increasing student fees and widely ignoring centrally issued student quotas (Abutu, 2020). However, by admitting more students than they can handle, institutions are making it more difficult for students to learn. Some classes now have as many as 500 students. At some universities, students have to stand in and around the lecture halls to receive lectures because there are not enough seats (2,000 students crammed into a 500-seat hall is not uncommon). Students report that during such lectures they can barely hear what the lecturers are saying and it is difficult to access the lecturers after class to seek clarification (Abutu, 2020).

The NPE was a response to general dissatisfaction with the then-existing education system, which was widely regarded as irrelevant to national needs, aspirations and goals. The first edition was published in 1997. Subsequent editions (with the latest being the sixth) have been designed to reflect changes in the national economy, the emergence of globalisation and developments in education, but major concerns remain regarding the relevance of some current Nigerian HE provision to graduate employability.

In summary, Nigerian HE provision is already insufficient to meet current demand in terms of capacity, quality, availability and relevance. Future population increases and developments in the economy, driven by further industrialisation, urbanisation and globalisation, seem likely to only exacerbate this situation.

## Future options for Nigerian HE

Clearly 'do nothing' is not a viable option. As observed by Peter Okebukola, Distinguished Professor of Science and Computer Education at Lagos State University and former NUC Executive Secretary, 'With more than two million candidates striving to fill about 750,000 available spaces in the universities, polytechnics and colleges of education, the challenge of opening the doors for more to enter the higher education system and ensure that quality graduates come out of it in the face of resource handicaps is stark' (The PIE News, 2018). The situation is particularly acute in the face of rapid population growth and potential loss of crucial revenue as a result of falling oil exports in the wake of a COVID-19-induced global recession.

### Enlarge existing or build more universities

Nigeria already has approximately 43 federal, 48 state and 79 private universities, making a total of 170 universities (Jegede, 2016). However, federal universities account for around 40 per cent of university places and, despite the rapid establishment of large numbers of private universities since 1999, the latter still account for less than 4 per cent (Ramon-Yusuf, n.d.). Speaking in April 2018 at the annual conference of the UK's Quality Assurance Agency, Professor Abdulrasheed Abubakar said that more than 290 new universities were planned for the country (The PIE News, 2018). Nigeria was also aiming to recruit an extra 10,000 university lecturers in the next five years, which would take the total number to about 72,000 by 2023 – an improvement, but still short of the 'about 88,000' needed (The PIE News, 2018). How this level of expansion would be achieved is not clear. Despite the large number of private universities, most Nigerian HE places are in the public sector, which, as we have seen, lacks sufficient capacity to meet even current demand. Reflecting on this, one leading Nigerian educationalist has commented:

> Given the huge numbers of unmet demand for education at all levels staring us in the face, there will not be enough resources to meet the needs of the population. Besides, there will not be enough resources to build all the classrooms, all the furnishing and all the infrastructure needed to meet the needs of the population. Besides, there will not be

time and people to train all the teachers and lecturers and other ancillary staff needed to work in the educational establishments. The only answer, known to nations ready to confront their educational needs, that we know is ODL. (Jegede, 2016)

## Employ more ODL

Nigeria has a long history of ODL provision, stretching back to correspondence courses provided by British HEIs prior to Independence. The University of the Air (Ahmadu Bello University), 1972, the University of Lagos, 1974, and the National Teachers Institute, 1978, are more recent examples (Jegede, 2016). In 1997, the first NPE stated that ODL should be an integral part of education that needed to be organised nationwide (Jegede, 2016). The National Open University was launched in 1984 but was suspended in the wake of a coup d'état. It was relaunched as the National Open University of Nigeria (NOUN) in 2002. Significantly, the Nigerian government recently lifted a suspension order on ODL programmes (Jegede, 2016) and the most recent NPE (2013) reiterates the need to have flexible learning modes, including open and distance education (Federal Republic of Nigeria, 2013).

Strong foundations therefore exist for increasing the capacity of ODL in Nigerian HE. As of 2022, NOUN already enrols around 515,000 students. Many conventional universities in good standing with respect to quality have been encouraged by the NUC to switch to a dual mode, with a strong ODL delivery system alongside conventional face-to-face provision to increase capacity (The PIE News, 2018). From 2016, around 20 institutions of higher learning have been, or are developing, dual-mode systems that use both ODL and traditional face-to-face as instructional modes (Jegede, 2016).

Notwithstanding these strengths, successful scaling up of ODL nationally and institutionally faces some significant challenges. These include insufficient, although fast-improving, internet and mobile phone network coverage, high access costs and limited institutional capacity and capability for ODL pedagogy design skills, technical development skills and 24/7 support capability.

## Capacity building for ODL

It was against the backdrop of rapidly escalating demand for relevant, accessible HE provision, colossal undercapacity to meet that demand and an effective moratorium in Nigeria on all new online delivery by private and/or international providers that, in 2017, the NUC invited the University of London (UoL) to explore possible support for the development of ODL in Nigeria. NUC believes that ODL is the only feasible and affordable way in which the nation, with the largest and fastest growing population in Africa, can meet current, let alone future, needs for HE.

Historically, ODL has not been regarded highly across much of Africa because of its long association with low-quality correspondence courses. In particular, some professional groups argue that educational quality cannot be maintained, distance learners cannot adapt and time-tested methods are better (Jegede, 2016). UoL was seen as an attractive partner in the development of ODL, having a very strong global academic reputation, long experience of distance learning and familiarity with Nigeria. For example, the University of Ibadan was established in 1948 as a college of UoL.

Following early conversations between the NUC's Executive Secretary Professor Abdulrasheed Abubakar and his senior team and UoL, plans were made to explore and share good practice at a joint policy symposium in Abuja in November 2017. As a follow-up, the NUC and UoL planned a workshop in London in March 2018, devised and delivered by UoL's CODE.

It was at this point, in the context of the developing relationship between the NUC and UoL and its potential impact on the Nigerian university sector, that the NUC expressed a wish to sign a Memorandum of Understanding (MoU) encapsulating joint aspirations. For the NUC, a Nigerian government body, this represented a suitable vehicle for signalling official intent. For UoL, the MoU offered a non-binding agreement that provided a welcome focus for joint endeavour over the next few years.

The MoU envisages a programme of cooperation in areas to be determined by both parties, including:

- ODL policy development
- course material development
- assessment in ODL
- research and development in ODL
- tutor capacity development
- pedagogical considerations and innovations in ODL
- management of ODL
- technological developments in ODL
- development and deployment of massive open online courses
- quality assurance and quality enhancement in ODL

- establishment of parallel degrees with selected Nigerian universities in fields including banking, finance, management, economics, computing, data science, international relations and law
- provision of ODL postgraduate programmes in sectors of interest, including education, law, Masters of Business Administration (MBA), environmental management, sustainable development, information security, petroleum geoscience and accounting.

## Workshops in London

Annual development workshops have been run in London for Nigerian University senior managers, including vice chancellors, deputy vice chancellors, pro-vice chancellors and heads of support services with a particular interest in ODL. The workshops provide a combination of input, question and answer, discussions and activities. Participants have been encouraged throughout to explore implications for their own institutions and time and support for action planning are included.

Sessions in 2020 included presentations from the UoL Student Experience Team and workshop sessions on policy for student support, face-to-face summer schools as an element in ODL, the importance of online community for distance learning students, listening to and using feedback from students, staff development for ODL, approaches to researching ODL practice and course and learning design.

These workshops are run in association with the annual CODE Research in Distance Education (RIDE) conference, discussed further below.

## RIDE conferences

The London workshops for the NUC are run on the days immediately prior to CODE's RIDE conferences. Through plenaries and parallel sessions, these established conferences provide overviews of current major issues in distance education and accounts of, and opportunities to explore, recent advances in the standing and practice of distance education. This timing has enabled NUC colleagues to attend, participate and present at the RIDE conferences, helping to build a dialogue between the NUC and UoL and opening up Nigerian issues to discussion by a wider audience.

## Annual conference/symposium in Nigeria

These large two-day events are attended by staff from the NUC and by vice chancellors and other senior staff of universities across Nigeria with an interest in ODL. As an example, the title theme of the 2018 event was 'Delivering Open and Distance Learning Degree Programmes Fit for Purpose'. Presentations are made by leading Nigerian ODL experts and by CODE staff. Issues explored in presentations and panel sessions include national and institutional strategy, the vital importance of quality assurance in raising the reputation of ODL in Nigeria, the development of national and local support systems and structures, the need to achieve a better match between graduate attributes and the requirements of Nigerian employers, forms of cooperation between UoL and HE in Nigeria, the uses of IT in ODL and cultural, resource, organisation and policy issues involved in the increased use of ODL in Nigeria.

## Workshops in Nigeria

Training and development events in Nigeria in HE have typically been formal, conference or symposium-style events such as those described earlier. Lectures, usually illustrated with slides, are followed by question-and-answer sessions, along with panel discussions. This style reflects the predominant didactic pedagogy in Nigerian HE and in many other countries besides. Such an approach was used in some of the London and Abuja events, especially those involving senior university managers.

However, for the July 2018 event in Abuja, CODE agreed with the NUC to take a different approach. This would be more practical, hands-on and fully integrating practice, theory and strategy. Unusually, participants worked over the three days, for the most part in a café-style setting, with six or eight people per table, rather than in an auditorium. Participants were allocated to tables to maximise mixing and mutual learning between institutions and roles. Table allocations were changed during the three-day event to further increase sharing and networking and to expose participants to new people and perspectives.

The main aim of the workshop was to provide information, ideas and resources to support participants to plan the next stages of development of ODL in their institutions, whatever their role. A further important aim was to help participants to form networks that would continue to provide peer support after the workshop was over.

### The shape of the workshop
Each day comprised five 75-minute sessions, with additional private study time. Each session was supported by a workbook containing structured exercises with explicit aims and expected outcomes, information, links to resources and space for participants to work on

reflective exercises and action planning. By the end of the workshop, this made the final completed workbook a tangible and personalised resource for each individual and their institution.

Important features of the event included:

- a Nigerian national expert speaker each day
- large amounts of collaborative work culminating in a competitive poster event
- detailed individual action planning during and after each session, using a workbook produced for the workshop.

Questions participants were asked to consider at the end of each session included the following:

- What are the main ideas that you are taking away from this session?
- How do you plan to use these ideas to advance your own and your institution's practice in ODL during the next few months or years?
- What are you going to do with each of these ideas?
- How are you going to implement them?
- Who else will you need to talk to, to put these ideas into practice?
- How will you persuade them that these are good ideas?
- What objections may they raise?
- How will you negotiate with them?
- What will success look like?
- What will you do from this session about ODL on Monday?

These questions implement some of the approaches to evaluation described in Chapter 19.

Participants were thus invited to work not just on ODL but also on educational change and how to achieve it in their own setting.

Putting the emphasis on the 'work' in workshop – by reducing the proportion of lectures and obliging participants to work collaboratively – initially took many participants well out of their comfort zone. Mid-morning on the first day, participants were asking the facilitators, 'When are you going to tell us how to do open and distance learning?' However, as participants engaged more and more with the activities and challenges they were set, they became engrossed in this new style of learning. Later on the first day, they were saying, 'Please could you bring our afternoon tea to us at our tables, we have a lot of work to do and don't have time to break for tea?'

More formal end-of-workshop feedback data identified things that worked particularly well, including:

- Allocating participants to specific tables and moving them around at specific times to foster interaction between participants from different institutions. Initially, tables were organised to mix participants from different institutions, geographical locations, seniority and gender. For the final poster presentations, participants were put with colleagues and neighbouring institutions that have a natural affinity to facilitate future networking.
- More light-hearted elements, including getting participants to come up with a name for their groups during the first poster session. This went down well. The best name award went to 'Boko Halal' (which means 'the book is good').
- The competition element on the final day, 'Preparing and judging posters on an ODL course', lifted the energy levels in the final sessions still further. Getting participants to vote for the winner rather than leaving it to the facilitators added to the credibility and encouraged participants to actively engage with and critically appraise each other's posters.

Despite the event being a considerable change from conventional local culture and practice, participants reported a considerable positive impact on their thinking and planning.

## Impact of the NUC/CODE programme of work to date

An initial evaluation of work under the MoU was carried out by interviewing some of the participants from a selection of Nigerian universities. Responses show the following:

- The perception of the status of ODL on campus has improved since exposure to CODE contributions.
- The necessary NUC accreditation of some universities to offer ODL programmes has been gained as a result of quality enhancement following work with CODE.
- A wide range of ODL-related reforms in universities has been undertaken as a result of CODE contributions.
- There are significant opportunities to support quality and programmes, as dual-mode universities have ambitious plans to grow their ODL provision.

- Directors of ODL centres are a significant professional grouping in Nigeria who meet and support each other. They could form the basis of a community of practice network that could work productively with CODE.

Nevertheless, most universities are at an early stage in terms of ODL student numbers and the digital transition is particularly challenging due to poor infrastructure for staff and students.

## Changing culture and practice

Nigeria's plans for increasing the scale of university teaching through greatly increased use of ODL are enormously ambitious. Despite strong foundations on which to build in some institutions, the rate at which ODL can be scaled up nationally is limited: by the availability of skilled practitioners, institutional experience and resources; by understandable caution and concern for quality on the part of the NUC; and by persisting negative perceptions of the quality of distance learning among staff, students and employers.

The supporting work by CODE, commissioned by the NUC, aims to accelerate this process by focusing on the development of robust quality assurance mechanisms and capacity building to address the key issues of trust and capacity. Support is being provided at institutional senior and middle management levels. Attention is being paid both to policy and to practice at institutional level. Possible future directions of work include what is conventionally called 'training the trainers'; that is, supporting institutions to become better able to further develop the capabilities of their own staff, thus building an effective community of practice. This is the only feasible long-term approach given the scale of development required.

What the experience of the 2018 Abuja development workshop in particular has demonstrated is that culture and practice can change rapidly when participants see the value of a new way of working. This discovery has much wider implications.

A common theme in accounts of development work is the importance of respecting local culture. Our work here suggests that being constructively (albeit implicitly) critical and offering well-grounded alternatives can also be productive, as long as the alternative approaches are found by participants to be productive. Part of the skill may lie in helping, supporting and reassuring participants as they cross into unfamiliar, uncertain, even dangerous-feeling territory, which, hopefully, soon comes to feel secure and valuable. This is true for the development of, as well as for studying by, ODL.

## Acknowledgements

We are grateful to the NUC, and in particular to Executive Secretary Professor Abdulrasheed Abubakar, Professors Peter Okebukola and Olugbemiro Jegede, former Director of Open and Distance Learning Dr Olamide Adesina and current director, Engineer Kayode Odedina, for support and encouragement with this work.

We thank colleagues in CODE, and more widely the UoL, and in particular CODE Director Dr Linda Amrane-Cooper, Dr Akanimo Odon and Professor Alan Tait and Mike Winter OBE for their contributions to this work and this chapter.

## References

Abutu, A. (2018) 'Overcrowded universities fail to reduce student intake'. *University World News*, 27 June. Accessed 14 January 2019. https://www.universityworldnews.com/post.php?story=20180626152203560.

Abutu, A. (2020). 'Universities close as coronavirus threat spreads'. *University World News*, 20 March. Accessed 14 December 2021. https://www.universityworldnews.com/post.php?story=20200320124504312.

Federal Republic of Nigeria (2013) 'National Policy on Education'. Accessed 14 January 2019. https://educatetolead.wordpress.com/2016/02/22/national-policy-on-education-6th-edition-2013/.

*The Guardian* (n.d.) 'Boko Haram'. Accessed 14 December 2021. https://www.theguardian.com/world/boko-haram.

Jegede, O. (2016) 'Open and distance learning practices in Nigerian higher institutions of learning'. Keynote address, 3rd University of Ibadan Annual Distance Learning Centre Distinguished Lecture and Stakeholders' Forum, International Conference Centre, University of Ibadan, 14–15 July. Accessed 14 December 2021. https://www.olugbemirojegede.com/odl_practices_in_tertiary_institutions_in_nigeria.pdf.

The PIE News (2018) '2 million applicants for 750K places: Nigeria's bid to tackle its capacity issue'. Accessed 14 January 2019. https://thepienews.com/analysis/two-million-applicants-for-750k-places-nigerias-bid-to-tackle-its-capacity-issue/.

Ramon-Yusuf, S. (n.d.) 'Trends in open and distance learning in the Nigerian university system'. Accessed 14 December 2021. https://www.academia.edu/33817047/TRENDS_IN_OPEN_AND_DISTANCE_LEARNING_IN_THE_NIGERIAN_UNIVERSITY?auto=download.

UK Government (n.d.) 'Foreign travel advice: Nigeria'. Accessed 14 December 2021. https://www.gov.uk/foreign-travel-advice/nigeria/terrorism.

# Section 2
**Doing distance education**

# Introduction to Section 2
Stephen Brown

Section 2 sets the scene for practitioners with Chapter 8. This chapter suggests a growing convergence between distance and face-to-face education. It proposes an intimate relationship between course design and pedagogy and explores a range of course design issues and approaches. The chapter also discusses staff development for distance education. Many methods and models can be used to design learning, both in-person and at a distance. Some of these models work better than others for actually designing a structure or scaffold for student learning. The chapter argues that there is a need to transform thoughts and practices on structuring, scaffolding and supporting learning in this new world to reflect what we know about learning. This transformation in course design will occur better and faster when lecturers combine their talents with those with other skills, including learning designers, technologists and librarians, in a cooperative setting.

Chapter 9 takes the idea of pedagogical design a step further by discussing participatory approaches that promote social interaction and interactive group learning in the online environment. These approaches include student peer support, peer feedback and collaborative exercises and activities, as well as encouragement for informal student interaction and conversation, quite possibly outside the virtual learning environment. Interactive social learning, based on individual or group interactions, has proven to be effective in the delivery of student-centred learning. The development of learning communities is facilitated by group or social activities that open up new opportunities for collaborations and peer support – both synchronous and asynchronous. Fostering successful learning communities also requires clarification and management of expectations, designated motivators, formative feedback, constant listening and a scaffolded structure for the learners to seek support when necessary. Some of these activities can occur spontaneously or can be ad hoc in face-to-face education. In distance education, they have to be designed in and students may need to be encouraged to engage with them. These approaches may be used by academic, non-academic and student teams, working separately or together. Interactive social learning may sometimes be resource intensive, both in design and implementation. However, with experience, innovative approaches may also be delivered at low cost to effectively support learning communities. Using examples, this chapter describes methods and techniques to foster learning communities and provides a theoretical analysis of current concepts that underpin interactive social learning.

A specific example of fostering interactive social learning through deliberate pedagogical design is shown in Chapter 10, which looks at the Icarus simulation tool. Icarus is an airport management integrated activity used in an online MSc programme. It seeks to identify to what degree a range of measures reflected within the simulation design overcome a number of key challenges often associated with online learning programmes, including learner isolation and disconnection. A caveat to note is that this case study provides a snapshot rather than a comprehensive catalogue of insights into its intentions. However, this case study has relevance for online learning in that it shows the possibilities and merits of harnessing the use of simulated activity to add value to online learning experiences. It also serves as an example of research through evaluation discussed later in Section 3.

Chapter 11 focuses on digital assessment and feedback practices in distance learning contexts. The contexts and cases discussed in this chapter have been drawn from member institutions across the University of London (UoL) Federation. It reviews some previous work conducted within a subset of the federation based in Bloomsbury, which aimed to provide a snapshot of current assessment practice within credit-bearing distance learning programmes. It also looks beyond the current mainstream of practices, through consideration of some additional cases of emerging practice within the massive open online course (MOOC) space. In recent years, there have been considerable innovations in digitally supported assessments, driven in large part by the MOOC model of online education, which is characterised by the ability to scale to very large numbers of students with very limited input from tutors, resulting in a focus on automated and peer assessment.

The challenge of massively upscaling assessment using online methods is the topic of the second case study chapter in this section, Chapter 12. This case study has two main elements: an account of the principal issues involved in undertaking online assessment and in moving to online assessment and a contemporaneous (summer 2020) account of the first stages of putting the UoL's 110,000 examinations online in response to the 2020 COVID-19 outbreak.

These issues and the account address: fairness and student and staff concerns under changed examination conditions; implications for, and working with, policy; doing without examinations altogether; analysing conventional examinations in changed times; using technology; opportunities and difficulties; ethical behaviour under changed examination conditions; revisiting and extending the idea of 'reasonable' accommodations; and commercial examination, invigilation/proctoring and other such services. The case study deals with some of the main, often interrelated, features of conventional university examinations under changed circumstances: seen or unseen examinations; distribution/release and receipt of examination papers; open or closed book examinations when students are taking the examination alone or with internet access; typed or handwritten answers; timing of examinations under changed conditions; invigilation or proctoring; candidate identification; and issues in student language.

One of the key value propositions of distance education is its potential for removing or reducing barriers to accessing learning opportunities. This is particularly apparent in the context of inclusion. Chapter 13 examines issues of inclusion today for students with disabilities in distance and online teaching in the context of the UoL home-based study system. The authors critically examine how the discourse of disability is constructed and note the complexities that extend beyond physical disability and hidden disability to contextual issues such as language and culture. An analysis is made of a range of practices that support inclusion in online environments in a range of higher education (HE) institutions in the UK and internationally. The authors note that, as inclusion is mainstreamed in HE practice, the need for sophisticated rather than simplistic understanding must be accompanied by careful and conscientious practice.

Design for inclusivity is an important strategy for helping students to survive and succeed at university. Chapter 14 explores innovations in promoting retention – or from the student point of view, persistence – in online distance learning that could enable more students to be successful. While retention of students is of concern for HE in general, the issue is often assumed to be more acute in distance education. This chapter examines two main approaches to enabling retention online:

- Academic engagement of students through the use of online tools, which can not only help students and tutors to communicate and present ideas but can also track and present data about student

engagement and learning. It explores the fundamental role of assessment and feedback in enabling student progression and shows how strong alignment between online activities and assessment and use of ipsative assessment (that is, measures of progress rather than outcome) can promote sustained learning over a module.
- Social integration or developing a sense of online identity and belonging. It describes a range of tools, communications and support options deployed at UoL, including onboarding strategies, social-psychological interventions, well-being support and social belonging exercises.

Finally, the chapter offers some tentative recommendations for improving retention online with the caution that there is no straightforward solution and every context will be unique.

The third and final case study in this section, Chapter 15, addresses these issues of inclusion, retention and success through an example of a MOOC in the field of healthcare training. An urgent increase in the provision of both pre- and in-service healthcare training is needed to produce the 20 million additional healthcare workers required to deliver the Sustainable Development Goals – a shared blueprint for achieving the United Nations' 2030 Agenda for Sustainable Development (UN General Assembly, 2015). This is a challenging prospect in many health systems that face ongoing and severe shortfalls in clinical staff, training financing, institutions and faculty (WHO, 2016). MOOCs, which can provide low-cost access to professional development training to hundreds or thousands of learners at a time, may provide a way forward if MOOC producers can balance the three long-standing and closely intertwined educational challenges of quality, efficiency and equity. This case study shares the experiences and lessons learned by one MOOC producer in response to this global training challenge by collaboratively developing a MOOC to deliver a specialist healthcare curriculum at scale across many countries and contexts to health teams who would otherwise not have access to the training. The study discusses how the project addressed the challenges of quality, efficiency and equity and shares evaluation findings on the patterns of participation in the course (efficiency), impact on eye care delivery (quality) and cascading of the training beyond the platform (equity).

The concept of low-cost MOOCs takes us back to the idea of open education, discussed briefly at the start of this introductory chapter. Chapter 16 explores and applies two pairs of closely related concepts in current and future distance learning. The first pair is 'open', as contrasted with (the rarely so labelled but nonetheless) 'closed' education. The chapter considers the relationship between open educational practices

(OEP) and open educational resources. The nature, emergence, continuing development and implementation of these two concepts and practices, and some of the many synergies between them, are described, critiqued and illustrated with examples and case studies. Open/closed is not a simple dichotomy but rather a spectrum, possibly even a matrix, of possible forms of provision of education. The chapter explores some of the dimensions of openness and closedness and some of the implications of these for distance learning policy and practice. The chapter considers the future for OEP in a complex and evolving educational landscape and reflects on how open practices and their adoption might become part of the everyday educational landscape. We suggest that for this to happen there needs to be closer alignment between educational policy, response to market demand and alignment with technological development. We hope that this chapter will help you to locate your current practice on these various dimensions and, more importantly, to plan realistic, ambitious and appropriate educational futures.

Arguably, one of the original and most successful open learning resources is the public library. Chapter 17, the final chapter in Section 2, takes us back to basics with an extensive analysis of the function of libraries in the analogue and digital ages and their role in supporting learning in HE. The authors focus on the contemporary online library with special reference to two distance education institutions, the UoL and the Open University. Accepting that an online library should do anything a physical library has historically done, the chapter goes on to examine student user needs as providing the more important defining characteristic of best practice in online libraries as they develop. The lack of equity between library services for campus-based students and those available remotely for distance and online students is critically examined and a particular focus is given to the need for online literacy development courses for online learners. Lastly, the chapter offers a range of suggestions as to how good-quality online library services can be managed and emphasises the importance of a partnership between academic course leaders and library professionals.

## References

UN General Assembly (2015) 'Transforming our world: The 2030 Agenda for Sustainable Development', A/RES/70/1, 21 October. Accessed 25 July 2022. https://sustainabledevelopment.un.org/post2015/transformingourworld.

WHO (World Health Organization) (2016) 'Global strategy on human resources for health: Workforce 2030', 7 July. Accessed 31 July 2022. https://www.who.int/publications/i/item/9789241511131.

# 8
# Course design, pedagogy and staff development

David Baume and Matthew Philpott

This chapter suggests a growing convergence between distance, online and face-to-face education. An intimate relationship between course design and pedagogy is also suggested.

A range of course design issues and approaches is explored. Seven things that we know, with some confidence, about the conditions for student learning are outlined and their implications for online and distance learning pedagogy and hence also for elements of in-person education are explored. The chapter concludes with some notes on staff development for online and distance education.

## The basics

Distance learning can get fabulously complicated, with huge teams, corresponding budgets, lengthy course design and approvals processes and intricate technology and administration. It need not.

The essentials for an effective distance learning course are probably:

- evidence and/or confidence that there is demand and market for a course
- a very small number of clear and appropriate high-level learning outcomes for the course, so that everyone – course planners and writers, tutors and students – knows where they are headed, what is to be attained, what success will look like
- a collection of engaging learning activities, which clearly contribute to attainment of the outcomes

- ready student access to relevant sources of information and expertise
- a supportive space where students and staff work together, sharing ideas and information, providing mutual support and encouragement and constructive challenge
- very good admin and assistance, so that staff and students know at all times where they are on the course and any problems are quickly resolved
- feedback to students on their work, from staff and/or peers
- valid and authentic assessment
- frequent reviews of, and subsequent improvements to, the course.

One academic, preferably with administrative support, can design and run a good small, specialist distance education course, if backed by a shared online working space and a library (see Chapter 17) or website for materials and resources. Early additions to this core team are likely to be a learning technologist, whose working relationship with the academic is explored later in this chapter, and a library or information specialist, as explored in much more detail in Chapter 17. A small, close team can have all the necessary expertise. There needs to be a good reason for every complication beyond this minimum. Hipwell and Baume (1977) describe a basic distance learning course in underwater engineering. The study guide for each unit of this course typically comprised one side of A4, which provided a unit aim, learning outcomes and relevant student activities and questions. Content was provided separately, using published sources. Students gave positive feedback.

## Distance and face-to-face learning

The biggest difference in pedagogy between online or distance and face-to-face or in-person education may be, not so much the fact of distance, but more the need to plan in much greater detail the pedagogy for distance education.

One reason for this need for detailed planning has been the comparative inflexibility of distance learning platforms, where the production and rendering processes, once the course has left the academic authors and editors, have been long and complex. Like most other aspects of technology, this is changing. Recent developments automate an increasing number of these processes of production and implementation. Such developments also make it possible for academics to make changes to the course while it is running, although care and attention are still essential for the course information and links to remain consistent and coherent. But this growing flexibility is progress, so it will continue.

The other reason more detailed planning is needed for distance education is that studying online is much less likely to be synchronous than is in-person, in-class study. More precisely, a smaller proportion of online studying is likely to be synchronous than is the case for in-person study. At its most basic, in class, whether in person or online, if a student does not understand something, either about course content or course process, they may (in a small class at least) be able to put up their hand and ask. Asynchronous, online study builds in a lag. A well-designed course will anticipate many of these questions and provide as many responses as possible, perhaps through a growing FAQ list. Where possible, the course authors will have designed out most of the questions in the first place, although there will always be new students and therefore new questions. Students will still be able to ask, and hopefully receive prompt answers to, questions online, from the course team and/or from peers. But some delay is almost inevitable.

In in-person education, the teacher can usually adapt from week to week, speeding up when it is clear that students are learning faster than expected, spending extra time on content that is proving unexpectedly problematic, improvising new teaching and learning approaches when the need or opportunity arises, adding content that is more current and replacing content that has become less relevant – at least until the assessment task is finalised.

In distance education, the freedom is differently distributed. Distance education typically includes a much lower proportion of synchronous working than in-person education. Distance education allows students much more freedom during the week about when to study and the tutor much more freedom over when they will react to student work, within any service-level specifications. This freedom is very valuable to those with other commitments. It is also valuable for those who can respond better after taking some time to reflect and consider. But the overall shape of a distance education course, the determination of what is taught and learned and carried out each week, is typically more constrained than for an in-person course, although the scope for adaptation is increasing.

We should hope that, after more than 150 years of distance education from the University of London (UoL) (see the Preface of this book), and decades from other reputable providers besides, the stigma attached to distance learning is beginning to fade. However, some jurisdictions still explicitly value contact hours more highly than distance learning hours. The evidence base for doing this is not clear. The COVID-19 pandemic, and the associated Great Leap Online, may be speeding up the recognition of the value and effectiveness of distance learning.

In an ideal world it would be possible to pilot courses and adapt the presentation in the light of feedback. In the real world, this is rarely possible. However, even if piloting were possible, every student, and every cohort of students, is different in some significant ways. Fundamentally, learning is an individual activity, even when undertaken on a structured distance learning course and even when substantial student collaboration is involved.

It is useful to analyse two dimensions of education – time and distance. This is also considered in Chapter 3.

Those parts of the staff and student week labelled as 'contact' are, logically, synchronous. But they are not the only parts of education that deserve the term 'contact'. Many students experience feedback from the teacher on their work as a very real, immediate and personal form of contact. 'Asynchronous contact' may sound odd, but feedback is a valued form of one-to-one contact. However, live streaming of lectures means that the student and teacher do not need to be in the same place. Online conferencing means that other kinds of classes, such as seminars and workshops, can also be synchronous while participants are physically remote.

Lecture capture means that events that currently have some elements of 'contact' can now be used asynchronously, although they are no longer obviously 'contact'. However, even for the student who is both synchronously and physically present for a large lecture, the term 'contact' may be largely aspirational or even misleading. The distinctions, the meanings, blur.

A recorded seminar or workshop may well have value to those hearing or watching a recording of it, although a somewhat different value from that obtained by participants. The recorded lecture becomes more of a resource and less of an experience, now allowing for pause, rewind and, of course, fast forward. But text-based conversation (we avoid the somewhat trivialising term 'chat'), whether synchronous or asynchronous, about any recording, whether of a lecture, seminar or something else, could have value to the participants. We and our students will need to continue to become more versatile, as teachers and as learners.

A newly encountered virtual learning environment (VLE) can be a daunting experience to a student. A Facebook or Instagram native or resident is not necessarily a VLE native or resident. There is no single 'digital literacy' or 'digital fluency' beyond perhaps a degree of confidence in the ability to learn to use a new platform or technology and facility for clicking and swiping – a small repertoire of approaches, conceptual models and actions that sometimes work. Individual induction and continued support are likely to be required for both students and staff to become confident and effective users of the particular VLE and the tools embedded in and associated with it.

Learning activities may not directly involve a tutor, other than perhaps in providing oversight rather than direction. Examples are forums, quizzes and interactive tutorials. Such activities may require much more detail and explanation to guide students through the content and learning process than is the case where a tutor is immediately available, in person or online, synchronously. Here, as elsewhere, distance learning requires investment, which is hopefully repaid through a greater efficiency of course operation, perhaps over a few years, if student numbers are high enough and the economics of the course are properly planned. Assinder et al. (2010) explore course design, and in particular the design of learning activities, as in part an economic activity. One important conclusion from this paper is that the design of good learning activities can be a very effective and efficient use of staff time. Each hour spent designing a learning activity can generate tens or hundreds of hours of productive student work.

Many of the same resources and activities can be used for distance and for face-to-face learning. Distance and face-to-face education are blurring into each other.

How can we find a secure base to plan our pedagogy in this typically more fixed online regime? This chapter suggests one reasonably secure basis for planning: what we know about the conditions under which students learn.

Before that, however, we provide some further thoughts on relationships between distance and face-to-face learning and on different approaches to the planning of courses and pedagogy.

## Problems with language and reality

Current terminology is not entirely helpful. Via an online conferencing system you can be face to face with somebody half the world away. Perhaps the important distinction here is between in person and online. But the importance of this distinction is fading, too, and will fade further, as the reliability and the bandwidth, the fidelity, of online communications improve and as travel, particularly long-distance travel, is likely to become more expensive, more restricted and less acceptable.

A growing proportion of student work, both on distance and face-to-face courses, is done through the VLE. 'Virtual learning environment' is another problematic term. Hopefully, the learning that occurs in a VLE is real, so it must be the environment that is virtual? This is not helpful. When we are teaching or learning in it, the VLE is as real as an office, study, various screens or a kitchen table. It is a real workspace in which real teaching and real learning happen. So, in what useful sense is it virtual? Other terms with very similar meanings are used, including 'managed learning environments' and 'learning management systems' (LMSs). But perhaps all we need are learning environments, each with a particular cluster of characteristics, using a particular mixture of physical and online presence. We might call them 'universities'. Of course, we all know what 'VLE' means, but the term remains unhelpful.

Increasingly, the VLE provides learning resources, study materials, access to references and sources. It provides the space where learning activities, both individual and collaborative, are undertaken. It may also be the place where assessments are undertaken, marked and given feedback and where much or all of the administration of the course happens.

While definitions are problematic, expectations are more troubling. VLEs are often, at least initially, understood by tutors, academics and students as file repositories to support classes. It remains difficult to encourage more experimental and imaginative uses of VLEs and their tools, although this is now happening. This is not just a problem of knowledge or time, but of how the VLE is viewed, treated and used. Similarly, back in 2012, massive open online courses (MOOCs) were seen by some as a solution – an innovation or disruptor that enabled tutors to reach students in more interesting and pedagogically sound ways. But in the years since, MOOCs have shown themselves to have their own limitations and challenges, particularly economic ones, often being free to study (but not to produce), perhaps with a paid-for, added-on assessment providing a certificate or badge. Expectations have settled on what a MOOC is and on what a VLE or LMS is. Neither has fully managed to break free of these initial expectations, although there is movement.

Then there is 'the class', with its much longer history. Whether the class takes the form of a lecture, tutorial, seminar, workshop or something else, it can now increasingly be undertaken online. A combination of synchronous and asynchronous classes is more common than wholly synchronous in online and distance courses, to exploit the flexibility that distance learning can provide.

It is not necessary or helpful to look at distance and face-to-face learning as different beasts. They represent two zones with increasing overlap, along a spectrum that ranges from considerable to no physical or temporal contiguity between teacher and student and among students. Or we can use a two-axis model, with the axes representing distance and time.

Both approaches, in person and online, have things to learn from the other. Many educational resources and processes work equally well in distance and face-to-face settings. This commonality between some elements of and resources for online and in person education – above all, in the provision of course content – allows economies in course development and production.

We can also use a combination of these two approaches, distance and in person, depending on current local circumstances. This combined approach is often called blended learning. The word 'blended' here is sometimes optimistic. 'Mixed' may be more accurate.

The flexibility that this blend or mixture provides, the opportunity to shift rapidly the proportions of in person and online, may be valued over the coming years for reasons of cost and inclusion, rather than just as a response to pandemics and other disruptions.

## Course planning and pedagogy

There is, or should be, an intimate relationship between course planning and pedagogy. One of the things that we know about learning is that learning has to be an active business. Students learn most effectively by being appropriately active. A major part of course planning is therefore planning what students do and how teachers can support them in doing those productive things in productive ways. For better and for worse, course planning includes the planning of pedagogy.

### Course design as the sequencing of content: a slippery slope

One common approach to course planning is to sequence the content to be taught. For example, consider a 22-week, perhaps one-semester, course, with a week at the start for induction, perhaps one or two reading or consolidation weeks (usually meaning weeks in which there is no teaching, although hopefully still some learning) and with a week or two at the end for revision and examination. This course may be planned by dividing the content into, say, 18 weeks, and teaching one-eighteenth of the content each week in some hopefully logical sequence.

This content-centred, teaching-centred and transmission-centred approach is widely used in in-person and distance learning. This approach often leads to the course being planned, undertaken and experienced as a content delivery process. It also leads to students experiencing learning as primarily a process of reception and memorisation, hopefully with some sense-making. In turn, assessment may well be experienced as a test of what has been memorised, perhaps lightly processed and applied. This is necessarily true for a closed-book examination, which, whatever else we may hope it tests, inevitably tests memory. Other forms of assessment can test a wider range of capabilities. Falchikov (2013) describes valuable ways of improving students in assessment.

Somehow, the unseen written examination has become, in many subjects, the gold standard. False gold, we suggest, and inauthentic. An in-person closed-book examination provides strong assurance (not quite a guarantee) that the candidate is who they claim to be and that what they put onto the examination paper comes only from inside their head. But this is a poor benefit from the much-reduced, indeed impoverished, set of capabilities that it can test. Chapters 11 and 12 address assessment in online and distance learning in far more detail. This sequence (we would suggest, this fall) towards content and its memorisation is not automatic or inevitable, but it is common. We wonder to what extent memorisation and recall comprise degree-level learning. This fall can be resisted with courage and ingenuity. The learning outcome should determine the assessment task, not the sad tradition of the examination room.

## Course design as using the capabilities of the VLE

Another approach to distance learning course design and pedagogy starts with the capabilities of the VLE. Learning designers and learning technologists may be keen to explain and demonstrate the many features and many kinds of learning activities available to the course designer and teacher and in due course to the student. Part of the design of each module, and then of each week of study, may involve the selection of learning activities from the catalogue of riches offered by the VLE.

There can be a real tension here. The academic may retreat in apprehension back to the, perhaps relatively modest, range of learning and teaching methods with which they are familiar in in-person education. This may feel safe. However, not all methods used in in-person education have a natural, appropriate counterpart in the VLE. The long lecture is a good example, even when transcript and recording are provided. A long lecture can still be a somewhat pre-Gutenberg, let alone pre-worldwide web, experience, despite the use of PowerPoint. Bligh (1971) provides valuable evidence on the relative ineffectiveness of the lecture for any function beyond the transmission of information.

Also, not all of the methods used in in-person education may be particularly effective, or have a particularly sound educational rationale, even in person. These teaching methods may be familiar, even sometimes comfortable, to teacher and students, rather than being of proven effectiveness, so new and potentially valuable and appropriate teaching and learning methods may not be adopted online. The course, and the students, may be much poorer as a result.

Alternatively, the academic may rush to embrace new methods, perhaps with mixed results in the absence of a sound rationale for choosing particular methods. A productive relationship between learning technologist or learning designer and lecturer may take some time and effort to develop and maintain. They cannot fully become members of each other's world, but some mutual respect, preferably evidence-based respect, is essential for the development of good online education.

Educational or pedagogic expertise – that is, knowing enough about learning to make educationally sound decisions about course design and pedagogy – can lie awkwardly at the interface between learning designer or technologist and lecturer. The lecturer is undoubtedly an expert in the subject, but they may or may not have expertise in learning and what makes it happen, let alone in the newer technologies of learning. The learning designer or technologist will obviously have expertise in learning design and learning technology, hopefully also in learning, but quite possibly not in the discipline of the course. Lecturers and learning technologists may defer inappropriately to each other. For example, the lecturer may accept uncritically the pedagogic suggestions of the learning designer or learning technologist, or the lecturer may retreat into replicating their repertoire of face-to-face teaching methods, as discussed.

Again, a productive relationship between learning technologist or learning designer and lecturer may take some time and effort to develop and maintain. And it may be a while before the lecturer designs another course, during which time their recently acquired expertise may fade and new learning technologies will become available.

## Starting at the end: outcomes-based course design for distance learning

We suggest another approach to course planning and pedagogy. This process starts with the identification of a small number of accounts of what students need to be able to do in order to complete the course successfully. These are often known as module learning outcomes. Baume (2009) offers and illustrates advice on writing good learning outcomes. It makes no difference whether these learning outcomes are for an in-person or an online course.

It is necessary that these learning outcomes form the basis for assessment. Biggs (1999) describes how learning outcomes, learning activities and assessment must align and be consistent with each other. He also makes a strong case for learning as a process of making sense, rather than as simple absorption or memorisation. He brings these two powerful ideas together in his account of con-structive alignment.

From these course learning outcomes, the learning outcomes for blocks, typically weeks, of study can be devised. Each block, each week, is then planned as a process to help the students to achieve the learning outcome for the week and always with the course learning outcomes in view and making progress towards those larger goals.

Of course, learning is more complex than the accumulation of learning outcomes, just as it is more complex than the accumulation of content and knowledge. Successive weeks of study should explicitly build on, integrate, perhaps also critique, what has been learned and what capabilities have been developed in previous weeks. Returning to topics previously studied can be a problem, summed up in an eight-year-old's complaint, 'The Romans! We did the Romans last year!' (Grandchild, personal communication). For such iterative approaches to work, it is essential to signpost how each block or week builds on its predecessors and how it all fits together overall. Doing this helps the student to make the best use of the learning and teaching. Students need a map to understand the design of, and plan for, their learning.

## Knowledge and capability

This outcomes-based approach seeks to adjust the relationship between knowledge and capability. It seeks to value, perhaps more than we currently do, the critical and reflective use of knowledge and to value a little less the accumulation of knowledge.

Why is such a shift needed?

- The half-life of many particular items of true, useful knowledge is reducing.
- Knowledge is becoming much more readily available, although always to be approached and used critically.
- The teacher's role as the gatekeeper to knowledge has been much reduced.
- Graduates are increasingly valued for what they can do, for who and how they are over what they know.
- The concept of 'knowledge', or certainly of what comprises 'valid knowledge', is being increasingly problematised, for example, through concerns over decolonisation of the curriculum (see, for example, Baume, n.d.; Demiray and Sharma, 2009; DUKC, 2020). These concerns may in turn usefully be seen as part of a wider movement towards inclusion and respect for diversity.

Current courses, in their pedagogy and in their assessment, do not always fully reflect these shifts, which continue to accelerate.

These shifts do not deny the importance of knowledge. However, when you look back at your undergraduate studies, how much of what you were taught then as essential, basic and fundamental to the discipline still has that status? Discuss your answers with younger and older colleagues.

A personal story may make the point:

I went to see my GP. I described my symptoms. He paused, and then said:

'I am sorry, I'm just back from two weeks of holiday, and my brain seems to have emptied itself completely. Do you mind if I look this up?'

'Hm. Would I rather you guessed, possibly wrong, and failed to cure me, or even made things worse? Or would I prefer you to look it up?'

(We had a good relationship, and he knew I worked in education. My response was not intended or heard as rude.)

He took my questions as encouragement to look the symptoms up. He used what he looked up – no doubt alongside his fast-returning memory – to prescribe a course of treatment. It worked.

### The ABC course design approach

It may be useful to see a specific, well-developed methodology for an outcomes-based approach to course design.

The outcomes-led and learning activities-led ABC course design approach (Young and Perović, 2016) is based on Laurillard's 'conversational framework' account of adult learning (Laurillard, 2013). The framework outlines six particular types of learning activity: discussion, collaboration, enquiry, acquisition, production and practice.

Before the ABC workshop is held, the subject matter experts undertake an online activity. They are asked to watch some short videos about the conversational framework and the six types of learning activities. They are then encouraged to think about how they can implement these activity types into their module. They are also encouraged to write module learning outcomes.

During the workshop, participants storyboard their module at a high level, using colour-coded cards related to the six activity types described. (This colour coding enables the design team to check at a glance whether they have used a mix of different activity types.)

Different subjects typically use a different balance of activity types. For example, mathematical subjects are often acquisition heavy and need students to read, synthesise and practice complex theorems and techniques. In a little more detail, in a business forecasting module, the subject matter expert used many demonstrations of using formulae and Excel spreadsheets for calculations. The module uses many practical video demonstrations (acquisition), problem solving (practice) and data manipulation (production), but not much discussion.

By contrast, on a consumer behaviour module there are many discursive activities around, for example, effective marketing campaigns, and there is collaboration in the course wiki where students collect and discuss examples of good and bad practice.

The subject matter experts start the ABC workshop by deciding where in the module their mid-term and final assessments will go and what learning outcomes will be addressed. Then they work backwards to make sure that the topics before the mid-term and final assessments help students to attain these learning outcomes.

The subject matter experts split the overall module learning outcome into smaller topic learning outcomes, often for each topic or week of study. They plan what learning activities, taken from a range of examples on the activity cards, they could appropriately use to help the students achieve these learning outcomes.

After the workshop, the subject matter expert uses the storyboard they created in the workshop to write a more detailed module design plan with the continuing support of their learning designer.

## Starting at the bottom

A conventional view, embedded in many historic and some current programmes, is that students first acquire knowledge and then learn how to use this knowledge. This view is embedded in and reinforced by one of the most widely known and used models in higher education, Bloom's taxonomy (Bloom, 1956, 2000). We shall critique this view in a moment, but first give a quick overview of Bloom's ideas.

The problem that Bloom is addressing is how to classify in some usable way the multiple types and levels of learning that we might see, expect, hope for or teach towards. His taxonomy was originally devised within a behaviourist educational paradigm. This paradigm saw teaching as providing prompts and stimuli that would provoke appropriate student responses, learning and evidence of learning, which were then rewarded. The paradigm worked for rats and pigeons – why not for students?

Bloom produced classifications, taxonomies, for the cognitive, affective and psychomotor domains (see Table 8.1). Those for the cognitive domain, considered here, have endured longest. They still feature, sometimes in their updated (2000) version, in courses to train and accredit university teachers. They classify types of educational objectives or, as we now say, learning outcomes, things people can do, using their rational brains as distinct from feelings or psychomotor skills.

The shift from 1956 to 2000 from nouns to verbs is welcome – we are concerned with capabilities, not with objects. The swapping of the order of levels 5 and 6, evaluating and creating, might have been better resolved by putting them on the same level and noting that much knowledge creation and sense making results from alternating or cycling between creating or synthesising new ideas and then evaluating or testing them, rather than from a linear progression.

Nonetheless, the taxonomy has some use as a tool for analysis, particularly at level 1, knowledge/remembering. It's good if we can be honest with ourselves and our learners and say, 'you need to know/remember this – which may mean either recall or recognise from a list, which of course are spectacularly different abilities'.

However, in a connected world awash with well-indexed knowledge that is only a skilful click or swipe or two away, our students may, when feeling bold and not under immediate threat of assessment, ask *why* they

Table 8.1  Bloom's taxonomy. Adapted from Bloom (1956, 2000).

| Bloom Version | Level | | | | | |
|---|---|---|---|---|---|---|
| | 1 | 2 | 3 | 4 | 5 | 6 |
| 1956 | Knowledge | Comprehension | Explanation | Analysis | Synthesis | Evaluation |
| 2000 | Remembering | Understanding | Applying | Analysing | Evaluating | Creating |

need to know. This is a conversation well worth having. There is a strong case for suggesting that degree-level study should involve working primarily at Bloom levels 4, 5 and 6, with excursions to level 3, applying ideas and theories to practice. Work at these higher levels should, of course, be informed by remembering or, intelligently and critically, looking up; understanding, making sense or recalling sense that others have made; and applying or using what is known and understood – or, again, repeating applications that have previously been made, perhaps with slight modifications (adapted from Baume, 2015b).

However valuable it is as a tool for analysis, Bloom's taxonomy fails as a tool for course design.

Faced with a blank sheet of paper or blank screen, it is tempting to use the taxonomy as a guide to course design – starting at the lower levels, then building up. Firstly, teach them the facts, then teach them to understand the facts, then to apply them; finally, to analyse and then to evaluate and synthesise, in whichever order. As easy as Lego. Just another brick in the wall.

The trouble is, this is not how people learn. It may or not be a useful description of levels of learning, but as a way to plan learning, it is, again, most unhelpful.

Consider a course you know. What are a few basic bits of knowledge in your subject? Imagine teaching students to remember these facts: either to recall them or to recognise them among wrong facts in a multiple-choice question, but with no context for the knowledge, no account of why it is important, or what it might mean, or how it may be useful. Just the facts. Remembered, then recalled or recognised.

Now consider moving on to understanding these facts – to explaining them and expressing them in different ways. Then, moving on to applying this knowledge and understanding, to using it …

This, we suggest, is not how we learn. So, it should not be how we teach.

So, how should we teach?

## Starting with questions

Questions and problems are much better starting points for many learners. Perhaps rather fancifully, we see the question mark at the end of a question as a hook – to engage the brain, the spirit and the imagination.

Below is a generic form of teacher's script; it is also an effective learner's script, a possible process for a course, whether implemented face to face or online or in some combination, individual or en masse. It will play out very differently in different disciplines and different academic levels. What would be your version of it?

'Given the title and topic of the course, what kinds of questions and problems would you expect, or hope, that we are going to learn to tackle here? Here are a few ... Add your own ...

'Why are these questions important? How do these questions and problems relate to other questions and problems that we have already decided are important, in the current or related subjects?

'What kinds of things do we want or need to be able to do by the end of this course? What do we want to be like? What should the assessment tasks look like? And again, why do these outcomes, abilities and qualities matter?

'Here's a simple, small question or problem in this area – or maybe, suggest some questions or problems yourself ... Before you try to answer it – what would a good answer or solution look like? How would we know it was a good or acceptable answer? Maybe, if it helps, what would a poor answer look like?

'Now, what do we know and what can we already do that may be relevant to this question or problem? How far can we get by using what we already know and what we can already do?

'We got this far ... what's stopping us? Here are a couple of possible ways through or around the obstacle(s) that we've identified. Or you, the learner, suggest a couple of possible approaches.

'There are some powerful ideas underlying these possible ways forward. Let's spend some time studying them, making sense of them, applying them to this simplified version of the kinds of problems we want to be able to solve, to the kinds of questions that we want to be able to answer by the end of the course.

'And as we learn, make sense of, these ideas and methods, we'll immediately apply them, and test them, to see how and when they work and don't work and to see what's involved in using them; what are their capabilities and limitations and what more we need to know understand or be able to do ...?'

This is more like how good learners learn and how good teachers support, prompt and indeed challenge this learning. The account was written, implicitly, as a classroom conversation, but it could equally well be conducted online, synchronously (live) or asynchronously; that is, in discrete segments, allowing time to think at each stage, valuing reflection and consideration over speed, except perhaps for trauma surgeons and the pilot landing my flight.

Learning outcomes are answers to questions – questions about the purpose and goals of the course, about the subject, about what it means to be able to practise the subject and to do good work in the subject (adapted from Baume, 2015a).

## What the research says about learning

The rest of this chapter uses an account of what we know about the conditions for learning in higher education (Baume and Scanlon, 2018). From the introduction to that chapter:

> ... here are seven things we know about learning, seven principles for learning. We know these with reasonable confidence, because each of them can be seen in at least two of the four very large syntheses of meta-analyses of, in total, many hundreds of thousands of individual studies. Most of the results here come from the two meta-studies, which mainly focus on learning (Chickering and Gamson, 1987; James and Pollard, 2011).
>
> However, there is some confirmation, and no contradiction, from the other two meta-studies, which are more concerned with teaching (Hattie, 2015; Pascarella and Terenzini, 2005).
> Learning is most effective when:
>
> 1) A clear structure, framework, scaffolding surrounds, supports and informs learning.
> 2) High standards are expected of learners, and are made explicit.
> 3) Learners acknowledge and use their prior learning and their particular approaches to learning.
> 4) Learning is an active process.
> 5) Learners spend lots of time on task; that is, doing relevant things and practising.
> 6) Learning is undertaken, at least in part as a collaborative activity, both among students and between students and staff.
> 7) Learners receive and use feedback on their work. (Baume and Scanlon, 2018: 2)

## Some implications for pedagogy in online and distance learning

**Principle 1 Learning is most effective when a clear structure, framework or scaffolding surrounds, supports and informs learning**

This structure may have several elements, including learning outcomes, curriculum or syllabus, learning activities, learning resources, a weekly schedule, a schedule for handing in and receiving feedback on assignments and, of course, the overall assessment schedule.

A difficulty with distance education can be that there is too much structure rather than an insufficient amount. Students can feel deluged with information, drowned in help and lost in the maze. Students may find it easier to be faced with a single text; essentially, a study schedule that summarises the learning outcomes, the learning activities and the main resources for each week or topic of study. These summaries can be very concise because the student can click through each of them to see more detail. But students always know, wherever they are in their studies, that they have a safe familiar place to come back to, preferably with one click; a place, a home (button), that reminds them where they are in the complex scheme of the course and what they should be doing this week and why.

If they can also use this document or study schedule to log their progress, so much the better. The VLE may have an automatic way of recording and showing at least some information about what screens the student has accessed, although this won't be a complete account of what they have done.

**Principle 2 Learning is most effective when high standards are expected of learners, and are made explicit**

This can be achieved through the following.

**Clear, high-level learning outcomes:** The comments earlier about learning outcomes offer guidance here. We suggest that the great majority of degree level work should be at Bloom levels 5 and 6, synthesis and evaluation. Synthesis means, not necessarily being entirely or globally original (Baume 2013), but certainly achieving some degree of local originality, creating solutions that are new, original, to the learner, rather than repeating or perhaps slightly adapting existing solutions. Because existing solutions are already out there, accessible, waiting to be adapted and used.

**Examples of good and less good work:** However skilfully written, learning outcomes can sometimes feel rather remote or abstract to students. Sadler (1989) argues that these learning outcomes have to be brought to life through examples. It is preferable to offer several examples; one example can become a model or ideal type, which isn't always helpful.

**Discussions of what makes good work good and less good work less good:** Beyond learning outcomes and examples of them being achieved, it is valuable to discuss with students what they think are the qualities of good and less good work and how these qualities relate to learning outcomes. A useful prompt for discussion would be: 'Analyse the ways in which this particular piece of work does and does not show that the author has achieved the learning outcome.'

The discussion could usefully broaden into other ways in which the work was and was not good. This would be an easy activity to set online. It would help students to externalise and explore their own, perhaps impressionistic, ideas about what was and was not good work in this particular case.

**Principle 3 Learning is most effective when learners acknowledge and use their prior learning and their particular approaches to learning**

How can this be achieved in distance learning?

**Ask students what they already know about the subject:** Icebreakers and introductions, more and less formal, are common and valued features of many in-person courses, although they can become a cliché. They can also be unnecessary, especially for students who already know each other, as there may not be any ice.

Icebreakers may also have a valuable role in distance education. Like most features of distance learning, icebreakers and introductions need to be structured rather more than is necessary in an in-person course, because there is usually less opportunity for informal mingling and getting to know others. Such informal spaces are available, for example, at Wonder.me. We should note that informal student-led groups, often using WhatsApp, sometimes run in parallel alongside more formal channels. These are to be welcomed by staff but ignored, unless the staff are invited to join, as staff presence will inevitably affect the conversations.

'What do you already know about [the subject of the module]?' 'What previous contact have you had with the subject?' And, if this is a postgraduate or post-experience course, 'What work have you done/are you currently doing in the subject?' can be productive icebreakers. Such questions help students to get to know each other in the context of the course and the subject, to form a view as to whom it may be worth asking about what during the course. Such questions also help students to get to know themselves in relation to the subject.

Throughout the course, it is appropriate to invite students to bring questions and ideas from outside the course as well as from within it. Students will thereby learn both to value and to interrogate any information, expertise and questions that they bring. This increases their engagement with the subject, their connecting of study to the real world outside the university.

Ask students how they prefer to learn – but don't be afraid to help them learn in new ways! Get them thinking about their learning: The concept of learning styles is attractive, but suspect. The concept of preferred learning styles, or even learning preferences, probably has greater validity (Fleming and Baume, 2006).

It may help students get off to a comfortable start on the course if they are asked about their preferred ways of learning and if they see in the rich mix of the course some learning activities and methods that play to their preferences.

However, one goal of a course of study must be to extend students' range of learning approaches, to help them become more versatile as learners. For example, if a 'lurker' in groups only continues to lurk, they are unlikely to develop valuable skills of participation, of engaging in debate, whatever they learn while lurking.

The value of being explicit about preferred learning styles or learning preferences is that it makes it easier for the course to, quite explicitly, help students to increase their range of learning approaches, uncomfortable though some of these may initially be.

**Principle 4 Learning is most effective when it is an active process**

Learning outcomes describe what students need to be able to do at the end of the course. Assessment identifies to what extent the students have achieved these learning outcomes. Learning activities provide a bridge between learning outcomes and the ability to succeed at assessment.

For in-person courses, lecturers are often advised to break up the lecture with activities, as if lecturing was the natural form of education that needs occasional interruptions to keep the students alert.

Principle 4 inverts this model of education. It suggests that the natural state of student learning is being active, undertaking – thoughtfully, critically, intelligently and making full use of resources and information provided – a carefully crafted and curated set of learning activities, which are most likely to generate learning and attainment of the course learning outcomes.

Appropriate learning activities lie at the heart of good distance learning. They also lie at the heart of good in-person education, but that is not our topic here.

What are appropriate learning activities? They are activities that help the student to achieve the learning outcomes. These learning activities may take different forms, different sequences, in different subjects. In some subjects the learning activities may comprise at first simple and then increasingly complex versions of the module learning outcome, the final assessment task. In other subjects they may comprise a more linear sequence of activities, each adding a new idea and combining it with what has been learnt previously. Some subjects may use a mixture of these approaches, these structures.

Where do content, syllabus, reading and presentations fit into this model? They are the resources that the students use in order to undertake the activities, to answer the questions and to solve the problems.

Of course, this is an extreme account. Students will value short presentations and will need to read and study before as well as during and in support of activities. But listening to a presentation, even reading, can be a passive process. If the students bring a few prior questions to the listening and their reading, then the listening and reading are likely to be more productive. Perhaps the account of outcomes-led, activity-led learning was not so extreme after all.

VLEs may provide a spectacular range of possible learning activities, as we have suggested. Those planning a course should select or design activities primarily on the basis of their educational appropriateness. However, students will appreciate occasional variety or novelty, as long as it is not wildly inappropriate. And lecturers contemplating an unfamiliar feature within the VLE may find that it has unexpected educational merit. They may increase their view of what comprises appropriate forms of learning activity. Lecturers can learn, too.

**Principle 5 Learners spend lots of time on task – doing relevant things and practising**

This principle is closely related to principle 4. It further emphasises that appropriate learning activities are a core of the course, not an addition. Students should be supported and challenged to undertake the activities.

Some students may have previously taken a much less active approach to their learning because of the environment and the pedagogic culture in which they were studying. A gentle, even slow, induction into this new, far more student-active approach to learning may be required. Recent research (Brown and Baume, 2022) suggests that distance learning students do not value learning activities, and in particular do not value collaborative learning activities, as highly as they value content.

It would be useful to share and discuss these principles for learning with the students, so they can see the rationale for this change of pedagogy.

**Principle 6 Learning is most effective when it is undertaken as a collaborative activity, both among students and between students and staff**

Growing concern about plagiarism means that students will welcome some help to identify legitimate and illegitimate forms of cooperation. The basic idea – in academic work everything you write is assumed to be your own work unless either it is common knowledge or you expressly credit it to someone else, whether to a colleague or to a published source – is reasonably straightforward to understand and apply. Essentially, it is an appeal to fairness.

With plagiarism sorted, many productive forms of cooperation are available:

- An assignment can be broken down into small tasks, different students undertake different elements of it, and then the students can combine their work into a coherent whole.
- Several students can undertake the same assignment, then compare notes on what they have done and perhaps produce an agreed version that includes the best of all of their work.
- Students can work together to produce a wiki of the key concepts in the course, adding to and editing each other's comments, as with Wikipedia.

Each subject presents its own opportunities for collaboration. Many of the approaches taken to collaboration in in-person courses can work equally well, although perhaps differently in detail, online. An important difference is that most of the collaboration online is likely to happen asynchronously. This will typically mean that shared activities take longer than they might take on an in-person course. The timing of activities has to reflect that.

Collaboration between students and staff may sound unrealistic in these resource-light times. Staff participation in online forums can take a number of forms. They may come in as judge and arbiter of student contributions, which may rapidly shut down conversation. Alternatively, they can collaborate, facilitate, ask productive questions, react to what students have said and perhaps steer the conversation, adding their information and expertise where appropriate, but for the most part acting as a member, not leader, of the conversation.

**Principle 7 Learning is most effective when learners receive and use feedback on their work**

In online and distance learning, once the course has been written and produced, a major part of the tutor's role may be online participation, as suggested in principle 6, and then giving feedback to students on their assignments. This is one of the returns on the investment made in producing the course – the time and attention that can now be spent responding to the work of individual students.

Feedback need not come from those who wrote the course. In the UK Open University, a separate group of staff, associate lecturers, give feedback as well as providing online or, sometimes, in-person tutoring. Staff in the UoL Recognised Teaching Centres, where many students study, as well as teaching, give feedback on student work.

Perhaps counterintuitively, students can learn to give useful feedback on the work of peers (Falchikov, 2013) and on their own work (Boud, 1995). Students learn both from giving and then from receiving feedback.

Whoever provides the feedback, it is essential that the feedback is both helpful and usable. Such feedback: explains what the person giving feedback sees as good and less good features of the work; explains why these are seen variously as good and less good features; and provides constructive suggestions on how this, or future work, might be improved – again with reasons. Nicol and Macfarlane-Dick (2006) provide valuable guidance on giving feedback to students.

## Staff development for distance education

The effective planning and operation of large-scale distance education requires a wide range of talents, working together productively. A sophisticated distance education operation probably contains most of the following functions and quite possibly others besides: course design, learning design, library, learning technologies, teaching, student support and guidance on educational, administrative, personal and technical matters, assessment, market intelligence and marketing, student recruitment and admission, management and administration, finance and fees, quality assurance and course review and evaluation.

We shall not provide a detailed account of all possible staff development goals and methods across this full range of functions. Rather, we shall suggest a strategic approach. We hope you will find this approach productive in planning appropriate forms of staff development for online and distance education in your own setting.

A conventional approach would:

- start by analysing the capabilities that your new distance education operation will require
- identify the current capabilities of the team
- identify any capability gaps
- undertake the necessary staff development to fill these gaps
- review and revise as required.

It is worth keeping this generic account of learning needs analysis and staff development planning in mind, as elements of it will need to be used. But the situation for a new distance education operation presents both challenges and opportunities, which may somewhat modify this approach.

## Not a whole new world ...

Distance education is not completely different from in-person education. Many of the academic, technical, management and administrative functions described in this chapter have some equivalent in in-person education. You are already starting from a strong position of capability. So, identify and use the strengths you have in your team. If you are lucky enough to be able to select a team, select a team with those capabilities. Also, beyond capability, select for enthusiasm and for commitment to both quality and innovation. Select people who see their involvement in distance learning as a way of advancing their own career. Ambition can be a very positive quality.

## ... but partly a new world

However, there are significant differences in moving to online and distance education. We suggested that both the special requirements of online and distance education and the things we know about the conditions for student learning have strong implications for the design and the pedagogy of courses. Developing a distance learning course requires, at a senior level in the development process, an expert distance education champion. It requires someone who is familiar with, capable in and passionate about distance education, and who can identify when current practices and expertise are relevant and readily applicable to distance education and when new or modified approaches are required. Without even this one expert champion, progress will be difficult. Of course, that champion may be you.

External advice and support can be valuable; see, for example, the case study in Chapter 7.

## Timing and teamwork

A conventional approach would be to identify the development needs and undertake the staff development and training before the course development started. This would be too slow for distance education. It would also be a bad idea, indeed a wasted opportunity. Why?

Details of the particular capabilities required will become apparent as the course is designed. Every course is a little different and every institution's approach is a little different. Every course in every subject in every institution needs some different capabilities.

Some broad academic, administrative and technical capabilities will obviously be needed, but it will be better if the development of the course is undertaken as a team activity. Team members will bring and apply their expertise, which will be shared among the team, and expertise gaps can be identified and filled rapidly. The course and the course team will develop or be developed together.

# Conclusion: building high on firm foundations

In summary, many methods and models can be used to design learning, both in person and at a distance. The differences between in-person and online and distance learning pedagogies may not be as great as is sometimes assumed. As suggested, some of these models work better than others for actually designing a structure or scaffold for student learning. We see great merit in a learning outcomes-based approach. For distance learning, in particular, the best models break the mould of traditional learning, which is often content and delivery led rather than outcomes and learning led. Sometimes much of the traditional structure and process of in-person education seems to be retained in the VLE, even when the course is to be run mainly asynchronously.

We have suggested here that we all need to adapt our thoughts and practices on structuring, scaffolding and supporting learning and use what we know about learning, as well as about the changed arrangements for teaching and learning at a distance. This change in course design will occur better and faster when lecturers work with those having other skills, including learning designers and technologists and librarians. This is a time for cooperation.

This chapter offers prompts and support for anyone developing or redeveloping courses to be taught at a distance. We all need to ensure that what we build is pedagogically sound, in the new online and distant environment, and is also suited to students with differing digital literacies and other capabilities. The inclusive Universal Design for Learning approach (see CAST, 2021, for a useful overview), which is widely informing the design of in-person courses, also has implications for the design of distance learning courses. We need to support students into using new VLEs and other digital tools. In doing so, we can usefully remember how we learnt, perhaps only recently, to use these tools ourselves.

We also need to acknowledge that students have varying access to technology and the technology itself may have varying capabilities, most obviously bandwidth or reliability of service. We have to be realistic about, and honest with, our current and potential students in relation to the technologies required to study the course successfully. A great option may be 4K video, but can our students access and afford it, and is it essential? Might audio, or indeed text and some still images, do the job?

And, widening attention beyond technology, lots of synchronous learning activities may be great, but are they compatible with the many other work- and life-related commitments, as well as current capabilities and learning preferences, of our students? At an early stage of course planning and production, we need to reality-check the technologies and the patterns of study that we are considering.

Above all, in this chapter we have offered ways to put pedagogy and knowledge about our students and their circumstances alongside subject expertise at the heart of course design and operation.

## Acknowledgements

We are grateful to Vicky Devaney, Learning Designer at UoL, for information on the ABC course design process and to Emily Wilson for feedback on an earlier draft.

# References

Assinder, S., Baume, D. and Bates, I. (2010) 'Focusing on student learning to guide the use of staff time'. *Innovations in Education and Teaching International*, 47 (4), 357–67.

Baume, D. (2009) *Writing and Using Good Learning Outcomes*. Leeds: Leeds Beckett University. Accessed 5 April 2017. http://eprints.leedsbeckett.ac.uk/2837/.

Baume, D. (2013) 'Originality and education'. *All Ireland Journal of Higher Education*, 5(2). Accessed 15 June 2020. https://ojs.aishe.org/index.php/aishe-j/article/view/128.

Baume, D. (2015a) 'Bloom and course design: Disaster strikes!' David Baume's Blog, 6 October. Accessed 28 April 2020. https://davidbaume.com/2015/10/06/bloom-and-course-design-disaster-strikes/.

Baume, D. (2015b) 'Learning and knowledge: Bloomin' obvious?' David Baume's Blog, 28 September. Accessed 28 April 2020. https://davidbaume.com/2015/09/28/learning-and-knowledge-bloomin-obvious/.

Baume, D. (n.d.) 'Some possible accounts of a (partially) decolonized curriculum, of a decolonisation process, and of what success might look like'. Accessed 19 January 2022. https://docs.google.com/document/d/1ElaiDODy9OOKTxK1bd_dsmTLU0TQ8Hprs7E_FzJknbM/edit?usp=sharing.

Baume, D. and Scanlon, R. (2018) 'What the research says about how and why learning happens'. In R. Luckin (ed.), *Enhancing Learning and Teaching with Technology – What the Research Says*, 1st edn. London: UCL IoE Press, 2–13.

Biggs, J. (1999) 'What the student does: Teaching for enhanced learning'. *Higher Education Research & Development*, 18 (1), 57–75.

Bligh, D. A. (1971) *What's the Use of Lectures?* (1st edn). Exeter: Intellect Books.

Bloom, B. S. (1956) *The Taxonomy of Educational Objectives: Handbook 1* (1st edn). London: Longman Higher Education.

Bloom, B. S. (2000) *A Taxonomy for Learning, Teaching, and Assessing: A revision of Bloom's taxonomy of educational objectives, complete edition*, ed. L. W. Anderson and D. R. Krathwohl. New York: Longman Publishing Group.

Boud, D. (1995) *Enhancing Learning through Self-Assessment*. Philadelphia: Routledge Falmer.

Brown, S. and Baume, D. (2022) '"Not another group activity!" Student attitudes to individual and collaborative learning activities, and some implications for distance learning course design and operation'. *Innovations in Education and Teaching International*. Accessed 5 July 2022. https://doi.org/10.1080/14703297.2022.2062424.

CAST (2021) 'About Universal Design for Learning: CAST'. Accessed 15 December 2021. https://www.cast.org/impact/universal-design-for-learning-udl.

Chickering, A. W. and Gamson, Z. F. (1987) 'Seven principles for good practice in undergraduate education'. *AAHE Bulletin*, 39 (7), 3–7.

Demiray, U. and Sharma, R. C. (2009) *Ethical Practices and Implications in Distance Learning* (1st edn). Hershey, PA: Information Science Reference.

DUKC (Decolonise University of Kent Collective) (2020) *Towards Decolonising the University: A kaleidoscope for empowered action* (1st edn). Oxford: Counterpress.

Falchikov, N. (2013) *Improving Assessment through Student Involvement* (1st edn). London: Taylor & Francis.

Fleming, N. and Baume, D. (2006) 'Learning styles again: VARKing up the right tree!' *Educational Developments, SEDA Ltd*, 7 (4), 4–7.

Hattie, J. (2015) 'The applicability of visible learning to higher education'. *Scholarship of Teaching and Learning in Psychology*, 1 (1), 79–91. Accessed 5 July 2022. https://doi.org/doi:10.1037/stl0000021.

Hipwell, J. and Baume, D. (1977) 'Adaptable correspondence studies for offshore engineers: A course that learns'. *Teaching at a Distance*, 9, 27–35.

James, M. and Pollard, A. (2011) 'TLRP's ten principles for effective pedagogy: Rationale, development, evidence, argument and impact'. *Research Papers in Education*, 26 (3), 275–328. Accessed 5 July 2022. https://doi.org/10.1080/02671522.2011.590007.

Laurillard, D. (2013) *Rethinking University Teaching*. Hoboken, NJ: Taylor & Francis.

Nicol, D. and Macfarlane-Dick, D. (2006) 'Formative assessment and self-regulated learning: A model and seven principles of good feedback practice'. *Studies in Higher Education*, 31 (2), 199–218.

Pascarella, E. T. and Terenzini, P. T. (2005) *How College Affects Students*. Vol. 2: *A third decade of research* (2nd edn). San Francisco: Jossey-Bass.

Sadler, D. (1989) 'Formative assessment and the design of instructional systems'. *Instructional Science*, 18 (2), 119–44.

Young, C. and Perović, N. (2016) 'Rapid and creative course design: As easy as ABC?' *Procedia – Social and Behavioral Sciences*, 228, 390–5. Accessed 5 July 2022. https://doi.org/10.1016/j.sbspro.2016.07.058.

# 9
# Interactive social learning and fostering learning communities

Ayona Silva-Fletcher and
Christine Thuranira-McKeever

Interactive learning based on individual or group interactions has proven to be effective in the delivery of student-centred learning. This chapter describes participatory approaches that promote social interaction and interactive group learning in the online environment.

The development of learning communities is facilitated by group social activities that open up new opportunities for collaborations and peer support. To foster successful learning communities also requires clarification and management of expectations, designated motivators, formative feedback, constant listening and a scaffolded structure to provide support for the learners when they need it. These approaches may be used by academic, non-academic and student teams, working separately or together. Interactive social learning may sometimes be resource intensive, but experience shows that novel and innovative approaches may also be delivered at low cost to effectively support online learning communities. Using examples, this chapter describes methods and techniques to foster online learning communities and provides a theoretical analysis of current concepts that underpin interactive social learning. The focus is mainly on the strengths and limitations of learning management systems (LMSs) or virtual learning environments (VLEs) in the application of social learning theories. Specific technologies for online learning, such as assistive technologies, use of multimedia technologies, mobile and social networking technologies and gaming, simulations and virtual reality can all enhance social learning, but are not discussed in detail in this chapter.

During what may be called the early period in distance education, from the mid-nineteenth century, printed materials were sent by post. These were later expanded and/or supplemented using the opportunities of radio and television as new media for teaching. As the popularity, uptake and acceptance of distance education grew, a considerable amount of effort was invested to explore how to support the 'lone long-distance learner', as they came to be called. The social isolation of the distance learner is considered one of the key reasons for high dropout rates in distance education. With the advent of the internet in the late twentieth century and the growth of LMSs, distance education became online education. The adoption of the LMS as a vehicle for teaching, learning and assessment has given a new meaning and value to distance education. LMSs provide a more efficient and effective means to disseminate educational materials to a wider audience. They use an internet-based platform; some common examples are Moodle, Saki, Canvas and Blackboard. These browser-based systems provide a dedicated learning environment for students and teachers to work together. This may include an online (sometimes called virtual) classroom as a site in which to teach, learn, access study materials, submit assignments and provide teacher feedback.

The potential to support and enhance distance learning via LMS-based media seems endless. During the COVID-19 pandemic, the LMS-based virtual classroom became the most effective, certainly the most widely used, solution for teaching, learning and assessment.

However, can an internet-based LMS bring the distance learner out of social isolation? Can we promote student–teacher and student–student interactions that enhance the experience and support the 'lone long-distance learner'? What is the feasibility and justification for addressing social isolation in course design, online teaching and assessment in higher education (HE) today? These are some of the questions that will be explored in this chapter as we describe concepts in interactive social learning and how they may be used to foster successful learning communities.

The focus will be on the three following themes:

- social and adaptive learning; conceptual frameworks designed to underpin social learning
- how participatory approaches promote social interaction and offer learning opportunities to students in an online learning environment
- how academic and non-academic scaffolding and structuring may be used to foster learning communities whose members are at a considerable physical distance from each other.

## What is social learning?

Early work by Bandura (1977: 1–3) described social learning as learning related to an individual who acquires new patterns of behaviour through direct experience, or by observing the behaviours of others in a social context. The individual then experiments with his/her own behavioural change and 'observes the differential consequences accompanying their various actions. On the basis of this informative feedback, they develop thoughts or hypotheses about the types of behaviour most likely to succeed' (Bandura, 1977: 3).

Today, this type of social learning may occur in the online environment as individuals observe and model themselves on others and change their behaviours accordingly. This, however, is a rather narrow definition of social learning. The fundamental concept of 'individual learning in a social context resulting in behavioural change' is naturally limited to learning by an individual. A wider definition of social learning, in which groups of people learn from each other and which in turn may lead to societal learning, is a more commonly adopted concept today (Bawden et al., 2007). This concept of group learning is further supported by social theories that define learning as active social participation in communities with effective interaction between people (Lave and Wenger, 1991; Wenger, 1998). Some would now describe social learning in terms of a shift away from transmissive expert-based teaching and towards transformative community-based learning (Capra, 2007: 13). Others would argue that there is no universal theoretical basis or terminology for social learning (Wals and Van der Leij, 2007: 18).

Social learning at both individual and group levels can potentially occur in the LMS-based online environment. Based on a curriculum design that provides opportunities for learners to meet each other online, long-lasting trusting networks may develop, which are somewhat similar to those that arise from more traditional face-to-face learning situations.

For the purpose of this chapter, we will define social learning as:

- learning that occurs through social interactions between learners and teachers within an LMS-based online environment
- learning that goes beyond the individual and becomes situated within wider social units or communities of practice.

## Online social interactions and learning

There is evidence that social interactions promote student learning (Bligh, 1993; Laurillard, 1993; Ramsden, 1992). When appropriate teaching materials, teaching methods, student-to-student interaction and timely teacher-to-student feedback is given (Moore and Thompson, 1990; Verduin and Clark, 1991), grade outcomes of face-to-face and LMS-based online learners are similar (Ali and Smith, 2014).

These concepts have been used to design LMS programmes that provide a comprehensive learning environment. Learning materials have been developed utilising pedagogical principles; for example, to promote student-centred learning, appropriate materials promote activities that direct students to learn by doing (see Chapter 8) (Biggs, 1999). Additional software has been developed that supports reflection to conceptualise learning (Kolb, 1984) and provides tools to self-assess and evaluate a student's own progress as they move through a self-regulated learning cycle (Grow, 1991). The face-to-face campus has been recreated using LMS, students are inducted via online tours that show classrooms, a library, café, discussion forums, access to online course materials, assignment submission, how to get feedback and where to find the non-academic course support teams. As social learning may occur by observing and modelling others' behaviours (Bandura, 1977), unless the learners can see others in the LMS opportunities for social learning may be limited. The most challenging component in recreating face-to-face learning in the LMS is online social presence. Without adequate social presence, learners cannot observe the behaviour of other students. Neither can they contribute to social constructions of knowledge by exposing their own conceptual understandings to their peers, limiting their opportunity to explore different learning perspectives and shared understandings.

What types of social presence and interactions can be created in LMS programmes? Moore (1989) identified different types of interactions in education: learner with study content, learner with teacher, learner with learner and learner with technology. All these types of interactions are essential for online education, are not necessarily separated by space and time and can occur simultaneously. While the interactions of the learner with content, teacher and technology are embedded in the LMS, the learner–learner interactions are not automatic and have to be included in the pedagogical design of a course.

With the advent of LMSs in the early 1990s the online discussion forum became the tool of choice to foster learner-to-learner interactions.

The online discussion forum was similar to a rolling seminar that could be synchronous, asynchronous or both. Online discussion fora became the main location for social presence and a considerable amount of effort was invested to make them attractive, user-friendly and even informal. They have been the subject of much research since the mid-1990s. After reviewing 62 studies on asynchronous online discussions, Hammond (2005) suggested that curriculum design, teacher role, student responsibilities and software in the LMS all play key roles in their success or failure. Table 9.1 shows the conditions under which learners best engage with asynchronous discussions.

Although most of the reported research is encouraging about promoting participation in asynchronous online discussions, researchers agree that learner participation is not assured. Furthermore, it is clear that participation in itself is not sufficient to ensure that learning takes place (Hammond, 2005). There is evidence that participatory processes may stimulate and facilitate learning (Cundill, 2010), but there is no guarantee that participation leads to learning (Bull et al., 2008).

This begs the question whether following pedagogical principles designed for face-to-face teaching are suitable for online course design to foster learner-to-learner interactions. A more fundamental approach based on a conceptual framework at the LMS design stage could be more productive in achieving learning objectives (Wilson and Cole, 1991). The features as outlined in Table 9.1 also suggest that a comprehensive design is essential to foster online learner engagement that benefits from social interactions and social presence. Liu (2005) argued that a LMS design based on cognitive apprenticeship theory will create a better student-centred learning environment that leads to collaboration and joint intellectual effort. Cognitive apprenticeship theory aims to foster a culture in which learners intuitively believe that they can learn better if they share knowledge among themselves and interact with each other. Discussions in this learning process will facilitate individual cognitive growth so that learners will come to their own conclusions based on collaboration through interpersonal communication. The theory aligns with Bandura's (1977) social learning theory that social presence and observation are key to learning. Modern technologies that include multimedia in the design and delivery of curriculum and assessments, gaming, simulations and virtual reality are used effectively to promote social interactivity and engagement.

There is growing interest in the novel and popular digital tools used in social networking (such as Facebook, WhatsApp, Twitter and Snapchat) as social learning tools. These tools are also used to broadcast or

Table 9.1  Key features to maximise learner participation in an asynchronous online discussion forum. Based on Hammond (2005).

| Curriculum designers should… | Teachers/instructors should… | Learners should… | Software should… |
|---|---|---|---|
| Encourage formative peer assessment | Draw on past experience but appreciate the unique features of the online environment | Have knowledge, experience and understanding of the benefits of group work | Allow permanent storage and threading of messages |
| Provide summative assessment of process and credit for participation | Show teaching presence but encourage critique and divergence | Have access to ICT and be confident in and have some level of proficiency in ICT | Be robust and provide reliable access to messages |
| Provide summative assessment of group products | Fade as appropriate; have an administrative role (e.g., notify students of assessment arrangements) | Not be able to meet face-to-face easily | Be intuitive, easy to use and offer good visual representation |
| Make group work and problem-based learning explicit in learning outcomes | Have a pastoral role (e.g., identify and support non-participants) | Be ready to critique the authority of the tutor | Enable files to be easily attached and downloaded |

| | | |
|---|---|---|
| Require a minimum level of participation; set explicit tasks (e.g., discussion of cases, readings, or shared events) | Be aware of their pedagogic role (e.g., respond where appropriate) | Find that text-based communication suits preferred learning approach |
| Build in review of group work process | Suggest activities and roles to generate debate | Have proactively chosen to take part in online learning |
| Adjust workload to allow time for discussion | Take responsibility for monitoring the nature and scope of discussion and group processes | Be confident in contributing to public forums and ready to constructively critique other points of view |
| Make conceptual learning and higher order reasoning explicit and appropriate learning outcomes | | Be proficient in language of the forum and fluent writers |
| Build in appearances of online guests; and rotate roles within the group | | Be aware of an information gap and eager to cross it |

disseminate media. Facebook can be used to disseminate educational content, specifically for rural communities, but they are not designed for knowledge construction and knowledge creation (Kirschner, 2015).

## Social learning and learning strategies

Social learning has become a major research topic in non-human mammal societies and the results of these investigations may inform and improve social learning by human students.

Studies on animals in captivity have revealed that information is passed between individuals and diffuses through groups, leading to the formation of group-level patterns of behaviour and traditions (Whiten and Mesoudi, 2008). Both animals and humans develop social learning strategies to their own advantage. Empirical evidence suggests that 'copy when uncertain, copy the majority, and copy if better' are the commonest learning strategies employed by animals and humans (Laland, 2004).

The literature on human copying behaviour is extensive and includes theoretical analyses of social, asocial and adaptive learning. The question of who to copy and the emergence of a social hierarchy in copying has been studied in children to help understand how social learning develops. Children are social learners (Horner and Whiten, 2005) who copy with great fidelity (Wood et al., 2013). Children between four and seven years old show selectivity in copying others when deciding whether to follow the competent or the majority (Burdett et al., 2016; Laland, 2004) suggests that social learning strategies in non-human mammals are developed on a basis of when and who to copy. 'When' strategies to copy include when established behaviour is unproductive, when asocial learning is costly or when it is uncertain. Who strategies are context dependent, but often involve 'copy the majority', 'copy if rare', 'copy successful individuals', 'copy if better', 'copy if dissatisfied', 'copy good social learners', 'copy kin', 'copy friends' and 'copy older individuals'. These tendencies can also be seen in human social learning, but there are more complex factors that determine copying strategies.

There are pronounced individual differences in social learning strategies among humans. Molleman et al. (2014) have demonstrated that human individuals 'tend to employ the same learning strategy irrespective of the interaction context'. The learning strategies of learners on an LMS have not been studied in detail. The behaviour and participation of learners on an LMS have been explored through LMS analytics, but how these behaviours are related to learning or learning strategies is uncertain.

Plagiarism and learning through copying from others are different. Copying and adapting for one's own developmental goals is part of social learning. In social learning, individuals observe others, copy and adapt. With the advent of the LMS and the online discussion forum, copying other learners' written work became easier. The promotion of peer assessment and peer discussion on the LMS led to the possibility of presenting others' work as one's own. This is plagiarism. Today, almost all LMSs have plagiarism detection software embedded in them to discourage plagiarism on assessed work. Learners are also offered details on plagiarism and how to avoid it and are encouraged to learn good writing skills.

## Individual and group learning through social interaction and societal impact

Can social learning cause changes to society and traditions? What precisely is a tradition? The broad definition of 'tradition' proposed by Fragaszy and Perry (2003: 6) as 'a distinctive behaviour pattern shared by two or more individuals in a social unit, which persists over time and that new practitioners acquire in part through socially aided learning' is an important outcome of social learning. Social learning can give rise to varied local cultures (Richerson and Boyd, 2005). A good example is the entertainment-education that promotes social learning to change group behaviours and local cultures. The application of entertainment-education to promote social, health and development-oriented goals has increased tremendously (Shen and Han, 2014). In the promotion of social learning in distance and online education, it is plausible that changes to group behaviours can occur. Can such group behaviours diffuse through local society or professional groups and make a societal impact? These are not easy questions to research; change must be attributed to social and group learning to be confident that the societal change is directly linked to social learning. Detailed studies that triangulate evidence from learners, society and online courses must be conducted to ascertain this. An example that demonstrates the evidence needed to demonstrate individual learning through social interaction that led to societal impact follows.

> **Example**
>
> **Multi-level impact of continuing professional development using distance and online learning on Sri Lanka's veterinary sector**
>
> This research used a case-study approach to assess the impact of a postgraduate online learning programme's impact at different levels: individual, institutional, institution's students, the profession, the public and animals. The study was based on two groups of veterinarians who participated in online and distance learning programmes offered by the Royal Veterinary College (RVC) in the UK. One group were field veterinarians working for the government who undertook an MSc related to livestock health and production. The other group were academic staff who studied a postgraduate certificate in teaching and learning. As they were all veterinarians studying for two online qualifications by the same university, a greater collaboration between the participants was established. To study the impact on society, the employers of all the postgraduate participants, colleagues and undergraduate students who were taught by the academic staff were interviewed. Data was transcribed and qualitative content analysis conducted. Participants had achieved personal satisfaction, gained new knowledge and skills and progressed professionally. These impacts translated to societal impacts including disseminating understanding of the One Health concept, improving animal welfare laws and assisting the development of the undergraduate veterinary curriculum. The graduates from these distance learning programmes are experts at the centre of a new community of practice and have the ability to inspire future generations of Sri Lankan veterinary surgeons (Kinnison et al., 2020).

## Concepts in social learning and examples

In the next section, 'Fostering learning communities', examples that are used in online courses to promote social interactions to enhance learning will be used to discuss the three following concepts in social interactions and learning:

- learning as an emergent property of the reinforcing interactions between students in the online environment

- learning that is situated within wider social units or communities of practice
- learning through individual interactivities with input from peers.

---

**Concept 1: Learning as an emergent property of the reinforcing interactions between students in the online environment**

*Online Peer Review Workshops*
This is a participatory activity that is designed as part of the PG certificate in teaching and learning offered by the University of London (UoL) Worldwide programme.[1]

Purpose of the activity: To develop reflective writing

Task 1: Individual
Participants start by doing two tasks: an interactive plagiarism quiz and an activity based on reading a plagiarism similarity report downloaded via Turnitin software.

Task 2: Individual
Participants consider their experience of doing the quiz and the Turnitin activity from different perspectives and use a framework to write a short reflective piece of no more than 500 words about it. They submit the reflective piece to peer review workshop, phase 1.

Task 3: Individual and peer related
Each participant is allocated to see two written submissions of their peers and have to provide constructive feedback using a set of assessment criteria.

Task 4: Individual and peer related
The participant reads the feedback that he/she received from two peers on their work, reflects on it and captures some thoughts in the reflective workbook.

The peer review workshop provides the following learning opportunities:

1) Active learning by doing – participants do two tasks, self-assess their understanding regarding plagiarism, reflect on

the experience and own self-knowledge and then do a piece of reflective writing.
2) Critical evaluation of self and peer – first-hand experience of own peers' work to relate to own, how to give formative feedback.

**Concept 2: Learning that is situated within wider social units or communities of practice**

This is an activity in the module on Securing Human Rights UHM 020 in the MA in human rights offered by the School of Advanced Studies, UoL.

Task 1: On campaigning strategies – participants have to develop their own campaign idea and create a series of campaign messages. Participants can use the organisations where they work or volunteer as the basis of the exercise.

Participants are given the following information:

- Creating public awareness and mobilising public opinion around human rights causes is a major part of any NGO's work.
- Social media tools are a cheap and effective way to reach wider audiences.

Devise your own campaign cause and prepare the following:

1) A series of three tweets to generate interest in your campaign (think about your target audience(s).
2) A hashtag for your campaign.
3) One Facebook post or Instagram image to generate interest in your campaign.

Invite other participants to comment on your work.

Task 2: Peer review – give feedback to your fellow participants regarding their campaign message and whether the messages could be adapted to better draw attention to the cause.

Overall feedback: Peers and a campaign consultant such as the ex-Deputy of Campaigns at Amnesty International will be invited to give feedback on their campaign message, the effectiveness of the approach to generate interest, which has a direct application on their real-world practice.

**Concept 3: Learning through individual interactivities with input from peers** *Bring Back Activities (BBAs)*

These are activities that are designed to bring together peers and tutors to be involved in a task that the participant has to do in relation to the core study material to encourage participants to discuss their thoughts with peers and tutors. This is designed as part of the PG certificate in veterinary education at the RVC.

Purpose of the activity: To construct learning through peer and tutor discussion.

Task 1: Individual
Participants start by doing a task. An example of a BBA is as follows: in relation to study content on student learning theories, interview three students to find out how they approach their learning. Critically reflect on how students learn and how they fit the mould. Create a post in your tutor discussion forum and discuss thoughts and findings with your peers.

Task 2: Individual
Participants write a critically reflective post (500–700 words) answering the BBA in their own BBA tutor discussion forum (four to five participants per forum). Participants are also encouraged to upload a photo, drawing or recording if they have used one to aid reflection.

Example post: 'I have decided to interview a range of learners who have very different backgrounds with regards to their qualifications. The first learner I talked to was my postdoc who is currently working in my lab. I thought she would be a good starter as she has taken a similar career path to myself and would have had similar experiences with regards to teaching as I had. I was however wrong and her teaching experience was very different. From research I think my postdoc's learning style is a mixture of theorist (De Vita, 2001) but learning in the right environment (Canfield, 1992). From her information it was obvious that to learn she needed to be motivated but also in the right place, and she has said even now in the lab she prefers learning new skills and techniques by reading first before heading to the practical side. Something that was very different to myself, where I like to learn practically.'

Task 3: Peer related
Participants must comment on one or two peer postings.

Example post: 'A theme discussed by xxxx that I did not deliberate, was that students very rarely fit one of the moulds we learned about. Upon reflection, I think I subconsciously try to fit students into a "category" or "box" for ease in the classroom. To consider students being fluid learners that adapt between lessons or indeed even topics, makes catering to that very challenging, but is a possibility I will not neglect in the future. By using a variety of teaching methods, hopefully I can include learners of all approaches in my sessions.'

Task 4: Tutor related
The tutor provides feedback to the whole group.

Example post: 'I'd like to just tease apart the concept of approaches to learning versus learning styles – some of you used the term interchangeably (this is often done when people are new to learning theory). Approaches to learning comprise motivation and strategies and can lead to deep/surface/strategic learning. Learning styles are different and are usually measured using some sort of "inventory" – there has been a lot of criticism in the literature about teaching to specific learning styles, such as Visual-Auditory-Kinaesthetic (VAK) or Honey and Mumford, or Kolb learning styles, with there being no evidence that teaching students in their preferred format works (Kirschner, 2015). This has been compounded by the 'Universal Design for Learning' initiative (Rose and Meyer, 2002), which is important and has merit because it recognises learner diversity, promoting inclusion, and encourages educators to allow students to represent their learning in different ways, but unfortunately also draws on the learning styles myth.'

> Learning opportunities: The peer review workshop provides several learning opportunities:
>
> 1) Active learning by doing – participants do two tasks, explore concepts in study materials, gain first-hand experience of how their own students learn, reflect on the experience and own self-knowledge and explore how their peers learned through this activity.
> 2) Feedback from peer and tutor – an experiential learning episode that supports and constructs their developing understanding on how others learn.

## Fostering learning communities

The term 'community' has been defined in various ways, but it is fundamentally premised on notions of togetherness among a group of people. According to McMillan and Chavis (1986: 9) it is 'a feeling that members have of belonging, a feeling that members matter to one another and to the group and a shared faith that members' needs will be met through their commitment to be together'. The sense of community that emerges among members is described by Westheimer and Kahne (1993) as being the result of interaction and deliberation by people brought together by similar interests and common goals.

The concept of learning communities borrows from this general notion of human communities and the benefits that an individual gains from being a part of a group with common interests as they work towards sharing understandings, skills and knowledge for shared purposes (Kilpatrick et al., 2012).

Learning communities are a manifestation of the shift of focus from learning as an individual to the social constructivist (Vygotsky, 1978) emphasis of learning as part of a community. Social constructivism views learning as a process in which a learner works to construct new meaning through active involvement. The role of the educator here is to establish an environment in which active participation between and among learners and the instructor can occur. The learner must engage in interaction with his or her instructor, peers and content and attempt to make sense of what they encounter. In Lave and Wenger's (1991) work on situated learning and Wenger's (1998) subsequent work on communities of practice, they raise the concept of communities of practice and consider learning to be 'an integral aspect of social practice' within the classroom community.

In terms of the community in a learning context, this has traditionally been viewed as the domain of a classroom setting where learners are physically present and can interact on a face-to-face basis. However, distance learners in virtual classrooms can and do transcend geographical barriers to form online communities of learning. Wellman (1999) suggests that, when community is viewed as what people do together rather than where or through what means they do them, community becomes separated from geography, physical neighbourhoods and campuses.

The creation and sustaining of distance learning communities has been found to have a number of benefits. Some of these positive aspects are related to the development of strong interpersonal links, sharing of information and resources, collaborative learning and peer support (Haythornthwaite, 2002). The presence of a community in learning has been recognised as being critical to increasing student satisfaction and improving retention, an element of distance learning that remains problematic as rates of attrition are generally higher than those of campus-based courses (Simpson, 2003). A number of studies have found that the lack of interaction is often cited as a major cause of dissatisfaction among distance learners. Associated with this are feelings of isolation and disconnection that can lead to low retention rates as students drop out of their courses. Tinto (1993) suggests that there is a greater likelihood of students continuing with their studies if they feel involved and able to develop relationships with members of their learning community.

An example of how a learning community develops within a distance learning course is given below.

### Building a learning community in a cohort of dispersed distant learners in the RVC

The RVC's distance learners studying for MSc courses are dispersed learners all studying independently in locations around the world. Their connection to their peers and their tutors is primarily through the LMS; they also have an administrative support structure that is accessed online via a variety of media, including the LMS.

The community of learning that emerges with every cohort does so with academic, technical and administrative staff, creating a scaffolded structure that underpins the students' learning. These three areas of support undertake a number of activities – they design learning content, provide information and technical support and provide the overall signposting that directs the learners towards ways in which they can engage with their course and become an integrated part of a cohort, which eventually develops into a community of practice.

The broad design of learning activities is outlined below.

### Induction

The students' learning journey begins with online induction tutorials that are held at the beginning of the academic year. This is their first introduction to their peers and to the support structures that will be present for the duration of their studies. The key features of these induction tutorials are:

- Whole cohort: they include the whole cohort of learners, so everyone is beginning the experience at the same time.
- Non-threatening: the tutorials are informal and invite the students to introduce themselves and share some information about their location, their work and their interests. Students are encouraged to upload a photo of themselves onto a Padlet wall with a world map as a background; the photo is placed onto their geographical location. This adds a visual aspect to the induction and allows the students to get a sense of who and where their new peers are.

### Generic study skills

The induction tutorials are soon followed by tutorials on generic academic skills, such as studying at Masters level, how to write a tutor-marked assignment and plagiarism. These tutorials are also directed at the whole cohort and are meant to be the beginning of the shared academic journey.

### Module-specific tutorials

Following on from the whole-cohort interactions, students then break into smaller groups for module-specific online tutorials. By the time they join these smaller groups, they have had the experience of learning with the whole cohort, have some understanding of how their LMS platform works and have a general sense of being part of a learning community. This sense of community grows as they work in, and interact with, peers within a smaller group for the module-specific work.

In time, the learners become more independent in developing and managing their interactions, either via student-led discussion groups on the LMS or sometimes via use of alternative social media of their own choosing.

As learners progress through these different levels of activity, the expectation is that they develop a sense of belonging and feel that they have a shared purpose and work with others towards a common goal. This sense of belonging in a learning community plays an important role in the retention of students.

## Conclusions

Over the years, a considerable amount of effort has been invested in addressing the social isolation of the 'lone long-distance learner'. With the advent of the internet and the wider use of technology-based media, a parallel VLE was created that transformed the learning experiences of such learners.

Today, the learner is at the centre of a learning community and is connected to other learners, teachers and non-teachers, who together foster this learning community. The learning experience is maximised with opportunities to learn from others, give and receive feedback and develop skills through interactive social learning. The pedagogical underpinning of these developments has neither been easy nor straightforward. Costly experiments have been conducted with learning and the learner as the focus, with a shift from teaching and the teacher. Evidence from human and animal learning approaches have been used to inform, guide and lead the way. New approaches are continuously being developed, practised, evaluated and adopted, with course design and pedagogies recognising the need for learner interaction at various steps of the learning journey. The increasing use of artificial intelligence in teaching and disruptive learning modes such as massive open online courses have not been discussed here, but these new technologies and educational fora are likely to have an effect on interactions in learning and on learning communities.

As the educator community moves forward and continues to develop and change, the two key issues of interactive social learning and fostering the learning community remain essential in supporting the 'lone long-distance learner' and hopefully helping them to become a little less alone.

## Note

1   PGCert: Learning and Teaching in Higher Education, https://london.ac.uk/courses/learning-teaching.

## References

Ali, A. and Smith, D. (2014) 'Comparing students' performance in online versus face-to-face courses in computer literacy courses'. *Competitiveness Forum*, 12 (2), 118–23.

Bandura, A. (1977) *Social Learning Theory*. Englewood Cliffs, NJ: Prentice Hall.

Bawden, R., Guijt, I. and Woodhill, J. (2007) 'The critical role of civil society in fostering societal learning for a sustainable world'. In A. E. Wals (ed.), *Social Learning towards a Sustainable World: Principles, perspectives, and praxis*. Wagenigen: Wageningen Academic Publishers, 133–48.

Biggs, J. (1999) 'What the student does: Teaching for enhanced learning'. *Higher Education Research & Development*, 18 (1), 57–75. Accessed 7 July 2022. https://doi.org/10.1080/0729436990180105.

Bligh, D. (1993) 'Learning to teach in higher education'. *Studies in Higher Education*, 18 (1), 105–11.

Bull, R., Petts, J. and Evans, J. (2008) 'Social learning from public engagement: Dreaming the impossible?' *Journal of Environmental Planning and Management*, 51 (5), 701–16.

Burdett, E. R., Lucas, A. J., Buchsbaum, D., McGuigan, N., Wood, L. A. and Whiten, A. (2016) 'Do children copy an expert or a majority? Examining selective learning in instrumental and normative contexts'. *PLoS ONE*, 11 (10), e0164698. Accessed 7 July 2022. https://doi.org/10.1371/journal.pone.0164698.

Canfield, A. (1992) *Canfield Learning Styles Inventory Manual*. Los Angeles: Western Psychological Services.

Capra, F. (2007) 'Foreword'. In A. E. Wals (ed.), *Social Learning towards a Sustainable World: Principles, perspectives, and praxis*. Wagenigen: Wageningen Academic Publishers, 13–15.

Cundill, G. (2010) 'Monitoring social learning processes in adaptive comanagement: Three case studies from South Africa'. *Ecology and Society*, 15 (3). Accessed 7 July 2022. http://www.jstor.org/stable/26268171.

De Vita, G. (2001) 'Learning styles, culture and inclusive instruction in the multicultural classroom: A business and management perspective'. *Innovations in Education and Teaching International*, 38 (2), 165–74. Accessed 7 July 2022. https://doi.org/10.1080/14703290110035437.

Fragaszy, D. M. and Perry, S. (2003) 'Towards a biology of traditions'. In D. Fragaszy and S. Perry (eds), *The Biology of Traditions: Models and evidence*. Cambridge: Cambridge University Press, 1–32.

Grow, G. O. (1991) 'Teaching learners to be self-directed'. *Adult Education Quarterly*, 41 (3) 125–49. Accessed 7 July 2022. https://doi.org/10.1177/0001848191041003001.

Hammond, M. (2005) 'A review of recent papers on online discussion in teaching and learning in higher education'. *Journal of Asynchronous Learning Networks*, 9 (3), 9–23.

Haythornthwaite, C. (2002) 'Strong, weak and latent ties and the impact of new media'. *The Information Society*, 18 (5), 385–401.

Horner, V. and Whiten, A. (2005) 'Causal knowledge and imitation/emulation switching in chimpanzees (*Pan troglodytes*) and children (*Homo sapiens*)'. *Animal Cognition*, 8, 164–81. Accessed 7 July 2022. https://doi.org/10.1007/s10071-004-0239-6.

Kilpatrick, S., Barrett, M. and Jones, T. (2012) 'Defining learning communities contact: Defining learning communities', CRLRA Discussion Paper Series, Discussion Paper D1/2003. Accessed 7 July 2022. https://doi.org/10.13140/RG.2.2.18041.08806.

Kinnison, T., Thuranira-McKeever, C., Kalupahana, R. and Silva-Fletcher, A. (2020) 'Multi-level impact of continuing professional development on Sri Lanka's veterinary sector'. *Open Learning: The Journal of Open, Distance and e-Learning*, 1–18. Accessed 7 July 2022. https://doi.org/10.1080/02680513.2020.1758650.

Kirschner, P. A. (2015) 'Facebook as learning platform: Argumentation superhighway or dead-end street?' *Computers in Human Behaviour*, 53, 621–5.

Kolb, D. A. (1984) *Experiential Learning*. Englewood Cliffs, NJ: Prentice Hall.

Laland, K. N. (2004) 'Social learning strategies'. *Animal Learning & Behavior*, 32, 4–14. Accessed 7 July 2022. https://doi.org/10.3758/BF03196002.

Laurillard, D. (1993) *Rethinking University Teaching: A framework for the effective use of educational technology*. New York: Routledge.

Lave, J. and Wenger, E. (1991) *Situated Learning: Legitimate peripheral participation*. Cambridge: Cambridge University Press.

Liu, T. C. (2005) 'Web-based cognitive apprenticeship model for improving pre-service teachers' performances and attitudes towards instructional planning: Design and field experiment'. *Educational Technology & Society*, 8 (2), 136–49.

McMillan, D. W. and Chavis, D. M. (1986) 'Sense of community: A definition and theory'. *Journal of Community Psychology*, 14 (1), 6–23.

Molleman, L., Van den Berg, P. and Weissing, F. (2014) 'Consistent individual differences in human social learning strategies'. *Nature Communications*, 5, 3570. Accessed 7 July 2022. https://doi.org/10.1038/ncomms4570.

Moore, M. G. (1989) 'Editorial: Three types of interaction'. *American Journal of Distance Education*, 3, 1–6.

Moore, M. G. and Thompson, M. M. (1990) 'The effects of distance learning: A summary of literature', Research monograph no. 2, American Center for the Study of Distance Education, Pennsylvania. Accessed 7 July 2022. https://eric.ed.gov/?id=ED330321.

Ramsden, P. (1992) *Learning to Teach in Higher Education*. London: Routledge.

Richerson, P. J. and Boyd, R. (2005) *Not by Genes Alone: How culture transformed human evolution*. Chicago: University of Chicago Press.

Rose, D. H. and Meyer, A. (2002) *Teaching Every Student in the Digital Age: Universal Design for Learning*. Alexandria, VA: Association for Supervision and Curriculum Development.

Shen, F. and Han, J. (2014) 'Effectiveness of entertainment education in communicating health information: A systematic review'. *Asian Journal of Communication*, 24 (6), 605–16. Accessed 7 July 2022. https://doi.org/10.1080/01292986.2014.927895.

Simpson, O. (2003) *Student Retention in Online, Open and Distance Learning* (1st edn). London: Routledge.

Tinto, V. (1993) *Leaving College: Rethinking the causes and cures of student attrition* (2nd edn). Chicago: University of Chicago Press.

Verduin, J. R. and Clark, T. A. (1991) *Distance Education: The foundations of effective practice*. San Francisco: Jossey-Bass.

Vygotsky, L. (1978) *Mind in Society*. Cambridge, MA: Harvard University Press.

Wals, A. E. and Van der Leij, T. (2007) 'Introduction'. In A. E. Wals (ed.), *Social Learning towards a Sustainable World: Principles, perspectives, and praxis*. Wagenigen: Wageningen Academic Publishers, 17–32.

Wellman, B. (1999) 'The network community: An introduction to networks in the global village'. In B. Wellman (ed.), *Networks in the Global Village*. New York: Routledge, 1–48.

Wenger, E. (1998) *Communities of Practice: Learning, meaning and identity*. Cambridge: Cambridge University Press.

Westheimer, J. and Kahne, J. (1993) 'Building school communities: An experience-based model'. *Phi Delta Kappan*, 75 (4), 324–8.

Whiten, A. and Mesoudi, A. (2008) 'Establishing an experimental science of culture: Animal social diffusion experiments'. *Philosophical Transactions of the Royal Society of London. Series B, Biological Sciences*, 363 (1509), 3477–88. Accessed 7 July 2022. https://doi.org/10.1098/rstb.2008.0134.

Wilson, B. and Cole, P. (1991) 'A review of cognitive teaching models'. *Educational Technology Research and Development*, 39 (4), 47–64.

Wood, L. A., Kendal, R. L. and Flynn, E. G. (2013) 'Whom do children copy? Model-based biases in social learning'. *Developmental Review*, 33, 387–94.

# 10
# The Icarus simulation tool: a case study

Lynsie Chew and Alan Parkinson

The focus of this chapter is an evaluation of a business/financial simulation, 'Icarus'. The evaluation seeks to identify how far measures embodied within the simulation design overcome challenges commonly associated with online learning programmes, namely high attrition rates, lack of engagement, loneliness and negative passivity.

The Icarus simulation is part of a global online MSc in professional accountancy (MPAcc). The programme is aimed at finance professionals who are members or affiliates of the Association of Chartered Certified Accountants (ACCA). MPAcc is a collaboration between ACCA, the University of London (UoL) and UCL. It includes a capstone Strategic Financial Project (SFP) module, which introduces business research skills leading to the preparation of a business plan, including financial forecasts concerning an organisational strategic initiative. The Icarus simulation is part of this SFP module and is intended to rehearse and test the skills taught in the module.

The programme was launched in 2016 and has since had over 6,000 students from over 150 countries. MPAcc students are assigned online tutors who respond to student queries and questions and monitor forum discussions, intervening and supporting as and when necessary. The core study materials are videos, self-paced formative activities, selected book chapters and specialist journal articles. There is a facility for some students to pay an extra local tuition fee to one of a number of local teaching support centres, notably in Hong Kong, Singapore and Malaysia. However, since registrations in such centres have been consistently low, never exceeding more than

3 per cent of intake, most students study the online programme as distance education learners.

## Icarus design

The Icarus simulation is based on a macro-enabled Excel file. Its plotline is a struggling airport requiring strategic change. Students, in groups of five, assume key roles as an incoming senior management team responsible for developing and implementing required changes. The exercise is managed across five weeks, with each week equating to one financial year. Each week, students rotate management roles and responsibilities. Given the global nature of MPAcc, teams are grouped according to world time zones.

Their task is to assess the current situation within the simulated context, identify objectives and associated targets, analyse financial and other data and make strategic decisions about the short- and longer-term future in pursuit of the stated objectives. These include financial returns, growth, customer and staff satisfaction. Students are required to think critically and creatively in order to make decisions about strategic and operational matters to achieve targets and objectives. In addition to financial matters, students have to take account of strategy, operations, marketing and human resource management. They set an annual plan with a budget, based on their decisions and consequential forecasts. Their inputs are set against a 'real-world' model and results returned.

As in the real world, rarely do plans match reality. Teams must explore why what they planned to happen has not happened. They then need to apply their insights based on lessons learned to the next financial period.

Specifically, Icarus is intended to:

- develop learners' research, analysis and decision-making skills
- create a sense of community and identity
- help learners to make sense of meaning through shared challenges and building on experience
- help learners to move from passive to active learning and knowledge construction.

## Icarus design rationale

While online learning can offer many benefits to learners, it is not without its own challenges and limitations, such as high attrition rates, lack of engagement, loneliness and negative passivity (Bates, 2019; Dron and Ostashewski, 2015).[1]

Looking at some of these challenges in more detail, Latchem and Jung (2010) contend that, globally, up to 40 per cent of adult online learners fail to complete an online programme, with that figure reaching up to 90 per cent in some developing countries.

Burns (2013) cites the descriptor 'the loneliness of the long-distance learner' as an overarching umbrella heading, under which rests a number of contributory factors to a poor learning experience and consequential dropout rates. It is not unusual for online learners to be impacted by feelings of isolation and disconnection, lack of interactivity and lack of community.

Given that MPAcc students do not meet physically (because the course is carried out online, at a distance), the MPAcc programme team sought pedagogical approaches that would avoid or at least reduce the impacts of these kinds of challenges for online distance learners, while supporting the development of the business research skills introduced in the SFP module.

Gerstein (2014), Dron et al. (2015) and Bates (2019) advocate a constructivist approach to elicit problem-solving and enquiry-based learning. At the heart of this is the need to help students to formulate and test ideas, draw conclusions and inferences and share and convey knowledge in a collaborative learning environment. Students seek to understand how the world works by applying existing knowledge and real-world experience and learning to hypothesise, test ideas and draw conclusions from findings. This approach is based on the premise that knowledge is subjective in nature and is constructed from perceptions and mutually agreed upon conventions. Accordingly, individuals build or construct knowledge rather than acquire it through instructivism; that is, transmission from an expert with knowledge. Meaning or understanding is achieved by assimilating information, relating it to existing knowledge and cognitively processing it by reflecting on new information. This approach is applicable to education across a range of disciplines, particularly in the social sciences. Drawing on and endorsing Gerstein's thoughts, Jackson (2016) contends that learning in general, and especially so in blended, hybrid and online environments, needs to move from being instructivist in nature to being constructivist (at a minimum) and, wherever possible, also connectivist. Accordingly, the team opted for a broadly constructivist approach, combining problem-solving and enquiry-based learning with connectivist elements of collaboration and sharing.

## Impact of Icarus

Icarus was evaluated to establish whether or not, and how far, it is successful. The specific research questions were as follows:

- Do students benefit from engaging with Icarus as they develop research skills in preparation for their capstone project?
- In the eyes of the students does Icarus create a sense of community and identity that enhances their learning experience?
- Are students able to make sense of their learning through sharing challenges with others?
- Does Icarus allow them to draw upon and build on their experience as finance professionals?
- To what degree does the use of Icarus facilitate active learning and knowledge construction rather than passive learning?

Data was collected through a generic survey of all students in mid-2018 (by which time around 2,800 students had engaged with Icarus) and a specific questionnaire to a sample of students (n=116) based on purposive sampling. The generic survey concerned MPAcc as a whole and no ratings or rankings related specifically to Icarus. Rather, qualitative comments were used to inform the questions asked in the purposive sampling survey. For the latter, a Likert scale of 1–5 (with 5 being positive and/or in agreement) was applied and open comments were encouraged to add richness and illuminate the responses.

Comments regarding the role of Icarus collected via the generic survey were overwhelmingly positive, as in the following examples:

> 'Overall, my experience in the Icarus activities and building my business plan has improved my research and analysis skills, my professional writing skills, my team working skills, organisational skills and, most especially, time management, which I found very difficult as a new parent.'

> 'Icarus was an exciting, challenging, realistic and thought-provoking five-week activity. Icarus simulation is a unique exercise which was very interactive and engaging not just for me, but my whole team. This exercise helped to understand the whole operation of a business. Even though the simulation was of an airport, there were the basic operations that every company has.'

> 'Working in a group who have different cultural, religious and environmental backgrounds is not an easy task. Thanks to this course I am fully exposed to working together with different people.'

> 'As an accountant a natural tendency is to focus only on core financial KPIs [key performance indicators] around income, costs, margins and liquidity. Icarus demonstrated to me the need to satisfy and optimise a much wider set of performance measures – staff satisfaction, customer satisfaction and brand awareness, for example.'

> 'I enjoyed the simulation as it brought ideas to life. That said, more time should be devoted to it.'

The purposive sampling survey with n = 116 received a response rate of 76.7 per cent (89 responses). The questions/focus areas and the accompanying Likert scale ratings are shown in Table 10.1. Students were also asked to identify areas for potential improvement.

As with the generic survey, illuminating comments were overwhelmingly positive, as illustrated by these examples:

> 'For me, Icarus was the highlight. It brought everything to life. It should be used wherever possible in other modules.'

> 'Well, it was an insightful activity, providing opportunities for rational cogitations and interaction with foreign team members.'

> 'Icarus was a great experience, especially because it was the first time to get such an exposure to all the things that were interrelated. It enhanced the strategic thinking skills as well as team collaboration.'

> 'I had engaged in forum discussions but not many others did. The simulation brought us together as a group and I felt a real sense of companionship.'

> 'I enjoyed the Icarus activity as it allowed me to network with other professionals and understand how different people have different perspectives on various levels of decision making.'

> 'Through being engaged with lots of activities all the time I got the feeling I was learning by doing rather than being just told what to do.'

> 'You should have a simulation activity across all modules.'

**Table 10.1** Questions/focus areas in purposive sampling survey and responses.

| Question/focus area | Rating (rounded) on Likert scale of 1–5 (1 = strongly disagree; 5 = strongly agree) |
|---|---|
| 1. Developing research skills: The use of Icarus helped me to develop research skills in preparation for the final capstone project. | 4.3 |
| 2. Creating a sense of community and identity: Engagement with Icarus created a sense of community and identity, which enhanced my learning experience. | 4.6 |
| 3. Learning from sharing with other colleagues: I was able to make sense of my learning and derive meaning through sharing challenges with others. | 4.5 |
| 4. Drawing upon and building on financial experience: Icarus enabled and allowed me to draw upon and build on my experience as an accountant/finance professional. | 4.5 |
| 5. Engaging meaningfully with ideas: The use of Icarus facilitates active learning and knowledge construction rather than passive learning. | 4.6 |

The analysis of the data collected indicates that the purposes of including Icarus in the SFP module are valid and have, in the main, been achieved. The generic survey certainly contains many positive comments. Of more significance, the Likert scale survey suggests that the most respondents feel that Icarus helped to engender a sense of engagement with, and belonging to, an online peer group of active learners. The lowest rating of 4.3 is for question/focus 1 ('Developing research skills'), but that is still an equivalent agreement rating of 86 per cent.

Where criticisms were voiced, they linked to team dynamics and time. Very few groups had issues with 'free-riders' or non-contributors. Individuals are required to submit minutes of meetings, with tasks allocated to team members, with the next meeting recording whether or not agreed allocated tasks were completed and reported back on. Where teams were unable to resolve matters informally, the use of participation surveys, direct requests and the minutes of meetings proved helpful for the module leader to intervene, usually resulting in a positive recalibration of team dynamics. Regarding time constraints, for busy professionals, often with family and/or domestic responsibilities, this can sometimes be challenging. Students are encouraged to plan ahead and make time for Icarus just as they do for their study of core readings and other activities.

## Limitations of the study

An obvious weakness of this evaluation study is that the 89 respondents to the purposive sampling survey represent only a very small percentage of the over 6,000 student numbers to date. Additionally, as there is no stratified sampling in place, there is no opportunity as yet to identify commonalities and differences between various categories of students. This means that no cause-and-effect correlations exist and no meaningful inferences can be drawn from the data.

However, in addition to the surveys, three other sources of data strongly suggest that Icarus plays a meaningful role in enhancing the student experience and reducing attrition rates. One source is that of MPAcc programme statistics, revealing that approximately 85 per cent of students complete the programme, with an 89 per cent pass rate for those completing. Icarus itself has a 95 per cent participation figure, tending not to drop off after week one as the activity progresses.

A second source is in the *UoL Graduation Alumni* book. This book highlights the profiles of students from all UoL programmes, including MPAcc. Students are asked to identify and comment on one aspect of their programme that stands out for them as a highlight. In the May 2019 edition of the book, nearly 60 per cent of profiled MPAcc students cited Icarus as one of their highlights.

A third source is independent of students. In 2017, Icarus was entered for the UK National Learning Technology Awards. In November 2017 it received the Gold Award for Best Use of Simulation.

Thus, when taken with the Gold Award and the graduation book comments, there is enough in the data collected and analysed to indicate that the MPAcc team is moving in the right direction in its attempts to minimise the loneliness of the long-distance learner and encourage a more active approach to learning.

While Icarus had been used primarily in MPAcc, at the time of writing it is also being used in a range of programmes including MBAs, management, business analytics and entrepreneurship and in professional development within the medical profession and airline industry. The simulation has since been developed into an app to allow its use on mobile devices running Android and iOS operating systems, as well as laptops running Windows 10, making access and participation 'on the go' an added possibility.

## Note

1   For further analyses of challenges to distance and online learning at macro, meso and micro levels, see chapters in Zawacki-Richter and Anderson (2014), particularly Chapter 13 'Major movements in instructional design' (by Campbell and Schwier); Chapter 14 'Interaction and communication in online learning communities: Toward an engaged and flexible future' (by Conrad) and Chapter 15 'Quantitative analysis of interaction patterns in online distance education' (by Jeong).

## References

Bates, A. W. (2019) *Teaching in a Digital Age: Second edition*. Vancouver: Tony Bates Associates. Accessed 7 July 2022. https://pressbooks.bccampus.ca/teachinginadigitalagev2/.

Burns, M. (2013) *The Loneliness of the Long-Distance Learner*. Washington D.C.: Global Partnership for Education, Accessed 7 July 2022. https://www.globalpartnership.org/blog/loneliness-long-distance-learner.

Dron, J. and Ostashewski, N. (2015) 'Seeking connectivist and instructivist safety in a MOOC', *Educación XXI*, 18 (2), 51–76.

Gerstein, J. (2014) 'Moving from education 1.0 through education 2.0 towards education 3.0', *Experiences in Self-Determined Learning*. Seattle, WA: Amazon, 83–98.

Jackson, N. J. (2016) *Exploring Learning Ecologies*. Betchworth: Chalk Mountain. Accessed 7 July 2022. http://www.normanjackson.co.uk/uploads/1/0/8/4/10842717/lulu_print_file.pdf.

Latchem, C. and Jung, I. (2010) *Distance and Blended Learning in Asia*. New York: Routledge.

Zawacki-Richter, O. and Anderson, T. (2014) *Online Distance Education: Towards a research agenda*. Athabasca: Athabasca University Press. Accessed 7 July 2022. https://doi.org/10.15215/aupress/9781927356623.01.

# 11
# Digitally supported assessment

Leo Havemann, Simon Katan,
Edward Anstead, Marco Gillies,
Joanna Stroud and Sarah Sherman

This chapter focuses on digital assessment and feedback practices in distance education. Providing evidence of learning through assessment is at the heart of students' experience of higher education (HE), whatever their mode of study. Open and distance education-focused institutions have justifiably been proud of their technical innovation, tending to move rapidly to harness available technologies (from post to broadcast media and, most recently, online media) in their mission to enable education for remote, distributed groups of learners. In recent years, distance education courses have, in the main, moved from paper and digital media delivered physically to wholly online delivery, except where the circumstances of target learners preclude reliance on a reliable and fast internet connection. In terms of content, discussion and collaboration, where distance education has forged ahead, campus-based, blended programmes have generally followed. However, in terms of assessment and feedback, distance education has remained somewhat conservative. While most assessment in distance education has taken place online along with content and communication, there has been a tendency to replicate fairly traditional assessment formats using digital tools.

The contexts and cases discussed in this chapter have been drawn from member institutions across the University of London (UoL) Federation. This chapter considers the future of assessment in distance education. It reviews some previous work conducted within a subset of the federation based in Bloomsbury, which aimed to provide a snapshot of current assessment practice within credit-bearing distance education programmes (Weitz and Seddon, 2017). It then attempts to look beyond the current mainstream of practices by considering additional cases of emerging practice within the massive open online course (MOOC) space.

During their rise to prominence in the early 2010s, MOOCs were widely heralded by their proponents as a completely new and innovative educational format and, conversely, critiqued by detractors as simply a rebranding exercise for online distance education. Taking a view from somewhere between these points, this chapter goes on to discuss that while MOOCs certainly represent a form of distance education, they also possess features that distinguish them from 'traditional' distance education programmes.

## A snapshot of mainstream distance education practice

The pre-COVID-19 practice in digitally supported assessment is explored through findings of a review of assessment activity in several programmes offered via the UoL network. The distance education programmes forming the UoL portfolio are run by a subset of UoL member institutions. The findings of this current practice review, which was conducted by the Bloomsbury Learning Exchange (BLE) as part of a larger focus on assessment throughout its member institutions (Havemann and Sherman, 2017), are categorised according to three broad approaches: functional, enhanced functional and innovative, defined as follows:

- A functional approach, in which compliance processes are met. Resources and results are generally available through technology. Summative assessment is more prevalent than formative assessment.
- An enhanced functional approach, where there is an increase in the use of formative assessment with tutor interaction and individual feedback enabled through technology.
- An innovative approach, with a strong collaborative pedagogical rationale and increased variety of learning activities.

Taken together, the examples discussed provide a 'snapshot' of typical practices, rather than representing an exhaustive documentation or evaluation. Furthermore, the examples highlighted do not discuss the tools employed in significant detail, instead focusing on assessment contexts, tasks and outcomes.

## Functional approach

All departments, programmes and modules explored and referenced as part of the BLE review that can be grouped within the functional approach fulfil, at a minimum, the standards of academic quality expected by their respective institutions, inclusive of learning, teaching and assessment practices. Nevertheless, these courses may be termed 'legacy', having originally been delivered via correspondence with posted, hard-copy material and now updated with modern content delivery and communication tools rather than explicitly designed for an online context. The courses are now mostly paperless, with content and some aspects of assessment activity (such as provision of marks and feedback) available online or supported by technology. Summative assessment dominates the courses featured, although there are occasions when formative assessments are also present and delivered.

Several departments, including those at the School of Oriental and African Studies (SOAS), the London School of Hygiene & Tropical Medicine (LSHTM) and the Royal Veterinary College (RVC), indicated that their programmes operated summative assessment models primarily weighted towards examinations taken in traditional, invigilated face-to-face contexts, such as in local examination centres. These examinations take a variety of forms, including seen and unseen essay question papers and multiple-choice question (MCQ) tests. Weightings for these activities were typically up to 80 per cent of the grades and made little use of technology given the context within which they were completed. Nevertheless, programmes at LSHTM suggested that exam scripts completed in local centres were scanned and marked electronically.

Coursework activities within this approach were completed through varied assessment tasks appropriate to the discipline of study, such as reports, essays, audio-visual presentations, case studies, journals, logs and scientific or mathematical exercises. These were frequently weighted at approximately 20 per cent of the module mark and were more likely to be supported by technology, either through a pedagogic delivery mechanism inherent within the virtual learning environment (VLE) or by means of an upload through a VLE-based online submission facility (Birkbeck, LSHTM, RVC, SOAS and UCL). Marks and feedback for coursework submitted online were in most cases also made available via the VLE assignment facility or proprietary tools such as Turnitin, with the UCL Institute of Education noting that feedback was provided for drafts in advance of the final summative submission.

## Enhanced functional approach

Courses following the enhanced functional approach were common among reviewed institutions, building on the functional approach to demonstrate greater recognition and use of formative assessment and feedback. These activities were typically enabled or enhanced by technology and would often feature an increased focus on tutor or peer interaction with individual students.

As with summative assessments, formative tasks take a variety of forms across member institutions, including essays, mock examinations, quizzes and portfolios, each with a strong focus on feedback. Several of these offer opportunities for students to engage with the actions and processes of self-regulated learning (Zimmerman, 1990) that have a defined relationship to academic achievement in both face-to-face and learning contexts. For instance, both LSHTM and the RVC offer quizzes that promote self-efficacy and assessment in relation to the individual's understanding of specific topics, while UoL has further developed its own custom self-assessment VLE plugin for essay questions, giving students the ability to mark and evaluate their responses against a series of model answers.

Programmes from LSHTM, RVC and UCL Institute of Education each identify discussion fora as environments in which peer-to-peer and peer-to-tutor interactions are used to generate formative feedback.

Synchronous tools such as Skype and Blackboard Collaborate are further identified by Birkbeck, LSHTM, RVC, SOAS and UCL as mechanisms for individual and group-based interactive tasks. These routinely take the form of tutorials, being an opportunity to review material but, as described by SOAS, additionally promote student voice and engagement in personal goal setting.

The UCL Institute of Education additionally reported tutors' use of audio to deliver feedback, offering greater flexibility in both the generation of the feedback and the potential to make feedback feel more personal, thereby building more meaningful connections with students studying at a distance.

## Innovative approach

The key feature of this innovative approach is the collaborative, pedagogic rationale taken by departments, programmes and modules, which facilitate much more student interaction.

In such examples there typically exist an increased diversity of learning activities, which are often drawn from cultural or socially driven learning theories such as social constructivism. While this rationale broadly informs course learning design, it is also evident within the assessment methods employed, with formative and peer-supported tasks being prevalent.

Multiple programmes considered as part of the BLE review featured assessment activity that could be grouped under the innovative approach and, notably, through formatively assessed tasks. Alongside traditional forms of assessment such as presentations and essays, UCL's MSc in paediatric dentistry further requires that students complete a logbook using the iPad minis with which they are supplied. The logbook is populated with treatment approaches and requires some peer interaction in relation to the rationale for the selections made.

Students enrolled on Birkbeck's MSc in geochemistry are provided with high-quality digital learning resources to analyse through Xerte tutorials. The initial analyses are used as the basis for collaborative discussions between peers and tutors, which subsequently inform the assessed portions of the course.

The SOAS MSc in financial sector management operates predominantly within the functional and enhanced functional approaches. However, one module uses a strategic simulation model in which students are placed in teams of five to conduct research and build a strategic case study. Within this case study there are specific assessed activities, including development of a business plan, a risk analysis and scenario planning, while long-term collaboration is established as a significant factor in the awarding of marks. Formative feedback is given at key milestones within the simulation and students can benchmark their progress against both their own plans and that of other teams.

The programme featured as part of the review that most fully embraces collaboration between students and tutors in its activities and assessments is the SOAS MA in global diplomacy. The course demonstrates constructive alignment in its learning and assessment design and course activities are explicitly mapped to assessments and learning outcomes (Biggs, 2003), with each module featuring five written online assessments or 'e-tivities' (based on the work of Salmon, 2002) comprising 30 per cent of the module mark and a longer-form essay for the remaining 70 per cent. The concept of e-tivities is drawn from the framework for participatory online learning in which learners are supported through five stages of progressive participation in an online learning community: access and motivation, online socialisation, information exchange, knowledge construction and development (Rofe, 2011; Salmon, 2002).

# Emerging good practices in assessment at scale

## Blurred boundaries: traditional and non-credit-bearing online assessments

MOOCs are generally delivered to large numbers of learners across diverse geographical and cultural contexts and are open in the sense of being at least initially free of fees or formal entry requirements. The bulk of such courses are made available as a result of HE or specialist providers' formal relationship with a privately operated platform provider, such as Coursera, FutureLearn or edX. Course content is typically designed using pedagogic patterns familiar within the distance education context (Bali, 2014; Daradoumis et al., 2013; Glance et al., 2013), such as text, video, audio and downloadable files of supplementary or longer-form material. However, the fundamental differences in delivery have seen implications for the administration and learning design of such courses, leading to a departure from the types of assessment activity most frequently employed as part of more traditional distance education. Tutor-led review, marking and feedback is a labour-intensive process and, on that basis, cannot be replicated at scale, meaning that MOOCs and their delivery platforms have instead adopted pedagogic strategies more appropriate for large cohorts. These strategies focus on peer-to-peer interaction, opportunities for self-regulated and self-evaluated learning activities and automated assessments.

The tools or pedagogic approaches in place to support assessment activity as part of MOOCs are ultimately dependent on the platform being used. However, those that are offered as standard across platforms include:

- In-content pause points, such as those delivered within video material. These are typically lightweight, ungraded MCQs that assess understanding and provide immediate contextual feedback.
- Discussion prompts, whereby learners are encouraged to engage with one another in social spaces by answering questions posited by tutors within the body of content. Although there may be occasional tutor interaction, learners are often asked to read and respond to the comments of others.
- Quizzes containing a range of automated question types, such as multiple choice, multiple answer and numeric response. These can be used in both a formative and summative context with pass/fail functions, but automatic grading and delivery of pre-generated

feedback is paramount to both accommodate large numbers of learners and deliver uniform results across the cohort.
- Peer-supported assignments, in which open-ended assessment tasks can be delivered and learners grade one another's work using a rubric or criteria provided within the course.
- Programming assignments that require learners to submit computer code, then a platform technology reviews and grades the script.

A light touch, automated tutor facilitation and lack of summative assessment has led these tools to exist solely in a non-credit-bearing context. This means that they exist outside of the assessment regulations and accreditation frameworks that govern delivery of more traditional distance education modules and programmes.

However, while the at-scale nature of MOOCs has seen them occupy a distinct space within the provision of education internationally, there are lessons to be learned or pedagogies that might be borrowed from the delivery format. This can happen through the application of at-scale pedagogies and formative assessment tasks to award-bearing courses and is happening in the sense that full, credit-bearing programmes are now being delivered via MOOC platforms. Practical examples of both are explored in the subsequent illustrations of innovative practice.

## Formative peer review

In one assignment, learners are asked to select any single issue that negatively affects the lives of the residents of an African city or neighbourhood of their choice. The task assignment is an essay between 500 and 1,000 words that cannot be delivered at scale with the tutor support available. On that basis it is delivered as a peer review activity, with significant scaffolding to support its completion.

Learners are encouraged to draw upon and combine their prior personal, professional and educational experiences with their learning around issues and concepts as part of the course in their submitted response. A number of key and open-ended questions serve to implicitly scaffold the learner's response, asking them what the issue is, who is most affected by it and why, what issues underpin it, what factors and processes have contributed to it and how and which actors could contribute to its solution. Some basic examples of issues are provided but learners are encouraged to select their own.

The second stage of the assessment is to review the submission of another learner. It is only possible to progress and complete this stage once an individual has submitted their own work. Learners do not provide a mark as part of their review but are asked to actively engage with the content of another learner's assignment and reflect upon it in a positive and constructive way. Assignments are reviewed using the same generic criteria applied to more traditional assignments, such as quality of critical reflection and originality, use of evidence, use of concepts and materials to illustrate the issue and build an argument, coherence and clarity and relevance and focus. Additionally, they are asked to write a short reflection guided by open questions relating to the subject matter, such as their thoughts on the assignment's most interesting points, what it made them think about, the connections they had made between the subject location of the assignment and a different place or situation and whether anything was missing that could have helped to better elucidate the situation or problem.

## Autograding

Autograding is the automatic grading of student work by a computer program rather than a human tutor. Students submit work in digital form to a VLE. The work is then marked algorithmically by a computer program, which would normally be on a remote server, such as a VLE server, so that the student cannot tamper with the grading software. Autograding, together with peer grading, is a key enabler of MOOCs, because it allows students to receive grades and feedback without tutor input. For example, it is a key element of the new MOOC-based BSc in computer science by Goldsmiths and UoL (though it should be noted that as it is a full degree, all modules also contain tutor-marked assessments).

The simplest and most common form of autograding is the MCQ test. Since MCQs have a well-defined correct answer, and they can easily be implemented digitally as check boxes, automatically grading them is straightforward. They are a very common form of assessment that underpins MOOCs and other online courses. In the BSc in computer science, for example, they are used extensively both as formative practice and summative assessment. Most VLE platforms generalise these types of quizzes to other types of questions that also have a clear correct answer and are easily assessed by a computer; for example, numerical answer questions or simple text matching. Quizzes are therefore an easily implemented and efficient form of autograding. However, they are limited in the depth of the learning outcomes they are able to assess. In most cases they are used for simple factual recall, though more sophisticated question design can improve them, for example, by careful choice of alternative answers for MCQ. An example of the use of a quiz for more sophisticated learning is in the module 'How Computers Work' in the BSc in computer science. In the module, quizzes are used as a prompt for independent research as students are asked to use the internet to research a particular topic that has not been covered in the course (for example, a particular computer virus called Mirai) and then must complete a quiz on the topic.

Other forms of autograding require more sophisticated grading algorithms. Apart from quizzes, the most common use of autograding is for computer programming. Students upload the programs they have written and an algorithm checks this program. This is normally done by checking the output the program produces with a number of different inputs (though there are other approaches, such as analysis of the source code for correctness against the programming language's syntax). This checking process normally mirrors the testing process used in professional programming practice. It uses a type of checking software method known as unit testing, which was originally developed for professional software testing. The assessment is therefore very close to industry-standard ways of working.

Another approach to autograding used in the BSc in computer science is simulation. This is an interactive activity that models an element to be learned; for example, the workings of a computer processor or a particular algorithm. It can be a very engaging, hands-on way of learning and can also provide feedback. Simulation can be designed as an open-ended formative activity that allows students to explore the functioning of a computational system. It is also possible to design simulations that function more like a computer game, in which there are certain correct 'winning' strategies and students get more direct feedback through either a score or a 'win' condition (which can be checked automatically by the simulation software). In this latter case the simulations can be used as more summative assessment, with grades being calculated from students' scores on the simulation.

Beyond computer programming, autograding is relatively rare. It requires defining algorithms to assess a piece of work, which might be straightforward in the case of a clearly defined programming exercise as above, but in other cases can be very challenging or beyond the current technological 'state of the art'. Even in areas such as mathematics or computer programming there are many aspects that cannot easily be autograded (the 'working' and problem solving in mathematics or coding style and open-ended software design in programming). In other subject areas, such as humanities, very little can be automated. This is still a very active research area and there are even claims of machine learning software that can grade humanities essays (though these should be judged with caution), so progress may be made in other disciplines (Arikat, 2012).

The most obvious benefit of autograding is that human tutors no longer have to mark assessments. This is a potentially significant re-education in labour for individual teachers or a considerable cost saving for institutions, though these are balanced by the much larger upfront costs of developing the autograded exercise. Developing grading software or simulations can take considerable and costly effort.

However, as with many forms of automation, autograding is not simply about reducing the cost of existing approaches to assessment, but radically changing assessment, particularly through scale. The cost and effort of marking work is a considerable bottleneck in traditional education and removing it can allow assessment to increase in scale in a number of ways. The most obvious is increasing the number of students. MOOCs can support thousands of learners at low or zero cost because all assessments are automated. Scaling up can also qualitatively change the nature of assessment. As well as efficiently assessing more students, each individual student has access to many more assessments for practice and formal evaluation. A typical course in a BSc in computer science will have several quizzes and/or programming exercises per week, allowing students to get frequent and instant feedback on their work. Since marking the work is not costly, students can also attempt an assessment multiple times and get feedback on them all, thus gradually improving their work. This enables radically new approaches to learning that would not have been possible or would have been very costly with tutor marking. For example, variants of Bloom's *mastery learning* (Bloom, 1984) discuss an approach where students can make multiple attempts at tasks, watch lectures multiple times and go through materials in a much more self-paced manner than would be possible in a traditional campus environment.

## Gamification

Sleuth (Katan and Anstead, 2020) is a series of gamified (Deterding et al., 2011) code puzzles themed around a film-noir detective story. The project was developed for the introductory programming module that runs on campus at Goldsmiths College and through UoL and Coursera. Goldsmiths follows a 'learning by doing' approach to teaching programming. In the module, students build fluency in rudimentary techniques and patterns through the repeated practice of programming exercises. This raises challenges around content generation, scalability and student motivation to which the design of Sleuth responds.

Students access Sleuth via a personalised web app. From here they can check their current grade and feedback, download puzzles and upload them to get them graded. The web app is themed as a detective agency 'Sleuth & Co', with students playing the character of a fledgling detective. They are guided by 'the Chief' who gives them feedback on individual puzzle attempts as well as their general progress in the game.

Primarily, Sleuth aims to facilitate a greater amount of practice of rudimentary programming tasks in a way that is scalable for module tutors. This is achieved through the employment of two techniques: procedural content generation and autograding. To facilitate procedural content, each student is allocated a user ID within the game. The ID is used to generate unique puzzles for students to complete, containing distinct numeric values, naming conventions and coding styles. When a student downloads a puzzle to solve, the unique version they receive is sufficiently different from other students' versions in the class so that collusion and other forms of plagiarism are eliminated from the assessment. The autograder recognises the student's user ID and marks the correct variation of the puzzle. Uploading another student's work would be rejected by the system as the variations in the code would not match the ones given to the colluding student.

The downloaded puzzle comprises a sketch template (a set of files defining a program in the programming environment employed) containing a unique puzzle task written as text comments and starter code for the student to complete. Included in these comments is a reference that identifies the puzzle variant to the autograder. Students attempt the puzzle and upload it for grading. They receive immediate feedback from 'the Chief', which includes any compile or runtime errors and tells them what parts of the task they have achieved and what parts they still need to work on. Students get five attempts to complete a puzzle, after which 'the Chief' suspends them from that particular task for one hour. On returning, students must start afresh by downloading a new variant. Through this design, students are provided with as much practice as they need to master topics without placing extra burden on the teacher.

The design also aims to provide differentiated outcomes for students of varying experience levels, which is carried out through the arrangement of puzzles and the scoring system. The puzzles are arranged into 16 cases, each based on a particular topic from the syllabus and consisting of four stages. Students can attempt the cases in any order and need not complete them before starting another. However, the stages of each case progress in order of difficulty and are unlocked in sequence as the student solves them. While more experienced students might complete the higher stages of most cases, less experienced students can still practise and achieve in all areas of the course by completing the lower stages of each case. Having built up their confidence, these same students might return to harder stages that they had previously abandoned. These types of behaviour are further supported through the scoring system. Students' grading comprises a 'rookie' score and 'pro' score. The 'rookie' score is made up of the average of the first nine cases that are made available to students from the start of the course. At the midpoint of the course, the students 'go pro'. Their 'rookie' score is frozen and the remaining seven cases are released. The 'pro' score is made up of the average of all the cases. This means that students are rewarded for completing their work in a timely manner but are also rewarded for continuing work on unfinished rookie cases after the midpoint deadline.

The aim to create an engaging environment in Sleuth that would motivate students to practise their code rudiments is in part achieved through the instant feedback and summative scoring design. However, the unit also used game-like theming to amuse students and arouse their curiosity. Each case tells a different story set around the criminal residents of Console City. As students solve more cases, they uncover further connections and evidence of a criminal conspiracy. Additionally, graphical content for the puzzles was produced by a professional illustrator.

At the time of completing this chapter (October 2022), Sleuth has so far run four times on campus and eight times online for approximately 5,000 degree-level learners. The results have been encouraging. In the initial on-campus run, students made a total of 42,534 code submissions – an average of 138 per student over a ten-week period. Despite perceiving the task's level as between fair and difficult, the class's achievement was high with a median grade of 90.67 per cent (quartile 1 mark: 75.79; quartile 3 mark: 96.49). These figures demonstrate that Sleuth has facilitated a very different environment for students to learn in. Such submission quantities are beyond the capacity of any team of human graders that could be resourced and the motivational, gamified aspects of the design have engendered altogether different levels of student engagement.

Another advantage of autograded assessment is that rich data can be collected about how students are responding to the assignments. Sleuth records the details of every student submission, including the submitted code, grade and feedback. In reviewing the data, several areas of improvement for subsequent iterations of Sleuth have been identified. Despite the conceived behaviour in the level design, less experienced students tend to persist in their attempts at the more difficult case stages instead of moving on to other cases. With this in mind, there is an aim to increase the interventions of 'the Chief', who will increase suspension times and recommend alternative cases for students to try. By reviewing the average number of attempts per puzzle it is possible to identify those cases that students find particularly challenging. For these cases, the unit plans to experiment with different forms of feedback to improve student performance. Currently, a significant proportion of students achieve full marks for the assignment. While passable at this level, a lack of differentiation at the top end of grades may be considered undesirable in assessment in HE. Therefore, an area of improvement might be to raise the difficulty level of the final stages of cases. It would be interesting here to see what proportion of students still continue to achieve the highest grades, given the automated feedback and unlimited attempts.

## Conclusion

Assessment in online and distance education has largely attempted to reproduce the forms of assessment used in traditional on campus settings in digital form. While this reproduction of existing forms is typical of initial experiments with new technology, assessment seems to be a particularly conservative area. This is due in part to concerns about the rigour and fairness of assessments, with new approaches being viewed with suspicion and traditional approaches such as paper exams viewed (perhaps overgenerously) as a rigorous 'gold standard'. This concern is held by many academics and universities and, in many countries, paper exams are enshrined in educational regulations.

While the examples gathered in this chapter pre-date the COVID-19 pandemic, we have seen similar tensions play out in the context of the 'pivot online', which saw campus-based teaching around the world replaced with 'emergency remote teaching' (Hodges et al., 2020). In many cases, traditional, in-person timed exams have been substituted with online, sometimes 'proctored' timed exams; however, the switch to online learning and assessment has also initiated a wider uptake of alternative forms of assessment. The case study in Chapter 12 explores many of the practical issues in how UoL moved to online assessment in 2020. It remains to be seen how many of the new practices that have been developed as a result of the pandemic will be retained and to what extent. However, there are encouraging signs that practices in both distance and campus-based assessment are evolving to take advantage of distinctly digital opportunities now that these are becoming more widely available and better understood.

Recent years have seen considerable innovations in digitally supported assessments. These have been driven in large part by the MOOC model of online education, which is characterised by the ability to scale to very large numbers of students with very limited input from tutors, resulting in a focus on automated and peer assessment. These MOOC-style approaches are now starting to be used in credit-bearing and degree programmes, allowing for greater scale and efficiency. However, their use in degrees raises new challenges due to concerns of rigour and quality of assessment. While automated and peer assessments can be used to evaluate many important learning outcomes in many subject areas, they also have considerable limitations. Automated assessments can work well for technical subjects such as mathematics and computer science, but there are many deeper aspects of work that cannot be assessed in this way. Many disciplines, such as humanities, may have little scope for using automated assessments. Peer assessment is more flexible, but the quality of assessment is limited by students' own prior conceptions.

Students are also likely to question the validity of peer grading in high-stakes assessments. For these reasons, it is important to balance automated assessments with human-graded assessments. For example, UoL's BSc in computer science makes extensive use of both automated and peer assessment but has a policy of requiring that every module also includes human-graded assessments and that peer-graded assessments do not count towards final course grades.

However, many of the concerns listed here also relate to the summative function of assessment and there is a strong element to formative assessment that drives learning. This is where a typical MOOC style of assessment can be particularly valuable, since the scale it provides is not simply in terms of the number of students that can be assessed but the frequency of assessment for each student. Having several small assessments every week and giving feedback on them would be unfeasible for human tutors, but it becomes possible with MOOC-style assessment. Students are therefore able to test their learning and get fine-grained feedback on their learning more frequently. When used well, there is not simply a quantitative increase in feedback but a qualitative change in the nature of learning, as exemplified by the aforementioned Sleuth example. By offering instant feedback for many small exercises, Sleuth has been able to shift the style of learning towards one of intensive practice and sustained engagement, which are both vital when learning programming.

Peer assessment also has considerable formative benefits. It allows students to engage in tasks that are too complex for automated assessment without being restricted by the bottlenecks that arise in tutor grading. However, there are also important benefits not related to performing the task but to the fact that students are assessing the same task. Evaluating one's own work and that of others is a vital skill in academic and professional settings. On the one hand, an education system based purely on tutor grading is unlikely to develop these skills in students as they can feel reliant on others for feedback. The requirement to assess peers, on the other hand, ensures that students develop evaluation skills and engage deeply with the marking criteria to develop critical thinking and improve their own work.

The new approaches to digitally supported assessment that are currently emerging therefore have the potential to result in major changes in how students learn in distance settings, supporting more intensive engagement and deeper self-evaluation among other things. These changes will not result from simply viewing digital technology as a way of making traditional assessment more efficient or from a naive techno-optimism that sees any use of technology as automatically resulting in improved learning. They will result from the conscious use of technology to enable new pedagogies centred on improving students' learning.

# References

Arikat, Y. M. (2012) 'Subtractive neuro-fuzzy modeling techniques applied to short essay auto-grading problem'. In *6th International Conference on Sciences of Electronics, Technologies of Information and Telecommunications (SETIT) 2012*, Sousse, Tunisia. IEEE, 889–95. Accessed 18 July 2022. https://doi.org/10.1109/SETIT.2012.6482032.

Bali, M. (2014) 'MOOC pedagogy: Gleaning good practice from existing MOOCs'. *MERLOT Journal of Online Learning and Teaching*, 10 (1), 44–56.

Biggs, J. (2003) 'Aligning teaching and assessing to course objectives'. *Teaching and Learning in Higher Education: New Trends and Innovations*, 2 (April), 13–17.

Bloom, B. S. (1984) 'The 2 sigma problem: The search for methods of group instruction as effective as one-to-one tutoring'. *Educational Researcher*, 13 (6), 4–16. Accessed 18 July 2022. https://doi.org/10.3102/0013189X013006004.

Daradoumis, T., Bassi, R., Xhafa, F. and Caballé, S. (2013) 'A review on massive e-learning (MOOC) design, delivery and assessment'. In *Eighth International Conference on P2P, Parallel, Grid, Cloud and Internet Computing*. 28–30 October 2013, Compiègne, France. IEEE, 208–13. Accessed 18 July 2022. https://doi.org/10.1109/3PGCIC.2013.37.

Deterding, S., Sicart, M., Nacke, L., O'Hara, K. and Dixon, D. (2011) 'Gamification: Using game-design elements in non-gaming contexts'. *CHI '11 Extended Abstracts on Human Factors in Computing Systems (CHI EA '11)*. New York: ACM, 2425–8. Accessed 18 July 2022. https://doi.org/10.1145/1979742.1979575.

Glance, D. G., Forsey, M. and Riley, M. (2013) 'The pedagogical foundations of massive open online courses'. *First Monday*, 18 (5), 1–10.

Havemann, L. and Sherman, S. (2017) *Assessment, Feedback and Technology: Contexts and case studies in Bloomsbury*. London: Bloomsbury Learning Environment. Accessed 18 July 2022. https://doi.org/10.6084/m9.figshare.5315224.

Hodges, C., Moore, S., Lockee, B., Trust, T. and Bond, A. (2020) 'The difference between emergency remote teaching and online learning'. *Educause Review*, 27 March. Accessed 18 July 2022. https://er.educause.edu/articles/2020/3/the-difference-between-emergency-remote-teaching-and-online-learning.

Katan, S. and Anstead, E. (2020) 'Work in progress: Sleuth, a programming environment for testing gamification'. In *IEEE Global Engineering Education Conference (EDUCON)*. IEEE, 1503–7. Accessed 18 July 2022. https://doi.org/10.1109/EDUCON45650.2020.9125098.

Rofe, J. Simon (2011) 'The IR model and e-moderating'. In G. Salmon (ed.), *E-moderating: The key to teaching and learning online* (3rd edn). London: Routledge Falmer.

Salmon, G. (2002) *E-tivities: The key to active online learning*. New York and London: Routledge Falmer.

Weitz, N. and Seddon, K. (2017) 'Assessment, technology and innovation in distance learning in the Bloomsbury Learning Environment institutions'. In L. Havemann and S. Sherman (eds), *Assessment, Feedback and Technology: Contexts and case studies in Bloomsbury*. London: Bloomsbury Learning Environment, 23–37. Accessed 18 July 2022. https://doi.org/10.6084/m9.figshare.5315224.

Zimmerman, B. (1990) 'Self-regulated learning and academic achievement: An overview'. *Educational Psychologist*, 25, 3–17. Accessed 18 July 2022. https://doi.org/10.1207/s15326985ep2501_2.

# 12
# Taking assessment online – systems, issues and practices: a case study

Linda Amrane-Cooper, David Baume, Stylianos Hatzipanagos, Gwyneth Hughes and Alan Tait

Taking assessment online – as with taking course design, teaching, feedback, collaboration and all other aspects of education online – requires greater rigour, more detailed planning and, ideally, a longer lead time than is required for in-person education and assessment. Clear and robust systems are needed. There is less scope for improvisation and last-minute changes.

These unremarkable assertions, particularly those relating to 'less scope for last-minute changes', would have produced at best a hollow laugh among members of the University of London (UoL), who suddenly found themselves, early in 2020, tasked with moving approximately 110,000 examinations online in just a few weeks at the start of the COVID-19 pandemic.

This case study frames, analyses and reviews the main learning from that experience. It identifies issues about systems for online assessment and explores issues and identifies particular practices in the conduct of online assessment. It is adapted from an evaluation report prepared for UoL.

## The assessment system

The following elements are common to any system for summative assessment (that is, for assessment intended to provide marks, grades or other forms of information on student attainment):

- communication with students about the assessment, including format, expectations, dates, support options, preparation activities and resources
- specification, writing and quality assurance of the assessment task – often the examination paper
- production and distribution to candidates of the examination paper
- invigilation of the assessment process
- return of examination scripts to assessors, usually via the awarding university (in this case, UoL)
- marking and quality assurance of marking
- communication of marks to students
- dealing with issues or concerns at any stage.

For UoL, until 2020, the bulk of end-of-unit study assessment was conducted via pen-and-paper examinations, delivered in over 600 approved examination centres around the world. The distance learning model available to most UoL students separates the cost of learning from the cost of assessment. This separation provides flexibility and allows students to control their progress route through their studies. Students register and pay UoL for their selection of exams. They pay an additional fee to the examination centre they plan to attend, usually relatively local to them. In January 2020, approximately 35,000 students had registered their intention to engage with examinations in May and June 2020 at examination centres and approximately 110,000 examination events were lined up.

## Moving assessment online

In late March 2020, the COVID-19 pandemic began in earnest in the UK. The challenge to UK universities, and to many other higher education institutions around the world, was essentially the same – how to move online, very quickly. Uniquely, UoL was challenged further – in the global and distributed nature of its student body and in the range of universities in partnerships in the UoL family. The response to the pandemic was made in emergency mode. In the event, 33,000 students, 93 per cent of those eligible, sat approximately 110,000 examination events of different types, which was around 8 per cent more than in 2019.

On 25 March, UoL communicated to all students that examinations in 2020 would have to move online, as conventional examinations in examination centres would not be possible due to COVID-19. Programme teams also communicated to students about the modes and formats of assessment that would replace the conventional examinations. A range of examination formats was adopted differentially by programme teams. These were delivered via one of two approaches:

- The examination paper was downloaded by the student from the virtual learning environment (VLE). The submission from the student (typed or handwritten and then scanned) was returned within a prescribed time. The window of submission varied across the programmes from one hour to seven days. Unseen examination papers delivered via the VLE were, in practice, open world exams, as no restrictions could be applied to the materials and resources students could access. This approach allowed for online timed assessments to be delivered at scale across 23 time zones.
- Digitally proctored (invigilated) examinations were taken on an enterprise solution platform where students engaged with the examination in a shorter assessment window (a few hours) and completed their work directly in the online system.

## Evaluation of the move to online assessment

University leadership and the Student Voice Group were keen to understand the impact of the rapid move to online timed assessment for the key stakeholders involved: students, staff, programme teams and examiners. Additionally, it was important to explore the successes and challenges of the assessment system itself.

A plan for the evaluation of the move to online assessment in summer 2020 was developed by a multidisciplinary team of academics in the Centre for Online and Distance Education and professional services colleagues at UoL.

Four key areas were identified for the focus of the evaluation:

- student behaviours
- student sentiment
- student outcomes
- operational issues.

**Student behaviours**: Data from the VLE was captured and reviewed to identify how students interacted with the online environment.

The areas of investigation

| Student behaviours | Student sentiment | Student outcome | Operational |
|---|---|---|---|
| • Exam take up<br>• Usage patterns of VLE<br>• Issues around proctoring<br>• Submissions of answers | • Survey<br>• 2 weeks after<br>• Before marks confirmed<br>• Interviews<br>• CDE Student Research Fellows | • Average marks<br>• Across four years<br>• Distribution of awards | • Assessment choices<br>• Assessment offences<br>• Logistical issues<br>• Experience of programme and marking teams |

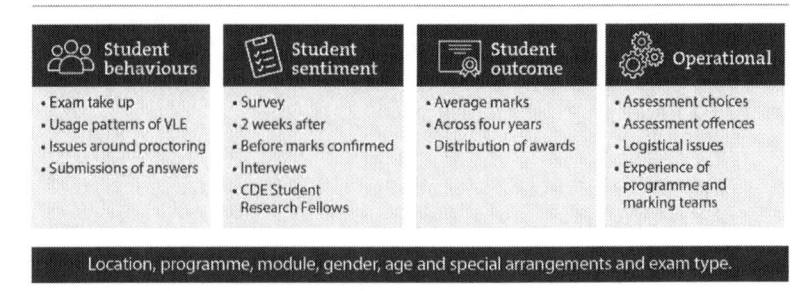

Location, programme, module, gender, age and special arrangements and exam type.

Figure 12.1  Focus of project evaluation. Source: Authors.

Student survey: A survey with a target audience of approximately 35,000 was disseminated, including all students who had booked to take exams in the summer. The survey ran from 8 July to 31 August 2020. A total of 8,595 responses were received during the live survey period, with an overall response rate of 29.5 per cent. An extensive report covering the quantitative and qualitative data was prepared in conjunction with a data management company.

Each programme team received a summary of the survey data from their student body and this informed development of assessment approaches after summer 2020.

Student interviews: Fourteen undergraduates and eight postgraduate students were interviewed across a representative sample of programmes. These semi-structured interviews were conducted to elaborate on issues identified in the student survey.

Programme director interviews: Twelve semi-structured interviews were conducted to collect the views from a sample of programme directors.

Examiner attitudes from the survey: A survey was undertaken with a target audience of 621 examiners who had engaged with marking the submitted work in summer 2020. A total of 176 responses were received: an overall response rate of 27 per cent.

# Major findings and some implications for developing practice in digital assessment

Table 12.1  Findings and implications: student behaviours.

| Findings | Implications |
|---|---|
| Overall, 93 per cent of students, registered for an examination in summer 2020, undertook their assessment. This is a higher rate than previous years, when pen and paper exams took place in exam centres.<br><br>UoL students studying at a distance are required to have a suitable computer or device and WiFi access in commencing study with the university. The uptake of exams in summer 2020 indicated that, overall, students were not excluded from assessment by the rapid pivot to online timed assessment.<br><br>A small minority of students who would normally request special examination arrangements noted that they could not engage with assessment in summer 2020. Reasons included health and anxiety linked to the pandemic.<br><br>Conversely, a large proportion of students who would normally request special examination arrangements noted that the move to digital assessment allowed them to engage with their exams safely without having to travel to examination centres during the pandemic. | Digital assessment may provide a more accessible form of assessment.<br><br>Meeting the needs of all students needs careful management and appropriate adjustments. |
| Often, students logged into the VLE and accessed their examination at the point the exam opened.<br><br>Similarly, there was often very high traffic at the point when the exam submission window was due to close, even for papers where students had a 24-hour-plus window in which to submit. This occasionally led the VLE to crash. Action was taken to mitigate this as the examination session progressed. | Technical mitigation for peak-load demands on the system.<br><br>Training for students to deploy strategies for engagement with assessment over a longer time period than traditional pen and paper exams. |

(continued)

*(continued)*

| Findings | Implications |
|---|---|
| A considerable volume of traffic, via email and the student enquiry system, resulted from students being unclear about whether they had successfully uploaded their submission file(s) or failed to complete the upload within the time allocated for the examination. The costs and time taken to distribute paper-based assessments and answer booklets for a distance provider like UoL, with students studying in over 190 countries, can be substantial. The move to online assessment is cost and time efficient. However, considerable reorganisation of staff activity to support the summer 2020 online assessments was required. | Robust and clear instructions and routes for students to submit their work. Notification to students by the system of successful upload. Clarity over expectations and regulations related to technical issues encountered with the upload of student work. Mitigation procedures to support students. Upskilling and redeployment of staff to support digital assessment may be required. |

Table 12.2  Findings and implications: student sentiment from survey and interviews.

| Findings | Implications |
|---|---|
| Most students indicated a positive experience with online assessment. 82 per cent agreed that they were able to take the online assessment in a suitable environment, 80 per cent agreed that the platform used for online assessment worked well and 79 per cent agreed that they were able to demonstrate their learning through the online assessment. | Review of approaches to delivery of assessment and assessment timeframes. |

| Findings | Implications |
|---|---|
| On average, satisfaction levels were higher among independent learners than among students at teaching centres and higher among postgraduates. | |
| Satisfaction levels were significantly lower among programmes that experienced well-acknowledged problems with online invigilation arrangements, as well as among programmes where the assessment submission period was five hours or less. | |
| Two-thirds of respondents (66 per cent) to the survey agreed they would like to see online assessment continue in the future. Agreement with this statement was correlated with students feeling well prepared to use the online assessment platform and able to demonstrate their learning. | Online timed assessment is likely to continue for most students across the UK HE sector and beyond. |
| Men (68 per cent agree) were slightly more likely than women (65 per cent) to indicate interest in continued online assessment. | Support for student skills and confidence development, in using online assessment platforms and also in approaching the variety of assessment formats, including open-book/open-world, fixed-time assessments. |
| Students aged 25 or over (74 per cent) were more open to its continued use than younger students (60 per cent). | |
| Analysis of the open-text comments suggest that many students recognise that online forms of assessment are cheaper and easier logistically (for example, no exam centre, travel or accommodation costs) and can afford greater flexibility and security for students in terms of where they take their exams. | Training for students to understand strategies for engagement with assessment over a longer time period than traditional pen-and-paper exams. |
| A good majority of students interviewed (16/22) would like digital assessment to continue in the future. | |

*(continued)*

*(continued)*

| Findings | Implications |
|---|---|
| Overall, students interviewed indicated they had a positive experience with the online assessment. In terms of process, no student reported any significant technological problems during the exams. A few students said that the technology created anxiety for them. Advantages were perceived mainly to be flexibility and lower cost (including travelling and accommodation). In terms of content, students did not have any objections to the alternative formats used or the open-book exam format. The added advantage of moving to the alternative assessment for most students interviewed that had a wider submission window was having extra time to complete their exam. For some of them this was not viewed as a positive change as it was anxiety inducing and might encourage academic offences. Most students interviewed did not feel that their performance in the exams was affected by the alternative format. Students felt that there was no difference between the in-person and the online exam experience. For those who did feel that it affected them, most felt their results were affected positively. Again, flexibility was the main reason cited for this positive effect. | |
| The survey indicated that students who undertook online assessment in summer 2020 had significant support needs. 54 per cent of survey respondents said they needed to ask a question about online assessment, with undergraduates, | Improved communication of expectations, format, timing and technical requirements have been put in place. |

| Findings | Implications |
|---|---|
| those at teaching centres and those in countries with developing digital infrastructure (for example, Pakistan, Malaysia and Sri Lanka) more likely than the average student to have needed to contact the university.<br><br>Most students interviewed believed the information provided by UoL was adequate (summer 2020). However, in a few cases they felt that there was some confusion, with information coming both centrally and from programme teams, and a lack of timeliness or delay to their communication. | Summer 2021 saw a significantly lower rate of support needed. Training for students in using the online system, managing their time during assessment and example assessment papers all help to prepare students for online timed assessments.<br><br>Longer planning periods allow for more effective communication strategies. |
| Personal circumstances and online assessment. 98 per cent of survey respondents said that they were able to complete either all or some of the online assessment they had registered for.<br><br>Among those who did not sit all or some of their online assessment, the top three reasons given for this were that:<br><br>• COVID 19 had impacted on the time they had available for their studies<br>• they did not feel academically ready for assessment<br>• COVID-19 had impacted on their mental health and well-being.<br><br>82 per cent of respondents agreed that they were able to take their online assessment in a suitable environment. Postgraduates and independent learners | Student well-being and mental health support have continued to be a significant area of responsibility for the HE sector. Delivering effective support at a distance is evolving. Further exploration of this is provided in Chapter 14. |

*(continued)*

*(continued)*

| Findings | Implications |
|---|---|
| were more likely to agree than their undergraduate or teaching centre-based counterparts.<br><br>There was some evidence in the open-text comments that those students who thought they had a suitable environment felt that doing assessment online contributed to them feeling lower levels of stress regarding their assessment compared to previous years when they had been assessed in examination centres. | |
| A minority of respondents (12 per cent) believed that the use of online assessment had a negative impact on the grades they thought they would obtain through the 2020 assessment round.<br><br>• Survey respondents who require special arrangements due to disability or other reasons were more likely to believe they had done better (27 per cent) through online assessment compared to an unseen written examination than their counterparts (20 per cent).<br><br>The opportunity to type their exams rather than write them by hand was well received by most students interviewed. However, some felt that this could be problematic for some disciplines (for example, STEM). | Close attention needs to be paid to the ways in which students with disabilities, or those in specific circumstances (such as students on deployment with the armed forces) will access, engage with and upload their online timed assessments.<br><br>Training in use of software tools such as text-to-speech and information management tools is useful for all students. |

**Table 12.3** Findings and implications: academic integrity.

| Findings | Implications |
|---|---|
| A majority of students (55 per cent) said that online forms of assessment made no difference to the risk of students cheating compared to unseen written examinations.<br><br>A significant minority (39 per cent) believed that the risk of cheating was higher.<br><br>In interviews, a number of students stressed the need to maintain the credibility of their programme if online assessment were to continue. Students were divided on whether cheating was more likely with the online assessment they had undertaken. In particular, many felt that it was down to the particular discipline, as some subjects made it more difficult than others to cheat.<br><br>During interviews, students underlined the importance of making academic integrity a key issue in online examinations in order to retain credibility for their qualification. Some of them referred to the need to introduce online invigilation to maintain the rigour of assessment. | Two approaches to academic integrity may be considered:<br><br>• through technological intervention (including automated identity checking, proctoring and locked-down browsers)<br>• adapting the assessment task to allow for authenticity and validity.<br><br>This is discussed further in Chapter 7. |
| Online proctoring (via the enterprise solution platform) did not work for students in some locations and circumstances because of broadband limitations. | A no-detriment procedure was applied to allow students to re-engage with assessment when technology prevented engagement. |

**Table 12.4** Findings and implications: academic sentiment (from programme director interviews).

| Findings | Implications |
|---|---|
| In most programmes delivered in summer 2020, exams remained the predominant assessment format. Programme directors cited the following reasons for this:<br><br>• the perceived academic rigour of the summative assessment process<br>• the recognition of the exams by professional bodies and regional regulators as a rigorous assessment format<br>• the impact any radical change might have on confidence in the quality of degrees.<br><br>Changes to assessment included adoption of alternative forms of assessment – broadly coursework (in some cases submitted online) to complement or to replace the exam.<br><br>Alternative forms of assessment, including coursework, group work and peer learning were considered advantageous. This is because they allowed students to develop and demonstrate a range of skills.<br><br>Changes in most cases consisted of moving to open-book exams and redesigning questions to discourage plagiarism (including self-plagiarism from student's previous assessed work). The rationale was to reduce reliance on rote learning and to introduce an element of flexibility and ease anxiety by establishing windows of submission of variable length. | Assessment design and purpose is being reconceived for digital contexts. Design that offers the opportunity for authentic, valid and reliable assessment is an area of rapid innovation. Technology plays a part in this, but the pedagogical underpinnings of the role of assessment in relation to student learning are also coming to the foreground.<br><br>A need for academic staff development and sharing of best practice was indicated.<br><br>Quality assurance processes, including programme approval or reapproval, may need adjustment to facilitate timely changes to assessment.<br><br>Regulation updates will need to ensure that expectations of ethical student behaviour are effectively delineated and clearly communicated to all stakeholders.<br><br>Support for students (and in some cases academic and professional services staff) is needed to understand subject disciplinary approaches to student engagement with, and possible inclusion of, work that is not their own. |

| Findings | Implications |
|---|---|
| For some disciplinary areas, particularly those with professional body or regional/national recognition, the expectations around assessment predicated against open-world examinations.<br><br>Most programme directors reported that they would continue with the online exams.<br><br>For some programme teams, the rapid pivot to online exams in summer 2020, although challenging organisationally, made visible some limitations of exams and enabled enhancements to student learning that might otherwise have taken much longer to achieve.<br><br>When interviewing the programme directors, the evaluation team was also able to focus on the ways in which the academic programme teams adapted their assessment processes and design to include assessment *for* learning as well as judgement of performance (assessment *of* learning). | Expectations around citations in pen-and-paper exam hall assessments are quite different to online timed assessments that are submitted through text-matching software.<br><br>A shift to include more assessment for learning (for example, with the inclusion of more coursework), alongside the established practice of assessment of learning is already taking place among the programme directors and their teams (with a shift in views about the value of assessment for learning for the student journey). However, with the range of institutions, cohort sizes and disciplines involved, the picture is not surprisingly very mixed (see https://london.ac.uk/sites/default/files/cdc/assessment-reforms-tra-report.pdf – accessed 19 July 2022). |

**Table 12.5** Findings and implications: academic sentiment (from examiner survey).

| Findings | Implications |
|---|---|
| • Most examiners welcomed the move to mark typed examination scripts compared to handwritten scripts, as typed examination scripts tend to be more legible and easier to access. | There are implications to asking students to type their work within time constraints:<br><br>• for students for whom English is not their first language, typing in English may be challenging and require practice<br>• keyboards may not be configured to English<br>• students may not be able to type accurately or with speed, or may have physical challenges with time at a computer<br>• diagrams, illustrations, STEM and language fonts may not be easily produced in typed format<br>• students who may need a scribe similarly need to be supported online<br>• text-to-speech software is useful, but students need to develop skills to write academically while dictating. |
| • Efficiency was a concern for examiners. Areas that require technical and procedural improvement to help examiners engage with scripts efficiently online included:<br><br>   ◦ speed of locating, opening and reading of scripts<br>   ◦ recording of marks and comments<br>   ◦ reviewing of marks and comments of other markers<br>   ◦ flagging of answers for possible plagiarism<br>   ◦ agreement and confirmation of final marks. | Development of the digital platform to support effective use by examiners. This could include development of the VLE or engagement with enterprise solutions that provide an end-to-end service to support exam preparation, distribution and engagement with/by students, marking and moderation. |

| Findings | Implications |
|---|---|
| - Over half (51 per cent) of examiners said the move to online assessment helped students achieve higher academic standards in submitted work than previously.<br>- Examiners also flagged concerns in respect of plagiarism, cheating and academic integrity issues they had encountered during the marking process. We asked examiners to identify the top adjustments they would recommend the university makes for future online assessment to minimise assessment offences. The top two responses were:<br>   ◦ for exams to be invigilated<br>   ◦ for exams to be converted into open-world/open-book format, which made use of text-matching software during submission.<br><br>The open-text comments called for greater levels of student training on academic integrity and for avoiding plagiarism and collusion. | Students need help to support appropriate citations and resource utilisation in online timed assessments. Clear policy is needed around use of text-matching software and training for students and staff to understand the affordances and limitations of such software. |

## Technology and assessment

Technology for assessment can bring significant benefits. For example, the use of end-to-end assessment platforms facilitates effective and efficient ways of creating and distributing assessments. These platforms can include question banks, multimedia resources and a very wide range of question and assessment types. Students can engage with the platform, either from home, using their own device, or at an approved exam centre where they can use a device provided or bring their own device. Lockdown of browsers, when coupled with exam centres or digital invigilation, can provide an alternative to open-book/open-world assessments. Distribution of marking to examining teams via digital provision, along with the ability to manage moderation and quality assurance processes in the digital space, lead to opportunities for greater speed and efficiency. However, replacing paper-based in-centre examinations with online proctored assessments that provide a short, fixed time for engagement may do little to move practice from assessment of learning to a more student-centred assessment-for-learning approach.

## Conclusion

In a time of major disruption to both normal and academic life across the world, the rapid move to online timed assessment described here allowed a large, geographically distributed group of distance education students to access and succeed in assessment.

The move has also developed our understanding of the implications for the changing practices to provide opportunities for all students to demonstrate, authentically and honestly, their achievements in a regulated and global system.

# 13
# Inclusive practice

Shoshi Ish-Horowicz, Diana Maniati, Nicholas Charlton, Danielle Johnson, Beatrice Hyams, Sarah Sherman and Sarah Gonnet

Distance education is arguably one of the most flexible means of studying, so it should be the most accessible. A variety of student learning needs can be supported by distance educators taking an inclusive practice approach to their pedagogic work and to curriculum design. This chapter explores definitions of inclusive education and brings together a broad range of accessibility challenges with a specific focus on distance education. Educators have both a legal and educational responsibility to support all students' learning journeys. While the topic is addressed here as a discrete chapter, in best practice it would be embedded across all elements of distance learning.

This chapter starts with a history of inclusion in higher education (HE) and outlines key debates, many of which are still relevant; for example, ensuring that the pedagogy used to design a course meets the needs of all learners equally. Even with a well-designed inclusive course, all students still need to be provided with equitable access to materials and this chapter explores some of the challenges and solutions related to this, including the application of assistive technology. The chapter describes the need for designing and creating inclusive courses to benefit students and also to meet regulations and legal responsibilities.

Some of the common issues in improving inclusivity of existing courses are outlined, along with guidance and recommendations for making distance learning courses accessible for all.

This chapter also models an inclusive approach, enabling it to grapple with the realities that students and institutions face. A team of six writers from different institutions, based across the world, collaborated synchronously and asynchronously to plan, draft and edit the chapter. They used a range of technologies to produce the chapter, including: Skype for Business, Skype, email and WhatsApp for communication; a variety of online academic and legal resources for research; Mendeley for collating references; Google Docs and Microsoft OneDrive for planning and writing. The reason for this large selection of technology was due to the accessibility needs of the team members; for example, the need to collaborate across time zones and compatibility with Job Access with Speech (JAWS) screen reader accessibility software for text-to-speech functionality. It was often challenging to find suitable collaborative tools that can be accessed with screen reading software and there were difficulties using Business Enterprise versions of software for a multi-team project. Overall, however, the process was positive, with the benefit of enabling the authors to live the experience of inclusive practice while writing about it.

## Definitions and models of disability

There are two frequently mentioned models of disability: the 'social' and the 'medical'.

The 'medical' model sees disabled people as being restricted by their impairment. If the impairment is cured, the issue of how disabled people fit into society goes away. Society does not have to change to accommodate them. This has been criticised as being a 'deficit' model of disability, leading, for example, to disabled students being seen as lacking in comparison with an idealised norm.

According to the 'social' model of disability, disabled people are seen as being restricted not by their impairments but by society's failure to take their needs into account. Being disabled is part of the normal spectrum of human life: society must accept disabled people and include them. For example, if a wheelchair user has restricted access into a building because of some steps, the medical model would suggest that this is because of the wheelchair rather than the steps. The social model would see the steps as the disabling barrier.

The social model sees disability as the result of the interaction between people living with impairments and an environment filled with physical, attitudinal, communication and social barriers. The physical, attitudinal, communication and social environment must change to enable people living with impairments to participate in society on an equal footing with others. Barriers should be removed to accommodate an impairment as an expected incident of human diversity.

This model is more inclusive in approach. Proactive thought is given to how disabled people can participate in activities, everyday life and education on an equal basis with non-disabled people.

The social model is internationally recognised and supported by the legislation discussed below. Universities must have an inclusive approach to their provision, including teaching and learning, student services, student activities and online provision. The onus is on the institution to make sure that their provision is accessible and adjustments are made to ensure that disabled people are not excluded.

## Inclusion and distance education

In 1859, Charles Dickens' new magazine, *All the Year Round*, contained a laudatory article headlined 'The English people's university'. In it, the author extolled the admission policies of the new University of London (UoL), where 'every hard worker who can prove his competence may come for a degree' (Dickens, 1859: 281). This headline hints at the revolutionary aims of this new university, at which 'every' student would be accepted and the only barriers to study would be proof of competence.

In the twenty-first century, issues with the phrasing of this ideal can be seen. The pronoun used is problematic. UoL would not award degrees to women until 1880, reminding us that blanket terms such as 'every student' are often misleading and depend on the speaker's own definition of what a 'student' should be. Inclusivity in HE can demand changes in both perception and infrastructure for institutions. For Sutherland (1990: 36), 'the great, the revolutionary feature about UoL was that it did not require residence of its students ... this great fact allowed the separation of the question of *how* and *in what context* you learned'. Sutherland (1990) and Tait (2004) argue that it was this separation that enabled women to be included as students on an equal footing with their male counterparts, with the distance educational model providing the basis for radically increased access to HE.

The levels of determination and agency required for students in this new educational landscape were necessarily high. Returning to the Dickens quotation, the image of the 'hard worker who can prove his [sic] competence' places the burden of proof and work squarely with the student. The direction of action is also explicit: the student will 'come' for a degree, rather than the university reaching out or meeting them halfway. Even as the *All the Year Round* article was published, the new distance learning university was struggling with the problem that 'access' is not enough to remove inequalities (Lee, 2017). In 1865 over 70 per cent of 'private' students did not pass their degrees, a trend only corrected when the university introduced and supported the work of correspondence colleges to help prepare independent students. Interestingly, one student who did successfully sit his examination before then was Daniel Conolly, a blind student who was assessed in 1862 through a combination of *viva voce* and scribed written examinations (Kenyon-Jones, 2008). Here, the university recognised its responsibility to facilitate a 'hard worker' who might otherwise be barred from demonstrating their competence.

As a distance learning institution, UoL was able to circumvent what Dolmage (2017) calls the exceptionalism and ableism of HE, physically manifested in the imposing, inaccessible steps of traditional university architecture. With technological developments, online education has been conceptualised as equally revolutionary in widening access (Adelman and Vogel, 2006; Richardson, 2009). This is reflected in more recent research; for example, a survey commissioned by the Inclusive Panel of the UoL found that around 20 per cent of students with disabilities stated that their disability was the main factor in choosing distance learning (Simpson, n.d.).

It is worth noting, however, that the architecture and structures of online education are not universally accessible. There is a cost associated with education, whether online or face to face and, as argued by Marginson (2004: 90), extreme cost savings 'can only be obtained when there is unmet demand and low expectations about teaching services'. Some of these costs may be met nationally, for example, in countries with high-quality internet access. Many costs and barriers, however, are passed on to students. For example, Hersh and Mouroutsou (2019) concluded that differing levels in accessing learning technologies exist both between and within countries, with income and language being the main factors affecting availability. Groups traditionally excluded from in-person tertiary education are also less likely to engage with online education, as digital divides echo existing social divides (Hersh and Mouroutsou, 2019; Stich and Reeves, 2017).

Inclusion in distance and online education needs to be explored critically. The paradigm of accessibility set out in the early days of UoL is embedded within a specific societal viewpoint; one in which students are expected to rise above their disability or societal disadvantage (Lovern, 2018) with the support of an institution that will accommodate their prior situations and needs (Haughey, 2007; Lee, 2017). In recent decades, this view has been challenged by calls to explore how individuals and communities can be 'disabled' by society (Kent, 2015), with intersectional feminist and race analysis of disability critiquing the deficit-oriented understanding of disability as affecting individuals who are lacking something or have something wrong with them (Boxall et al., 2004; Harry and Klingner, 2007; Liasidou, 2015). This widens the debate to include questions of agency and responsibility for students and for institutions. By exploring how different communities can be excluded from education, labelled as 'other' and defined against a homogeneous elite rather than on their own terms, inclusivity in education can be expanded to encompass the issues of decolonising the curriculum and effective teaching and learning for diverse online and distance learning cohorts.

The experiences of Daniel Conolly from the 1860s would be familiar to anyone working in education today; a student discloses their disability to the appropriate department in the university, which then invests in accommodating their specific requirement(s). Recent research, however, has critiqued this 'self-advocacy' model (Osborne, 2019; Terras et al., 2015), which can imply that a student is to blame for poor engagement with their studies if they do not actively identify themselves through mechanisms that inherently evoke a deficit model of disability (Osborne, 2019). This can be challenging for students who may not be prepared to take on this responsibility, which was often the legal obligation of schools before university-level education (Barnard-Brak et al., 2009; Getzel and Thoma, 2008). It also demands students either self-accommodate (Phillips et al., 2012) or 'accept their disability' (Getzel and Thoma, 2008: 80), navigate any associated bureaucracy (Fossey et al., 2017; Mullins and Preyde, 2013) and categorise themselves according to definitions set out by an able-bodied and privileged society (Guillaume, 2011; Jacklin et al., 2007). Crucially, it ignores the ways in which human identity is fluid; with students 'involved in many different aspects of identity exploration and development whilst at university … addressing their relationship to the construct of disability is only one aspect of a much wider process' (Moriña, 2017: 40). Disclosure is a complex issue for students and can be misunderstood by instructors (Lindsay et al., 2018; Phillips et al., 2012; Venville et al., 2014). The history of UoL shows how inclusion that is premised on self-disclosure has enabled students to succeed, but recent scholarship has exposed its practical and theoretical limitations.

It has been argued that disclosure is less problematic when learning takes place entirely online, as students have found the 'invisibility' afforded by such learning environments 'erased feelings of stigmatization, judgement and discrimination' (Verdinelli and Kutner, 2016: 364). It should be noted, however, that these findings do not resolve the more complex issues around disclosure explored above. Although online and blended learning can increase participation, it has also been found that it may result in a greater dropout rate and lower retention (Paniagua and Simpson, 2018). There is also a problem with assuming disabled students will have different attitudes to learning than their peers. UoL research into the disabled student experience found that, while approximately 20 per cent of disabled students stated their disability was the main factor in choosing the international (now online, distance learning) programme 'even for them the brand of the London University and the choice of appropriate courses were still very important' (Simpson, n.d.).

To claim that the online environment is inherently inclusive and accessible can mean falling into an unjustifiably deterministic approach that ignores the complexities of how technologies are designed and experienced (Adelman and Vogel, 2006; Hamilton and Friesen, 2013). Technology is a 'double-edged sword' that can both empower and disable groups of users. Compounding this, as technologies evolve, previous assistive technologies can become outdated, the results of a negative 'accessibility cycle' in which technologies are designed without considering accessibility and the requirements of specific user groups (Katseva, 2004). For example, the addition of voice chat in the virtual online world Second Life created a barrier for the deaf and hard of hearing where there had not been one before (Carr, 2011). Universal Design for Learning (UDL) aims to reduce this effect by insisting that 'pedagogical and technical issues must be addressed in order for courses to be welcoming to, accessible to, and usable by all students' (Burgstahler, 2015: 71). UDL has its roots in universal design principles for physical and built environments (Connell et al., 1997) and has been the basis for a number of frameworks for postsecondary instruction and curriculum (McGuire, 2014). Indeed, with its principled and practical approach, UDL has often been conflated with 'just good teaching' (Edyburn, 2010: 38). We have already seen how infrastructure and design greatly increased the inclusivity of UoL in the nineteenth century, with female students taking advantage of the 'invisibility' of distance education. As discussed in Chapter 8, UDL provides a method for capitalising on the potential for inclusion as technology advances by investigating how all students use and interact with their learning environments.

## Inclusion and multiculturalism

The deficit model of disability has affected attitudes towards inclusion in HE. Understanding the dangerous and damaging limitations of this model is the starting point for inclusive education and pedagogy. Deficit thinking does not only apply to conceptions of (dis)ability; research into multiculturalism and education has explored deficit thinking with regards to race and cultural heritage (Brandon, 2003; Ippolito, 2007; Valencia, 2010). Writing specifically about online environments in which invisibility or anonymity could be seen as creating a level playing field for all students, Nakamura (2013: 4) critiques this 'ideology of liberation from marginalised and devalued bodies'. While anonymity may free students from fears of stigma or prejudice, it does this by insisting users adhere to normative notions of behaviour, identity and expression (Pitcan et al., 2018). Such a view also discounts the cultural specificity that users bring to online spaces. Even images and icons have been found to have different meanings depending on the cultural context or background of the viewer (Griffin et al., 1995) and, although members of a community will assume their way of constructing knowledge is universal (Mor and Abdu, 2018), this assumption implicitly undermines and excludes students from different regions or cultures (Bozkurt et al., 2017). Rather than being universal and neutral, instructional design is culturally grounded (Chen et al., 1999; Mor and Abdu, 2018; Parrish and Linder-VanBerschot, 2010).

It has been argued that the first step towards inclusion based on a knowledge of diverse students, as opposed to inclusion based on ignorance of differences, is for course designers and instructors to become aware that their own pedagogical assumptions are the product of a distinct, often European, educational tradition (Altbach, 2014; Henderson, 1996; Mor and Abdu, 2018; Parrish and Linder-VanBerschot, 2010). McLoughlin (2001: 9) argues that 'the cultural dimensions of learning must be constantly problematised and not marginalised'. For McLoughlin, this means internationalising the curriculum, valuing cultural differences and designing for sharing, collaborative learning opportunities. At an institutional level, the UK's Office for Students recommends a holistic approach to addressing inequalities for specific minority ethnic groups 'ensuring a balance of interventions across the full student lifecycle' (Stevenson et al., 2019: 7).

**Example**

**A student story: the educational experiences of a learner with a hidden disability**

As a child I had an extremely complex relationship with school. I was very bookish and keen to learn, but I was put off by constant bullying from reception class onward and the teaching hierarchy where the student never knows best. The way I was ill made both of those situations much worse. From age 11 onwards the signs of my mental health condition were readily evident and I found myself often unable to engage with traditional education. When I wasn't at school, I was intent on teaching myself. I have always read constantly, and SparkNotes also supplemented the worksheets I was sent home from teachers. I attempted to teach myself A-level subjects whilst in a psychiatric hospital in my late teens. It turns out that powerful sedatives, hallucinating spitting evil cats and teaching yourself how to write an essay don't go well together. I wished there was a way to prove my capability and knowledge without being in mainstream education. That's when I began engaging with distance learning. It was a way of learning that enabled me to be properly supported whilst essentially teaching myself.

My relationship with distance learning is complex. In long periods where I have been unable to leave the house, or a hospital, I have seen distance learning as a way of maintaining my study skills and a degree of hope for a future where I can return to a classroom. However, it hasn't always worked out like that. Distance learning has its pros and cons. There is no doubt that some courses out there are around purely to make money and quality varies severely.

There are many positives to be found in distance learning, especially when looking at access. It is comparably easy to enrol on courses and people who have missed out on a high school education, due to illness or other circumstances, can often get a place despite not having a solid set of A levels. It can be more practical than having to go into a classroom, especially for people who are unable to leave home or a hospital. You can also often build up credits towards courses from a variety of subject areas; this particularly helped me as, due to the way my brain is structured, I often leap from interest to interest.

> I was also able to take part in a distance learning course from a psychiatric hospital. This helped give me something to do during a difficult period. At that time, it was possible to send in coursework, etc., via post rather than online. Now that there is a definite shift to online only, I think that many people in hospital without internet access will no longer be able to study distance learning courses.
>
> There are a number of prominent areas for improvement with distance learning. For example, the shift upwards in price means that people are no longer able to learn for personal interest reasons. Personal interest learning is something which is not currently seen as valuable to society. Yet education allows people to think for themselves and I feel that learning for personal interest should be encouraged, whilst the price of courses at the moment is causing the opposite to occur. This particularly affects disabled people who may have previously used learning for personal interest as a stepping stone to further engagement in society.

## Accessible teaching and learning content

This section addresses the removal of barriers or inequalities to increase access to materials used as part of a distance learning course. However, it should be mentioned that it does not cover access to courses and degree programmes more generally. Without access to courses, there is no access to content. This level of access is affected by acceptance criteria, entry requirements or financial costs (Prodan et al., 2015). Addressed here are aspects of accessible teaching and learning content and why there is a need to aim for equitable access to materials.

### Non-technical solutions to content accessibility

Technology can both increase access and reduce it; making content more accessible does not always require a technological solution or approach. Using an inclusive practice approach can mean making content easier to understand. The Jisc (2017) guide, 'Meeting the requirements of learners with special educational needs' includes the following recommendations:

- a clear outline of each lesson
- clear, unambiguous language
- information in a variety of forms

- repetition
- signpost changes to: routines; class or group work; new or additional content; new language or concepts.

It states that these recommendations will be of particular relevance to those with disabilities but will help all learners. The recommendations would certainly benefit those students with invisible or unreported disabilities, as well as those with officially registered needs for accommodation. These are students who require special mention here, as demonstrated by the previous student story, as well as research indicating that staff appear to be less confident in supporting students with hidden disabilities, particularly mental health and autism (Pearson et al., 2019).

## Access in the global university

Making content accessible should be about making it available at all times to meet the needs of all users. Content that must be accessed live, such as a video or audio webinar, can reduce access for certain users. In the global world of distance and online learning, students could be spread across multiple time zones or, more simply, students may choose distance education because of the flexibility it provides compared to having to be at lectures or tutorials at specific times. Unless live content is recorded and made available after the event, these students' access is substantially diminished. Similarly, activities that are built around synchronous interactions may exclude users not available at the time needed. As such, asynchronous interactions, such as discussion forums, are common communication methods in modern virtual learning environments (VLEs).

As the context here is one of distance education, which is often assumed to have evolved into online education (Lee, 2017), connection to the web is crucial. In some cases, improving access to the internet can increase access to distance education courses. In areas where internet service or electricity supply is intermittent or low compared to the average expected in more economically developed regions such as Europe and North America, access to content can be a problem (Bolger, 2009). Content that requires high bandwidth becomes inaccessible in the context of a global classroom where some students have connectivity limitations (Czerniewicz, 2018; Hilbert, 2014). Furthermore, global and local digital divides limit the availability for disabled students of the very technologies that may provide inclusivity to online resources (Wu and Taneja, 2016). Even where access to such technologies exists, students may have limited knowledge of their availability or how they technically work to address accessibility needs. Distance learners may need to be taught the vocabulary to find and navigate assistive technologies and features.

## Assistive technology

There is a wide variety of software and hardware that can be used by disabled people to interact with digital content. Typically, these take the form of alternative input and display technologies: a screen reader like JAWS can enable a visually impaired user to consume text content in aural form, alternative devices are used by those with mobility impairments that prevent them from using a keyboard or mouse and speech recognition software can allow voice commands and speech-to-text input. These are vital to distance education that is delivered in digital formats, as are features in web browsers that allow personalisation for accessibility, such as zooming, changing colour contrast or switching to more readable fonts. Being aware of assistive technologies is vital to designing inclusive distance learning and, by meeting Web Content Accessibility Guidelines (WCAG) standards (discussed later in the chapter), content should become compatible with common assistive technologies.

VLEs are effectively websites and should have been built and updated using the WCAG 2.1 standards. Blackboard Learn, for example, has accessibility features such as full support for captions on all media types and there are a variety of accessibility-related plug-ins available for use with Moodle. Similarly, many content authoring or creation tools will have been built with web accessibility in mind and already have features built in to make content more accessible. However, this is not always a given and technology providers and maintainers should be held to account for the conformity of their technologies to accessibility standards.

Furthermore, alignment of content creation tools to standards does not ensure that all content created with them will be accessible. Despite technology allowing content to be accessible, it still needs content creators to follow correct procedures. If not, content may be assumed to be accessible until it is tested. For example, a PDF constructed without tagging images may appear fine, but a screen reader will not detect the content of such images, excluding any students reliant on this assistive technology from these components of the resource. Research has shown that a technically accessible VLE cannot make up for exclusionary pedagogy and design of learning (Parsons, 2017). Policies (which link governance to practice and provide a point of reference for stakeholders) and guides (which form the link between the recommendations and the processes involved in making accessible content) can help content creators successfully produce accessible materials. Some of these will be explored later in this chapter.

## Legislation

There is a legal obligation to promote and protect the rights of disabled people. For example, the United Nations Convention on the Rights of Persons with Disabilities (CRPD), which was adopted in 2006, is an international legal agreement covering a wide range of areas, including education and access to information (United Nations, 2007). As of May 2022, 164 countries have signed the treaty, including the UK, Australia and the USA (United Nations, n.d.). The successes of the CRPD, however, should not mask the fact that that the global situation is complex and inconsistent; the 'GEM report summary on disabilities and education' found that 'data remains insufficient to assess progress, leaving widespread inequality related to disabilities still concealed' (UNESCO, 2018: 1). It is also worth noting that the CRPD relates to all levels of education. This means that the primary focus is compulsory schooling for children; only where this is sufficiently inclusive can tertiary education begin to meet its obligations towards disabled students.

Of relevance to UoL's distance learning provision, in 2009, the UK ratified the CRPD and agreed that they would work to 'Ensure the education system at all levels is inclusive and geared towards supporting disabled people to achieve their full potential and participate equally in society' (Disability Rights UK, 2019). This applies to all students studying in UK institutions, whether they are UK citizens or not and regardless of their country of residence during their studies (Britishcouncil.org, n.d.), meaning it is equally applicable to international distance learning students. For UoL, the CRPD is a new step within a recognised framework. The UK had already been developing anti-disability discrimination laws and its 1998 Human Rights Act was based on principles such as dignity, fairness, equality, respect and autonomy, including the concept that everybody has the right to an effective education (Disability Rights UK, 2019). This was in line with international trends in disability legislation. In the late twentieth century, many countries passed acts protecting the rights of disabled citizens, such as the Americans with Disabilities Act in 1990 and Australia's Disability Discrimination Act in 1992.

Since signing the CRPD, the UK's 2010 Equality Act has provided greater legal protection against discrimination and has emphasised education providers' legal duty to make reasonable adjustments so disabled people can take part in education. Under this Act, HE institutions must have 'due regard' for the need to eliminate unlawful discrimination, to advance equality of opportunity and foster good relations between people who have particular protected characteristics, including those with a disability and without (UK Government, 2010: 149).

Legislation can have a large impact on improving inclusion, firstly by providing a definition of disability and discrimination and secondly by requiring bodies to demonstrate compliance. For example, under the Equality Act, disability is defined as any physical or mental impairment that has a substantial adverse effect on the person's ability to carry out normal day-to-day activities and is likely to last more than 12 months (UK Government, 2010: 6). The Act also sets out the two different types of unlawful discrimination:

- Direct discrimination is when a university treats a student less favourably because of their disability.
- Indirect discrimination is when a university has policies and procedures in place that have a worse impact on disabled students compared to students who are not disabled. Failure to make reasonable adjustments for a disabled student is also considered discrimination under this legislation.

The UK Equality Act requires public bodies, including universities, to set themselves specific, measurable equality objectives for combatting discrimination against those with disabilities, including making reasonable adjustments to meet the needs of disabled students. This is an anticipatory duty, which means service providers and people exercising public functions must anticipate the needs of disabled people and make appropriate reasonable adjustments (section 20 of the Act).[1] The anticipatory duty requires institutions to prepare all learning environments to provide for disabled students and to consider accessibility throughout the development of all provisions. Institutions must anticipate the types of barriers that students with various impairments may face. They must also anticipate the adjustments they can make to remove these barriers. This includes accessibility of buildings, teaching and student services (Disability Rights UK, 2019).

Compliance with equality legislation promotes inclusion. A university that is able to provide services to meet the diverse needs of its students will support all students, including those with different learning styles. While legislation is not the only reason for prioritising inclusion in education, it is invaluable as a basis for producing and supporting policies and strategies to increase inclusion in universities.

## Web content accessibility guidelines

Online content presents new challenges for accessibility and inclusion. In 1999, WCAG 1.0, comprising 14 key guidelines, became a World Wide Web Consortium (W3C) recommendation. These were updated in 2008 as WCAG 2.0 and again in 2018 as WCAG 2.1. However, as the name suggests, these were developed as guidelines rather than legislation (W3C, n.d.).

### WCAG 2.1 Guidelines

Principle 1: Perceivable – information and user interface components must be presentable to users in ways they can perceive.

> Guideline 1.1 Text alternatives. Provide text alternatives for any non-text component so that it can be changed into other forms people need.
> Guideline 1.2 Time-based media. Provide alternatives for time-based media, such as video and audio recordings.
> Guideline 1.3 Adaptable. Create content that can be presented in different ways without losing information or structure.
> Guideline 1.4 Distinguishable. Make it easier for users to see and hear content, including separating foreground from background.

Principle 2: Operable – user interface components and navigation must be operable.

> Guideline 2.1 Keyboard accessibility. Make all functionality available from a keyboard.
> Guideline 2.2 Enough time. Provide users enough time to read and use content.
> Guideline 2.3 Seizures and physical reactions. Do not design content in a way that is known to cause seizures or physical reactions.
> Guideline 2.4 Navigable. Provide ways to help users navigate, find content and determine where they are.
> Guideline 2.5 Input modalities. Make it easier for users to operate functionality through various inputs beyond keyboard.

Principle 3: Understandable – information and the operation of user interface must be understandable.

Guideline 3.1 Readability. Make text content readable and understandable.
Guideline 3.2 Predictable. Make web pages appear and operate in predictable ways.
Guideline 3.3 Input assistance. Help users avoid and correct mistakes.

Principle 4: Robust – content must be robust enough to be interpreted reliably by a wide variety of user agents, including assistive technologies.

Guideline 4.1 Compatible. Maximise compatibility with current and future user agents, including assistive technologies.

In June 2018, the EU set out the first implementation deadlines for the EU Web Accessibility Directive, which added enforcement mechanisms to WCAG 2.1, requiring member states to transpose the directive into their national laws by September 2018. To comply with the directive, all public sector websites and apps (including VLEs and password-protected institutional intranets) had to:

- comply with WCAG 2.1 guidelines
- have a publicly posted, regularly updated accessibility statement, explaining accessible content standards
- have an accessible feedback mechanism.

As with the anti-discrimination legislation discussed, it can be hard to assess international compliance with these guidelines, both in terms of monitoring and enforcing (Lewthwaite and James, 2020; UNESCO, 2018). However, they do stand as a vital resource for institutions seeking to meet their obligations to diverse students, especially those who are reliant on the internet for their university education.

## Improving inclusivity

### Common issues across universities

Possibly the most intimidating difficulty facing anyone working towards this is the size of the challenge; infrastructure and attitudes create realities of experience for students and staff alike and these can be extremely hard to change. Issues of inclusion can impact every aspect of an institution and, as explored, are complex, requiring operational and strategic planning. As concluded by May and Bridger (2010), change is required at both an institutional and individual level to bring about inclusive policy and practice, a finding supported by Terras et al. (2015: 335): 'successful online accommodation are a result of specific efforts made by students, instructors, and the institution'.

An initial challenge within an institution can be the establishment of a shared vocabulary. The word 'inclusion' can be interpreted differently in different contexts, but how it is understood has a central and iterative impact on policy decisions and stakeholder experience across the institution.

Given the scope and centrality of inclusion in distance education, early stakeholder involvement is crucial for its effective practise across an institution. Even where key stakeholders are in general agreement about theories around inclusion, they may not necessarily agree on how, or even if, these should affect the practical day-to-day work management and operations of an institution. It can also be a challenge to move from a focus on a specific issue to do with access, equality and inclusion to a more comprehensive approach and strategy (Jørgensen and Claeys-Kulik, 2018).

However, if a stakeholder's interpretation of inclusion is that immediate action and reflection is needed, this can lead to a culture change that will feed into positive responses to new strategies and policies around inclusion. For example, in their report on change initiatives across ten UK universities, May and Bridger (2010: 78) found:

> The changing of particular words or phrases (such as using the word 'entitlement' rather than 'need') or the use of inclusive messages (such as 'inclusive practices enhance the learning of all students') were found to make a substantial impact upon stakeholders and promote a culture that fosters the success of all students.

Inclusion in education means being both proactive (ensuring all learners are supported and catered for) and reactive (removing barriers to individuals or groups of learners). It requires buy-in and infrastructure to support staff and students (Macy et al., 2018; May and Bridger, 2010; Pettigrew and Tropp, 2006; Terras et al., 2015). The range of stakeholders within institutions can be broad, including students, support staff, teaching staff and management, and all of them can be impacted by improvements in inclusivity:

- Students can often be the benefactors of improvements, but should also be consulted at times.

- Support and teaching staff are often those who create or curate course content that needs to be inclusive, from curriculum design to the addition of specific learning materials.
- Management at many levels need to be involved in terms of the moral and legal institutional responsibility, as well as making decisions and implementing changes at department or institution level.

Understanding who is involved and impacted by improvements to inclusivity is extremely important in deciding who is going to make the changes. Successful inclusion in education is tied directly to a university's culture and mission and will be supported by appropriate policies and strategies that speak to stakeholders' experiences and understanding of this.

With staff turnover, changes in student population and developments in assistive technology it is important to facilitate training on how to improve inclusivity and produce accessible resources so that inclusive practices can be sustained. For example, incorporating inclusion or accessibility as a topic into existing continuing professional development courses can show a more integrated approach to inclusion and demonstrates how it is embedded into the institution's ethos far more successfully than standalone sessions covering a range of inclusion training needs. Creating opportunities for sharing good practice prevents isolated members of staff 'reinventing the wheel' and also models a respectful, inclusive approach, contributing to improved standards and awareness of inclusion in the university.

In conclusion, despite the range of complex issues and individual factors involved, there are some key recommendations for addressing common issues in improving inclusion across institutions. Firstly, it is always worth investing in the preliminary stages of any new initiative, by starting early with the planning, engaging stakeholders as soon as possible and managing the project carefully. Pilots can be useful in this, though the key is to embed strategy and sustain momentum (Wray, 2013). Secondly, it is also recommended to engage the support of high-level managers and work with staff from across the university in developing strategy and driving forward change (May and Bridger, 2010). Finally, promoting and disseminating strategy and best practice across an institution can help inclusion by creating a shared vocabulary and culture (May and Bridger, 2010). For example, UoL has a publicly available Inclusive Practice Policy,[2] which sets out its aim and expectations for inclusive practices across the university. Although the size of the challenge can be daunting and will vary depending on the area of focus and the specific institutional conditions, there are common guidelines for a strategic approach to inclusive practice (Jisc, 2017). By investing in stakeholder engagement, institutional culture and robust and appropriate strategy and policy, for example, the challenge can be addressed with sustainable impact on students and staff.

## Common issues in improving inclusivity and accessibility of existing courses

One key challenge in improving inclusion is the fact that systems, attitudes and resources already exist and updating these can be an intimidatingly large and demoralising task. Ideally, inclusive practice will have been built into course design from the start. In reality, however, this may not be the case, especially with established, older courses.

Initially, a decision will have to be made about resourcing. A balance needs to be struck between time spent reviewing and updating existing materials and time spent developing new courses based on universal design principles, with the idea that these will be more future-proof due to their sound theoretical underpinnings. Ideally, a consistent approach can be found for both, for example, by auditing existing courses using the same checklist as that developed for creating new courses. Such a checklist could include:

- text on screen added by users
- video content
- audio content
- hyperlinks
- files, such as PDFs and Microsoft Office documents
- images, photos, figures and graphs
- third-party resources or tools.

Universal design principles cannot be applied to courses retroactively, but the inclusivity of existing courses can be improved by addressing deficits in the current provision. In the first instance, improvements can be made by ensuring all new materials for existing courses comply with inclusivity best practice; for example, by using this checklist to audit how existing materials adhere to WAG 2.1 guidelines. There is still likely to be a considerable backlog, however, which will need to be tackled systematically and realistically; for example, by prioritising and streamlining processes to address the most pressing concerns, be they captioning for videos, the production of accessible PDFs or the addition of 'alt-text' for images.

Similarly, on a content level, existing readings, case studies and examples should be reviewed with a focus on how they could be received by diverse student groups. For example, do such materials represent only a certain limited section of society and thus imply that those that do not belong to this privileged group are less connected to the subject being covered? Additional, specifically chosen readings or images can address this in the short term, without requiring extensive content revision. It is not necessary to radically rewrite a course in order for it to reflect a more mindful, inclusive approach on the part of its author.

## Considerations for designing new courses

The ideal time to enact and embed inclusive practices is when new courses are being designed. Planning a course with universal design principles in mind means that accommodation for students can become a natural and integral component of the course, rather than a 'bolt-on' requiring additional resources.

The development of new courses can be an opportunity for staff and students to explore new tools, ideas and ways of learning; for example, employing UDL principles (Burgstahler, 2009) by:

- adopting practices that reflect high values with respect to diversity and inclusiveness
- encouraging regular and effective interactions between students and the instructor (and ensuring that communication methods are accessible to all participants)
- ensuring that materials, activities, equipment and facilities are physically accessible to, and usable by, all students
- using multiple, accessible instructional methods
- ensuring that course materials, notes and other information resources are engaging, flexible and accessible for all students
- providing specific feedback on a regular basis
- regularly assessing student progress using multiple accessible methods and tools – and adjusting instruction accordingly
- planning for accommodation for students whose needs are not met by the instructional design.

This requires a collaborative approach, with support from different members of staff beyond an individual instructor. As with inclusive education itself, there is no 'one-size-fits-all' model for producing courses that meet a specific institution's inclusion needs. Training and support in line with the guidance and examples below can be adapted to work within different contexts, but with the same aim of improving inclusivity for all students.

## Practical summary with examples of good practice

### UCL: accessibility materials

UCL provides guidance on its website for creating accessible content plus an e-learning wiki that includes accessibility as a topic.[3] The information here mainly describes how to ensure content meets accessibility requirements. The wiki has been created with a Creative Commons licence, which allows sharing and adaptation with attribution (CC BY-SA 4.0).[4] This addition makes it easier for the creators to share good practice and allows others to compare what they are doing in order that they can learn from them. It also means other institutions can use the information in this resource without reinventing it or starting from scratch, making standards more consistent across institutions and countries and reducing the individual workloads for making content more inclusive.

Additionally, UCL's page on assistive technology (UCL, n.d.) is aimed at students who may benefit from assistive technologies and provides lists of free alternatives to paid versions. This includes accessibility options that help with reading screens, information on tools for helping time management and planning and accessibility tools built into devices. This highlights an important part of improving inclusivity – that of empowering the students to help themselves. Without guidance, students may not be able to help themselves due to a lack of information about the options, tools or assistance available to them.

### UoL Inclusive Practice Panel

UoL's distance education department has an Inclusive Practice Panel, which is responsible for its policies and procedures relating to inclusive practice and accessibility (UoL Panel, n.d.). Its aims include raising awareness of inclusive practice and ensuring learning resources are accessible to all. As a committee of mixed roles and responsibilities, with both internal and external members, the panel is able to connect to higher levels of management with an advisory function and also connect with staff who have experience of working directly with inclusive practice issues and procedures. Having a separate committee dedicated to inclusive practice has brought about positive changes, such as reviewing and changing special examination arrangements and the development of a VLE inclusive practice policy. These may have been difficult to implement or identify without the specific focus on improving inclusivity.

### University of Edinburgh: accessibility materials
The University of Edinburgh has provided detailed accessibility information on its website (University of Edinburgh, n.d.). This includes information and helpful links for staff, students and the public on assistive technology and creation of accessible materials. By providing this information in a central location, easily available to users, it is more likely to be found and benefit those who need it.

### University of Auckland: accessibility materials
The University of Auckland has created a framework of expectations for students and staff for the inclusion of students with impairments within their university (University of Auckland, n.d.b). This includes guidelines for specified groups, including students with impairments, teaching staff and faculties. Although some of the information is only relevant to the physical environment, most of it is applicable to distance learning. Providing guidelines for all in a single location allows different groups to see what the expectations are for themselves as well as others.

A broader policy related to inclusivity is one of equitable education (University of Auckland, n.d.a). This policy applies to all members of the university, but also includes information specific to New Zealand in recognition of 'the distinct status of Māori' and aiming achieving equity for them and other groups. This highlights differences in improving inclusivity in different nations or regions of the world, where specific peoples may need to be acknowledged in inclusivity policies and practices.

### UDL, Ministry of Education, New Zealand
The Ministry of Education in New Zealand has produced a guide to UDL (New Zealand Government, n.d.). Although this resource was created for the school education system in New Zealand, it is included here because of the style and format of delivering the information to educators online. By making the information interesting, engaging and accessible, educators are more likely to learn from it and to understand the why and the how of making their teaching more inclusive.

## Conclusions

This chapter has provided an outline of key issues around inclusion in HE, with a focus on those that have affected the practices and policies of UoL. Located in the UK and serving a diverse, global, student cohort, UoL has unique, but by no means exceptional, challenges in ensuring equitable access to education and materials. By bringing together geographically disparate authors with a range of access requirements and personal situations, this chapter demonstrates the benefits of an inclusive approach. Although there have been challenges, exacerbated by the disruption of the COVID-19 pandemic, this approach has demonstrated the strength of designing for inclusion and sharing a vision and common vocabulary for addressing the topic. With the potentially disabling effects of the global pandemic, inclusion is more important than ever in helping institutions and students achieve their goals for HE.

## Notes

1. See https://www.legislation.gov.uk/ukpga/2010/15/section/20.
2. See https://london.ac.uk/sites/default/files/governance/inclusive-practice-policy.pdf.
3. For more information see the following: https://www.ucl.ac.uk/isd/services/websites-apps/creating-accessible-content/documents; https://wiki.ucl.ac.uk/display/UCLELearning; https://wiki.ucl.ac.uk/display/UCLELearning/Accessibility.
4. https://creativecommons.org/licenses/by-sa/4.0/.

## References

Adelman, P. B. and Vogel, S. A. (2006) 'College graduates with learning disabilities: Employment attainment and career patterns'. *Learning Disability Quarterly*, 13 (3), 154–66. Accessed 23 July 2022. https://doi.org/10.2307/1510698.

Altbach, P. G. (2014) 'MOOCs as neocolonialism: Who controls knowledge?' *International Higher Education*, 75, 5–7. Accessed 24 July 2022. https://doi.org/10.6017/ihe.2014.75.5426.

Barnard-Brak, L., Davis, T., Tate, A. and Sulak, T. (2009) 'Attitudes as a predictor of college students requesting accommodations'. *Journal of Vocational Rehabilitation*, 31 (3), 189–98. Accessed 24 July 2022. https://doi.org/10.3233/JVR-2009-0488.

Bolger, M. (2009) 'Globalization: An opportunity for the "uneducated" to become "learned" or further "excluded"?' In U. Bernath, A. Szücs, A. Tait and M. Vida (eds), *Distance and e-Learning in Transition: Learning innovation, technology and social challenges*. London: ISTE Ltd, 303–10.

Boxall, K., Carson, I. and Docherty, D. (2004) 'Room at the academy? People with learning difficulties and higher education'. *Disability and Society*, 19 (2), 99–112. Accessed 24 July 2022. https://doi.org/10.1080/0968759042000181749.

Bozkurt, A., Yazıcı, M. and Aydın, İ. E. (2017) 'Cultural diversity and its implications in online networked learning spaces'. In E. Toprak and E. G. Kumtepe (eds), *Supporting Multiculturalism in Open and Distance Learning Spaces*. Hershey, PA: IGI-Global, 56–81. Accessed 24 July 2022. https://doi.org/10.4018/978-1-5225-3076-3.ch004.

Brandon, W. W. (2003) 'Toward a white teachers' guide to playing fair: Exploring the cultural politics of multicultural teaching?' *International Journal of Qualitative Studies in Education*, 16 (1), 31–50. Accessed 24 July 2022. https://doi.org/10.1080/0951839032000033518.

Britishcouncil.org (n.d.) 'Study-UK: Disability and special needs'. Accessed 23 June 2020. https://study-uk.britishcouncil.org/moving-uk/support-guidance/disability.

Burgstahler, S. (2009) 'Universal Design of Instruction (UDI): Definition, principles, guidelines, and examples', DO-IT. Accessed 24 July 2022. https://www.washington.edu/doit/universal-design-instruction-udi-definition-principles-guidelines-and-examples.

Burgstahler, S. (2015) 'Opening doors or slamming them shut? Online learning practices and students with disabilities'. *Social Inclusion*, 3 (6), 69–79. Accessed 24 July 2022. https://doi.org/10.17645/si.v3i6.420.

Carr, D. (2011) 'Constructing disability in online worlds; Conceptualising disability in online research'. In A. Peachey and M. Childs (eds), *Reinventing Ourselves: Contemporary concepts of identity in virtual worlds*. London: Springer, 177–90. Accessed 24 July 2022. https://doi.org/10.1007/978-0-85729-361-9.

Chen, A.-Y., Mashhadi, A., Ang, D. and Harkrider, N. (1999) 'Cultural issues in the design of technology-enhanced learning systems'. *British Journal of Educational Technology*, 30 (3), 217–30. Accessed 24 July 2022. https://doi.org/10.1111/1467-8535.00111.

Connell, B., Jones, M., Mace, R., Mueller, J., Mullick, A., Ostroff, E., Sanford, J., Steinfeld, E., Story, M. and Vanderheiden, G. (1997) 'The principles of universal design: Version 2.0', Center for Universal Design poster. Accessed 10 June 2019. https://projects.ncsu.edu/design/cud/pubs_p/docs/poster.pdf.

Czerniewicz, L. (2018) 'Inequality as higher education goes online'. In N. Bonderup Dohn, S. Cranmer, J. A. Sime, M. de Laat and T. Ryberg (eds), *Networked Learning: Research in networked learning*. Cham: Springer, 95–106.

Dickens, C. (ed.) (1859) 'The English people's university'. *All the Year Round: A Weekly Journal*, 16 July, 279–83.

Disability Rights UK (2019) 'Understanding the Equality Act: Information for disabled students', Disability Rights UK Factsheet F56. Accessed 11 September 2019. https://www.disabilityrightsuk.org/understanding-equality-act-information-disabled-students.

Dolmage, J. T. (2017) *Academic Ableism: Disability and higher education*. Ann Arbor: University of Michigan Press.

Edyburn, D. L. (2010) 'Would you recognize Universal Design for Learning if you saw it? Ten propositions for new directions for the second decade of UDL'. *Learning Disability Quarterly*, 33 (1), 33–41. Accessed 24 July 2022. https://doi.org/10.1177/073194871003300103.

Fossey, E., Chaffey, L., Venville, A., Ennals, P., Douglas, J. and Bigby, C. (2017) 'Navigating the complexity of disability support in tertiary education: Perspectives of students and disability service staff'. *International Journal of Inclusive Education*, 21 (8), 822–32. Accessed 24 July 2022. https://doi.org/10.1080/13603116.2017.1278798.

Getzel, E. E. and Thoma, C. A. (2008) 'Experiences of college students with disabilities and the importance of self-determination in higher education settings'. *Career Development for Exceptional Individuals*, 31 (2), 77–84. Accessed 24 July 2022. https://doi.org/10.1177/0885728808317658.

Griffin, R. E., Pettersson, R., Somali, L. and Takakuwa, Y. (1995) 'Using symbols in international business presentations: How well are they understood'. In D. G. Beauchamp, A. B. Roberts and R. E. Griffin (eds), *Imagery and Visual Literacy: Selected readings*. Loretto, PA: International Visual Literacy Association, 182–9. Accessed 24 July 2022. https://files.eric.ed.gov/fulltext/ED380079.pdf.

Guillaume, L. (2011) 'Critical race and disability framework. A new paradigm for understanding discrimination against people from non-English speaking backgrounds and Indigenous people with disability'. *Critical Race and Whiteness Studies*, 7, 6–19.

Hamilton, E. C. and Friesen, N. (2013) 'Online education: A science and technology studies perspective/Éducation en ligne: Perspective des études en science et technologie'. *CJLT/RCAT (Canadian Journal of Learning and Technology/La Revue canadienne de l'apprentissage et de la technologie)*, 39 (2). Accessed 24 July 2022. https://doi.org/10.21432/T2001C.

Harry, B. and Klingner, J. (2007) 'Discarding the deficit model minorities in special ed'. *Educational Leadership*, 64 (5), 16–21.

Haughey, D. J. (2007) 'Ethical relationships between instructor, learner and institution'. *Open Learning: The Journal of Open, Distance and e-Learning*, 22 (2) 139–47. Accessed 24 July 2022. https://doi.org/10.1080/02680510701306681.

Henderson, L. (1996) 'Instructional design of interactive multimedia: A cultural critique'. *ETR&D*, 44 (4), 85–104.

Hersh, M. and Mouroutsou, S. (2019) 'Learning technology and disability – overcoming barriers to inclusion: Evidence from a multicountry study'. *British Journal of Educational Technology*, 50 (6), 3329–44.

Hilbert, M. (2014) 'Technological information inequality as an incessantly moving target: The redistribution of information and communication capacities between 1986 and 2010'. *Journal of the Association for Information Science and Technology*, 65 (4), 821–35. Accessed 24 July 2022. https://doi.org/10.1002/asi.23020.

Ippolito, K. (2007) 'Promoting intercultural learning in a multicultural university: Ideals and realities'. *Teaching in Higher Education*, 12 (5–6), 749–63. Accessed 24 July 2022. https://doi.org/10.1080/13562510701596356.

Jacklin, A., Robinson, C., O'Meara, L. and Harris, A. (2007) 'Improving the experiences of disabled students in higher education'. *Higher Education*, 1. Accessed 24 July 2022. https://www.researchgate.net/publication/253525979_Improving_the_Experiences_of_Disabled_Students_in_Higher_Education.

Jisc (2017) 'Meeting the requirements of learners with special educational needs', guide. Accessed 24 July 2022. https://www.jisc.ac.uk/full-guide/meeting-the-requirements-of-learners-with-special-educational-needs.

Jørgensen, T. E. and Claeys-Kulik, A.-L. (2018) *Universities' Strategies and Approaches towards Diversity, Equity and Inclusion: Examples from across Europe*. Brussels: European University Association.

Katseva, A. (2004) 'The case for pervasive accessibility'. Paper presented at the Center on Disabilities: Technology and Persons with Disabilities Conference 2004. Accessed 24 July 2022. http://www.csun.edu/~hfdss006/conf/2004/proceedings/114.htm.

Kent, M. (2015) 'Disability and eLearning: Opportunities and barriers'. *Disability Studies Quarterly*, 35 (1). Accessed 24 July 2022. http://dsq-sds.org/article/view/3815/3830.

Kenyon-Jones, C. (2008) *The People's University: 150 years of the University of London and its external students*. London: University of London External System.

Lee, K. (2017) 'Rethinking the accessibility of online higher education: A historical review'. *Internet and Higher Education*, 33, 15–23. Accessed 24 July 2022. https://doi.org/10.1016/j.iheduc.2017.01.001.

Lewthwaite, S. and James, A. (2020) 'Accessible at last? What do new European digital accessibility laws mean for disabled people in the UK?' *Disability & Society*, 35 (8), 1360–5. Accessed 24 July 2022. https://doi.org/10.1080/09687599.2020.1717446.

Liasidou, A. (2015) *Inclusive Education and the Issue of Change*. London: Palgrave Macmillan UK. Accessed 24 July 2022. https://doi.org/10.1057/9781137333704.

Lindsay, S., Cagliostro, E. and Carafa, G. (2018) 'A systematic review of barriers and facilitators of disability disclosure and accommodations for youth in post-secondary education'. *International Journal of Disability, Development and Education*, 65 (5), 526–56. Accessed 24 July 2022. https://doi.org/10.1080/1034912X.2018.1430352.

Lovern, L. L. (2018) *Fostering a Climate of Inclusion in the College Classroom: The missing voice of the humanities*. Cham: Palgrave Macmillan. Accessed 24 July 2022. https://doi.org/10.1007/978-3-319-75367-6.

McGuire, J. M. (2014) 'Universally accessible instruction: Oxymoron or opportunity?' *Journal of Postsecondary Education and Disability*, 27 (4), 387–98.

McLoughlin, C. (2001) 'Inclusivity and alignment: Principles of pedagogy, task and assessment design for effective cross-cultural online learning'. *Distance Education*, 22 (1), 7–29. Accessed 24 July 2022. https://doi.org/10.1080/0158791010220102.

Macy, M., Macy, R. and Shaw, M. (2018) 'Bringing the ivory tower into students' homes: Promoting accessibility in online courses'. *Ubiquitous Learning: An International Journal*, 11 (1), 13–21. Accessed 24 July 2022. https://doi.org/10.18848/1835-9795/cgp/v11i01/13-21.

Marginson, S. (2004) 'Don't leave me hanging on the old anglophone: The potential for online distance higher education in the Asia Pacific region'. *Higher Education Quarterly*, 58 (2–3), 74–113.

May, H. and Bridger, K. (2010) 'Developing and embedding inclusive policy and practice in higher education', Higher Education Academy report, January. Accessed 24 July 2022. https://s3.eu-west-2.amazonaws.com/assets.creode.advancehe-document-manager/documents/hea/private/developingembeddinginclusivepp_report_1568036692.pdf.

Mor, Y. and Abdu, R. (2018) 'Responsive learning design: Epistemic fluency and generative pedagogical practices'. *British Journal of Educational Technology*, 49 (6), 1162–73. Accessed 24 July 2022. https://doi.org/10.1111/bjet.12704.

Moriña, A. (2017) 'Inclusive education in higher education: Challenges and opportunities'. *European Journal of Special Needs Education*, 32 (1), 3–17. Accessed 24 July 2022. https://doi.org/10.1080/08856257.2016.1254964.

Mullins, L. and Preyde, M. (2013) 'The lived experience of students with an invisible disability at a Canadian university'. *Disability and Society*, 28 (2), 147–60. Accessed 24 July 2022. https://doi.org/10.1080/09687599.2012.752127.

Nakamura, L. (2013) *Cybertypes: Race, ethnicity, and identity on the internet*. New York: Routledge.

New Zealand Government (n.d.) 'Guide to Universal Design for Learning'. Accessed 22 July 2021. https://www.inclusive.tki.org.nz/guides/universal-design-for-learning/.

Osborne, T. (2019) 'Not lazy, not faking: Teaching and learning experiences of university students with disabilities'. *Disability and Society*, 34 (2), 228–52. Accessed 24 July 2022. https://doi.org/10.1080/09687599.2018.1515724.

Paniagua, A. S.-E. and Simpson, O. (2018) 'Developing student support for open and distance learning: The EMPOWER project'. *Journal of Interactive Media in Education*, 2018 (1), 9. Accessed 24 July 2022. https://doi.org/10.5334/jime.470.

Parrish, P. and Linder-VanBerschot, J. A. (2010) 'Cultural dimensions of learning: Addressing the challenges of multicultural instruction'. *International Review of Research in Open and Distance Learning*, 11 (2), 1–19. Accessed 24 July 2022. https://doi.org/10.19173/irrodl.v11i2.809.

Parsons, A. (2017) 'Accessibility and use of VLEs by students in further education'. *Research in Post-Compulsory Education*, 22 (2), 271–88. Accessed 24 July 2022. https://doi.org/10.1080/13596748.2017.1314684.

Pearson, V., Lister, K., McPherson, E., Gallen A.-M., Davies, G., Colwell, C., Bradshaw, K., Braithwaite, N. and Collins, T. (2019) 'Embedding and sustaining inclusive practice to support disabled students in online and blended learning'. *Journal of Interactive Media in Education*, 2019 (1), 1–10. Accessed 24 July 2022. https://doi.org/10.5334/jime.500.

Pettigrew, T. F. and Tropp, L. R. (2006) 'A meta-analytic test of intergroup contact theory'. *Journal of Personality and Social Psychology*, 90 (5), 751–83. Accessed 24 July 2022. https://doi.org/10.1037/0022-3514.90.5.751.

Phillips, A., Terras, K., Swinney, L. and Schneweis, C. (2012) 'Online disability accommodations: Faculty experiences at one public university'. *Journal of Postsecondary Education and Disability*, 25 (4), 331–44.

Pitcan, M., Marwick, A. E. and Boyd, D. (2018) 'Performing a vanilla self: Respectability politics, social class, and the digital world'. *Journal of Computer-Mediated Communication*, 23 (3), 163–79. Accessed 24 July 2022. https://doi.org/10.1093/jcmc/zmy008.

Prodan, A., Maxim, E., Manolescu, I., Arustei, C. C. and Guta, A. L. (2015) 'Access to higher education: Influences and possible implications'. *Procedia Economics and Finance*, 20, 535–43. Accessed 24 July 2022. https://doi.org/10.1016/s2212-5671(15)00106-9.

Richardson, J. T. E. (2009) 'The attainment and experiences of disabled students in distance education'. *Distance Education*, 30 (1), 87–102. Accessed 24 July 2022. https://doi.org/10.1080/01587910902845931.

Simpson, O. (n.d.) 'The student voices: Feedback'. Accessed 24 July 2022. https://london.ac.uk/centre-distance-education-cde/cde-activities/cde-projects#the-student-voices---feedback-13240.

Stevenson, J., O'Mahony, J., Khan, O., Ghaffar, F. and Stiell, B. (2019) 'Understanding and overcoming the challenges of targeting students from under-represented and disadvantaged ethnic backgrounds'. Report to the Office for Students, February. Accessed 24 July 2022. https://www.officeforstudents.org.uk/media/d21cb263-526d-401c-bc74-299c748e9ecd/ethnicity-targeting-research-report.pdf.

Stich, A. E. and Reeves, T. D. (2017) 'Massive open online courses and underserved students in the United States'. *Internet and Higher Education*, 32, 58–71.

Sutherland, G. (1990) 'The plainest principles of justice: The University of London and the higher education of women'. In F. M. L. Thompson (ed.), *The University of London and the World of Learning 1836–1986*. London: Hambledon Press, 35–56.

Tait, A. (2004) 'On institutional models and concepts of student support services: The case of the Open University UK'. In J. E. Brindley, C. Walti and O. Zawacki-Richter (eds), *Learner Support in Open, Distance and Online Learning Environments*. Oldenburg: BIS-Verlag der Carl von Ossietzky Universität, 283–93.

Terras, K., Leggio, J. and Phillips, A. (2015) 'Disability accommodations in online courses: The graduate student experience'. *Journal of Postsecondary Education and Disability*, 28 (3), 329–40.

UCL (n.d.) 'Digital Accessibility Hub'. Accessed 22 July 2021. https://www.ucl.ac.uk/isd/services/digital-accessibility-hub.

UK Government (2010) 'Equality Act 2010'. UK Public General Acts: 2010 c. 15. Accessed 24 July 2022. http://www.legislation.gov.uk/ukpga/2010/15/contents.

UNESCO (United Nations Educational, Scientific and Cultural Organization) (2018) 'GEM report summary on disabilities and education', Global Education Monitoring Report ED/GEM/MRT/2018/SN/1. Accessed 24 July 2022. http://unesdoc.unesco.org/images/0026/002653/265353e.pdf.

United Nations (2006) Convention on the Rights of Persons with Disabilities. Accessed 11 September 2019. http://www.un.org/esa/socdev/enable/rights/convtexte.htm.

United Nations (n.d.) 'Treaty collection'. Accessed 24 July 2022. https://www.un.org/esa/socdev/enable/rights/convtexte.htm.

University of Auckland (n.d.a) 'Equity policy'. Accessed 22 July 2021. https://www.auckland.ac.nz/en/about/the-university/how-university-works/policy-and-administration/equity/equity-policy-and-procedures-.html.

University of Auckland (n.d.b) 'Inclusive learning and teaching of students with impairments guidelines'. Accessed 22 July 2021. https://www.auckland.ac.nz/en/about/the-university/how-university-works/policy-and-administration/teaching-and-learning/general/inclusive-teaching-and-learning-guidelines.html.

University of Edinburgh (n.d.) 'Information services and accessibility'. Accessed 22 July 2021. https://www.ed.ac.uk/information-services/help-consultancy/accessibility.

UoL Panel (University of London Panel) (n.d.) 'Inclusive Practice Panel'. Accessed 22 July 2021. https://prod.london.ac.uk/about-us/how-university-run/university-governance/committees/inclusive-practice-panel.

Valencia, R. R. (2010) *Dismantling Contemporary Deficit Thinking* (1st edn). New York: Routledge.

Venville, A., Street, A. F. and Fossey, E. (2014) 'Good intentions: Teaching and specialist support staff perspectives of student disclosure of mental health issues in post-secondary education'. *International Journal of Inclusive Education*, 18 (11), 1172–88. Accessed 24 July 2022. https://doi.org/10.1080/13603116.2014.881568.

Verdinelli, S. and Kutner, D. (2016) 'Persistence factors among online graduate students with disabilities'. *Journal of Diversity in Higher Education*, 9 (4), 353–68. Accessed 24 July 2022. https://doi.org/10.1037/a0039791.

W3C (n.d.) 'All standards and drafts'. Accessed 11 September 2019. https://www.w3.org/TR/?tag=accessibility.

Wray, M. (2013) *Developing an Inclusive Culture in Higher Education: Final report*. York: Higher Education Academy.

Wu, A. X. and Taneja, H. (2016) 'Reimagining internet geographies: A user-centric ethnological mapping of the world wide web'. *Journal of Computer-Mediated Communication*, 21 (3), 230–46. Accessed 24 July 2022. https://doi.org/10.1111/jcc4.12157.

# 14
# Retention and success: approaches and tools for making a difference

Gwyneth Hughes and Joanne Harris

One of the mostly common criticisms of distance learning is that too many students do not complete the course (Simpson, 2013). While retention of students is of concern for higher education (HE) in general, the 'distance' part of distance education is thought to lead to more disengagement from students than does in-person education. In an increasingly online world, much distance learning is now online. Going digital may reduce the distance that these students experience through online activities, but there is no guarantee that students will engage.

This book argues that distance education can be a flexible and enriching experience for students in a world of instability and uncertainty. But what about those who struggle and may leave – can they be helped? This chapter will explore some innovations in promoting retention – or from the student point of view, persistence – in online distance learning that could enable more students to be successful. Retention and persistence are two sides of the same coin, but with a difference of interest: retention expresses the institutional interest of keeping students, while persistence reflects the student perspective of motivation for staying on the programme of study (Tinto, 2017). This chapter, written by representatives of a large distance learning institution, focuses on what we can do to improve retention from our perspective. We also believe that the institution and the course of study shape student persistence, as well as myriad factors that students bring from their complex lives. The chapter might be very different were it written by students – each with a different story about their individual learning journey.

Student engagement is a complex and much-explored topic. Engagement can be viewed as behavioural, such as the time a student spends on academic tasks; psychological, including cognitive and motivational factors; or sociocultural, a perspective that focuses on the context and the background of the student (Kahu, 2013). All these types of engagement are interdependent and Kahu has developed a holistic framework for student engagement that integrates affect, cognition and behaviour into the wider sociocultural context to consider the many activities that educators and their institutions might use to influence and promote engagement.

In this chapter we explore two main approaches to enabling retention on campus, which Tinto (1987) identified many years ago: promoting academic engagement and success of students and providing social integration or a sense of belonging. While we focus on these aspects, we are mindful of Kahu's holistic view of engagement. For example, academic and social engagement are important for learning online, but there is an additional sociocultural factor of practical access to the technology, such as experiencing stable internet access and technical support. Hughes (2010) has argued that these three aspects of engagement are dependent on nurturing a student's online identity: an academic identity, a sense of social belonging and an identity congruence that enables a learner to operate the online systems. Although students with a strong academic identity and ability to navigate the online world might learn online as independent learners, it is now well established that student psychological motivation, through online peer interactivity and proactive tutoring, is key for student persistence and online identity building in distance education (Macdonald, 2001; Simpson, 2013).

In this chapter we will firstly explore online academic engagement through the use of online tools. These can not only help students and tutors to communicate and present ideas but can also track and present data about student behaviour and learning. Such online tools include information on last date of access, student self-tracking, posting to discussion fora and engagement with peer review activities. All of these can be supported with tutor guidance and intervention with students who are falling behind. It is often assumed that discussion forum engagement is a predicator of success (Romero et al., 2013). However, a study of a distance learning module at the University of London (UoL) has suggested that using discussion forum activity as a single tool to identify student engagement may not be a good predictor of student outcomes and success. We shall present data from this study.

Secondly, the chapter will explore the fundamental role of assessment and feedback in enabling student progression. The same study considered how assessment design to include an ipsative assessment criterion – that is, one that measures or judges progress rather than outcome (Hughes, 2014) – can promote sustained learning over a module. Early assessment and feedback can also ensure that students know what is expected from them, while strong alignment between online activities and the assessment can help ensure that students do not defer work on assessments until it is too late to succeed.

Thirdly, the chapter moves to the issue of social integration of students and access and support. We will explore onboarding – induction and support strategies that enable retention and progression. Onboarding of students refers to more than just university or course orientation. It addresses first impressions, breaking down barriers, encouraging participation, mentoring, support mechanisms and student life outside the academic curriculum.

Using data and sentiment from UoL's internal student experience survey, a digital Student Experience Survey and anecdotal student feedback, we were able to define a series of learner types. These learner types all have characteristics or attributes that suggest the causes of achievement disparity could not simply be reduced to financial difficulties, language barriers and internet access. Among a range of issues there seems to be trepidation over engaging with an unfamiliar online learning environment and a fear of being judged negatively by peers and tutors. This led us to develop and provide a number of tools, communication and support options for our student body to increase retention, completion, satisfaction and success. Psychological interventions, well-being support and social-belonging exercises can also all help to build an online community that is suitable for the truly globally diverse UoL student body.

Finally, returning to Kahu (2013), the chapter acknowledges that engagement and retention do not depend on single factors. There are many influences on a student online learning identity, including the student's history, social context and emotional state. Nevertheless, the chapter makes some tentative recommendations for improving retention online, with the caution that there is no straightforward solution and every context will be unique.

## Online activities to promote academic engagement

The following information and activities – date of access and tracking, participation in discussion fora, tutor feedback and peer review – are available in virtual learning environments (VLEs). We suggest how they may help with both monitoring and promoting student engagement.

### Information on last date of access and student self-tracking

Last-date-of-access data generated by the system can be useful in identifying students who have not engaged for some time. These students can then be followed up. However, this is a very crude indicator. Students can also track completion of tasks, the results of which are then presented to them and to tutors in a dashboard. This information is also likely to be unreliable, as students may either not bother to record completed activities or may try to 'play' the system by recording tasks as completed even if they are not. Students can be encouraged to complete short 'quizzes' or click an emoji to note their understanding of a subject by rating their knowledge and confidence from 1–10, or via a confused or smiley face, to assess their perceived learning gains and to provide further data on engagement.

### Posting to discussion fora

Tutor support through a discussion forum has long been practised in online distance learning (Tait, 2004; Thorpe, 2002). The number of discussion posts gives a straightforward measure of student activity. Discussion online can be for educational, social or procedural purposes (Hughes, 2010). Students may post social messages or messages about access and technical difficulties, but not engage in knowledge dissemination and discussion. Tracking of engagement in disciplinary learning means that only discussion postings that are content related are counted.

### Online tutor guidance and feedback

Effective feedback is defined by Molloy and Boud (2013) as enabling students actively to compare their work with the expected standards and criteria and not just passively receive feedback. It has long been argued that early formative feedback helps students improve their work (Black and Wiliam, 2009) if the feedback is future orientated and can be applied in subsequent assignments (Hattie and Timperley, 2007). However, feedback is too often corrective and critical. This can demoralise students who have not performed well. Feedback needs to encourage but should not be based on empty praise either. Hughes (2010, 2014, 2017) has argued that feedback that takes a longer-term view is particularly useful to motivate students to see their progress over time and to develop positive online learning identities and persistence. Encouraging students to self-monitor their actions taken in response to feedback is one way of taking such a longitudinal approach to feedback.

## Engagement with peer review activities

Peer review can provide a useful mechanism for engaging students in feedback practice. Nicol et al. (2014) have argued that peer review enables students to see problems in the work of others that they might not see immediately in their own work. Thus, giving peer feedback may be more useful than receiving peer feedback. Being active in a feedback dialogue with peers also helps students to understand assessment criteria and standards, so that they can undertake self-review and self-critique and become less dependent on tutor feedback and instruction (Nicol and Macfarlane-Dick, 2006).

Online tools are available that can support these activities, but how effective these tools are in practice needs some exploration and we turn to one of the studies presented in this chapter.

## A study of retention at UoL

UoL has designed a new online distance learning Postgraduate Certificate in Learning and Teaching in Higher Education. This is aimed at developing staff who tutor in distance learning as well as in person. The programme aims to model good pedagogic practice in use of online and classroom tools. It includes aspects of distance online learning that encourage retention, such as regular tutor support, clear structure, discussion with peers, reflection, tracking of progress and digital videos (Doig and Hogg, 2013). The programme consists of two 30-credit modules.

The initial module, 'Supporting, Learning, Teachings and Assessment', was designed to include innovations in online learning to support both reflection on learning and peer engagement. In the module, learners are prompted to write about their current teaching practice and ways in which they can develop their practice in a reflective journal, which they complete throughout the module. A mid-point assessment ensures that students have tutor feedback on reflective writing, as reflective writing might be a difficult concept for some. For peer interaction, the module offers four evenly spread peer review activities, as well as opportunities for presenting and discussing ideas with peers in a weekly topic discussion forum.

By 2020, the module had run with two cohorts consisting of a total of 50 student lecturers and these have been evaluated using data that was captured online. The aim was to explore how the innovative online tools contributed to retention and success in the assessment. The cohorts had an identical presentation of the module but different tutors. However, marks were moderated by the same moderator, and we assumed that there would not be significant differences between measured outcomes for the two cohorts.

## Data collection

Three sets of data were used for the evaluation.

Firstly, the number of discussion postings that demonstrated engagement in learning were counted. Student contribution to the forum postings were categorised as over 30 messages = very good, 10–30 messages = good, below 10 = poor, 0 messages = no engagement. The categories arose because the majority of students posted between 10 and 20 messages and over 30 was exceptional.

Secondly, student engagement in the peer review processes was recorded to include both the giving and receiving of feedback. There were four peer review workshops throughout the module. Engagement with three or four workshops was considered to be high, engagement with two, moderate, one workshop was low and no workshops equated with zero engagement in peer review.

Thirdly, the study explored any links between online activity and module outcomes – in other words, with retention and success. Assessments were given numerical marks, but these equated with levels of fail, pass, merit and distinction. The outcomes of two assessments for the module were recorded in this non-numeric way. Students with both assessments as distinctions or merits were classified as high achieving, those with one merit or passes were recorded as moderate achievers and those with fails or non-submission were classified as low achievers.

## Findings of the study

Engagement with the discussion forum did not predict outcomes for high achievers. Out of the 15 highly successful students, nine had poor engagement with educational discussion, so this does not seem to be the cause of their success (see Table 14.1).

While engagement in the discussion forum was not linked to outcomes for the students who achieved, there was a clear association between engagement in peer review and outcomes. Out of the 15 high achievers, 14 had a strong or moderate engagement in peer review. The student who did succeed without taking part in peer review had a high

Table 14.1 Breakdown of high achievers' engagement in discussion forum and peer review (n=15).

| Educational discussion forum posting: number of students ||||
|---|---|---|---|
| Very good | Good | Poor | No posting |
| 3 | 3 | 9 | 0 |
| Engagement with peer review: number of students ||||
| Strong | Moderate | Weak | None |
| 9 | 5 | 1* | 0 |

* Student had very high discussion forum engagement.

engagement with the discussion forum, suggesting that either engaging in peer review or forum posting predicts success and different learners might prefer different approaches.

With moderate achievers, the number of postings again does not predict achievement, as the majority (10 out of 18) had low numbers of posts yet still passed (see Table 14.2). As with the high achievers, peer review participation does link to outcomes and 17 of the 18 students with strong or moderate engagement were moderately successful.

There was an outlier who did not fit the overall pattern and this was further investigated. One student did not engage in either peer review or the discussion forum yet passed. However, this student had downloaded all the materials and may have been working on them individually as would a traditional print-based distance learner who has an identity congruent with independent learning. The downloading option was provided for students with this aim in mind, as some were known to live in countries with erratic or slow internet connection.

All 19 non-submitters or fails had very low or no postings, as expected. Five of the 10 students who engaged minimally with the

Table 14.2 Breakdown of moderate achievers' engagement in discussion forum and peer review (n=18).

| Educational discussion forum posting: number of students ||||
|---|---|---|---|
| Very good | Good | Poor | No posting |
| 3 | 5 | 10 | 0 |
| Engagement with peer review: number of students ||||
| Strong | Moderate | Weak | None |
| 14 | 3 | 1** | 0 |

** This student also had low discussion forum engagement.

**Table 14.3** Breakdown of low achievers' engagement in discussion forum and peer review (n=19).

| Educational discussion forum posting: number of students ||||
|---|---|---|---|
| Very good | Good | Poor | No posting |
| 0 | 0 | 10 | 9 |
| Engagement with peer review: number of students ||||
| Strong | Moderate | Weak | None |
| 0 | 5 (early on) | 5 (early on) | 9 |

discussions submitted one assignment or withdrew, although these students may resubmit and pass in future (see Table 14.3). Thus, low posting might provide a warning for poor outcomes but, as we can see, students with low engagement in the discussion forum can also succeed.

There are two groups of students in the non-completion/fail group. One group consisted of those who did not engage in either the discussion or the peer review workshop; these nine non-starter students did not submit any assignments. The remainder engaged to a weak or moderate extent with the early activities of peer review. Five students in this group submitted one assignment and another student plans to re-enrol.

Some early weak or moderate peer review activity is associated with partial completion of the assessment. These students could retake the module and complete the outstanding peer reviews or engage in discussion, or they could retake a failed or non-submitted assessment. Once more, peer review activity correlates with outcomes for those who do not participate at all and also for those who exhibit some partial engagement. Lack of peer review activity is a better warning of poor outcomes than discussion activity and is well worth monitoring to pick up those in difficulty.

## Further discussion

These results call into question the widely held assumption (Romero et al., 2013) that discussion forum posting behaviour is an indicator of success in online distance learning. Students with a high posting rate were successful, but so were students with a low posting rate. However, taking part in the peer review was a strong predictor of success, with almost all those who engaged succeeding. Those who took part in early peer review activities but did not succeed overall did in many cases submit one assignment, so partial peer review activity seems to predict partial completion. Not surprisingly, most of those who did not take part in peer review at all did not submit any assignments.

In considering possible wider application of these results, we should remember that this course attracts participants already in the teaching profession and studying at postgraduate level. The results might be different for younger and undergraduate students and students studying different disciplines.

We might ask why these somewhat surprising findings emerged from the study. It seems that cognitive engagement with the materials in one way or another is important for success, whether through discussion forum, peer review or self-study of downloaded materials. Spending time on tasks is a predictor of success and this is consistent with Arum and Roksa's (2011) larger study of learning gain during a degree. Peer review has a particularly positive effect on learning because it provides insight into assessment, but it seems that discussion forum activities have less appeal to learners even though these too may promote reflective learning. We propose that peer review is viewed as a compulsory assessment activity in this module because it is managed by the system and students will feel they are letting peers down if they do not comply. The anonymity of the peer reviewing may also encourage those who are nervous about critiquing others to join in.

Assessment is always important in driving learning, and the module had an innovative assessment design.

## Assessment design and feedback

Assessment is key to retention, but students may not know that they are not making sufficient progress until they receive a poor mark or grade and it is too late to take action. Early intervention and feedback can help students with their learning but for many students feedback on a poor performance can be demoralising and they may not respond appropriately (Hughes, 2014). However, there is evidence that students are motivated by ipsative feedback, which informs them of the progress or personal learning gain they are making and helps them to identify areas that need attention (Hughes, 2017). Such feedback can improve student attainment and help with retention and progression. However, progress in response to feedback needs to be captured and made explicit, otherwise learners may not be aware that they are (or are not) making the personal learning gains that will enable them to succeed in the summative assessment (Hughes, 2017).

Therefore, the module assessment design aimed to encourage students to gather material for their assessment from the start, with an emphasis on rewarding progression as well as outcomes by including an ipsative component in summative assessment. The final summative assessment – a portfolio of development and achievement in teaching theory and practice – explicitly rewards awareness of personal learning gain by including the ipsative (learning gain) marking criterion:

> Evidence of development of own ideas, values and approaches in relation to critical analysis of effectiveness in teaching and learning, including within their own discipline.

The module includes an early piece of assessment that is both summative and formative and provides students with early feedback on their ability to reflect on their practice. The assessment is a reflection on practice in online learning. Students also had opportunities to benefit from tutor feedback in the weekly discussion forum.

The online tools such as peer feedback workshops and discussion activity are learning gain enablers and aim to help students meet this criterion through self-critique and reflection on their own learning as well as the learning of peers.

The study also looked at the feedback students were given in relation to this criterion, to explore how far participants were able to present their learning gains in teaching and learning theory and practice for this module.

*Outcomes of the study*

All the students who were successful had positive feedback about their development in thinking about teaching and learning during the module. Teacher feedback addressing criterion 4 was clear on this:

> Critical development of own ideas, values and approaches in relation to effectiveness in teaching practice within their own discipline. (Student with a distinction)

> Demonstrates knowledge gained in all aspects of teaching, learning, assessment referencing and practical application of theory. (Student with a pass)

While this does not necessarily mean that the ipsative assessment criteria prompted students to engage in online activities and monitor and record their progress, it does seem likely that the alignment between the assessment and the activities of the module was a contributor to their success. Furthermore, some students were inexperienced at the start but were able to demonstrate progress and succeed on the programme rather than feel inadequate compared to others who were more advanced. For example:

> Good development of ideas and values and theory starting from a low base. (Student with a merit)

Ipsative assessment has much potential to enhance the self-efficacy and motivation of learners and so this is where the greatest potential of ipsative assessment may lie (Hughes, 2014).

So far, we have considered how learning design and assessment can encourage retention, but there is a step before students begin their study – induction. The next section explores how it is important to get this right by presenting another piece of work that was undertaken at UoL.

## Student induction and support case study at UoL

Non-academic student support to improve the student experience of enrolment, induction and study support is important for fostering a sense of belonging to the university and the course (Tinto, 1987). However, activities for induction can be disjointed. Onboarding is a term that brings these processes together. The term 'onboarding' originally applied to the process of integrating a new employee into the workplace, with the aim of enhancing retention and productivity. Many universities have recognised the importance of onboarding to help students get to grips with university life and study. Onboarding of students refers to more than just university or course orientation. It is about first impressions, breaking down barriers, encouraging participation, mentoring, support mechanisms and student life outside of the academic curriculum. All of these can contribute to first impressions of the university and to that all-important sense of belonging. This next section will explore some examples from the projects.

At UoL, a series of onboarding projects have been set up to increase retention, completion, satisfaction and success. A number of tools, communication and support options have been developed and evaluated for the students, which we will share in this chapter. These include social-psychological interventions, well-being support and social-belonging exercises to help build a virtual community that is suitable for the globally diverse UoL student body.

We set the following 'student experience' objectives and evaluate each project we develop against them. We give some examples of each:

- embedding the student experience
- enhanced digital provision
- improving student satisfaction
- promoting opportunities to the stakeholder community.

## Embedding the student experience: pre-registration conversion campaigns and study planner

There is no guarantee that students who have been made an offer will proceed to enrol, but there are steps that can be taken to improve the conversion rate. The Student Experience Team coordinates conversion activities for a number of different programme sessions. For example, as well as automated emails after an offer has been made, nurture emails are sent using peer-led, authentic student and alumni voices in sections of the email to encourage conversion through motivation and aspiration.

In this particular campaign example, nurture emails were sent to 988 students. Comparing student records data showed that 318 of those who opened emails then went on to register. This gives a conversion percentage of 32.2 per cent.

In addition, all offer holders who had not taken up registration were phoned as part of our outbound calling activity. Webinars delivered by the programme team were also offered. This cumulative activity has helped secure 601 registrations, which is far above original target of 150.

We have started to implement the use of dynamic content in our conversion campaigns. This will include tailoring a significant amount of content in campaigns by geographic region or by teaching centre.

We have also created a multifunctional study planner for new starters. We evaluated its effectiveness and gathered student feedback via an online survey, printing QR codes in the planner. This study planner acts as a welcome to complement the study materials that some students receive by post. A student provided feedback on the planner:

> Absolutely delighted to receive my planner! This is a welcome development and so well put together ... excited for the year ahead!

## Enhanced digital provision: social media

We use our established presence on social media platforms to help our student community to form connections with each other and with the university. We post news, tips, quotes, articles and other topics to engage our global student body and create a sense of belonging. We actively promote student blog articles so that students can identify with their peers' experiences and encourage others to become contributors too. On average, the Student Experience Team publishes around 100 posts per month (across all social media platforms) with a community following across our platforms exceeding 820,000 (at the time of writing).

## Enhancing digital provision: student blog and My Digital project

We actively promote student blogging so that students can identify with their peers' experiences and in turn encourage others to become contributors too. We are also able to use the content provided by our students and alumni as collateral for our pastoral, well-being, conversion and retention campaigns. As noted, an authentic voice resonates most with our students. We can gauge the success of this from engagement with the blogs and feedback we receive from readers. In 2018, the blogs were viewed a total of 105,643 times by 56,952 unique users. These figures suggest that students are engaging in blogging and that they are developing an online social presence. We actively work with students to align the types of articles being published with their own priorities and those of the university. For instance, during an assessment period, there is a greater focus on content that offers guidance around revision, self-care and confidence building.

In addition, UoL has run a My Digital project, which enabled us to understand how current and future students will interact digitally and how we can best enhance their digital experience.

Examples of this are the use of Blackboard Collaborate Ultra for employability and conversion/retention activities, the Adobe Creative Suite to rapidly produce content for social media and induction activities and creating a virtual presence at graduation ceremonies outside the UK. We surveyed current students, alumni and prospective students. The results have driven the student-wide online resources and self-reflective activities and the implementation of an open online knowledge base to help resolve enquiries before they are logged.

Machine learning plays a key role in developing sophisticated answers to enquiries. A report by Gartner (Ingelbrecht and Lowendahl, 2018) suggested that by 2021 nearly one in six customer service interactions globally will be handled by artificial intelligence (AI). Mindful of this trend, we produced a prototype chatbot (machine learning software that responds to enquiries) to meet the demands of a 24/7 enquiry service for our students.

Since launch in April 2020 to November 2021, the UoL Chatbot has supported 49,330 users with an average of 81 chats per day. In 2021, the average was 86 chats per day. There have been 215,474 interactions in total during this time period. The chatbot is situated on the contact us page & the course pages of the website.

As noted in this chapter, UoL is generating more content for students. This non-course-specific content includes study skills, work wellness, employability activities, careers and webinars. The content is currently held on our portal as web pages or links to our platforms (iVent, Articulate Rise and PDFs).

Currently, the majority of VLEs do not take advantage of the data collection specifications available and rely on log files to provide analytics. This is a time-consuming activity with functional limitations. To better present this content to students we have developed a single platform (referred to as 'learn.london') that will capture analytics behind this content to confirm engagement and support our retention activities. The benefit will be more recordable student 'touchpoints', allowing us to trial initiatives such as micro-credentials and motivational design.

## Improving student satisfaction

We developed induction resources for students who have completed initial registration to act as an introduction to UoL, what to expect as a student and how to identify, understand and use the resources available. Previously, students completed registration and gained access to the VLE but did not receive any specific instructions on where to begin, where to find the resources they needed to engage with their programme or how to use them.

When a student registers for the first time, they must sign on to the Student Portal. We have created a welcome video that will automatically play once when they do so. The aim of the video is to familiarise the student with UoL and to begin creating a sense of belonging to our student community. The high production values of the video reflect the effort invested in creating a meaningful welcome for students. Staff members from some of the student services teams that students will interact with are showcased, providing a human face to UoL. We also show how-to content tutorials for the digital platforms students will use and the tasks they will need to complete. Video pop-ups throughout the induction break up the sections and provide audio-visual support. The induction resources are fully accessible and mobile responsive.

The induction also provides students with soft skills content that is not course specific and covers study skills, employability activities and support, careers webinars and self-reflective careers exercises, to focus students' career aspirations. Areas such as critical thinking, academic writing and time management augment their academic studies. We commissioned both the Careers Group and the Centre for Online and Distance Education to develop these resources and we will continue to provide new resources for our student body every year.

Additionally, we have built a course-specific orientation module that includes full information on programme structure, how to approach study, assessment and all other relevant information required to complete the degree successfully.

Statistics on the student induction were taken for the first five months after launch. The total number of hits to the induction home page was 49,212, an average of 9,842 each month. The busiest months were November and December, the initial registration date being 30 November. Elements of the VLE were viewed a total of 297,882 times in 2021 (24,834 monthly average) by 9,790 unique users. This represents 22 per cent of the total student population at that time.

The induction also provides expectation management, helping to reduce the gap between what students assume they will receive and have access to and the reality of the university's provision. Awareness of the provision should help decrease the number of enquiries directed to the Student Advice Centre.

We also believe that communication about support available during the critical parts of the student journey, such as revision and examination periods, improves retention and student outcomes. This initiative aims to create a sense of community and of feeling connected and supported by fellow students and the university across our digital platforms. An authentic, peer-led student voice is used within our campaigns, communications and social media.

An example of the cover note to a pastoral support email is below:

Revision Motivation

Preparing for Examinations

Dear [student name]

As the examination period draws nearer, we want to take this opportunity to send you some tips from your fellow students, motivational words from us and information that may spur you on to make a strong revision plan.

from your Pro-Vice Chancellor [PVC name]

## Promoting opportunities to the stakeholder community

Student clubs, societies, podcasts and community platforms serve to build a sense of community and belonging among the student cohort. Finding a way to offer this proposition to our students is a valuable investment to leverage support and connect our digital community. We have hosted our clubs and societies on our cloud-based VLE, which allows us to gather metrics and add micro-credentials. In addition to the Book Club and the World Recipes Society, we launched a Film and TV Club during the pandemic.

Giving students an opportunity to connect across borders, we have developed a community platform to host a wider portfolio of student-led clubs and societies, as well offering a space for peer-to-peer study support.

In total, the Online Societies pages and forums have been viewed 37,434 times by 4,129 unique users. This represents around 9.3 per cent of the total current student body.

Our UoL World Class podcast is another community-building avenue to engage our student audience. Episodes published feature programme directors, career experts and mental health and well-being specialists, as well as UoL staff and student specials. The pod has been downloaded in 155 countries over 8,000 times (at time of publication).

Research suggests that students with mental health conditions are less likely to continue registration, to attain their degree and to be employed or engage in future study (UUK, 2021). Therefore, early prevention is a moral and professional responsibility, which contributes to retention. Healthy students are more likely to succeed, continue on their programme of study without lapsing and ultimately complete their study successfully. Improving student outcomes enhances our reputation as an HE provider. Incident rates are low, but it only takes one tragic event to have a massive impact and ripple effect on the university and its students. Inclusivity and a sense of belonging are integral; students need to feel cared for. We need to get our students all over the world connecting with each other, especially in countries where there are fewer students who may be more isolated.

## Promoting well-being

> Research has clearly demonstrated that belonging and social integration are important, not just for student well-being, but also for academic achievement and persistence to graduation. (Hughes and Spanner, 2019)

Following the release of the 'University Mental Health Charter' in 2019, along with governmental and sector-wide demand for universities to take a more active approach in caring for student mental health and well-being, we are taking a number of steps to steadily increase and enhance our support offering.

We are focusing on early prevention, raising awareness and encouraging conversations surrounding mental health to better equip students with the tools and knowledge to care for their mental well-being.

We have partnered with TalkCampus, a free peer-supported app, which we launched in March 2020. Prior to that, we held a subscription with Nightline for all our students. The TalkCampus app is available 24/7, 365 days a year and is free at the point of use for all our students. It can be downloaded via the App Store or Google Play and students use their UoL email address to verify their account.

The platform has robust safeguarding measures and is monitored in four ways:

- by a professional safety team
- by trained student volunteers who undertake a six-week online training programme in basic counselling skills (Samaritans standard)
- by alerts that trigger to the safety team any posts identified by AI as using language that may indicate risk
- finally, by the users, peers, who are able to anonymously report posts.

If TalkCampus detects a student in crisis – which means when a risk to life, their own or others, is explicitly expressed – they implement real-time escalation processes, alerting designated university contacts, local authorities and crisis support services in the student's country of residence. It currently operates in over 100 countries. This offer, coupled with the crisis support helpline launched in December 2021, provides the support at scale we need to ensure our approximately 50,000 students globally have a safe space for their mental health and well-being that is easily accessible, as well as someone to talk to in a crisis if required. TalkCampus has approximately 10,000 master-level clinicians that support the crisis support helpline. They also provide counselling in other languages.

The university has put TalkCampus through rigorous assessment to ensure it is safe for students, that their data and privacy is protected and that everything adheres to all General Data Protection Regulation requirements.

The Student Experience Steering Group commissioned Mental Health First Aid training for 20 UoL staff in January 2020, meaning there are now a number of staff better equipped to respond to the immediate needs of student who reach out to us in mental distress throughout the year.

We developed a dedicated 'Well-being' hub on the Student Portal where we host a number of resources, articles and relevant information. We have collaborated with the Online Library to curate a self-help bibliography and we produce responsive content to world events; for example, producing articles on COVID-19 and looking after your mental well-being, and accompanying further reading. The Student Experience Steering Group designed the Well-being Toolkit short course to guide students through a reflective process that empowers them to create a personalised self-care plan.

We also introduced an examiner's protocol that allows our examiners to flag distressed students during assessment. Examiners can now immediately alert the Student Experience Steering Group to students who write concerning content on their examination papers, without removing them from the marking process, so we can provide efficient support where it is deemed necessary.

We are establishing a leading voice by engaging in public discourse around mental health and well-being, such as taking part in awareness days and producing and publishing relevant articles on our website and social media. We have launched a number of campaigns to de-stigmatise mental health issues. Our #IFeelBetterWhen video campaign has been developed with both staff and students sharing what they do to help themselves feel better. By initiating and showing that even staff are willing to talk about how they feel and sharing tips with the community, we are letting students know that they are safe to do so too.

The Student Experience Steering Group has drafted a Student Mental Health and Well-being Strategy and Policy for our distance and flexible learning students to feed into the overarching UoL strategy, as highlighted as best practice in the 'University Mental Health Charter'.

Another pilot that aimed to bolster our student pastoral care through alumni and student mentoring support was run in Sri Lanka for students on our two biggest undergraduate programmes pre-pandemic.

In March 2018, an email was sent to 20 undergraduate law alumni in Sri Lanka inviting them to become mentors. Eight were selected along with one who had mentored in the last period.

Twenty-nine students applied to be mentees out of 997 students invited, an increase of 11 from the previous year. All 29 were matched with a mentor.

A comment from one of the mentors is shown below:

> It was a great experience to mentor and help the mentee not just with the academic aspect but also the psychological aspect of the mentee by sharing experience and giving motivation.

During the pandemic we have developed an online community discord channel to foster peer to peer collaboration and access to Alumni ambassador support.

We hope to roll out further mentoring programmes in the future using a hybrid model of both online and in-person/country support.

## Employability

Working closely with the Careers Group, we provide both synchronous and asynchronous online careers support to students across our programmes. This support comes in a variety of forms. We facilitate live and interactive webinars (which are recorded), where larger groups of students take advantage of a presentation and Q&A with a senior careers consultant around a particular work-related topic, such as promoting their distance learning qualification, CV and interview skills. Furthermore, we provide career drop-in sessions where students are invited to discuss any issues with a senior careers consultant.

We used the Jisc survey platform to present attendees with a survey for each session attended, asking the same questions each time. These surveys saw 298 unique responses. Samples of free-form text feedback include the following:

> 'What did you learn?'

> 'I never considered my experience to be valuable to anyone. Now I understand that I should actually talk about it.'

> 'I learned the importance of matching my skill with what the job offers and what the job requires and tailoring my response accordingly.'

> 'I learnt how to navigate my way through the complexities of the workplace and to embrace change because work is constantly changing, growing over time.'

We have developed self-reflective exercises and online resources to augment our employability support. Students are encouraged to take a holistic approach to their employability, reflecting on what motivates them to succeed, the career path best suited to them and the steps they can take to get there. They have access to bespoke online resources that cover topics including CV building, interview skills, setting career development goals, understanding careers values and a library of short masterclasses.

In addition to this, we have created two certified micro-modules developed to work alongside a diverse range of distance learning curriculum programmes, which include content on global employment trends and how to plan a sustainable career in the Fourth Industrial Revolution.

Another ongoing initiative offers business placement opportunities for second-year and third-year students. The placements are with high-value organisations that can provide career-exploratory and career-confirmatory work experience to enhance each student's graduate potential. We placed over 200 students on business placements in 2019/20 in Pakistan, Bangladesh, India, Sri Lanka and the South-East Asian region. The project involved managing over 1,350 applications, as well as stakeholder engagement and logistical support. Undergraduate students benefited from work experience with high-value placement providers such as Grant Thornton, Deloitte, Coca Cola, Unilever, Ernst & Young, Vietnam Airlines and Nestlé. Many students had their placements extended and a number of students have been offered guaranteed jobs when they graduate. We aim to open placement opportunities for Malaysian, UK and European students when post-pandemic restrictions allow.

We seek to work with large multinationals that are present in many of our key markets, so that we can leverage our connections in one territory to open doors in others. Working with such high-value placement providers ensures the health and safety of our students undertaking work experience, as a robust HR infrastructure is already part of their set up.

In 2020/21, students were given the opportunity to take part in three virtual internship opportunities, as we were not able to provide in-person business placements. We ran these in partnership with Bright Network Internships across multiple sectors (from finance and law to technology and public policy), and the NatWest early career immersion week and Lloyds' RISE work experience programme, which focused on promoting opportunities for UK ethnic minority students.

Over 3,000 students took part in the Bright Network Internships with a 99 per cent positive feedback rating. The internship was a mixture of specialist talks about working in the sector from several employers, one-to-one networking sessions and a work project involving a professional consulting proposal.

The importance of employability among students is primary, so this initiative aims to attract prospective students as well as contribute to retention. Upon successful completion of their placement, students are reimbursed for expenses in the form of a reduction in their fees, as well as having the business placement noted on their final transcript.

Success can be measured through numbers of applications, sentiment (from feedback), additional skills gained (from feedback), the retention rate of the participants, examination success rate of participants, final award of participants, destination of participants, feedback from participating companies, offers of employment or extension of placement and applicants who cite business placements as a reason for applying.

When asked to elaborate on key skills students felt they had developed during their business placements, four stood out as most frequently selected by all participants in both Pakistan and Vietnam:

- confidence
- communication
- teamwork
- ability to work under pressure.

Every student has indicated significant growth in seven or more aptitudes.

The data below shows that the majority of students selected a ranking of 4 or 5 for skills developed.

Accolades are also a measure of success and UoL was a top five finalist from a field of 500 submissions, in the 'Most Improved Commitment to Employability' category for the National Undergraduate Employability Awards 2019.

We have provided our students with an industry skills initiative with a two-day boot camp providing 20 students per year, based in India, with the opportunity of working alongside industry professionals at the Bombay Stock Exchange. This boot camp included practical sessions on how to invest and trade using simulation software and real stock exchange data.

From the examples given we can assume that these onboarding projects have helped students engage with their online learning and gain a sense of belonging from enrolment, through the course and assessment and on to future careers. Although this is difficult to demonstrate empirically because of the large number of variables, we firmly believe that onboarding can only have a positive effect on retention and success.

We are continuing to monitor feedback, engagement and annual Student Experience Survey responses over a cycle of five years, to measure the impact of our current activities on students' experience with UoL and into their careers or further academic study.

## Recommendations for improving retention/persistence of distance learners

Good pedagogic design and effective student support and induction go some way towards enabling students to complete their studies. However, even when online learning identities are nurtured and students feel welcomed on the programme there are many reasons why students cannot succeed. These relate to external circumstances and personal situations in the wider sociocultural context. Clearly, no amount of good design can help students who are ill, overworked or under emotional or financial pressure. Others may not be academically prepared for the level of study or may lack self-belief and/or the goals to succeed (Bandura, 1997; Tinto, 2017). However, good design and support help as many students as possible to succeed. We recommend some effective strategies for addressing, but not solving, the student persistence challenge in distance learning. While some of our findings have been for a specific group of university students, we believe that they have wider resonance with undergraduates and learners from other disciplines.

The case studies reported in this chapter suggest a number of avenues for tutor development in online learning to encourage retention of professional learners that might also apply to other distance learning programmes:

- Include a variety of online tools that are time bound and well organised. This will encourage different learners to spend time on task. Peer review activities are particularly helpful for engaging distance learners and taking part in these also fosters a sense of both academic and social belonging.
- Learning is cumulative and builds throughout the course with ongoing support. Academic tutors can then be proactive and look for sustained student engagement or disengagement beyond the first few sessions to predict success and warn for non-completion or failure.
- Design assessments that include criteria for developmental progress (ipsative component) as well as outcome criteria. Such assessment

needs to be supported by peer review and early tutor feedback to develop student self-regulation and awareness of personal learning gains.
- Students can develop a sense of belonging in their programme and commitment at pre-enrolment as well as through support during the programme. Non-academic support through online induction, study planning, pastoral support, good access to digital media and opportunities to engage with wider stakeholders for career purposes can all contribute to both welcoming students and keeping students 'on board', to maximise the retention of any given student body.

# References

Arum, R. and Roksa, J. (2011) *Academically Adrift: Limited learning on college campuses*. Chicago and London: University of Chicago Press.

Bandura, A. (1997) *Self-Efficacy: The exercise of control*. New York: W. H. Freeman.

Black, P. and Wiliam, D. (2009) 'Developing the theory of formative assessment'. *Educational Assessment, Evaluation and Accountability*, 21, 5–31.

Doig, A. and Hogg, S. (2013) 'Engaging distance and blended learners online'. In C. Wankel and P. Blessinger (eds), *Increasing Student Engagement and Retention in e-Learning Environments: Web 2.0 and blended learning technologies*, Cutting-Edge Technologies in Higher Education Series, Vol. 6G. Bingley: Emerald, 229–60.

Hattie, J. and Timperley, H. (2007) 'The power of feedback'. *Review of Educational Research*, 77 (1), 81–112.

Hughes, G. (2010) 'Identity and belonging in social learning groups: The value of distinguishing the social, operational and knowledge-related dimensions'. *British Educational Research Journal*, 36 (1), 47–63.

Hughes, G. (2014) *Ipsative Assessment: Motivation through marking progress*. Basingstoke: Palgrave Macmillan.

Hughes. G. (ed.) (2017) *Ipsative Assessment and Personal Learning Gain: Exploring international case studies*. Basingstoke: Palgrave Macmillan.

Hughes, G. and Spanner, L. (2019) 'University Mental Health Charter', Student Minds. Accessed 24 July 2022. https://www.studentminds.org.uk/uploads/3/7/8/4/3784584/191208_umhc_artwork.pdf.

Ingelbrecht, N. and Lowendahl, J.-M. (2018) 'Use AI to take student success to the next level of personalization in higher education', Gartner. Accessed 17 October 2022. https://www.researchgate.net/profile/Kabir-Kharade/publication/359894024_Promise_Threats_And_Personalization_In_Higher_Education_With_Artificial_Intelligence/links/62553603d726197cfd50fb2c/Promise-Threats-And-Personalization-In-Higher-Education-With-Artificial-Intelligence.pdf..

Kahu, E. R. (2013) 'Framing student engagement in higher education'. *Studies in Higher Education*, 38 (5), 758–73. Accessed 24 July 2022. https://doi.org/10.1080/03075079.2011.598505.

Macdonald, J. (2001) 'Exploiting online interactivity to enhance assignment development'. *Open Learning: The Journal of Open, Distance and e-Learning*, 16 (2), 179–89.

Molloy, E. and Boud, D. (2013) 'Changing conceptions of feedback'. In D. Boud and E. Molloy (eds), *Feedback in Higher and Professional Education: Understanding it and doing it well*. London: Routledge, 11–23.

Nicol, D. J. and Macfarlane-Dick, D. (2006) 'Formative assessment and self-regulated learning: A model and seven principles of good feedback practice'. *Studies in Higher Education*, 31 (2), 199–218.

Nicol, D. J., Thomson, A. and Breslin, C. (2014) 'Rethinking feedback practice in higher education: A peer review perspective'. *Assessment and Evaluation in Higher Education*, 39 (1), 102–22.

Romero, C., López, M., Luna, J. M. and Ventura, S. (2013) 'Predicting students' final performance from participation in on-line discussion forums'. *Computers & Education*, 68 (C), 458–72.

Simpson, O. (2013) 'Student retention in distance education: Are we failing our students?' *Open Learning: The Journal of Open, Distance and e-Learning*, 28 (2), 105–19.

Tait, J. (2004) 'The tutor/facilitator role in student retention'. *Open Learning*, 19 (1), 97–109.

Thorpe, M. (2002) 'Rethinking learner support: The challenge of collaborative online learning'. *Open Learning*, 17 (2), 105–19.

Tinto, V. (1987) *Leaving College: Rethinking the causes and cures of student attrition*. Chicago: University of Chicago Press.

Tinto, V. (2017) 'Through the eyes of students'. *Journal of College Student Retention: Research, Theory & Practice*, 19 (3), 254–69.

UUK (Universities UK) (2021) 'Stepchange: Mentally healthy universities'. Accessed 24 July 2022. https://www.universitiesuk.ac.uk/sites/default/files/field/downloads/2021-07/uuk-stepchange-mhu.pdf.

# 15
# MOOCs for public health: a case study
Sally Parsley and Daksha Patel

An urgent increase in the provision of both pre- and in-service healthcare training is needed for the 20 million additional healthcare workers required to deliver the Sustainable Development Goals (a shared blueprint for achieving the United Nations' 2030 Agenda for Sustainable Development) (UN General Assembly, 2015). This is a challenging prospect in many health systems that face ongoing and severe shortfalls in clinical staff, training financing, institutions and faculty (WHO, 2016). Massive open online courses (MOOCs) can provide low-cost access to professional development training to hundreds or thousands of learners at a time and may provide a way forward if MOOC producers can balance three long-standing and closely intertwined educational challenges of quality, efficiency and equity (Daniel et al., 2009; Laurillard and Kennedy, 2017).

This case study shares the experiences and lessons learned by one MOOC producer in response to this global training challenge by collaboratively developing a MOOC to deliver a specialist healthcare curriculum at scale across many countries and contexts to health teams that would otherwise not have access to the training. The study discusses how the project addressed the challenges of quality, efficiency and equity and shares evaluation findings on the patterns of participation in the course (efficiency), impact on eye care delivery (quality) and cascading of the training beyond the platform (equity).

## Key lessons learned

- Global health MOOCs must connect global knowledge to local relevance for health worker participants. In the Global Blindness

MOOC, relevance was actively created through a shared approach in knowledge production and the inclusion of the local expert voice.
- Long-term, multi-level collaboration and partnerships can be used to drive quality and equity for global health MOOCs.
- The open educational resources (OER) and training partnerships did support further cascading of teaching and learning at the local level.
- Significant numbers of learners and stakeholders wanted formal accreditation for the course.
- Maintaining communication with learners and stakeholders beyond the MOOC platform is essential to promote equity and drive quality improvement and insight into practice.

## The Global Blindness MOOC: getting started

Globally, 253 million people are visually impaired or blind and 1 billion have a near vision impairment; 90 per cent of these live in low- and middle-income countries (LMICs) and 80 per cent have visual impairment from avoidable causes that could be prevented or treated with a simple operation or pair of spectacles (Bourne et al., 2017). There is international agreement on how to close this gap: health systems should adopt team-based, public health approaches to deliver comprehensive health services and an associated outline training curriculum. However, many health systems face severe shortfalls in the eye health specialists, training institutions and faculty needed to develop and deliver the training. For example, in 23 countries (mainly in Africa) there is still less than one ophthalmologist per million population compared to 49 ophthalmologists per million in the UK (Resnikoff et al., 2012).

To address this situation, the International Centre for Eye Health (ICEH) at the London School of Hygiene & Tropical Medicine (LSHTM)[1] obtained funding to develop 'Global Blindness: Planning and Managing Eye Care Services', the world's first public health eye care MOOC. This six-week online course was piloted in 2014, launched in 2015 and has run 12 times as of 2022. The course is now delivered on demand with professional accreditation certificate.

The project aimed to increase the scale and equity of participation in this training in three key ways. Firstly, the course was designed to be relevant, accessible and applicable by the whole eye health team across many health system settings, particularly limited resource settings with the greatest need for, and least access to, the training. Secondly, external funding enabled the course team to develop the content in agreement that the training would be free to all participants. Finally, additional activities aimed to facilitate the cascade of the training beyond the MOOC platform, for example, open copyright licences on the course materials, partnerships with training institutions and educator webinars.

A core course team of four was led by an experienced public health eye care academic with support from a design and production lead, part-time academic and a marketing and finance administrator. The team decided early on to drive success by focusing on educational quality:

- Global health MOOCs were, at that time, largely untried and there was uncertainty on the efficacy of MOOC learning, with various concerns raised in the literature: MOOC pedagogy can focus on passive consumption of content, they have high dropout rates, they may have limited reach in settings with low internet coverage and expensive data, global content may not be relevant locally and learners are required to have strong capabilities in using digital technology and engaging in self-directed learning (Laurillard, 2014; Liyanagunawardena et al., 2013; Onah et al., 2014).
- Delivering a high-quality course would drive demand for this component of the ophthalmic training curriculum.

To drive equity in who could benefit from the course, the team actively sought collaborations with eye health experts, leaders and educators from around the world throughout the project. Evidence from the development sector has shown that, without active management by stakeholders, digital innovations tend to increase inequalities of access and concentrations of power (World Bank, 2016). A key first step was recruiting a steering group with global expertise of eye health and distance learning to guide the project.

## Delivering the Global Blindness MOOC: a focus on quality

The course team adopted four key strategies to deliver quality throughout the project's activities and outputs:

- clearly defining the MOOC learners and stakeholders
- taking a learner-centred approach to the MOOC design
- extensive collaboration with stakeholders
- evaluating quality throughout (see Figure 15.1).

↙ **Stages 1-5: MOOC production cycle**

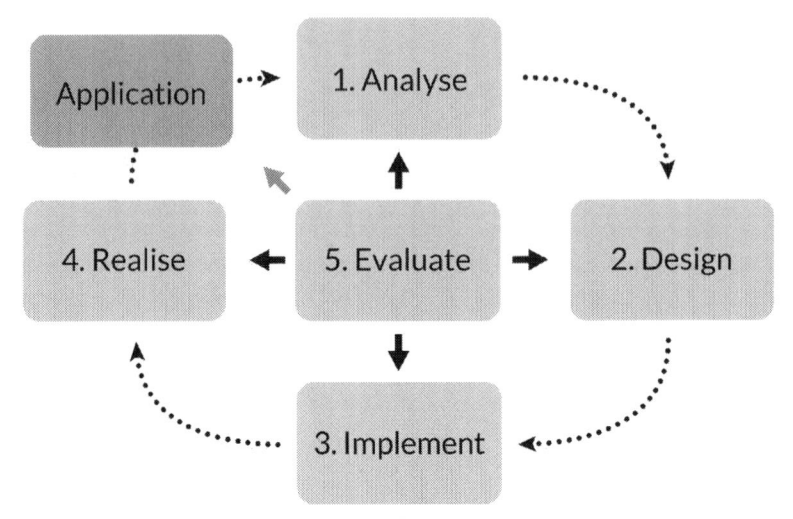

**Figure 15.1** Quality evaluated throughout the MOOC production cycle. Adapted from Stracke et al. (2018: 6–7).

*Clearly defining MOOC learners and stakeholders*
Agreeing the target MOOC learners and stakeholders (see Table 15.1) and their needs and goals (see Table 15.2) was useful for creating a shared vision of success. Evolving in response to feedback and evaluation as the project progressed, this was vital for guiding the course team, steering group and collaborators through the analysis, design, creation and delivery stages of the MOOC production.

*Taking a learner-centred design approach*
By applying a research-informed and learner-centred design approach (stages 2 and 3 of the MOOC production cycle, see Figure 15.1) the team, steering group and collaborators aimed to support the learners and stakeholders to achieve their course goals, with the achievement of learning outcomes at the core. Key elements of the design approach included the following:

- An existing international outline curriculum informed the training scope, which listed the course objectives, intended learning

Table 15.1 Global Blindness user types: target learners and key stakeholders.

| Target learners | |
|---|---|
| Members of health teams responsible for eye care service delivery at local level:<br>• Managers of eye health units and teams<br>• Clinicians working in remote and limited resource settings | Non-governmental organisation (NGO) staff |
| Future eye health managers and leaders:<br>• Providers with an interest in public health approaches<br>• Ophthalmic residents and nurses in training programmes | People with eye disease and families |
| **Stakeholders** | | | |
| Leaders and decision makers | Local trainers and managers | **Funders**<br>LSHTM and ICEH faculty and leadership | **Platforms**<br>Global eye health experts |

Table 15.2 Three examples of Global Blindness users' goals and needs.

| User type | Goals | Needs |
|---|---|---|
| Target learners | • Gain relevant knowledge and skills to improve eye health services<br>• Develop career | • Open registration and flexible access<br>• Relevant and applicable learning<br>• Recognition/certification |
| Local trainers and managers | • Provide relevant, applicable and affordable team training | • Good fit with health system's training needs<br>• Regular, low-cost, MOOC provision<br>• Easily adaptable OER materials |
| Health system leaders and decision makers | • Provide training to all who require it in the health system | • Accreditation<br>• Good fit with health system's training needs |

outcomes (ILOs), types of activities, feedback and assessment methods and hours of study required.
- Weekly learning designs visualised learners' journeys through short chunks of content and activity. This helped ensure activities aligned with the ILOs, that the learning was scaffolded and that an engaging variety of opportunities for active learning, reflection, self-assessment and feedback, note taking and dialogue were in place.
- Learning was designed to be relevant to, and applicable by, a diverse range of learners. A recurring, hypothetical case study highlighted common factors affecting many limited resource settings. Other techniques to promote inclusion included translations, plain English, non-culturally specific graphics and weekly facilitators from various contexts.
- The design was informed by evidence. For example, by applying findings on effective implementation of multimedia to support learning from video (Mayer, 2008).
- The design considered the platform affordances and constraints: for example, by leveraging the conversational learning theory embedded into the platform by encouraging note taking and discussion throughout, or by addressing the lack of bulk download and offline syncing by providing zipped content to download from the LSHTM website. Some issues could not be fully resolved; for example, data privacy regulations limited the teams' ability to follow up with learners after the course.
- OER: to promote longer-term use and contextualisation, an open copyright licence was applied to all course materials.

During the MOOC creation stage the team provided subject matter, pedagogical and editorial support to collaborating experts writing the content. Once these scripts and storyboards were finalised, the team reviewed them against the learning design before creating the final digital content and activities and uploading them to the platform. A final check of all activities and the learner journey from both the educator and learners' perspectives was carried out to ensure all the design elements were in place as planned.

A pilot course design was developed and tested across three limited resource settings in collaboration with Ministry of Health (MoH) personnel, eye health students and practitioners in Kenya, Botswana and Ghana. It found that participants from remote settings did engage and that the transnational and inter-professional content was relevant and applicable. These findings informed the scale up of the course on the

MOOC platform, which also went through a final testing process to ensure the platform's quality assurance standards were met.

## Extensive collaboration with stakeholders

As well as driving equity, collaborators were vital in delivering quality throughout the project's activities. Forty-four stakeholders from 16 countries, including 11 LMICs, worked with the course team as funders, steering group members, learning designers, content creators, educators and facilitators.

**MOOC production:** Collaboration with stakeholders throughout the analysis, design and creation stages ensured authentic, applicable learning experiences relevant to eye health teams across the multiple contexts and countries. Collaborators:

- reviewed the needs analysis findings (for example, identifying target learners)
- reviewed the course objectives and learning outcomes
- advised on the weekly learning designs
- advised on design and pedagogical decisions and best practices in open and distance learning
- facilitated the pilot study for the course
- volunteered as educators and weekly mentors during each course run
- marketed the course with their local networks.

**Cascading the training and supporting capacity building:** In 2016 and 2017, the team explored the potential for repurposing with local training institutions through collaborative partnerships, including south–south partnerships between educators and learning technologists in Kenya with the College of Ophthalmology of Eastern, Central, Southern Africa (COECSA) and in South Africa with the University of Cape Town (UCT).

The partnerships aimed to promote global linking, alliances and consortia between educational institutions and allied actors, including professional society organisations, and enable knowledge sharing and capacity building around eye health training.

A professor from UCT said:

> In Sub-Saharan Africa, we have limited health workers and big health needs. So, if you can adapt open training for local context, it can contribute to using the available health workers and trainers more efficiently and more effectively. Finally, when you get to

develop your staff, expand capacity and it extends your ability to run other training.

**Building interest in the training cascade:** To promote understanding among ophthalmic educators of the potential added value of the MOOC to their practice, the team collaborated with eight eye health and open educators to deliver two webinar series on developing open educational practices and building digital literacy skills for teaching and learning online (ICEH, n.d.).

**Providing feedback:** Collaborators shared useful information with the team throughout the project, both on the barriers and enablers to MOOC impact and on the collaboration processes themselves.

These collaborations were made possible by an actively maintained network of eye health leaders, decision makers and experienced practitioners who are alumni of the MSc in public health eye care. Although quality was the main driver for the approach, a secondary and important factor was to explore ways to build equity among eye health training institutions and address concerns that global MOOCs may exacerbate current power imbalances in the production of globalised knowledge (Czerniewicz et al., 2014; McKiernan, 2017).

*Evaluating quality throughout*
The team used three main data collection methods to gain insights into the patterns of course engagement and perceptions of impact on service delivery, training cascade and ways the MOOC could be improved:

- Platform analytics and pre- and post-course surveys provided anonymised data on learner demographics, patterns of engagement and perceptions of course experience and satisfaction.
- Perceptions of impact on practice were assessed using an online 'follow-up' survey sent by the MOOC platform provider one year after the first course run to all enrolees (August 2016).
- The team also collected informal feedback and case studies from stakeholders and collaborators on their views on course engagement, practice impacts and improvement ideas throughout the project.

The team obtained ethical permission from LSHTM and followed legal requirements to ensure data privacy and protection.

Insights gained were acted on by the team. For example, lack of engagement from West Africa drove the first translation into French. The team followed up on learners' challenges in obtaining certificates with the platform provider, both for individuals and as a general issue. Repeated requests for formal accreditation of the learning have informed strategic decision making around future decision making (see the 'In summary' section later in this chapter for more detail).

## Is it working? Evaluating the Global Blindness MOOC

### Participation and satisfaction

There were 11,380 enrolments on nine runs of the Global Blindness MOOC (between 2015 and 2019). Sixty-one per cent were based in 139 LMICs, 64 per cent were employed in the health and social care sector and 55 per cent were women.[2]

Participation followed a typical MOOC 'funnel pattern' (Clow, 2013), which remained consistent across the nine runs. Sixty per cent of enrolees logged in to become learners, 45 per cent of learners completed week 1,[3] 30 per cent fully participated,[4] and 19 per cent completed the course.[5]

Learners generally indicated high levels of satisfaction in their feedback. Ninety-five per cent reported in the post-course survey that their course experience had been excellent (58.4 per cent) or good (36.5 per cent) (runs 1 to 3, n=329). Satisfaction with the training's relevance and applicability to practice were common themes:

> This is a wonderful resource. Thank you for providing this course. I really appreciate your efforts in collecting the information and distilling it into clear, concise, manageable sections. The material will be very useful in helping me with clinics, my teaching and research. The information you provided is both up-to-date and specific. I really enjoyed the course and the format was perfect. I completed the first few weeks in a rush and then had to take a break due to work commitments and now I have a window to finish the course. This online platform is ideal for so many. Thanks again!! (Feedback on step 6.13, run 3, 2017)

> I am truly grateful to the whole team for bringing such good learning material together. It is very handy, lucid and with the creative commons license – makes it accessible to all at zero cost. Cheers to the whole team. (Post-course survey, run 9, 2019)

Some learners did also report challenges. Recurring themes include finding the time to study, paying for the completion or upgrade certificate, inadequate internet access, lack of translations and lack of experience or confidence with online learning.

> Travelled to the city twice a week [to participate] due to network challenges. ('Follow-up' survey, 2016)

> This is my first online course and it's been a bit challenging. I hope to get better at it on my next study online. ('Follow-up' survey, 2016)

Several themes emerged from learners' and stakeholders' suggestions on how to improve the course: formalise the accreditation, address issues around paying for and obtaining a copy of the certificate and further tailoring of the course to meet learners' needs, in particular:

- translations
- more content localisation
- more facilitation
- extended course run times.

> My humble suggestion is to take examples also from Asian countries too that could make someone like me practicing [sic] in developing countries like Nepal more useful. (Feedback on 'impact' survey, 2016)

## Perceptions of impact

### On eye health service delivery

**Individuals:** One hundred and thirty-nine participants on the first run of the Global Blindness MOOC responded to the 'follow-up' survey one year later (3.9 per cent response rate); 94 per cent worked in eye health and 82 per cent lived in an LMIC.

Eighty-five per cent reported being able to apply their learning from the course to their practice. In particular, 61 per cent had used their learning when planning eye care services and 50 per cent when assessing a community's eye care needs.

> Global Blindness course has really help[ed] me a lot to run [the] Vision 2020 Program, Post [Ebola Virus Disease] EVD survivor Program in Liberia (I got this assignment); after this course with

> International Medical corps and now in Eritrea I am working with [Fred Hollows Foundation] FHF to train cataract surgeon and ophthalmic officers, [and] ophthalmic nurses for [the] T Surgery in Trachoma program. ('Follow-up' survey, 2016)

> I have tried to improve on outreach activity and presently am writing a proposal that will enable us to do [a] screening of university students before the start of [the] next academic year. The course has been a motivation factor for my career. ('Follow-up' survey, 2016)

**Regional level:** In addition, the team has had informal feedback from the MoH official responsible for eye health service delivery in Kenya that participation had inspired three cataract surgeons managing eye health clinics in remote areas to make significant improvements, verified by the MoH, to their cataract surgery performance rate.

### On-training cascade

**Institutional level:** Working together and with the course team, the COECSA and UCT partners successfully adapted and localised the MOOC for their own training contexts:

- Creation of a blended learning diploma in community eye health accredited by the Health Professions Council of South Africa and UCT.
- Continuing professional development accreditation assigned by COECSA to a localised version of Global Blindness delivered using Google courses to eye health teams in ten countries in the COECSA region.

**Individual educators and training managers:** Fifty-four per cent of the respondents to the 'follow-up' survey had used their learning to teach others about eye care and 70 per cent reported having used the OER for learning or teaching:

- 50 per cent had downloaded and referred back to the OER
- 47 per cent had shared them with others
- 45 per cent had used them as teaching resources.

Informal feedback from educator stakeholders echoed many of the themes shared by learners, but also provided additional insights into further actions to improve the project's activities and process, especially around collaborations, which could further improve uptake, engagement and impact of the course at the local level.

> *Impact example: Dr Sabherwal's experience*
> Informal feedback from several participants showed that, for some at least, the MOOC led to a number of longer-term impacts on their professional practice. The experiences of Dr Sabherwal illustrate this well:
>
>> I studied the Global Blindness course while practising as an ophthalmologist in Delhi. I appreciated the flexible format which meant I could work and study at the same time. It was my first opportunity to learn about eye care planning and management.
>>
>> Learning from global experts and with other eye care professionals from different countries, cadres and local settings exposed me to many new experiences and ideas. It inspired me to think about how we could address some of the patient barriers we were seeing in a free rural outreach cataract programme. Around 25 per cent of the people offered surgery did not arrive at the hospital afterwards. A patient survey identified that many were afraid of a poor-quality surgical outcome and that, as we were carrying out surgeries during harvest, there was no-one to escort them to hospital. We addressed these barriers by counselling patients and their relatives about surgical quality and re-scheduled the timing of surgeries.
>>
>> Taking the Global Blindness course helped me reflect on and improve our eye care outreach programme. It also led me to become more interested in the public health approach to eye care and I came to London to study the LSHTM Masters in Public Health Eye Care in 2017. After successfully completing this, I took a new role at a not-for-profit eye health institute where my main responsibilities now include community ophthalmology and public health eye care research as well as my clinical work.
>>
>> Part of my role is providing practical training to the institute's excellent community team of programme managers and

> administrators. I encourage them to enrol in Global Blindness and run a supplementary weekly teaching hour where we relate the content to our own context, in Hindi if required. I also use online meeting software to widen the classes to include staff at our 4 remote secondary centres and a community team from another non-profit eye hospital about 500km away. The response has been great with lots of questions regarding the basics and it is really satisfying to share these concepts with people working in the field. The good reception for this training has led me to start to develop our own curriculum to train eye health programme managers.
>
> (Adapted from Ramasamy et al., 2017: 9–10)

## Limitations of the evaluation methodology

The limited resources and methods available to the course team mean that significant gaps remain in the team's insight as to the learning experience and its application to practice by the majority of Global Blindness participants. In particular:

- Only small numbers of self-selecting learners and stakeholders took part in the post-course and 'follow-up' surveys or provided informal feedback directly.
- The external platform provision combined with open registration constrained the evaluation's ability to gain insights useful to health system stakeholders; for example:
  ○ Which eye health teams were participating, to what extent, what learning was being achieved and what was being applied? Did application lead to performance improvement?
  ○ Which technical and socioeconomic factors were constraining and enabling participation and application of learning (Cox and Trotter, 2017; Littlejohn et al., 2019)?

## In summary

Despite the limited methodology and scope of insights gained, the evaluation findings do indicate that carefully and collaboratively produced MOOCs, such as Global Blindness, can deliver a high quality of education at scale to health teams across multiple contexts, including limited-resource settings. The localisation partnerships demonstrate capacity building and increasing equity at the health system level through a locally managed training cascade. The Dr Sabherwal example encapsulates the kinds of long-term and multifaceted practice impacts that this open approach to online education can inspire among individual health leaders at the local level.

Ongoing communication with multiple collaborators was an extremely important tool in driving quality and equity in the project – helping the team identify stakeholders' needs, adjust activities in response and, where the team was unable to respond immediately, informing discussions and planning for future developments (for example, sharing learner data ethically and legally across organisational boundaries).

## Ways forward

The current donor funding stream for the Global Blindness course ended in 2021 and a new training model is needed to enable it to continue to run. Based on the evaluation findings and on a survey of 173 eye health decision makers largely based in LMICs (March 2019), the course team is developing an approach that maintains focus on equitable widening of participation in health worker training but relies less heavily on donor funding. The model has two main strategies:

- continuing to manage Global Blindness and other public health eye care online courses developed by the team as open access MOOC / OER
- developing learner pathways and assessments building on LSHTM's eye health open courses to create a formal professional practice postgraduate certificate in public health eye care.

This development will contribute to addressing learner and stakeholder requests for more support for localisation, input into decision making around the course management and formal accreditation. It also aims to provide a way forward for eye health training managers and national stakeholders to gain deeper insight into the coverage and impact of this training within their health systems and better inform their eye health human resources strategy.

## Acknowledgements

The authors would like to thank the learners, colleagues, collaborators and funders who have contributed to helping improve eye health service delivery around the world through the Global Blindness course. In particular, we would like to acknowledge funders Seeing is Believing and the Queen Elizabeth Diamond Jubilee Trust, ICEH and LSHTM leadership, the LSHTM technology-enhanced learning and multimedia teams and, in particular, the Global Blindness steering group, course team, content contributors, educators, facilitators and localisation partners.

## Notes

1. See https://iceh.lshtm.ac.uk/ for more information.
2. LMIC figures extrapolated for runs 1 and 2 as IP data collected only on runs 3–9. VPN masking was not accounted for in IP data. N=704 for gender and n=631 for employment area.
3. Viewed ≥90 per cent of the learning activities in week 1.
4. Viewed ≥50 per cent of the course.
5. Viewed ≥90 per cent of the course.

## References

Bourne, R. R. A., Flaxman, S. R., Braithwaite, T., Cicinelli, M. V., Das, A., Jonas, J. B., Keeffe, J., Kempen, J. H., Leasher, J., Limburg, H., Naidoo, K., Pesudovs, K., Resnikoff, S., Silvester, A., Stevens, G. A., Tahhan, N., Wong, T. Y. and Taylor, H. R. (2017) 'Magnitude, temporal trends, and projections of the global prevalence of blindness and distance and near vision impairment: A systematic review and meta-analysis'. *Lancet Global Health*, 5 (9), e888–e897. Accessed 25 July 2022. https://doi.org/10.1016/S2214-109X(17)30293-0.

Clow, D. (2013) 'MOOCs and the funnel of participation'. *Proceedings of the Third International Conference on Learning Analytics and Knowledge – LAK '13*, April, 185–9. Accessed 25 July 2022. https://doi.org/10.1145/2460296.2460332.

Cox, G. and Trotter, H. (2017) 'Factors shaping lecturers' adoption of OER at three South African universities'. In C. Hodgkinson-Williams and P. B. Arinto (eds), *Adoption and Impact of OER in the Global South*. Cape Town: African Minds, International Development Research Centre & Research on Open Educational Resources for Development, 287–347. Accessed 25 July 2022. https://doi.org/10.5281/zenodo.601935.

Czerniewicz, L., Deacon, A., Small, J. and Walji, S. (2014) 'Developing world MOOCs: A curriculum view of the MOOC landscape'. *Journal of Global Literacies, Technologies, and Emerging Pedagogies*, 2 (3), 122–39.

Daniel, J., Kanwar, A. and Uvalić-Trumbić, S. (2009) 'Breaking higher education's iron triangle: Access, cost, and quality'. *Change: The Magazine of Higher Learning*, 41 (2), 30–5. Accessed 25 July 2022. https://www.doi.org/10.3200/CHNG.41.2.30-35.

ICEH (International Centre for Eye Health) (n.d.) 'Open Education (MOOCs)'. Accessed 16 October 2022. https://iceh.lshtm.ac.uk/open-education-moocs/.

Laurillard, D. (2014) 'Five myths about MOOCs'. *Times Higher Education*, 16 January. Accessed 28 September 2022. https://www.timeshighereducation.com/comment/opinion/five-myths-about-moocs/2010480.article.

Laurillard, D. and Kennedy, E. (2017) 'The potential of MOOCs for learning at scale in the Global South'. Centre for Global Higher Education working paper no. 31, December. Accessed 25 July

2022. http://www.researchcghe.org/publications/the-potential-of-moocs-for-learning-at-scale-in-the-global-south/.

Littlejohn, A., Charitonos, K., Kaatrakoski, H. and Seal, T. (2019) 'Professional learning to tackle global development challenges'. Paper presented at the Pan Commonwealth Forum 2019, 9–12 September, Edinburgh.

Liyanagunawardena, T. R., Williams, S. and Adams, A. (2013) 'The impact and reach of MOOCs: A developing countries' perspective'. *eLearning Papers*, 33, 1–8. Accessed 28 September 2022. https://www.researchgate.net/publication/282017429_The_impact_and_reach_of_MOOCs_A_developing_countries'_perspective.

McKiernan, E. C. (2017) 'Imagining the "open" university: Sharing scholarship to improve research and education'. *PLoS Biology*, 15 (10), e1002614. Accessed 25 July 2022. http://doi.org/10.1371/journal.pbio.1002614.

Mayer, R. E. (2008) 'Applying the science of learning: Evidence-based principles for the design of multimedia instruction'. *American Psychologist*, 63 (8), 760–9. Accessed 25 July 2022. https://doi.org/10.1037/0003-066X.63.8.760.

Onah, D., Sinclair, J. and Boyatt, R. (2014) 'Dropout rates of massive open online courses: Behavioural patterns'. In *6th International Conference on Education and New Learning Technologies*. EDULEARN14 Proceedings, Barcelona, 7–9 July. 5825–34. Accessed 25 July 2022. http://wrap.warwick.ac.uk/65543/.

Ramasamy, D., Gilbert, S. S., Puri, L. and Sabherwal, S. (2017) 'How to "do" CPD with your team (from the organisation's perspective)'. *Community Eye Health*, 30 (97), 9–10. Accessed 25 July 2022. https://www.cehjournal.org/article/how-to-do-cpd-with-your-team-from-the-organisations-perspective/.

Resnikoff, S., Felch, W., Gauthier, T. M. and Spivey, B. (2012) 'The number of ophthalmologists in practice and training worldwide: A growing gap despite more than 200,000 practitioners'. *British Journal of Ophthalmology*, 96 (6), 783–7. Accessed 25 July 2022. https://www.doi.org/10.1136/bjophthalmol-2011-301378.

Stracke, C. M., Tan, E., Texeira, A., Pinto, M., Vassiliadis, B., Kameas, A., Sgouropoulou, C. and Vidal, G. (2018) 'Quality reference framework (QRF) for the quality of massive open online courses (MOOCs)'. MOOQ and Open University of the Netherlands, 29 November. Accessed 25 July 2022. www.mooc-quality.eu/QRF.

UN General Assembly (2015) 'Transforming our world: The 2030 Agenda for Sustainable Development', A/RES/70/1, 21 October. Accessed 25 July 2022. https://sdgs.un.org/2030agenda.

WHO (World Health Organization) (2016) 'Global strategy on human resources for health: Workforce 2030', 7 July. Accessed 25 July 2022. https://www.who.int/publications/i/item/9789241511131.

World Bank (2016) *World Development Report 2016: Digital dividends*. Accessed 16 October 2022. https://openknowledge.worldbank.org/handle/10986/23347.

# 16
# Practising open education

Daksha Patel, Sally Parsley,
Pete Cannell and Leo Havemann

## Education as open (and closed)

> He who receives an idea from me, receives instruction himself without lessening mine; as he who lights his taper at mine, receives light without darkening me. That ideas should freely spread from one to another over the globe, for the moral and mutual instruction of man, and improvement of his condition, seems to have been peculiarly and benevolently designed by nature. (Thomas Jefferson, quoted in Lipscomb and Bergh, 1905)

Decades of debate have centred on definitions of openness in higher education (HE) and have considered the potential of open education to align, and even transform, the relationship between knowledge creation and knowledge needs. Proposals and tactics for extending the benefits of access to information and participation in education have a long history. In recent decades, much of this work has taken place under the banner of 'open', a descriptor that has been attached to universities, learning, resources, technology and even practices. Supporters of greater openness in education share the belief and aspiration that, through this route, educational opportunities can be provided to all as a human right and education can be the catalyst for global equalisation in sharing and receiving knowledge.

In practice, there are many 'opens' in education and any use is both contextual and potentially contested. Movements for open access to research outputs and open source software have played significant roles in HE and, in recent years, influenced diversification of open educational practices (OEP). Preceding the arrival of these newer influences, 'open' in an education context has most frequently been coupled with 'distance', as in open and distance education (ODE) or open and distance learning. Chapter 2 describes the nineteenth-century origins of distance education and the rapid expansion of open universities in the second half of the twentieth century. These new institutions embodied the aspirational concept of extending educational opportunities to all by:

- not disbarring applicants on account of their lack of educational qualifications
- not disbarring applicants on account of their location, by bridging geographical constraints, initially through correspondence courses and now through online courses
- promoting independent learning through appropriate pedagogy and teaching methods.

So, in a real sense, these universities have opened up access for sections of society for whom HE had previously been 'closed'. Nevertheless, as underlined in Chapter 3, this form of openness is far from total and is bounded by economic, social and attitudinal factors. Furthermore, 'open' in this sense does not automatically mean 'free'. The access policies and educational offers of open universities are also shaped by financial considerations. Similarly, a more recent collection of 'opens' (now detached from distance), such as open educational resources (OER), are open in their own specific sense and shaped by initiatives to network, share practices and promote education as a right.

What, then, does it mean to be open, as opposed to closed? An irony of the intense and ongoing debates prompted by the various movements for openness is that it has become easier to identify various forms of open practice than to precisely specify the implicated other of closed education (Havemann, 2020). There is a wide gamut of what can be described as 'closed' practices (usually thought of simply as 'normal' practices), including reliance upon educational materials that are restricted in their use by copyright or password protection, or limiting access to study as a result of either the relative scarcity of provision or the costs of fees or resources, such as textbooks. While 'open discourse' often seems to carry an implication that closed is bad, sometimes closed practices can be entirely necessary and appropriate; for example, the use of password-protected spaces in which students can discuss sensitive topics or even simply feel less exposed as they make tentative steps into new knowledge territories. There are also many practices that exhibit aspects of both openness and closure. For example, a site that showcases openly accessible materials or a course that allows open enrolment may officially permit both access and reuse of content, but not provide tools or interfaces that allow materials to be easily ported to other sites or remixed (Atenas and Havemann, 2014). Again, there are degrees of openness.

Open approaches in education are probably better understood by the values and aims that drive them, rather than by binary categorisation.[1] They place an emphasis on widening participation, overcoming barriers to engagement with knowledge and promoting equity (D'Antoni, 2009). However, such aspirations are not uniquely held by open educators. Open education is very often practised 'on the side' by educators who work in traditional ('closed') roles and institutions, either by opening up resources and participation to audiences beyond their own enrolled students, or by drawing in open content and practices to become part of students' education (Tur et al., 2020). Educational endeavours are therefore always produced through an interplay of openings and closures, rather than being completely open or closed (Edwards, 2015).

With this in mind, this chapter explores the affordances of a range of current OEP, such as the open licensing of resources and the associated downstream practices that this enables. We would encourage readers to reflect on their own experiences in the context of the opportunities for opening practice outlined in this chapter. It is useful to ask: in what particular respects the practices they are involved in are variously open and closed; why they currently take this form; what future moves towards openness might be possible and desired; and what the making of these moves would require.

## OER and Creative Commons

One of the most discussed aspects of open education in recent years is the development of open educational resources or OER. This term, coined by the United Nations Educational, Scientific and Cultural Organization (UNESCO, 2002), represented an evolution from 'open courseware' (an initiative originating from MIT, which referred to the open release of the learning resources of whole courses), towards the more inclusive notion that openness could be applied to content in any form or at any scale. Strictly speaking, the term OER indicates only those resources that have not simply been shared, but have been made legally, technically and practically available online and open, through application of permissive licensing, which enables them to be freely accessed, shared and adapted. Here there is an overlap between OER and open access publications, although a key point of difference is that open access does not automatically mean open to adaptation.

Central to the conditional openness of OER and their adoption by educators is copyright and a clear understanding of what is legally permitted by various licences. Typically, copyright is asserted to protect a resource from reproduction by parties other than the owner, without express permission, reliance on an exception or, often, payment. However (as in the case of open source software), new forms of licence have been developed in order to confer greater rights on the users of content. Although various forms of licence exist (including open government, general public, software and game licences), the most widely used in education is the suite of Creative Commons (CC) licences. These were developed in 2002 in response to the growing need across education and cultural sectors for an alternative to the binary choice of copyright/free. CC is fast becoming the gold standard that legally enables sharing and collaboration (Smith, 2019).

The CC licence framework provides options that allow the copyright holder to build the most appropriate level of 'openness' into their licence. These include the CC0 licence, which places the work in the public domain, allowing unrestricted use without attribution. Other CC licences require attribution as minimum and further provide creators with a modular range of additional options that set specific constraints on reuse:

- Attribution only (abbreviated as CC-BY), whereby the content can be used and adapted provided that the original creator is attributed, is the second most applied open CC licence after CC0.
- Including the share-alike (SA) agreement within the licence (CC-BY-SA) requires the user to carry forward the same conditions when creating new work that builds from the original content.
- Licences can include the stipulation that no derivatives of the work can be made (ND as indicated in CC-BY-ND and CC-BY-ND-SA) or no commercial exploitation is permitted (NC as in CC-BY-NC and CC-BY-NC-SA). These licences are often regarded as inappropriate for OER due to the restrictions they impose. However, works made available under these licences are still considerably more open than those in which all rights have been reserved.

## The evolution of OEP

In some of the literature on open education there has been a tendency to conflate open education with OER, or similarly, to define OEP as practices involved in the making and use of OER. For us, open education, considered more inclusively, has a longer history than is told in its 'OER chapter' and is inclusive of a broader range of practices. For example, ODE pioneered the use of novel pedagogies and technologies designed to support students' learning at a distance and we can consider these to be OEP even if they emerged before the term gained currency. However, it is true that the terminology of OEP and the development of a distinct community of practice around the concept is the product of recent decades and is linked to the rapid increase in the use of digital technologies throughout HE (including campus based, as well as in the context of distance education).

Digital technologies have changed the way in which learners, teachers and researchers interact and strengthen collaborations and communications within a global community of peers. They have also radically changed the availability and accessibility of learning resources and activities. Examples abound – myriad educational and 'how-to' videos on almost any topic are a mainstay of YouTube. Such freely accessible online resources are not necessarily openly licensed (although they could be). Massive open online courses (MOOCs), usually offered by universities in partnership with platforms, present a case for open learning in which the course content is often, unfortunately, not made available as an OER to be reused elsewhere. These examples demonstrate partially open practices at work, which could arguably be enhanced by extending to open licensing of the resources produced, but there are also open practices that simply have less to do with resources and more to do with community and connectivity.

An example of this latter kind is the set of practices involved in networked participatory scholarship (Veletsianos and Kimmons, 2012), in which educators open up their practices and reflections in order to share, gain feedback or collaborate within loose networks of peers. This kind of activity is typically digital and uses blogs or social media, sometimes also using hashtags or scheduled chat times. The boundary of what gets discussed as open practice is fuzzy in this space. Participation in special interest groups and conferences are more familiar forms of scholarship that can also be thought of as open. These also represent spaces that afford valuable opportunities to connect and share. However, compared with networked participatory scholarship, special interest groups or conferences tend to be more formalised spaces, in the sense that participation involves barriers such as needing to register, pay a joining fee, submit an abstract or be invited to join or speak.

A key subset of OEP are those educational practices designed to facilitate the use of OER. Initial developments in this area of practice were focused on technical developments to support educator practice. Much emphasis was placed on the creation and sharing of complex forms of content such as reusable learning objects, metadata for describing and discovering them and interoperability between online platforms used for hosting resources. Practice was therefore conceived largely through the lens of digital technology and was thought to require the involvement of specialist educational technologists. However, discussion of OEP has extended rapidly beyond the technological and embraced broader issues of pedagogy and context (Cronin and Maclaren, 2018). Some authors have extended their definition of OEP to include the social context of learners:

> Those educational practices that are concerned with and promote equity and openness. Our understanding of open builds on the freedoms associated with 'the 5 Rs' of OER (reuse, retain, revise, remix, redistribute) promoting a broader sense of open, emphasising social justice, and developing practices that open up opportunities for those distanced from education. (Cannell, 2017: 8)

Within more expansive definitions of OEP, the option to reuse and remix existing material allows for new approaches to design. These new approaches include participation and collaborative methods, in particular that facilitate student engagement and deconstruct the normally binary teacher–student discourse within a learning space. For a detailed example see Chapter 15, which explores the use of OER and MOOCs to scale up global access to specialist health worker training.

The development of a set of communities and practices around OER and OEP is sometimes referred to as the open education movement (Bliss and Smith, 2017), the emergence of which is shaped by initiatives to network and share practices and, simultaneously, is informed by the view that education is not a commodity but a right (Conole and Brown, 2018).

## The promise and the drivers

Open education promises a transformation for both teaching and learning, but this transformation requires fundamental strategic change of key attributes (Hodgkinson-Williams, 2010), including:

- technical open formats (connectivity, equipment and platforms)
- legal agreements (open licence knowledge and application)
- cultural relevance (curriculum and context)
- pedagogical framework (student demographic, engagement, assessment and accreditation)
- financial level (sustainable business model).

Open licences ensure that use and reuse of content is legitimate, providing the conditions of the open licence are observed. However, educational content is always contextual – embodying expectations of prior learning, cultural norms and assumptions about the student. As a result, the 'passive option', using good-quality 'found' material, may sometimes be 'good enough', but in other instances may also create barriers to learner participation. Therefore, realising the promise of open education requires a critical awareness that educational materials are created in diverse national and international settings, often characterised by sharp social inequalities, as well as growing awareness of the need to decolonise the curriculum. This is recognised through regional initiatives such as OER Africa.[2]

Developments in OEP are working towards a paradigm shift in HE, away from exclusivist systems that were based on power, privilege and scarcity and towards open and inclusive systems of HE based on justice and human rights and abundance. For example, internationally the Commonwealth of Learning is focused on using OER to meet the United Nations Sustainable Development Goals (SDGs).[3] The Open Education Research Hub has data on the use of OER from more than 170 countries.[4] Perryman and De Los Arcos (2016) have analysed how this is contributing to women's empowerment and the SDGs. In the UK there have been projects that have focused on redefining the boundaries of the academy, focusing on non-traditional learners and involving them in participative design of new courses (Cannell, 2017).

The drivers for OEP are complex. They include socioeconomic factors such as increases in demand for lifelong learning, on-the-job learning and continuous professional development. However, they also include the possibilities created by new digital networked technologies and the personal contexts of participants. We can think of this as an ecosystem – where technology plays a role but is not separated from the social, personal and economic drivers. Political and academic willingness to respond to these drivers by engaging actively with OEP varies across the range of stakeholders – from creators to users and from policy makers to managers.

### An example: MOOCs

In HE, MOOCs have gained a celebrated level of success in bridging the transactional distance between experts and learners in a flexible and informal space on a learning platform (see Chapter 15). The initial wave of 'connectivist' MOOCs ('cMOOCs') put into practice the principle that learning and knowledge sharing rest on the ability to define personal and collective learning aims, crowdsource knowledge, share opinions, make connections and collaboratively construct learning through organic interaction. This idea epitomised the model of the cMOOCs, which placed connectivism at the centre of the learning design, assigning emphasis to self-directed learning, user-generated and OER content and knowledge creation through dialogue. As MOOCs entered the mainstream and were being delivered via commercial platforms, the dominant mode of the later wave of 'xMOOCs' was instructor led, generally video heavy and presented proprietary content with knowledge creation through structured exercises and assessment.

Consistent across this wide spectrum of learning experiences is the fact that students are required to be self-directed and the user experience of the platform plays an integral role in engaging the learner with the content. Therefore, the learning pathway within MOOCs is built around a collaborative partnership, triangulated between the expert instructor, the platform and its business model and then finally the self-directed learner with their own digital capabilities and motivation.

## OEP and OER in practice

OEP, as defined by Cronin (2017: 18), emerge from an open mindset as

> collaborative practices that include the creation, use, and reuse of OER, as well as pedagogical practices employing participatory technologies and social networks for interaction, peer-learning, knowledge creation, and empowerment of learners.

Outsourcing to proprietary platforms or third-party publishers, and the contractual arrangements this involves, can restrict this collaborative vision of open practice (Cronin, 2017). Questions of standards, quality and accessibility are critical for academics and educational technologists who wish to make use of OER. Notwithstanding the power of internet search engines, finding relevant, high-quality resources that meet individual specific needs from among the huge number of learning objects and courses that are available online is a challenge. One response to the need for open access across institutions has been the development of online repositories that store and index digital resources such as OER.

Examples of OER repositories include:

- Directory of Open Access Books.[5]
- MIT OpenCourseWare.[6]

A prior example in the UK was the Jisc-funded Jorum repository, which aimed to host openly licensed material from across HE. However, an implicit premise that the availability of material for reuse would encourage widespread uptake proved to be false and levels of engagement with the resources were low. A survey of academics in Scotland in 2015 by the OEPS project found that only around 2 per cent of respondents had made use of Jorum (unpublished report).[7] Jorum and a number of similar sites no longer exist. Open repository functionality is dependent on how easy it is to find relevant, high-quality resources. Enablers for long-term use of repositories rely on the technology, tools and services attracting a community that includes a critical mass of active, engaged users, as well as contributors to create and improve quality of content (Atenas and Havemann, 2014). Institutional repositories designed for particular subject disciplines or professional interests have had greater longevity, providing subject depth and opportunities for collaboration.[8]

UoL's member institutions illustrate a range of approaches to hosting OER, including sites that are subject specific:

- UCL, one of the largest members of the University of London (UoL) Federation, hosts a variety of repositories, including an institutional OER repository (OpenEd@UCL), a video repository containing a substantial archive of publicly accessible material (mediacentral), as well as several topic-specific OER collections such as the online catalogues UCL Archaeology Collections and UCL Ethnographic Collections.[9]
- The London School of Economics (LSE), like several UoL member institutions, prefers to release material that is free to access and share rather than openly licensed material. Its LSE Player hosts regularly released podcasts and videos of LSE's public lectures, seminar series, launches and events.[10]

**UoL example: OER repository**

**Royal Holloway: Early Music Online**

Early Music Online (EMO)[11] is a freely available, searchable repository of digital images and catalogue records for more than 10,000 musical compositions from sixteenth-century printed anthologies held by the British Library. EMO was created in over four months in 2011 by a small team that emerged from an existing relationship between Royal Holloway and the British Library. Funding was provided by a grant of £75,521 from the Jisc Rapid Digitisation Programme.

The project's primary aim was to widen access to the material by HE academics and students and by interested musicians and music lovers outside education. This aim underpinned the decision to release the images and associated metadata under Jisc's Open Education User Licence, so they could be freely copied and adapted for education and research. A secondary aim for the project was to learn how to create a high-quality, easily searchable and sustainable repository for digitised music.

Impacts

- The repository has been well used since its release, especially in the first few years when it was the first of its kind. Professor Stephen Rose, the academic lead at Royal Holloway for EMO, still regularly receives emails from music faculty and musicians about the reuse of its materials.
- EMO material has been recycled by several other open websites and repositories; for example, the International Music Score Library Project, a Wiki site of digitised scores. The digitised images are now also available on the British Library's digital repository, using the Universal Viewer application developed since EMO was launched.
- Finally, the EMO material has been used by a variety of research projects at Royal Holloway and other universities, for example, Royal Holloway's Big Data History of Music,[12] Goldsmiths' F-TEMPO,[13] and the multi-institutional Transforming Musicology project.[14]

In summary/lessons learned

- Working in partnership promoted quality during the project through shared leadership responsibilities and complementary skills.
- To boost discoverability and to avoid creating separate digital silos, the catalogue data was put in existing library discovery systems (the British Library's Explore catalogue and Jisc Library Hub Discover), with links to the digitised repository.

- Institutional investment and a pragmatic approach were key to the initial success and longer-term sustainability of EMO. For example, using Royal Holloway's digital repository meant that the platform has been regularly upgraded as part of the institution's open research strategy.
- Opening up the EMO material did widen access and was used to support teaching and learning by universities and music colleges worldwide in what is an under-funded HE discipline.

It also enabled significant 'second-order' reuse for both education and research. This points up the kinds of broad, long-term impacts this kind of sustainable open education project can achieve within the HE sector.

More recently, many universities have established websites that showcase OER created by the institution. This trend is driven by a desire to enhance reputation and enables the institution to oversee quality. Such sites encourage reuse but rarely include tools for remixing and re-versioning, limiting the potential of collaboration under open practice.

As an example, UCL shares OER course material through UCLeXtend,[15] its free/low-cost course platform, publishes open access academic books through its university press, UCL Press,[16] and hosts a collection of openly available academic and student writing through its blogging platform Reflect at UCL.[17]

The wide spectrum of institutional open practice strategy ranges from 'show and share' to specific support for connective collaborative creation of new OER. Open University UK (OU) is unusual in hosting two OER sites:

- OpenLearn showcases OU OER, some of which is drawn from its mainstream provision, and offers options to freely study short courses. Here, dissemination of OER forms part of a systematic strategy that aims to recruit some users to undergraduate and postgraduate study programmes.
- OpenLearnCreate hosts OER from many institutions and provides open tools for creating new OER.

A number of non-institutional actors have also adopted support for OER and OEP as part of their business models. Wikimedia Commons is an example of a not-for-profit site that includes OER among a much wider range of openly licensed material. Commercial providers tend to offer a platform to host and showcase OER, while users are supported with design tools for OER creation and OEP if they (or, more often, their institution) subscribe. This is yet another example of the tensions and contradictions that characterise the open/closed matrix. Although they are commercial sites, YouTube and Flickr both include material shared under CC licences. Only some of this material is of relevance to formal education, but a great deal of it addresses the learning needs of people who wish to find out how to read their electricity meter, build a garden shed, fold paper napkins into exotic shapes, repair their washing machine and thousands of other practical skills. There is a blurring of boundaries between dedicated repositories and platforms that host OER and these sites. YouTube and Flickr have huge reach and an enormous user base, but OER coexist within a commercial framework.

When seeking to locate OER, practitioners are faced with a wide range of options and user experiences in the quest to extract the content they require. In navigating this complex landscape, it is worth noting that publishers or platforms may declare their content is open (as in, available) when in legal terms, it is not – a phenomenon sometimes known as 'open washing' (Villum, 2014). For example, Google Maps is often referred to as an open resource even though the data behind it is not openly available. Such content should be fine to use as is but will be harder to contextualise and most likely impossible to adapt.

We list here some interesting examples from within UoL of widening participation, active curation and networked practices. While reading them you may find it helpful to think about these examples through the lens of the 'open' versus 'closed'. What factors define these concepts within the digital arena and the ecology of an institution?

**Further examples**

The **UCL Centre for Holocaust Education** uses OER and low-cost training materials in its large-scale provision of teacher training to school teachers across England to strengthen commitment to genocide prevention. In the ten years from 2009 to 2019, they reached 12,477 teachers and this number continues to grow. The initiative is managed by an expert team that ensures the materials are based on the latest evidence.[18]

**Step up to Postgraduate Study in Arts** is a 'MOOC-inspired' Birkbeck College course (originally designed in 2012 and run annually since), which is free to attend for incoming MA students before they start their formal study. The course is mostly, but not completely, online and asynchronous, in contrast to Birkbeck's typical model of evening classes. Bookending face-to-face 'events' emphasise social learning and networking, thereby providing a foretaste of the 'Birkbeck experience', as well as skills development and practice. This example illustrates a role that open practices can play as part of the learning and teaching ecology of an institution, where interleaved open and closed practices are situated in both the digital and physical space (Havemann, 2020).

**Teaching translation through editing Wikipedia** was a Wikimedia-led 'editathon' for UCL translation studies students. The students translated women's health articles into several different target languages. The open practice involved using the tools correctly, working in edit mode, learning how to make a link and how to reference and Wikipedia etiquette to work within the sandbox of the target language.[19]

**Blogs by Birkbeck Arts** research students is an archive of freely available blogs, online diaries and podcasts from students on their research interests; for example, production practices in local community radio, the relationship between medicine and visual culture or synergies between thinking and writing in the arts.[20]

**Alumni and postgraduate students working together on dissertation and research topic decisions.** A database of openly available co-created short videos to enhance users' (future postgraduate students) awareness of how their choice of research questions and methodological approaches will impact successful completion of their dissertation/report.[21]

**The Economics of COVID-19 webinar series** is free to access and co-organised by the School of Oriental and African Studies (SOAS) Department of Economics and the SOAS Open Economics Forum. The aim of the series is to provide a critical perspective to the recent economic developments related to the COVID-19 crisis.[22]

**UoL example of open networked practice: the Bloomsbury Learning Exchange**

The Bloomsbury Learning Exchange (BLE)[23] is a digital education centre for six HE partner institutions co-located in Bloomsbury, central London: Birkbeck, London School of Hygiene & Tropical Medicine, Royal Veterinary College, SOAS, UCL and UoL. The BLE exists to share good practice between its partners and enable collaboration on technology-enhanced learning projects. We share two examples of the BLE's use of OER in this analysis.

**BLE OER book**: *Assessment, Feedback and Technology: Contexts and case studies in Bloomsbury* (Havemann and Sherman, 2017).[24]
Through 21 case studies, this book showcases technology-enabled pedagogy and technical development in the use of technology for assessment and feedback by BLE institutions. The book enables BLE partners and the wider HE landscape to see how institutions are using learning technologies to support assessment and feedback in both pedagogic and administrative senses, gain a better understanding of current practices and share good and innovative practices. As the editors noted following publication, although they selected a CC-BY-NC-ND licence to share the book, which allows open access and distribution but does not permit remixing or resale, they nonetheless consider the book a kind of OER, stating: 'part of the ethos of OER is that resources should be adaptable. We felt that here however, in this case of a collection of authored papers, that it is not the book or paper itself we are inviting someone to adapt, but the ideas contained within it' (Sherman and Havemann, 2018).

**BLE OER course**: 'Digital Skills Awareness'
The Digital Skills Awareness Course (DSAC)[25] is a self-directed OER course to help students new to HE to identify the key digital skills they already have and the ones they need to acquire or improve to succeed in their studies. Based on a CC licence, DSAC is a generic Moodle course available on request to HE institutions to install on their virtual learning environment. A memorandum of understanding is agreed between the BLE and the adopting institution and detailed guidance is shared on how institutions should customise the course for their students' needs and address support mechanisms for them.

A small project team of two ensured quality throughout in several ways:

- Carrying out two needs analysis surveys with tutors and students to guide curriculum development.
- Bringing together a working group from across the BLE institutions to guide major decisions. The working group pulled together the curriculum, found collaborators and reviewed content for the course. This included reviewing specially developed material and already existing OER content from other HE institutions.
- Carrying out informal conversations with various stakeholders throughout the project.

Originally, the course was to be made available only to the six BLE partners. However, the team decided to apply a CC-BY-NC-SA licence to the course and guidance materials to 'share back' with the wider HE community that had contributed OER material. DSAC was originally launched in late 2019 and a small annual budget has enabled the BLE team to regularly update the curriculum and materials and keep adopting institutions informed of the changes. In the year since its release, more than 50 UK HE institutions have requested a copy of the course so far, many more than the original scope of the six BLE institutions.

The project has also led to several additional outputs and new opportunities for the BLE; for example:

- Presentations by the project team to the Association of Learning Technologies conference, the UK Heads of e-Learning Forum and the Jisc Digital Capability Community of Practice in 2018 and a paper presentation at the Research in Distance Education conference in 2019.
- A new collaboration with a MOOC provider to adapt the course for a large-scale international audience.
- A request from BLE members for a similar OER course for teaching staff. This has been developed and is initially being implemented as part of UoL's postgraduate certificate in learning and teaching before being made available to other institutions.

> In summary, 'opening up' DSAC and ensuring the quality during project development and after launch have already led to it having a significantly larger and wider set of impacts than originally anticipated. In 2021, the team was presented with the Roger Mills Award for Innovation in Teaching and Learning for the open approach they took.

## Challenges in OEP

Thus far we have discussed the aspirations of the open education movement and illustrated some of the progress made with examples of OEP and OER from a range of organisations. However, OEP is not universally understood, let alone accepted as core to HE, despite various supranational and government initiatives and a large volume of supportive research findings. We turn now to consider the challenges faced by OEP and ways of meeting those challenges.

### Widening access

Widening access is not just about overcoming situational barriers. Kahle (2008: 35) explains that the practice of openness in education 'is measured by the degree to which it empowers users to take action, making technology [and content] their own, rather than imposing its own foreign and inflexible requirements and constraints'. Open education presupposes the participation of the learner and the educator. Self-determination, lifelong learning and personal agency take centre stage, defined by personal goals and outcomes, but also by how the process empowers them to take the action.

Evidence from an OER impact study (Masterman et al., 2011) found that engaging students with open content necessitates raising awareness and appreciation of copyright, intellectual property rights, plagiarism and information literacy. The study also highlighted that academics engaging with OER need to reconsider existing practices and appraise developing content that can be used across different settings through collaborative networking. Using OER can initiate new conversations about the learning experiences and how best to facilitate them.

In thinking about access, it is important to stress that the connection between the learner and the learning resource is neither simple nor linear, but shaped and reshaped by the context and history of both across spatial, temporal and process dimensions. Spatial access goes beyond geographical or physical barriers as access to digital devices becomes more widely available and affordable. Traditional distance learning models provided access, but opportunities for participants were often restricted to subject-specific or mono-disciplinary learning. Crossing these barriers through an open approach creates the opportunity to examine the potential of interdisciplinary approaches and rethink the constraints of traditional qualification frameworks. Providing learner contexts are integrated into the design process, OER that are created for one location can be adapted, shared and applied to another.

Digital resources and digital communication technologies enable both synchronous and asynchronous contact between students and between students and lecturers, which are driven by participants rather than a predetermined lecture timetable. In principle, open courses enable learning engagement and interaction through a personalised time framework – a utopia of participation and equity. This challenges the formal timetabled practice in education and provides a shift in practice as it empowers users to take control through technology. However, it also sets new challenges in developing collaborative pedagogies, which make space for student participation in design and delivery.

While the earliest MOOCs conformed to the cMOOC model, most of the subsequent MOOCs adopted pedagogy based more on the principles of an extended classroom, with plans to support a high level of student – content interaction but limited student – teacher interaction (xMOOCs) (Miyazoe and Anderson, 2013). Although most MOOC platforms offer a range of options for both synchronous and asynchronous student-to-student interactions such as discussion fora, chat, video conferencing and screen sharing, most of this is optional and take-up often depends on student motivation. Many of the MOOCs set up as 'runs' within set points in time within a year have started to develop an on-demand approach to enable personalised participation.

Collaborative networks start with educators but also invite learners to engage as participants and contributors. Both lecturers and students operate in a digital environment where online educational resources are ubiquitous. Recognising this requires a cultural shift for institutions and individual faculties. Democratising education through an open approach requires shifts in roles and boundaries and relocates traditional programmes into the broader setting of lifelong learning. The process and networked partnerships behind MOOCs have been a catalyst for change within the HE sector and for the involvement of a wide range of stakeholders from universities teaching online, with governments in countries including India, France, Mexico and China taking on active and investment roles around MOOCs and even edtech and industry. As the MOOC markets evolve, these collaborations and services are likely to require partners outside the HE sector and growing partnerships with technology companies. Governments correlate education with development and MOOCs offer the potential of large-scale, low-cost opportunities to increase the pace of innovation, social mobility and even social inclusion for target groups. In response, by way of an example, the European Association of Distance Teaching Universities' MOONLITE Hague Declaration in 2019 clearly set out MOOCs as a tool for social inclusion for refugee populations (Read, 2019).

The extent of institutional involvement in widening access through the use of OER is varied and dependent on motives ranging from altruistic (often subject specific or for the wider good), strategic adoption enabling cost-effective content development (sharing and using) or as means of innovative revenue generation (Hylén, 2002).

## Ensuring quality

The sharing of accumulated knowledge through appropriately developed resources, which go on to support and strengthen teaching and learning, is central to open education. Open pedagogy defines the framework for the transaction of sharing within which open principles and practice can be developed by practitioners.

Global developments in the use of digital resources are likely to affect curriculum, pedagogy and assessment directly or indirectly, whether or not institutions have developed formal policies (for more information on this see Chapters 8, 11 and 12). This is likely to accelerate in the field of personalised and independent learning. It is therefore important that concerns about the quality of OER are addressed through rigorous quality assurance processes. Measures of quality are highly debated. Traditionally, there is an assumption that it resides within the confines of exclusivity and distinctiveness (Harvey and Green, 1993). Educational institutions (particularly 'elite' universities) have built their reputations based on this notion. Open education challenges this definition.

Thinking about quality in a context where OER are freely available via the web and can be reused, revised and adapted requires a more expansive definition. There is a growing emphasis on evaluating quality through a framework that includes:

- an academically sound body of knowledge, ideally supported by research
- the creation of a pedagogically structured learning experience as a participatory process, involving local support and cultural contextualisation
- recognition of learning achievement through rigorously controlled assessment, accreditation and certification.

Bulathwela et al. (2019) propose five quality verticals when looking at the quality of open resources:

- understandability (includes language and cultural context)
- topic coverage (considers document or content entropy and broadly how the topic is considered)
- freshness of information (recognition of knowledge decay and validating content by date)
- presentation (video, audio and language)
- authority (academic authorship and reliability).

Beyond these criteria and the formal quality systems that may accompany them, students will need help to develop and bring to their studies their own critical standards and approaches.

## Affordability and business models

For more than two decades, digital technologies have been reshaping the traditional lecture-classroom approach to HE. The global impact of the COVID-19 pandemic, including the need for social distancing, has accelerated this process. Had open resources and practices already been ubiquitously distributed throughout the HE sector, the challenges of the pandemic should have been easier to mitigate, both in terms of staff time spent grappling with technology, pedagogy and sourcing e-resources to support learning at a distance and the cost to institutions (for example, to bolster holdings of e-resources). Encouragingly, though, educators do seem to have embraced networked sharing and discussion and a tolerance for experimentation and iteration in response to the uncertain and evolving situation (Havemann and Roberts, 2021). At the time of writing, the long-term impact of what many still see as temporary departures from 'normal' practice are not yet clear. However, the experience of the pandemic, combined with the ubiquity of online educational resources and a continuing growth in global demand for HE suggests that 2022 has proved to be a catalyst for change, enabled experimentation with innovation in modes of delivery through online, blended, hybrid curriculum designs, platforms, software and the potential to scale up flexible options.

In a largely marketised global HE system, paying for the exclusivity of the institution and faculty is being reshaped by the abundance of alternatives on the internet. Models of MOOCs that started as informal learning, where certification was not the central driver but rather the OEP and opportunity to learn, are being replaced by MOOCs with a different purpose.

The main question around sustainability of MOOC business models is centred on accreditation value for the career of the lifelong learner. Recognition for learning has been the key driver of the move towards 'freemium' models, such that access to content remains 'free', but certificates or badges need to be paid for at a level sufficient to cover fixed costs.

Major MOOC providers are now providing routes to accreditation through 'Nanodegrees' on Udacity, specialisations on Coursera and credit-bearing MOOCs and micro-credentials via FutureLearn that enable transfer of credit towards degrees. In India and Malaysia, MOOCs are being blended into university degrees. Swayam, an Indian platform, is fast becoming one of the largest MOOC providers and distinctively integrated into the Indian educational framework, simultaneously overcoming faculty shortages and geographical barriers.

Depending on the purpose of a MOOC, its development may be funded via grants or companies, especially if tailored to specific target groups. FutureLearn entered into a partnership with the British Council to pay for certification for MOOC participants from non-OECD (Organisation for Economic Co-operation and Development) countries, facilitating indirect benefits to both consumers and providers of MOOCs. Institutional benefits from investing in MOOCs may include an increased public profile that acts as a marketing tool for their on-campus or online courses, thereby potentially attracting more informed and motivated students and supporting improved retention and success rates.

Increasingly, institutions are required to rethink how and what they offer. Hitherto, at least in the view of many academics, it was high-quality content and accreditation. If content is free, then potentially the institutional focus will shift to the quality of teaching, effective pedagogy and strong support systems, while for the learner it will shift from just taking exams to acquiring relevant knowledge and skills.

More than a decade ago, an OECD report on the potential of OER argued that the case for their use was based on:

> Altruism, leveraging taxpayers' money; efficiency in cutting content development costs; providing a showcase to attract new students; offering potential students a taster of paid-for content; and to stimulate internal development and innovation. (OECD, 2007)

This list was extended by Stacey (2012) who suggested that the benefits to institutions adopting OER include:

> Increasing access to education; providing students with an opportunity to assess and plan their education choices; showcasing an institution's intellectual outputs, promoting its profile and attracting students; converting students into fee paying enrolments; accelerating learning; adding value to knowledge production; reducing faculty preparation time; generating cost savings; enhancing quality; and generating innovation through collaboration.

These early attempts to define the business case for open education, together with more recent developments, suggest the need for a radical change in approach from the traditional model of paying for exclusivity of the experience. Open education offers the possibility of increasing the number of learners but also of lowering the cost to learners. However, the need to attain high quality in OER means innovating.

There is much to be learned from the models established by open universities in the twentieth century – in particular, the importance of systemic approaches to organising education at large scale. However, these models largely pre-dated the internet and there is still enormous scope for combining established distance education models with the power of digital communication technologies, artificial intelligence and the affordances of OER. Current business models remain immature and more work is required to understand the balance between the immediate and lifetime institutional costs of producing, installing and maintaining support to users of the content and the cost to learners to acquire, upgrade, adopt and use it.

## Overcoming the skills gap

The ongoing digital and network revolution continues to put new options and tools at the disposal of educators, driving opportunities for new developments in OEP. The global growth of OEP includes sharing content (open papers and open publishing), sharing resources (all forms of OER, including structured courses, videos and data), as well as broadening opportunities for sharing views and opinions through blogs and social media.

Digital technology allows the expression of multidirectional openness. This can extend the relationship between teachers and students and involve wider collaborative experiences within the social and material context in which learning happens. Such approaches are sometimes referred to as post-web fusion pedagogy (Fawns, 2019), combining andragogy (adult learning) and heutagogy (self-directed learning) within the formal and informal curriculum.

> **Example: EU project for open-source educational gaming**
>
> Open learning and its practice through technology provides a wide range of opportunities within the classroom setting (blended learning) and in wider informal spaces, enabling self-driven learning on MOOCs, discussion boards, peer-to-peer learning and even learning from gaming.[26]

As we become more dependent on the use of technology in education and shift from participatory to collaborative openness, there are new challenges for educators and learners. There can be a gap between digital content creators and the digital learning skills required to receive online content, engage with it and become an active participant rather than simply a consumer. Overcoming this gap demands support for educators and learners alike to develop pedagogical and learning skills appropriate for these new environments. Freely available content on the internet can also lead to misinterpretations and lack of awareness of the role and application of intellectual property rights, open licensing and permissions to correctly use and reuse the content. Operating in an 'open' world offers new freedoms but also demands new skills. It is necessary to teach and support learners in the competences needed to extract the knowledge appropriately and apply it.

## Conclusion: the adoption of OEP

Environments and infrastructures that enable collaboration, as well as funding to support the development of OER and OEP, are essential if we are to foster the transformation and innovation that is required for equitable education. Adoption of OEP across universities is slow and entangled with:

- motivations to share or adopt resources and perceived uncertainty regarding quality
- the work of fostering collaborative cultures for content creation and understanding of licensing
- recognition from stakeholders and policy makers that business models are needed to support sustainability (Harvey and Green, 1993).

Enabling factors for the adoption of OEP and OER by individual academics are likely to include institutional or departmental 'norms', as well as their broader cultural and social context to accept and engage with OEP. The need for educators to accept and use OER within their teaching highlights that it is the individual who is the 'agent of change' that develops practice rather than the technology being used (Littlejohn and Hood, 2017). Academics often engage very deeply with their content and may feel that it is somehow wrong or inappropriate to use educational resources and practices developed by others.

The OER adoption pyramid from Cox and Trotter (2017) succinctly captures social norms, institutional strategic commitments and individual values that define OER readiness, and includes the following six factors:

- Access to appropriate infrastructure, such as the internet, computers, software and stability of electricity supply, which is relevant for many low-resource settings.
- Awareness of the conceptual difference between OER and other forms of free or copyright educational materials.
- Permission to license, which many academics lack under their institutional contract-linked intellectual property right policies. Academics will need to hold the copyright in their own teaching materials in order to make them OERs.
- Capacity, which is based on legal knowledge. At the individual level, this requires familiarity with the CC licensing and technical skills needed to apply it to one's own work, as well as for reusing and adapting OER content. At an institutional level there needs to be policies to recognise and enable public access to content.
- Availability of high-quality resources, which have local relevance and anticipated utility for local needs. This requires awareness of

the growing number of repositories but also a willingness and confidence on the part of the academic to make their own content available. Branding and sharing OER can add value to an institution and gain recognition as a collaborator.
- Volition to adopt open practices, as the use and creation of resources for sharing is driven by the individual academic's beliefs and teaching style. At an institutional level these are guided by strategic policies and educational philosophies.

In a collection of essays on OER in Asia (Dhanarajan and Porter, 2013), the contributors, from a wide range of different countries, find significant similarities in the challenges facing the further development of OEP. Prominent among these is a disjuncture between institutional policy and staff practice, with a strong culture of individual academics wanting to retain ownership and control of resources that they have developed. These examples suggest that wider adoption of OEP requires policy changes that support systematic development of the new skills needed to engage in the digital environment and build on existing best practice to develop new pedagogy.

Open practices promote a shift towards collaboration in education. This is a move away from the familiar idea of the lone teacher who develops and delivers content in isolation. Co-creation is an exchange that can involve the blurring of the boundary between the roles of students and educators. In the unprecedented disruption it has caused across HE, the COVID-19 pandemic has provided overwhelming evidence that the need for open practices and resources is great. One of the few silver linings of this traumatic period has been the collective responses of educators who have shared experiences and resources, supported colleagues and students and opened up new discussions about pedagogic success, failure and uncertainty through webinars, blogs and working groups. The good news, then, is that colleagues are already engaging in open practices; the challenge is to ensure that its potential and expansion can be supported and sustained at an institutional level.

## Notes

1 Cape Town Open Education Declaration, 2007, https://www.capetowndeclaration.org.
2 See https://www.oerafrica.org.
3 See https://sdgs.un.org/goals.
4 See http://oerhub.net/.
5 See https://www.doabooks.org/doab.
6 See https://ocw.mit.edu/index.htm.

7   A survey by the OEPS project of academics in Scotland in 2015 found that only around 2 per cent of respondents had made use of Jorum (unpublished report).
8   A rich resource is maintained by one UK academic: https://mickhealey.co.uk/resources.
9   See https://archcat.museums.ucl.ac.uk/; https://ethcat.museums.ucl.ac.uk/.
10  See https://www.lse.ac.uk/lse-player.
11  See http://www.earlymusiconline.org.
12  See https://www.royalholloway.ac.uk/research-and-teaching/departments-and-schools/music/research/research-projects-and-centres/big-data-history-of-music/.
13  See https://f-tempo.org/.
14  See https://tm.web.ox.ac.uk/.
15  See https://extend.ucl.ac.uk/.
16  See https://www.uclpress.co.uk/.
17  See https://reflect.ucl.ac.uk/.
18  See https://www.holocausteducation.org.uk/teacher-resources/.
19  See https://www.ucl.ac.uk/teaching-learning/case-studies/2015/jun/teaching-translation-through-editing-wikipedia.
20  See http://blogs.bbk.ac.uk/research/about/.
21  See https://www.ucl.ac.uk/teaching-learning/case-studies/2018/nov/alumni-and-postgraduate-students-working-together-dissertation-and-research.
22  See https://www.soas.ac.uk/economics/webinars/.
23  See https://www.ble.ac.uk/.
24  See https://www.ble.ac.uk/ebook.html.
25  See https://www.ble.ac.uk/digitalawareness.
26  See https://opengame-project.eu/.

# References

Atenas, J. and Havemann, L. (2014) 'Questions of quality in repositories of open educational resources: A literature review'. *Research in Learning Technology*, 22, 1–13. Accessed 26 July 2022. https://doi.org/10.3402/rlt.v22.20889.

Bliss, T. J. and Smith, M. (2017) 'A brief history of open educational resources'. In R. S. Jhangiani and R. Biswas-Diener (eds), *Open: The philosophy and practices that are revolutionizing education and science*. London: Ubiquity Press, 9–27. Accessed 26 July 2022. https://doi.org/10.5334/bbc.b.

Bulathwela, S., Yilmaz, E. and Shawe-Taylor, J. (2019) 'Towards automatic, scalable quality assurance in open education'. Paper presented at Workshop on AI and the United Nations SDGs at International Joint Conference on Artificial Intelligence. Accessed 26 July 2022. https://www.k4all.org/wp-content/uploads/2019/08/IJCAI_paper_on_quality.pdf.

Cannell, P. (2017) 'Open educational practices in Scotland: Final project report'. The Open University in Scotland, September. Accessed 26 July 2022. https://www.open.edu/openlearncreate/pluginfile.php/266560/mod_page/content/2/OEPS%20final%20report%20%28Web%29.pdf.

Cannell, P., Page, A. and Macintyre, R. (2016) 'Opening educational practices in Scotland (OEPS)'. *Journal of Interactive Media Education*, 1, 12.

Conole, G. and Brown, M. (2018) 'Reflecting on the impact of the open education movement'. *Journal of Learning Development*, 5 (3), 187–203.

Cox, G. and Trotter, H. (2017). 'Factors shaping lecturers' adoption of OER at three South African universities'. In C. Hodgkinson-Williams amd P. B. Arinto (eds), *Adoption and Impact of OER in the Global South*. Cape Town: African Minds, 287–347. https://doi.org/10.5281/zenodo.601935

Cronin, C. (2017) 'Openness and praxis: Exploring the use of open educational practices in higher education'. *International Review of Research in Open and Distributed Learning: IRRODL*, 18 (5), 15–34.

Cronin, C. and Maclaren, I. (2018) 'Conceptualising OEP: A review of theoretical and empirical literature in open educational practices'. *Open Praxis*, 10 (2), 127–43.

D'Antoni, S. (2009) 'Open educational resources: Reviewing initiatives and issues'. *Open Learning*, 24 (1), 3–10.

Dhanarajan, G. and Porter, D. (eds) (2013) 'Open educational resources: An Asian perspective'. The Commonwealth of Learning. Accessed 26 July 2022. https://www.oerknowledgecloud.org/archive/pub_PS_OER_Asia_web.pdf.

Edwards, R. (2015) 'Knowledge infrastructures and the inscrutability of openness in education'. *Learning, Media and Technology*, 40 (3), 251–64. Accessed 26 July 2022. https://doi.org/10.1080/17439884.2015.1006131.

Fawns, T. (2019) 'Postdigital education in design and practice'. *Postdigital Science and Education*, 1, 132–45. Accessed 26 July 2022. https://doi.org/10.1007/s42438-018-0021-8.

Harvey, L. and Green, D. (1993) 'Defining quality'. *Assessment & Evaluation in Higher Education*, 18 (1), 9–34.

Havemann, L. (2020) 'Open in the evening: Openings and closures in an ecology of practices'. In D. Conrad and P. Prinsloo (eds), *Open(ing) Education: Theory and practice*. Leiden: Brill Sense, 329–44. Accessed 26 July 2022. https://doi.org/10.1163/9789004422988_015.

Havemann, L. and Roberts, V. (2021) 'Pivoting open? Pandemic pedagogy and the search for openness in the viral learning environment'. *Journal of Interactive Media in Education*, 1 (27), 1–11. Accessed 26 July 2022. https://doi. org/10.5334/jime.676.

Havemann, L. and Sherman, S. eds (2017) *Assessment, Feedback and Technology: Contexts and case studies in Bloomsbury*. London: Bloomsbury Learning Environment. https://doi.org/10.6084/m9.figshare.5315224.v1.

Hodgkinson-Williams, C. (2010) 'Benefits and challenges of OER for higher education institutions'. Commonwealth of Learning report. Accessed 26 July 2022. http://hdl.handle.net/11599/3042.

Hylén, J. (2002) 'Open educational resources: Opportunities and challenges'. OECD. Accessed 26 July 2022. https://www.oecd.org/education/ceri/37351085.pdf.

Kahle, D. (2008) 'Designing open educational technology'. In T. Iiyoshi, M. S. V. Kumar (eds), *Opening Up Education: The collective advancement of education through open technology, open content, and open knowledge*. Cambridge, MA: MIT Press, 27–45.

Lipscomb, A. A. and Bergh, A. E. (1905) *The Writings of Thomas Jefferson*. Washington, D.C.: Thomas Jefferson Memorial Association.

Littlejohn, A. and Hood, N. (2017). 'How educators build knowledge and expand their practice: The case of open education resources'. *British Journal of Educational Technology*, 48 (2), 499–510.

Masterman, L., Wild, J., White, D. and Manton, M. (2011) 'JISC Open Educational Resources Programme: Phase 2 OER impact study'. Accessed 20 January 2023. https://www.openpractice.org/sites/default/files/jiscoerimpactstudyresearchreportv1-0.pdf.

Miyazoe, T. and Anderson, T. (2013) 'Interaction equivalency in an OER, MOOCS and informal learning era'. *Journal of Interactive Media in Education*, 2, 1–15.

OECD (Organisation for Economic Co-operation and Development) (2007) 'Giving knowledge for free: The emergence of open educational resources'. Accessed 26 July 2022. http://www.oecd.org/dataoecd/35/7/38654317.pdf.

Perryman, L. A. and De Los Arcos, B. (2016) 'Women's empowerment through openness: OER, OEP and the Sustainable Development Goals'. *Open Praxis*, 8 (2), 163–80.

Read, T. (ed.) (2019) 'MOONLITE: The Hague Declaration. Establishing MOOCs as a tool for societal change'. Accessed 5 August 2021. https://eadtu.eu/images/publicaties/2019_-_The_Hague_Declaration_MOOCs.pdf.

Sherman, S. and Havemann L. (2018) 'It's lovely out here: How we (self) published in the open'. UK Copyright Literacy, 13 April. Accessed 26 July 2022. https://copyrightliteracy.org/2018/04/13/its-lovely-out-here-how-we-self-published-in-the-open/.

Smith, D. E. (2019) 'The state of the Commons'. In D. E. Smith, *The People's House of Commons: Theories of Democracy in Contention*. Toronto: University of Toronto Press, 1–18. Accessed 26 July 2022. https://doi.org/10.3138/9781442685635.

Stacey, P. (2012) 'The economics of open', Musings on the Edtech Frontier blog post, 4 March. Accessed 26 July 2022. https://edtechfrontier.com/2012/03/04/the-economics-of-open/.

Tur, G., Havemann, L., Marsh, D., Keefer, J. M. and Nascimbeni, F. (2020) 'Becoming an open educator: Towards an open threshold framework'. *Research in Learning Technology*, 28. Accessed 26 July 2022. https://doi.org/10.25304/rlt.v28.2338.

UNESCO (United Nations Educational, Scientific and Cultural Organization) (2002) 'Forum on the impact of open courseware for higher education in developing countries: Final report'. UNESDOC Digital Library. Accessed 26 July 2022. Available at: https://unesdoc.unesco.org/ark:/48223/pf0000128515.

Veletsianos, G. and Kimmons, R. (2012) 'Networked participatory scholarship: Emergent techno-cultural pressures toward open and digital scholarship in online networks'. *Computers & Education*, 58 (2), 766–74. Accessed 26 July 2022. https://doi.org/10.1016/j.compedu.2011.10.001.

Villum, C. (2014) '"Open-washing": The difference between opening your data and simply making them available', Open Knowledge Foundation blog, 10 March. Accessed 26 July 2022. https://blog.okfn.org/2014/03/10/open-washing-the-difference-between-opening-your-data-and-simply-making-them-available/.

# 17
# Building the online library

Matthew Philpott, Sandra Tury and Shoshi Ish-Horowicz

The lost ancient library of Alexandria is considered to have been a great storehouse of knowledge. Traditionally, this is how libraries have been viewed and why they remain crucial to academic pursuits to this day. Indeed, it would be fair to say that libraries, alongside archives, are the core host for resources and repositories of knowledge and support on which academics, from undergraduate students to emeritus professors, rely to undertake research. Libraries, therefore, provide the foundation upon which new knowledge can be moulded and scaffolded. By association, the library is a manifestation of the core values and activities of academic life.

However, the traditional library has evolved. Since the 1990s, the internet has revolutionised the sharing and creation of information (and misinformation). While this has enabled libraries to reach out from the silos of buildings and institutions, it has also required them to redefine their worth in a crowded market. For instance, libraries now have a significant role in demonstrating why it is not safe academic practice for students to rely on Google searches, Open Access resources and Wikipedia alone, or without critical thinking about what it is they are looking at and discovering. To do so, libraries have had to emphasise how they provide reliable and trusted information resources and professional support in their use.

Additionally, rising out of this medley of opportunities and dangers that are offered by the online sphere, is the online library. As this chapter demonstrates, the online library shares many of the same concerns, services and requirements as an on-campus library, but there is a significant heightened need to consider the behaviour and specific needs of users when they are not physically present. This is new territory and therefore cannot entirely rely on traditional assumptions.

This chapter will address these needs by first explaining what is meant by the term 'online library' and why the distinction is important, before identifying the specific needs that distance learners have for library services, how the library can support these needs and, finally, where the online library should focus its efforts. In the process, discussion relies on two key examples of successful online libraries in UK higher education (HE). These are the Open University (OU) and the University of London (UoL) libraries.[1] These libraries have long histories and continue to be successfully implemented, maintained and developed and therefore provide a useful lens for the more technical and theoretical suggestions in this chapter.

## What is an online library?

All universities have an online library of one sort or another to complement their physical collections and expertise. At a minimum, these generally consist of an online catalogue, managed access to various e-resources and contact information for accessing the expertise of the librarians. In many cases, there is much more than this, including the use of digital tools to aid discovery, accessibility and statistical analysis. This is the traditional face-to-face library responding to the disruption of digital technologies and requires complex discussions around physical and digital collections in combination.

The online library differs in that all users are remote and because of geographical distance will not be able to enter a building to browse books or ask questions at any time. For some, the online library might not even be attached to a physical library at all and, even if it is, the physical infrastructure is of little or no use to the distance student.

While there are examples of remote library services that go back some time, the true online library has only really existed for the last decade or so. It came into being as a result of a combination of technological and societal changes, including access to faster and more reliable Wi-Fi connections, computerisation of mobile devices, the development of a wide variety of digital tools and a general infusion and acceptance of these technologies into daily life. During the same period (and linked to the above reasons) students studying their degrees remotely have begun to receive increasing acceptance and interest. Where OU and UoL were nearly alone in offering such an approach for students, now the market is flooded with options. The short-term and long-term changes wrought on universities and student studies by the COVID-19 pandemic only look to increase this trend.

In its most essential form, an online library should be a digital online replica of traditional libraries, relying on PDFs, e-resources, online catalogues, discovery tools and virtual communication tools to replace physical books, journals and in-person access to library experts. However, a true online library is much more than a simple transference of on-site practices and resources. It is an expansion and alteration of the library's role and one that involves more collaboration than previously as well. OU, for example, describes its online library in terms of access to 'e-books, e-journals and databases', but it also emphasises assistance (access to expert librarians), training and guidance (providing online guidance material, offering live webinar sessions and so on). Meanwhile, UoL's Online Library sees its core mission as developing and maintaining online resources and services in support of the present and future teaching, learning and research needs of UoL's distance learning community.

This suggests that closer ties to the syllabus and, thus, closer collaboration with academic departments and staff are increasingly important for the success of an online library. A successful online library must become more directly involved in the curriculum development processes to bring the library, its resources and expertise directly to the students. Before that can happen, however, it is important to first ask the question: what exactly do students need and want from a library and how might these needs and wants dovetail into a strategy linked to the academic departments upon which the library will serve?

## What do learners need?

When asked what challenges and barriers there are for distance learners, students have tended to cite a lack of time, limited access to support networks (including peers, tutors and librarians), delayed feedback and technology that can fail or is difficult to use, as their primary sticking points. Also, extensive studies by Tury (2014) and Tang and Tseng (2013), which involved a large number of distance learners, found that a significant proportion of distance learning students did not have the necessary information literacy skills required to successfully access and use the e-resources provided by modern online libraries.

One way to look at these results, then, would be to place more effort and focus on providing information literacy skills training, in the hope that many of the challenges related to the library are resolved by this route. However, why would a student put in the effort to learn specific skills to make use of specific resources when easier options such as Google searches can, theoretically, provide them with results.

Tury (2014) found that the most important resource selection criterion for students were 'easy to access' and easy to use. Indeed, these were the main reasons why students preferred unverified, poor-quality free internet sources over the reliable academic sources provided by the online library. Tury's recommendation was not just about the provision of training but a focus on the supply end of the chain. Implementing the best available technology and sophisticated web discovery tools to enable quick efficient and 'easy' access is crucial (Tury, 2014: 441).

Thus, the answer to the important question 'what do learners need?' should not be looked at only from the top-down approach of training students how to use the tools that we have but, more importantly, we should seek to understand their information-seeking behaviours and adjust our provision accordingly. Indeed, studies into information-seeking behaviour have emphasised the importance of understanding the learners' individual context when addressing their information needs, as well as their information literacy training requirements. One size does not fit all, especially when students are situated in their own settings and reliant on their own infrastructure.

For example, students at UoL are drawn from some of the poorest countries of the world. They are 'non-traditional', as they are largely formed of mature learners and a larger cohort of students with special needs. Disability, geographic, economic, environmental, professional, social factors and limited educational opportunities must all be factored into understanding what is needed from the online library. In contrast, students studying at OU are predominantly based in the UK but are again often 'non traditional'. Most students in HE in the UK, meanwhile, have come directly from a school or college and are in their late teens or early twenties. Is this also true of students that decide to study at a distance? Possibly not.

Returning to Tury (2014), there are significant factors that influence distance learners' information-seeking behaviour. The first is the learners themselves, especially the individual context in which they work, the barriers that stem from that specific context, such as those imposed by time, distance and instructional approaches (pedagogy), as well as ease of access to required information sources. Secondly, there is a need to understand needs in terms of demographic, interpersonal, psychological, environmental and logistical variables among the users of the library. Thirdly, an understanding of the user's social networks and their general information literacy skills is useful. Tury's study made a series of recommendations for supporting the needs of distance students, which can be adjusted for other circumstances. These include the following:

- consideration of the role of electronic provision versus other forms of provision
- design for ease of access and ease of use
- the need for access to physical libraries
- the need for technical support
- the need for student support in the broadest sense
- the responsibility of the institution for full provision of information resources and the provision of information literacy skills
- the design of distance learning programmes with integral information design rather than merely a translation of on-campus programmes
- the need for a communications strategy
- the role of the institution in education literacy skills for a better understanding and appreciation of the purpose of study.

Since the publication of this study, the UoL Online Library has made several significant improvements to its service, which enhance the students' learning experience and help to take into consideration the study's findings, including the implementation of a single sign-on authentication system, which enables students to access all their learning materials wherever they are held, whether in virtual learning environments (VLEs), the Student Portal or the Online Library, with one single username and password. Additionally, it has embedded information literacy into the postgraduate programmes and has introduced the Ask-A-Librarian live service, which enables students to chat in real time with reference librarians. The tagging system within the Ask-A-Librarian system enables the Online Library to obtain meaningful feedback and statistics about live chats, which can then be used to inform further service developments.

The delivery of a successful distance learning library service, therefore, requires a thorough understanding of the information and learning needs of distance learners and their information-seeking behaviour. When Mallon (2018: xiii) asked the question, 'how can we equip students with the skills to understand nuance and to critically navigate this digital world?', the answer would seem, in part, to be in how libraries design their collections and services and how they employ underpinning technologies that work for, rather than against, their users' information-seeking behaviour. Most important, however, is the quality of data and feedback that is sought and then used to adjust the approach taken.

Therefore, institutions and libraries must first understand the unique needs of their distance learning community and then work out the best way of meeting those needs that ensures the fastest and most reliable form of access. Library surveys are one place to start but are not enough. Egesah and Wahome (2017: 45), for instance, emphasise how HE institutions (HEIs) are increasingly interested in 'systematic feedback' from graduates to see how their products are used, perceived and provoke success. This is certainly another place to look, but both cases require the user to respond.

To develop an online library that suits all user needs, all available information must be used to identify information-seeking behaviour. For instance, any interaction with students should inform a picture around wider needs, statistics and information gleaned from systems must be analysed and understood, but in-depth research into student communities should also take place. Surveying, focus groups and similar methods for data collection and feedback are critical. They must consider the diversity of the stakeholder population, including variations between 'undergraduate', 'taught' and 'research post-graduate' and academic staff levels, differences and similarities between disciplines and the unique nature of studying at a distance and thus being entirely (or mostly) reliant on online support and access. This is a natural extension of the age-old library principle: know your users.

Establishing distance learners' needs is far more complex than establishing the needs of on-campus students because its requirement goes beyond understanding the collections and services that libraries and the institution provides, to understanding the learners' local environment and barriers to information access and use, including the learner's own personal characteristics, such as their educational background and information literacy skills level.

The other main challenge is that academic libraries do not own the digital collections that are required for teaching and learning; they simply license them from publishers, e-journal aggregators or database suppliers, among others. This means that if the supplier's database or e-book platform is clunky and ineffective, there is very little the online library can do to change this apart from choosing a different supplier. In many instances suitable alternatives cannot be obtained. Therefore, while the starting point should be the users themselves, significant consideration should be given over to what the library should, and can, offer considering restrictions such as finances, technologies and third-party suppliers.

## What should the library offer?

The question of 'what should the library offer?' comes down to a basic principle of equity. Library services are an important element in learner support and there is evidence that library users value the library more highly than many other university-supplied services (Tait, 2000). By their very nature, libraries are inextricably linked to distance learning because of the resource-based nature of this mode of study. Indeed, according to the Society of College, National and University Libraries (SCONUL), institutions that fail to capitalise on their libraries will find it hard to compete in the future. The SCONUL statement on the value of academic libraries states that 'satisfaction with library services was in the top ten (eighth) of the factors that prospective students would consider when deciding which university to apply for' (SCONUL, 2019).

Parnell (2002), meanwhile, stresses that it is also essential that academic libraries provide 24/7 access to online library and information resources, which should include:

- library catalogues
- access to citations, indexes and full-text electronic journals
- direct access by students to materials contained in general and research collections
- access to resources referred to in reading lists
- assistance from professional librarians via email, telephone, fax and face to face
- delivery of documents to students, both electronically and via courier or regular postal services
- training and user education programs and resources via the web, email, telephone, and face to face (including offshore)
- filtered access to websites via subject and course-based virtual libraries and facilitated access to the physical collections of other institutions.

Each of these factors needs to be provided for by the online library just as equally as it would be for on-campus study. The principle of equity is prominent in the requirements of accreditation agencies and quality assurance agencies (Tury, 2014) and it should be the basis for what the library seeks to offer.

In the USA, the Association of College and Research Libraries (ACRL), a division of the American Library Association that is responsible for distance learning library standards and guidelines, recommends that all HEIs must meet the needs of all their faculty, students and academic support personnel, regardless of where they are located. It recommends that the equity principle or access entitlement is applied to courses taken for credit or non-credit in continuing education programmes, in courses attended in person or to 'individuals at a distance' (ACRL, 2016: 1). The concern for ensuring the delivery of equivalent library services to college and university faculty, students and other personnel in remote settings was indeed the primary motivation for establishing and maintaining the guidelines since their inception in 1963.

The Canadian Association of College and University Libraries has similar guidelines that were written as early as 1963 and state that: 'The university library has an obligation to give service to all students enrolled in the university credit courses whether or not such courses or students are in the university town' (Horan, 2014: 21). Equivalent professional organisations in Australia and India have published guidelines for distance library provision (Horan, 2014), all of which assert the rights of distance learners to equivalent levels of library support as traditional students.

There are currently no official guidelines or standards for distance library provision in the UK. This might be related to the fact that under the original OU course model most of its students were assumed not to require a library service – an assumption that was influenced by the belief that the strong public library system in the UK could meet their needs (Parnell, 2002: 9). With the huge growth in distance learning programmes and a reduction in public library services this assumption is no longer valid. As an example, UoL has over 50,000 students from over 190 countries in the world. Many of these countries are developing countries and, in many cases, have varied and limited public library infrastructure. This is why many regional as well as discipline-oriented accreditation agencies are becoming increasingly more stringent in their expectations of standards that programmes taught at a distance have to meet, particularly with regard to the access that students in those programmes have to library services from the parent institution (Lebowitz, 1997: 304).

The 2001 briefing paper, 'Access for distance learners: Report of the SCONUL task force' (SCONUL, 2001), addresses the library and information needs of distance library services in the UK. In addition, the Society of Legal Scholars, which is the principal representative body for legal academics in the UK and Ireland, has published standards for law libraries (including distance law libraries) (SLS, 2010). The Quality Assurance Agency, which is responsible for ensuring that HEIs in the UK maintain their academic standards and quality, has also produced subject benchmarks, which stress the fundamental role of the library.[2]

According to Lebowitz (1997: 304), the concern for equity of library services for distance learners has been a long-standing issue for many accreditation agencies in the USA. In 1990, Howard Simmons, Chair of the Middle States Accreditation Association, wrote about the need for providing library services to off-campus students, saying, 'there can be no real differences in the quality of library support on or off campus. If the same level of quality is to be maintained, comparable – not necessarily the same – library resources and services are imperative' (Lebowitz, 1997: 304). Lebowitz also notes that in 1993, the Council for Adult and Experiential Learning and the American Council on Education jointly produced a document entitled 'Collaboration on adult degree programs: Quality issues, problem areas, and action', which asserted that provision of adequate, appropriate and available services that promote the success of adult students was key to a high-quality adult programme. Lebowitz (1997: 304) admits, however, that the lack of library support, particularly insufficient access to library and academic resources, remains a problem for most off-campus programmes.

Lebowitz (1997) also notes that, although many consider the library to be the heart of the university, the use of the library is often not incorporated into courses being prepared for distance learning delivery. She further mentions that while there is a growing body of literature, as well as specialised conferences, that discuss library services for off-campus students, the discussion appears primarily in library literature and, when library services are discussed in non-library literature, they are referred to as a type of service similar to advising and counselling, financial aid, registration and admissions and have little or no recognition.

Unwin et al. (1997) suggested that without ready access to a range of library resources and services, students face the risk that their learning experience will be unacceptably bound and controlled. Parnell (2002) asserts that significant differences in accessibility of learning resources and experience across study modes (distance learning versus on campus) raise serious questions within universities about the appropriateness of offering the same academic award to those students without equivalent access to learning resources.

Since students and faculty in distance programmes frequently do not have direct access to a full range of library services and materials, equitable distance learning library services are more personalised than might be expected on campus. At UoL, each programme has an individual gateway that contains resources that are directly relevant and tailored to the specific programme. Such personalisation enables students to find the resources that are relevant to their programmes in one place, thereby saving them time and allowing the online library to keep e-resource costs down through the licensing of specific e-resources for specific programmes. The traditional model of licensing resources based on the total student population of an institution is wasteful and it does not take into consideration distance learners' information-seeking behaviour, which is task oriented (Tury, 2014: 368).

Developments in information and communications technology, especially recent developments in mobile technology, have made 'equitable access' to distance learners much more achievable. While it was practically impossible to meet students' information and learning requirements with electronic collection only, these days it is possible to provide a decent library service completely online. Providing an online library service is the most equitable way of providing distance learners with access to learning materials and was behind the decision taken by UoL in 2001 to provide a completely online library service to its large and widely distributed distance learning community. It could be argued that students based in some poorer countries of the world are at a disadvantage because they do not have the same IT infrastructure as other countries (particularly good internet bandwidths and speeds). However, the barriers to digital provision are far fewer than those encountered when supplying physical learning materials to students based all over the world, for example, shipping costs, delays and items lost in transit, and physical provision is more harmful to the environment.

## Developing an online library

Considering what the student needs (and wants) and what an online library service should be offering, this chapter turns to how these general requirements can be translated into a functioning and successful library service, breaking down this question by looking at provision, accessibility and discoverability.

### Provision

As discussed, to be successful, the online library should provide e-resources and support that are appropriate to the users' needs and their behaviour. Therefore, this provision should be integrated further into the curricula offered by academic departments. A starting point is to ensure that the essential and further reading lists that tutors provide students are related to what the library provides. This involves collaboration between tutors and librarians, especially direct and active involvement for librarians in the curriculum development at the earliest possible time. Indeed, there is considerable benefit to including librarians in the development of programmes of study when they are first conceived. While this remains a challenge for many institutions (Thompson, 2002), the benefits are significant.

For instance, one obvious benefit is that the resultant provision of e-resources will be more appropriate to the user base, but there are also opportunities here to embed librarian support and training directly into students' curricula, making it more relevant and beneficial.

The provision of e-resources presents librarians with some unique challenges, one of which is managing the cost. The price of licences provided by publishers for the numerous databases that the online library must subscribe to increases every year and are often excessive. It is important to negotiate these prices as discounts can be obtained but, in general, sacrifices must be made. The huge cost of e-resources is further complicated by the fact that some e-resources, particularly e-books, have different licensing models with differing prices and access arrangements. Librarians must therefore select those models that offer the best value for money for their particular user base.

Focusing resources on the needs of the disciplines that the library will be serving and upon conclusions around the known characteristics and behaviours of the student user base is key here. Different disciplines generally require different resources and approaches to support. Understanding these needs is vital to the selection of e-resources that are most useful and appropriate. In many cases, discipline needs have changed. This is particularly obvious in subdisciplines such as digital science and the digital humanities, where complex statistical and analysing software is increasingly needed to undertake research using 'big data'. In the case of digital humanities in particular, subject librarians are unlikely to have previous experience of supporting learning and research using complex digital technologies and methodologies based on digital approaches. This has been largely unfamiliar territory to the various humanities disciplines until recently.

It is also important that an online library supports students' additional learning needs, particularly by providing extra reading materials to enable students to read more widely, thus resulting in better grades and understanding of the subject. Therefore, assumptions about needs are not enough. Meeting the changing needs of learners and the curriculum requires continuous assessment of the library resources and an acknowledgement that library provision needs to go beyond basic requirements to enable proper academic enquiry to take place.

It is necessary not only to consider the relevance of the collections to the taught curriculum but also the ease of access, as well as the skills needed to access core materials. The days when academic libraries needed to stock materials in case they were required may be coming to an end, certainly in the distance learning context. Instead, patron-driven acquisitions that are informed by learners' needs and their information-seeking behaviour are required. This targeted approach to collection development also helps to keep the library costs low or stretch resource budgets further, obtaining better value for money.

Included in such considerations is the need to be compliant with regulatory and contractual requirements, particularly in the fields of copyright, licensing and data protection, which is strictly enforced and has a significant impact on costs and control mechanisms.

Copyright/licensing in the digital environment is a challenging area and libraries are at the sharp end of policing and compliance. The area of law is complex and technical and the online library may need to have recourse to the institution's legal department for advice on occasion. For instance, in a physical library, users can be informed of copyright limitations and acceptable practices using physical notices and the use of photocopiers, scanners and handheld devices can be monitored and limited. In the digital environment, getting messages across is more challenging, particularly as many users lack copyright knowledge, extensive copying in the form of downloading can be easily done and violations can lead to access by the institution being withdrawn by the copyright owner.

It is essential that the terms of licences, once entered by the institution, are fully understood and implemented as far as possible in the control mechanisms of the online library. Licences will specify the period of use before renewal, the scope of the licence in terms of coverage of materials and the scope in terms of the user communities, perhaps limiting use to those registered on a specific programme or the number of concurrent users. The publisher will expect the institution to have in place authentication controls to protect databases from unlicensed use and these need to be actively managed and updated.

A licence may go further in specifying what use may be made of databases; access may include downloading of material but may place a limit on the extent. A user may find it is technically possible, for example, to download a large number of volumes of a journal, but the publisher might monitor and notify the institution of breaches of its licence, thus requiring the institution to establish better mechanisms and policies to limit individual usage. A clear policy to deal with and escalate measures applied to any breach will be required.

Although access to most e-resources from commercial publishers is governed by licence agreements negotiated and paid for by the institution, access to e-resources from other sources may be free at the point of use but subject to copyright. The institution and the user should be aware of the terms of use and underlying copyright in internet resources. There is also the resource-intensive exercise of tracking and maintaining accurate records of all items that are obtained and reproduced under the Copyright Licensing Agency (CLA) licence and reporting them annually to the CLA.

Data protection is also an issue. Although an institution will have oversight of its capture and management of personal data and will have a nominated manager responsible for data protection and a training programme for its staff, an online library will need to ensure its own practices are compliant with national regimes for data protection and with the professional ethics upheld by library bodies to protect their users. Large-scale data breaches are regularly reported and a library not only holds contact information and student data but potentially sensitive usage data. Compliance with data protection principles will involve basic procedures for personal interactions as well as technical measures to prevent system intrusions.

In summary, then, selections and sacrifices need to be made to balance budgets against e-resource requirements. These selections should be based upon the known needs of the disciplines being served and the student body. Online libraries should also ensure that more than a basic provision is supplied so that students can go beyond the strict requirements of module reading lists to fully explore topics and subjects. They should also consider the limitations to users in the copyright, data protection and general terms of the licence.

In all cases, the resources should be reviewed periodically and, where necessary, cancelled, replaced or enhanced. This can be achieved via a variety of mechanisms. An annual programme of review meetings is essential but, equally, balanced views taken from detailed statistics on key performance indicators are necessary. These might contain items such as expenditure, library resource use, reference desk use, faculty engagement, information literacy support, annual library surveys and feedback from university-wide student experience surveys.

## Accessibility

Providing e-resources is only worthwhile if those resources are accessible. Of course, there are all kinds of levels of accessibility that need to be considered and many challenges. The most obvious one is catering for various disabilities. How might a visually impaired user access the resources? What about someone who is deaf? How about physical disabilities that make keyboard, mouse or touchscreen options challenging or impossible? How can the online library cater to these users?

The OU has around 12,000 distance learning students a year who are registered as disabled (Smith, 2011). In the USA, Stitz and Blundell (2018: 37) found that approximately 11 per cent of enrolled undergraduate students reported having learning, visual, auditory or speech disabilities. Furthermore, many other users do not report their disabilities or are entirely unaware that these disabilities exist. As Stitz and Blundell argue, there is an ethical (as well as legal) need to educate all qualified students enrolled in a programme of study but, more than this, it is a further challenge to meet these needs when the user is studying or researching at a distance.

In December 2016, the EU put into law the Web Accessibility Directive, which required all EU states to ensure that all websites and apps are accessible to all users. The legislation was directed at everyone, not just users with disabilities. In September 2018, this EU directive became law in the UK in the form of the excitingly titled, the Public Sector Bodies (Websites and Mobile Applications) Accessibility Regulations.[3] These regulations included a requirement for educational institutions to ensure that their websites, including VLEs for students and library e-resources, portals and catalogues, are accessible to Web Content Accessibility Guidelines (WCAG) 2.1 AA standards.

It is therefore not only important that all library materials are created, curated and checked for universal accessibility for the benefit of students and researchers, but it is now a legal imperative as well. This is more challenging than it sounds. As already noted, most e-resource content is brought in by libraries via publisher subscriptions. How can an HEI ensure that external providers meet the same accessibility criteria? As yet, there is no easy solution to this conundrum. At the very minimum, the online library must enter accessibility into the equation when making e-resource purchasing decisions. While it is not necessarily the case that an e-resource would be refused if it had accessibility issues, where there is a choice between suppliers the accessibility of the item will help in making the final decision. OU, for instance, has taken a further step of attaching icons to the database pages, highlighting to students accessibility information based on their own user-testing processes (Smith, 2011).

Certainly, anyone developing an online library service must consider various accessibility issues, such as:

- creating captions and transcripts for videos
- evaluating text-to-speech functionality of resources
- checking if a database is compatible with screen readers and other adaptive technologies
- seeing if font size and colours can be adjusted.

However, part of the solution lies in creating a web accessibility policy in-house (Stitz and Blundell, 2018: 45). This does not guarantee adherence but it does provide a baseline upon which staff can be trained and online content organised, brought and created. Procurement processes, for example, should embed the web accessibility policy as a key element of consideration. Pereyaslavska et al. (2015: 104) suggest setting up a user advisory group to consider the accessibility and usability of tools and resources for the specific diversity of users who are expected to use the online library. Such a group can set out a required knowledge base of accessibility features that can be shared with potential and current third-party resource suppliers and provide a useful baseline and set of instructions for staff.

In the USA and Canada, the value of inclusive learning is also gaining rapid momentum. The core question that needs careful consideration is how to take leadership roles in becoming inclusive for all users. Pereyaslavska et al. (2015: 102) correctly argue (as the EU and UK legislation also confirm) that accessibility should not be focused exclusively on disability but on all user needs. Pereyaslavska et al. label accessibility as the removal of barriers. This is a useful way of thinking about the issue – what stops a user from accessing something? How can those barriers be removed? How can accessibility be made equitable to all?

Pereyaslavska et al. (2015: 104) also highlight staff training as vital, arguing that 'front line public services staff demonstrate knowledge and awareness of accessibility apps and adaptive technologies' and that 'all staff [are] well versed in most popular technologies such as screen readers or ZoomText'.

The technical infrastructure must therefore be carefully designed to manage such a complex task of providing access that is easy to use, robust, secure and equitable for all potential users. As mentioned, the starting point for establishing any library, especially a distance learning library service, is to establish the individual learning needs and information requirements of its distance learning community. In terms of technical infrastructure, this requires more personalisation than would normally be required in on-campus environments. For instance, if students are based in a developed country where there is a robust technology infrastructure, then standard e-book loan periods and download limits may be enough. However, if students are based in countries with poor technology infrastructure and bandwidth issues, then download speeds and download periods must be considered carefully to ensure that students have enough time to complete their assignments.

In an ideal world where resource licences are unlimited, such considerations may not be necessary. Today they must be considered because, increasingly, many e-book publishers and suppliers have single simultaneous user licences. This means that only one user can use the e-book at a time, which is very limiting and inconvenient, particularly for distance learners who often have severe time constraints because they are often juggling study with work and, as a result, try to fit in study at every possible opportunity. Therefore, if the item they need to read is not readily available at the time they are free, it could set them back a few days or even weeks.

Although an online library may provide comprehensive services, distance learning students may not have a suitable home learning environment, whether for personal or technical reasons, and in any case may prefer a collegial environment. A notable issue is that while some students can supplement their online learning with access to local physical libraries, this option is not available to all distance learners. Ideally, a worldwide digital library should be backed up by a network of local physical libraries, albeit libraries likely to be owned by other educational institutes, where distance learners have the option of local study space available to them if they need it.

## Discoverability

It is all well and good providing a range of e-resources that cover the basic and enhanced requirements of students and researchers, but provision and even accessibility is not enough. A simple and efficient means of discovering the content is the key to a successful online library. At one end of this spectrum is the need to anticipate all the needs of the end users, including those who have additional accessibility requirements. At the other end of the spectrum is a simple need to provide a seamless service that provides efficient and easily discoverable content that all users would not only benefit from but have come to expect.

*Discovery services*

Take, for instance, the provision of journal articles. These can be hidden away in various databases such as JSTOR, Muse, Science Direct, publisher websites and institutional repositories. Subscription to those databases behind a paywall alongside those that are available via open access poses a significant problem for students and researchers who need to learn of the existence of each database – including their individual strengths and weaknesses – before they can find any content at all. The division of databases also means that users will need to search several databases (if not more) before they can be certain that they have found all the material on a subject that is available to them. This is not only difficult but inefficient, annoying and requires knowledge about how e-resources are provided and what those e-resources are before a comprehensive search can even begin. Users should not need specialised training to find such content. It should be obvious, quick and easy.

There is a further but linked problem here. Mallon (2018: 20) suggests that many students come to university entirely unaware 'of the specialised resources available to them'. Google quickly becomes the default search mechanism, bypassing an unknown or perceived complex maze of institutional offerings. Students are therefore often restricted to a weaker (and potentially unreliable) availability of resources to aid their learning. Mallon argues that students expect information to be quick and easy to find and are often frustrated by the time it takes to search in academic or proprietary databases. How can the online library tackle such problems?

Web-scale discovery services such as EBSCO's Discovery Service or Ex Libris's Summon are two options available to the online librarian. These services are especially designed to index multiple databases and present to the end user a single set of search results, sometimes accommodating faceted options and/or user preferences, which help to present individual resources without the need to identify, know about or locate specific databases individually. Such discovery layers enable libraries to present search results that combine proprietary and open access holdings. However, these solutions are not cheap and many are not perfect.

As an example, Summon does not retrieve legal cases and legislation from many legal publishers' databases, including the main ones such as Westlaw. Nonetheless, UoL believed that a roughly 80 per cent coverage was much better than the previous use of multiple databases, which had led students to complain that 'it's easier to get information from friends than from the library' (Tury, 2014: 408). More needed to be done though to ensure that students were not confused and could trust the options available to them. Students were therefore advised to use JustisOne (JustCite) to locate legal cases and legislation and Summon for everything else (Tury, 2014).

Bengtson and Coleman (2019) provide a second example in the form of the Primo discovery layer used by Kansas State (K-State) University Library, which brought together most of their digital holdings, except for HathiTrust. The omission led to a swath of inaccurate records and resulted in over 30 complaints. The situation became more precarious as the librarians became reluctant to advertise the discovery layer to students. In the end, the K-State Library had to build their own application, which they called HathiGenius, to solve the problem and restore trust in the discovery layer (Bengtson and Coleman, 2019: 39–41).

The stories outlined by Tury (2014) and Bengtson and Coleman (2019) are warnings to online libraries to ensure that services always remain reliable and accurate. Failure to do so can lead to services being undermined. A carefully planned rollout and update procedure are therefore vital to ensure accuracy as well as discoverability of resources. As an example, the Senate House Library, UoL, has instigated accountability and confirmatory steps in any rollout of upgrades and digital developments. This is done via a monthly digital group supported by a SharePoint site containing mechanisms for requesting alterations to a service, receiving confirmation and discussion in group meetings and then rolling these alterations out during a monthly 'at risk' window. While such an approach does not preclude the possibility of error or failure in updates or rolling out of services, Senate House Library has found that it does provide a useful check to help institutions consider the risks more carefully (and hopefully, therefore, avoid as many of them as possible).

As Bengtson and Coleman (2019: 31) state, the online library needs to offer a 'seamless, easy flow from discovery through delivery', otherwise the service (and its reputation) will be undermined. While this point might seem obvious, it cannot be stated or emphasised enough. Users of online resources tend to expect that the systems they use provide no barriers at all and this expectation is often higher than might be the case if they were visiting a physical library where one-to-one interaction between user and librarian is possible and where expectations are different. Visitors to a library often expect some initial difficulty finding resources in a building that is unfamiliar to them. They do not expect the same for online resources.

*Using metadata*
Many online libraries have found that discoverability is often hampered by misunderstandings by users of what is available, how it is available and in what form. For instance, Bengtson and Coleman (2019) cite examples where users expect all textual sources to be available in full-text form (which is not always possible) and misunderstandings regarding the ownership of e-resource content. Moyo (2004: 221) argues that users do not necessarily grasp the idea that the catalogue contains resources that the library itself does not own.

There are various options open to the online librarian that attempt to aid the student in understanding what resources are available and how they might access them. The first is a good use of metadata. As Solomou et al. (2015: 246) argue, metadata should go beyond the obvious use of it to provide title, authorship, date, location and so forth, but also include the characteristics of its educational and pedagogical aspects. Who is the resource intended for? What type of learning does the resource promote? What is the institutional context (or rather, is this an in-house or purchased product)? Such an approach makes content more discoverable for students and embeds an understanding of context.

Various standard models exist for metadata and libraries should make use of these (or select the most useful). For example, the Dublin Core Metadata Initiative can be used for general web resources, while for educational materials there is the Institute of Electrical and Electronics Engineers Learning Object Metadata.

The provision of an online library catalogue can be enhanced via the purchase of a discovery layer, such as the one used by Kansas State University or UoL. In procuring such a system, the library needs to ensure that it will work with the type of metadata that the library uses and offers a way to enrich that metadata for greater discoverability of materials.

*Universal design*
The online library must focus on doing everything it can to provide comprehensive accessibility by setting out standards and guidelines for making web content (including e-resources) accessible to at least the WCAG 2.0 AA standard. This is incredibly challenging, not just in setting up content and resources to be accessible for as wide a diversity of students and researchers as possible, but also in maintaining and updating those materials. Stitz and Blundell (2018), for example, have tried to compile accessibility guideline rubrics based on various US institutions and US legal guidelines in an attempt to highlight best practice. In doing

so, they have encouraged libraries to follow a universal design principle when managing online resources.

Universal design is a concept that requires consideration of a wide variety of users as a core part of the design process, focusing on equitable use, flexibility, simple and intuitive access, perceptible information, tolerance for error, low physical effort and size and space (Stitz and Blundell, 2018: 43). Therefore, resources should be effective in a variety of device types (from desktop PC to mobile phone), which go beyond a simple responsive theme but into the structure of the content – thus, layout in different devices should be logical and simple to navigate and use. Directions used in the past, such as 'instructions are on the right' or 'for more details look below', no longer work as items can move around the page depending on the device. As another example, students with disabilities often rely on assistive technologies such as screen readers, text-to-speech, recording tools, predictive text and synthetic speech. Content, therefore, needs to be accessible for these different types of access. Does the resource, for example, require touchscreen or mouse clicks to work? If so, would a user who is navigating blind on your site using a screen reader be able to navigate the site successfully? Considering content as part of universal design, therefore, fits well with the core themes of WCAG 2.0 accessibility guidelines, which focus on the information being perceivable, operable, understandable and robust.

*Procurement*

To be successful, the online library needs to rely on a procurement service that puts accessibility and discoverability at the heart of purchases of e-resources. It must also be able to rely on a strong IT department or team of IT specialists, with strong knowledge and understanding of universal design and accessibility issues. As Bengtson and Coleman (2019) noted, the IT support would ideally be capable of 'sidewise development' or, in other words, the ability to creatively solve problems that are intractable within a proprietary or open source tool. However, careful thought needs to be put into these types of customisations – is there more than one person in the organisation able to provide support or further develop the customisation? How do you manage updates and errors? It is easy to focus on the here and now while building up a complex and costly legacy. This should be avoided by clear planning, processes and policies.

Providing access to resources and support, coupled with strong mechanisms for digital quality service and discoverability, are therefore vital for the online library to be a success. However, equally important is the support and teaching role that librarians need to actively pursue.

*Guidance and help*
Subject guides, research guides and library guides can all exist as documents that students can access in physical forms, such as a download or as online text (Courtney and Wilhoite-Mathews, 2015). These can take the form of curated lists of resources for students, which opens up the debate as to whether it is ideal to provide instant access, for example, to course texts, or if students are better served by having to use their own skills to find these within the online library or wider suite of recommended websites. Studies have indicated that curated lists of readings and other resources are perceived as more important by students than by lecturers, with the former appreciating them as a 'means to an end', while the latter fear they decrease learner autonomy and encourage dependence rather than assist the development of important literacy and research skills (Brewerton, 2014; Stokes and Martin, 2008). However, research has shown that even without direct guidance, students use online reading lists to develop information skills (McGuinn et al., 2017; Siddall and Rose, 2014).

Further questions around subject guides include what resources to include and how often these should, or can, be updated. Different disciplines will make use of different sources of information (Gardiner et al., 2006; Kim, 2011) and have different informational attitudes (Grafstein, 2002; Pinto and Sales, 2014). Decisions will need to be made about the inclusion of references to third-party resources; for example, to websites that may not comply with institutional or national policies around digital accessibility. With long lists of resources comes the responsibility for keeping these up to date. In 1999, Morris and Grimes found that 70 per cent of surveyed university libraries had no schedule for updating subject guides, although it is hoped that find-and-replace tools and link crawlers can make such processes easier for librarians and academics (Morris and Grimes, 1999). The OU has developed a content management system for library guides (Wales, 2005). Considering the role libraries play in developing research and information literacy skills, inconsistencies and errors in such guides are extremely problematic, giving poor examples rather than demonstrating best practice and leading to problems of confusion and loss of confidence and trust from students in their teachers (Siddall and Rose, 2014).

There are plenty of other options available to the online library to provide guidance and help. As one example, an enquiry service or reference desk is a vital part of a digital library. Users need easy access to help and support from knowledgeable professional librarians. Online support gives students more direct means of contacting librarians and being supported by their library, which is especially important given how little library and academic staff may know about whether and how students use pre-prepared guidance materials (Gourlay, 2015; Morris and Grimes, 1999). In order to support distance learners, for example, a 'real-time chat service goes some way towards reducing the inequalities that "distance" imposes' (Hinton and McGill, 2001: 59). Echoing issues with subject guides, the medium of online chat can exacerbate issues around library support – what Jacoby et al. (2016: 120) call a 'tug of war' between providing best practice guidance and pedagogy and the users' expectations for speed and convenience. There is an immediacy implied in the chat experience, which means expectations need to be clarified and transparent to users (Matteson et al., 2011).

The OU experimented with automated systems to provide a 24/7 service to deal with common requests from distance learners (Payne and Bradbury, 2002) and set up 'Librarians on call', a 'chat' or 'instant messaging' service, as its research findings suggested that users prefer chat to email or the phone. The value of chat services for distance learners was identified at an early stage (Hinton and McGill, 2001) and they are now commonly available in HE libraries (Radford and Connaway, 2013).

Recently, libraries have started looking at text and video messages as an alternative method for students to seek support. Chow and Croxton (2012: 258) concluded that, though this newer media was less common and less popular, 'libraries must carefully watch the trends, particularly among younger generations'. The synchronous communication of chat and text messages show how distance learning libraries can adapt how they communicate with students to take advantage of technological developments and conventions. Synchronous chat, however, also poses specific issues for global distance learning courses, with international network costs being a consideration for students, while the challenge of meeting possible expectations of 24-hour service is compounded by the practical difficulties of meeting the needs of a cohort studying across different time zones. For all libraries, there is a cost/benefit debate around synchronous support, with institutions, for example, outsourcing their chat service, joining partnerships and consortia and running instant messaging support for limited hours (Rawson et al., 2013).

In September 2018, the UoL Online Library implemented the Ask-A-Librarian live chat service, which enables students to chat in real time with reference librarians without incurring expensive long-distance call charges. The tagging of this system enables the online library to obtain meaningful statistics about live chats, which are used to inform service improvements. The chat service is used in conjunction with other support methods, including the virtual reference service using email and

'Cerberus' reference software, as well as by telephone. The online library has recently completely redeveloped its website, which has made it more user friendly, mobile compliant and easy to maintain by librarians with limited technical skills (not trained programmers).

As technologies and user habits develop there can be no conclusive answer to the best way of supporting distance learning students, although adoption of newer applications can be slow, with email remaining a dominant medium for reference requests despite a societal shift towards synchronous online communications (Sharpe and Norton, 2017). Still, although it seems that different media meet different information needs (Mawhinney and Kochkina, 2019) there are some consistent best practice guidelines for online support. Despite the anonymity of the media, libraries need to understand their user communities and librarians should follow basic virtual etiquette (such as greeting the patron and using enthusiastic, informal language to humanise the interaction) to best meet the needs and expectations of their users (Powers and Costello, 2019).

### Training

Subject guides can enable students to develop their literacy skills while support through email, chat or text message can assist with specific enquiries. Student needs can also be met through training modules that can be accessed on a VLE or through a link to an external module. For example, distance learning students can benefit from online synchronous library workshops (Kontos and Henkel, 2008), which seem to be as effective as traditional face-to-face instruction (Beile and Boote, 2004; Silver and Nickel, 2005). Online tutorials can take advantage of the affordances of online instruction, such as students being able to repeat or review content, pace themselves and decide individually when and where they choose to study (Bowles-Terry et al., 2010). Being involved in creating free online courses, such as massive open online courses (MOOCs), is another way for libraries to impact student learning, whilst also satisfying the libraries' need to reach wider audiences. MOOCs provide libraries with the opportunity to make a difference by supporting the needs of learners and researchers on a scale larger than distance learning currently affords.

Modules can include one or more of the following components:

- videos or screen recordings to talk students through finding resources, accessing the library tools and information literacy best practices
- quizzes for students to test their knowledge of literacy strategies and receive feedback
- synchronous elements such as scheduled webinars or chat windows for immediate communication relevant to the workshop.

The placement and distribution of training modules also need to be considered; for example, whether they should appear during orientation or at a specific academic point of need. Evidence has also shown the importance of cohort or discipline-specific instruction (Kumar and Ochoa, 2012) rather than a one-size-fits-all approach to developing training modules for large or generic student groups. Again, the question emerges: should this training be siloed from the course modules that are focused on the needs of sharing knowledge about the discipline or integrated directly within the learning objectives and assignments of the module as part of a constructive alignment approach?

Mallon (2018) argues that the online library should place a focus on outreach programmes, which target a variety of potential library users, including students, those returning to education after a long time away, distance students and research staff. Such a programme should offer a customised training package that helps users to understand library assets and develop various information, research and digital literacies.

As Mallon argues, research guides are not enough for distance students. While they can focus on topics of particular use to distance study, such as interlibrary loans, access to e-books and e-journals and other borrowing options, students studying at a distance need some other contact method. Mallon (2018: 23) suggests some form of virtual instruction such as online tutorials taking students step by step through a process or one-to-one consultations (virtual 'office hours') conducted via Skype or another video-conferencing tool.

Another option endorsed by Mallon is to provide 'liaison librarians'. These are librarians who are hired specifically to develop their role by actively engaging students and faculty in the entire academic cycle of teaching, learning and research (Mallon, 2018: 1). In essence, Mallon supports the move by librarians to nurture collaborations with departments, building on the subject librarian role. Embedding librarians, for instance, in the design of modules and in the design of materials in the VLE provides 'an obvious benefit of embedding digital resources directly into courses', thus providing access and discoverability at the point of need. Zabel calls this 'blended librarianship' (quoted in Shank and Bell, 2011: 106). Tutors and academics do not necessarily consider how a librarian might be able to help design a module or help with a research project by providing their subject expertise and familiarity with resources. The online library offers one means to help change this but does require flexibility, collaboration and integration across the institution as well as a certain 'letting go' of old models of working and control around programme design.

## The role of the librarian

University librarians are recognised as more than just 'keepers of the books' – they are instructional research partners who offer a valuable service to the future workforce and often have a direct-yet-silent hand in preparing students with important job skills. According to a 2010 report by Hart Research Associates, some of the most valued skill sets employer stakeholders ask universities to emphasise are: critical thinking and analytical thinking skills (81 per cent of employers); ability to analyse and solve complex problems (75 per cent); and the ability to locate, organise and evaluate information from multiple sources (68 per cent) – all skills academic librarians teach on a daily basis.

The role of the professional librarian has become more collaborative, focusing on close working with researchers and teaching staff with the purpose of continual renewal and reappraisal of the learning resources, their licensing, discoverability, accessibility and usability. Librarians, working in collaboration, are finding new ways to reach students remotely, with a view to embedded critical thinking and information/digital literacies that will enable them to engage with a complex, modern information landscape. Having answers to these kinds of questions helps to demonstrate the value and necessity of an online library to their institution's mission of facilitating student learning and creation. To do so libraries have taken a more active role than perhaps happened in the past.

These approaches of modern librarianship are being adopted and developed by professional librarians managing online libraries. Mallon (2018: xiv) shows that libraries are increasingly advertising for digital learning librarians and similarly titled roles, with the intention that these librarians will have expanded roles in the university that require further active engagement and collaboration with academic departments. The job descriptions describe the roles of professional librarians as educators, information architects and organisers; archivists and partners in the campus experience who actively engage and collaborate on instruction to students (in one-to-one and small group sessions), help design active learning materials and are aware of 'best practice', explore new methods for digital instruction, create online modules and provide virtual versions of reference and information services.

According to Kazakoff-Lane (2014: 31), questions about how libraries can support students and faculties should also extend beyond traditional learning activities into new opportunities and challenges, such as working on open educational resources or helping to build MOOCs. The emergence of open education on such a massive scale raises a number of challenges and opportunities for libraries, requiring them to address how they fit into this world based upon their support for openness, access to quality information for all, lifelong learning and support for teaching and learning.

As Egesah and Wahome (2017: 45) argue, there is increased pressure for institutions to continuously improve the quality of service. The focus is not just on curating resources and providing support but also on teaching and technology. An online library needs librarians who are allowed to be 'crucial partners in the effort to coach and teach students in developing critical thinking, information, and digital literacy skills' (Mallon, 2018: xviii). This is equally true for how the online library supports academic staff.

The ACRL Standards for Distance Library Provision note the importance of focusing responsibility for services:

> Libraries using innovative staffing models or distributed service models, which do not have a single specified distance learning librarian, must assign portions of that position among librarians with the requisite expertise throughout the library operation in order to carry out all the duties and responsibilities specified for the distance learning librarian in these Standards. (ACRL, 2016)

They go on to say that although many institutions have moved away from designating one person as distance learning librarian, campuses still need a designated person to bring focus, to function as an advocate and to coordinate distance learning librarians and services across a range of departments and services.

A digital library needs qualified, dedicated professional librarians with good technical abilities and team-working skills in order to function well and support students and faculty. In comparison to a physical library, a digital library requires a smaller team to run it. However, a digital library team must be flexible, work well together and have specialist skills and knowledge in areas including developing and maintaining web content, information literacy, copyright knowledge and licensing negotiation. As libraries become increasingly digital, librarianship course providers need to be able to cater for, and develop, these skill sets.

The Cambridge University Library, in partnership with their Office of Scholarly Communication, has recently introduced a staff development programme known as the 'Research Support Ambassadors Programme', which aims to develop their academic librarians' skills in new areas, including research data management and open access (Sewell and Kingsley, 2017).

The need for improved information skills training is a recurrent theme in the literature. Rowland and Rubbert's (2001: 741) study on the information needs and practices of distance education students in the UK found that the university libraries included in their sample 'often did not cater for the specific needs of part-time and distance learners, which leads to an increasing use of the internet as a substitute for traditional information channels'. Moreover, Catts and Lau (2008: 16) assert that users need a combination of 'cognitive and technical' skills in order to use the information available via digital technology and electronic databases. Furthermore, according to Kuhlthau et al. (2008: 66):

> Innovative approaches to the interaction between people and information are needed to bridge the divide between information behaviour, information literacy, and impact of information in order to address the issues of the twenty-first century.

Brooke et al.'s (2013) study found that the challenges that librarians face when supporting distance learners fell into three main categories: a lack of resources, diversity of student background and difficulties establishing collaborative relationships with course tutors.

Librarians believed that there was a lack of 'engagement', information sharing and understanding or appreciation by course tutors. Poor communication prevented them from knowing exactly what distance learners required and which students were registered as distance learners. They also found that that online guides and tutorials were the most popular methods of providing user education to distance learners, although other studies have suggested synchronous methods such as discussion forums and the virtual world Second Life offer better results (Hensley and Miller, 2010: 679; Meulemans et al., 2010; Ralph and Stahr, 2010).

Some HE libraries offer online information skills tutorials – sometimes within interactive resources, usually aimed at all students, be they campus based or distance learners. The University of Sunderland has introduced an accredited information skills half-module via the university's VLE, which gives users the flexibility to improve information skills in their own time. It has also developed customised units of information skills training to be embedded into the course content and a series of blogs, including one targeted at distance learners. Tutorials and guides aimed particularly at distance learners are described and discussed by Roberts and Hunter (2011).

The UoL Online Library has an ongoing programme of embedding information literacy training into academic programmes and is currently working with the Centre for Online and Distance Education on a project aimed at developing a university-wide policy on the embedding of information literacy into all programmes.

The OU, meanwhile, has established a credit-bearing 12-week-long Information Literacy Unit (MOSAIC) to improve information literacy across its programmes (Godwin and Parker, 2008; Parker, 2003). It has also developed flexible resources, such as the online information literacy package, 'Skills in Accessing, Finding and Reviewing Information' (SAFARI), which offers generic and interactive resources that can be used by individuals and course teams, and, more recently, 'Beyond Google: Working with Information Online'. SAFARI and MOSAIC involved close collaboration within the OU between the Information Literacy Unit, academics, and production and support staff.

## Conclusions

An online library is not just a repository of information but a range of proactive information services designed around a detailed evidence base. It has an ongoing understanding of the diversity of the student communities it serves and the range of barriers that they face in successfully accessing and using the information they need. The role of online library management as part of a multi-skilled team embraces: participation in course design; expertise in information sources; frontline student support and problem solving; teaching and coaching information literacy; management of resources; negotiation of licences and licence compliance; awareness of legal considerations in terms of copyright and data protection and participation in the design of technical infrastructure and authentication mechanisms.

When designing such an online library it is vital to consider and identify in detail what the user base needs and how they work. Users often need some form of information literacy skills training, but first there is a need to address the question of ease of access and use to ensure that students engage in the first place. Ensuring that resources are easy to find, access and use is essential to gaining the users' trust and engagement.

Any obstacles become larger barriers than they might in a physical setting.

Firstly, libraries need to identify (and continually reappraise) the users' information-seeking behaviours by employing surveys, recording informal and formal feedback from users and examining statistics from systems. Equally important is undertaking research projects to identify problems, seek improvements and assess existing structures. Research requires direct engagement with users in the form of, for example, questionnaires, focus groups, workshops and one-to-one interviews.

Essential to understanding users and ensuring that the online library offerings are the best that they can be is the principle of equity. This principle should be at the heart of all purchases, investment in digital infrastructure and engagement with users. Equity covers issues around access, discoverability and range of resources for all users, no matter their background, social and cultural context, capabilities and disabilities. The library not only needs to know its users but it also needs to ensure that it provides a service that is equitable to all.

Equitable provision of resources therefore does not just mean covering what is on the essential and further reading lists but also going beyond these to enable students to conduct academic enquiry and investigation. It should also encourage collaboration between academics, tutors and librarians to ensure that these resources are available, as needed, and to embed support and training within the curricula. The online library works best when it is embedded where the students will be undertaking their studies, but also needs to provide support beyond those locations in terms of live chat services, support guides, training programmes and email or telephone contact.

This chapter has highlighted how these resources and support mechanisms need to be accessible and discoverable if they are to be equitable. Accessibility goes beyond catering to specific disabilities to the wider needs of users. Planning the online library around universal design principles is a good place to start, but careful consideration of metadata schemas and means of highlighting accessibility issues in certain resources is crucial. One option is to consider a single sign-on authentication system, which means that users only need to log in once to access everything. Similarly, the use of discovery services is worthwhile, if costly. They offer a means of linking disparate resources together under one search and browse facility that should make ease of use better. None of these technical solutions are magic bullets but they do help.

The successful delivery of online library services will not only be crucial to the continued rapid growth of distance learning but also to many students who are nominally 'on campus' but through circumstances or preferences pursue their studies at least in part by virtual learning, combining online participation with physical attendance. Institutions are likely to continue to grow their online provision of courses to reach a global market, reduce per capita costs and achieve scalable delivery. Successful online libraries, which often attract and maintain the most regular contact with students (particularly those most challenged by their studies), have the opportunity to encourage and teach lifelong skills in information literacy and in the process enhance both retention for the institution and employability for the student.

## Notes

1 University of London Online Library Statement: https://onlinelibrary.london.ac.uk/about; The Open University Statement: https://www.open.ac.uk/library/help-and-support/getting-started-with-the-online-library.
2 These can be found at https://www.qaa.ac.uk/quality-code/subject-benchmark-statements.
3 See https://www.legislation.gov.uk/uksi/2018/852/pdfs/uksi_20180852_en.pdf.

## References

ACRL (2016) 'Standards for distance learning library services'. Accessed 3 March 2020. https://www.ala.org/acrl/standards/guidelinesdistancelearning.

Beile, P. M. and Boote, D. N. (2004) 'Does the medium matter? A comparison of a web-based tutorial with face-to-face library instruction on education students' self-efficacy levels and learning outcomes'. *Research Strategies*, 20 (1), 57–68. Accessed 27 July 2022. https://doi.org/10.1016/j.resstr.2005.07.002.

Bengtson, J. A. and Coleman, J. (2019) 'Taking the long way around: Improving the display of HathiTrust records in Primo'. *Information Technology and Libraries*, 38 (1), 27–39. Accessed 27 July 2022. https://doi.org/10.6017/ital.v38i1.10574.

Bowles-Terry, M., Hensley, M. K. and Hinchliffe, L. J. (2010) 'Best practices for online video tutorials in academic libraries: A study of student preferences and understanding'. *Communications in Information Literacy*, 4 (1), 17–28. Accessed 27 July 2022. https://doi.org/10.15760/comminfolit.2010.4.1.86.

Brewerton, G. (2014) 'Implications of student and lecturer qualitative views on reading lists: A case study at Loughborough University, UK'. *New Review of Academic Librarianship*, 20 (1), 78–90. Accessed 27 July 2022. https://doi.org/10.1080/13614533.2013.864688.

Brooke, C., McKinney, P. and Donoghue, A. (2013) 'Provision of distance learner support services at U.K. universities: Identification of best practice and institutional case study'. *Library Trends*, 61 (3), 613–35. Accessed 27 July 2022. https://doi.org/10.1353/lib.2013.0003.

Catts, R. and Lau, J. (2008) 'Towards information literacy indicators'. UNESCO programme and meeting document CI.2008/WS/1. Accessed 27 July 2022. https://unesdoc.unesco.org/ark:/48223/pf0000158723.

Chow, A. S. and Croxton, R. A. (2012) 'Information-seeking behavior and reference medium preferences: Differences between faculty, staff, and students'. *Reference and User Services Quarterly*, 51 (3), 246–62. Accessed 27 July 2022. https://dx.doi.org/10.5860/rusq.51n3.246.

Courtney, M. and Wilhoite-Mathews, S. (2015) 'From distance education to online learning: Practical approaches to information literacy instruction and collaborative learning in online environments'. *Journal of Library Administration*, 55 (4), 261–77. Accessed 27 July 2022. https://doi.org/10.1080/01930826.2015.1038924.

Egesah, O. B. and Wahome, M. N. (2017) 'University students' learning experiences: Nuanced voices from graduate tracer study'. *Journal of Higher Education in Africa*, 15 (1), 43–56.

Gardiner, D., McMenemy, D. and Chowdhury, G. (2006) 'A snapshot of information use patterns of academics in British universities'. *Online Information Review*, 30 (4), 341–59. Accessed 27 July 2022. https://doi.org/10.1108/14684520610686274.

Godwin, P. and Parker, J. (2008) *Information Literacy Meets Library 2.0*. London: Facet Publishing.

Gourlay, L. (2015) 'Posthuman texts: Nonhuman actors, *mediators* and the digital university'. *Social Semiotics*, 25 (4), 484–500. Accessed 27 July 2022. https://doi.org/10.1080/10350330.2015.1059578.

Grafstein, A. (2002) 'A discipline-based approach to information literacy'. *Journal of Academic Librarianship*, 28 (4), 197–204.

Hensley, M. and Miller, R. (2010) 'Listening from a distance: A survey of University of Illinois distance learners and its implication for meaningful instruction'. *Journal of Library Administration*, 50 (5–6), 670–83.

Hinton, D. and McGill, L. (2001) 'Chat to a librarian: 21st century reference for distance learners'. *VINE*, 31 (1), 59–64. Accessed 27 July 2022. https://doi.org/10.1108/03055720010803835.

Horan, M. (2014) 'No learner too far: A comparative study of the development of guidelines for distance education library services in Australia'. *Australian Academic & Research Libraries*, 45 (1), 19–34. Accessed 27 July 2022. https://doi.org/10.1080/00048623.2013.870523.

Jacoby, J., Ward, D., Avery, S. and Marcyk, E. (2016) 'The value of chat reference services: A pilot study'. *Portal: Libraries and the Academy*, 16 (1), 109–29. Accessed 27 July 2022. https://doi.org/10.1353/pla.2016.0013.

Kazakoff-Lane, C. (2014) 'Environmental scan and assessment of OERs, MOOCs and libraries: What effectiveness and sustainability means for libraries' impact on open education'. Association of College and Research Libraries. Accessed 27 July 2022. http://www.ala.org/acrl/sites/ala.org.acrl/files/content/publications/whitepapers/Environmental%20Scan%20and%20Assessment.pdf.

Kim, Y.-M. (2011) 'Why should I use university library website resources? Discipline differences'. *Journal of Academic Librarianship*, 37 (1), 9–18.

Kontos, F. and Henkel, H. (2008) 'Live instruction for distance students: Development of synchronous online workshops'. *Public Services Quarterly*, 4 (1), 1–14. Accessed 27 July 2022. https://doi.org/10.1080/15228950802135657.

Kuhlthau, C. C., Heinström, J. and Todd, R. J. (2008) 'The "information search process" revisited: Is the model still useful?' *Information Research*, 13 (4). Accessed 27 July 2022. http://InformationR.net/ir/13-4/paper355.html.

Kumar, S. and Ochoa, M. (2012) 'Program-integrated information literacy instruction for online graduate students'. *Journal of Library and Information Services in Distance Learning*, 6 (2), 67–78.

Lebowitz, G. (1997) 'Library services to distant students: An equity issue'. *Journal of Academic Librarianship*, 23 (4), 302–8.

McGuinn, K., Stone, G., Sharman, A. and Davison, E. (2017) 'Student reading lists: Evaluating the student experience at the University of Huddersfield'. *Electronic Library*, 35 (2), 322–32. Accessed 27 July 2022. https://doi.org/10.1108/EL-12-2015-0252.

Mallon, M. N. (2018) *The Pivotal Role of Academic Librarians in Digital Learning*. Santa Barbara, CA: Libraries Unlimited.

Matteson, M. L., Salamon, J. and Brewster, L. (2011) 'A systematic review of research on live chat service'. *Reference & User Services Quarterly*, 51 (2), 172–89. Accessed 27 July 2022. https://doi.org/10.5860/rusq.51n2.172.

Mawhinney, T. and Kochkina, S. (2019) 'Is the medium the message? Examining transactions conducted via text in comparison with traditional virtual reference methods'. *Journal of Library and Information Services in Distance Learning*, 13 (1–2), 56–73. Accessed 27 July 2022. https://doi.org/10.1080/1533290X.2018.1499236.

Meulemans, Y. N., Carr, A. and Ly, P. (2010) 'From a distance: Robust reference service via instant messaging'. *Journal of Library & Information Services in Distance Learning*, 4 (1–2), 3–17. Accessed 27 July 2022. https://doi.org/10.1080/15332901003667231.

Morris, S. E. and Grimes, M. (1999) 'A great deal of time and effort: An overview of creating and maintaining internet-based subject guides'. *Library Computing: Internet & Software Applications for Information Professionals*, 18 (3), 213–16.

Moyo, L. M. (2004) 'Electronic libraries and the emergence of new service paradigms'. *The Electronic Library*, 22 (3), 220–30. Accessed 27 July 2022. https://doi.org/10.1108/02640470410541615.

Parker, J. (2003) 'Putting the pieces together: Information literacy at the Open University'. *Library Management*, 24 (4–5), 223–8. Accessed 27 July 2022. https://doi.org/10.1108/01435120310475310.

Parnell, S. (2002) 'Redefining the cost and complexity of library services for open and distance learning'. *International Review of Research in Open and Distributed Learning*, 3 (2). Accessed 27 July 2022. https://doi.org/10.19173/irrodl.v3i2.102.

Payne, G. F. and Bradbury, D. (2002) 'An automated approach to online digital reference: The Open University Library OPAL Project'. *Program: Electronic Library and Information Systems*, 36 (1), 5–12. Accessed 27 July 2022. https://doi.org/10.1108/00330330210426076.

Pereyaslavska, K., Abba, C., Eva, N. and Shea, E. (2015) 'Don't be a reference "tool": How to use internal marketing to build staff competencies in the age of inclusive libraries'. *Reference & User Services Quarterly*, 55 (2), 102–8.

Pinto, M. and Sales, D. (2014) 'Uncovering information literacy's disciplinary differences through students' attitudes: An empirical study'. *Journal of Librarianship and Information Science*, 47 (3), 204–15. Accessed 27 July 2022. https://doi.org/10.1177/0961000614532675.

Powers, M. and Costello, L. (2019) *Reaching Diverse Audiences with Virtual Reference and Instruction: A practical guide for librarians*. London: Rowman & Littlefield.

Radford, M. L. and Connaway, L. S. (2013) 'Not dead yet! A longitudinal study of query type and ready reference accuracy in live chat and IM reference.' *Library & Information Science Research*, 35 (1), 2–13. Accessed 27 July 2022. https://doi.org/10.1016/j.lisr.2012.08.001.

Ralph, L. and Stahr, B. (2010) 'When off-campus means virtual campus: The academic library in Second Life'. *Journal of Library Administration*, 50 (7–8), 909–22. Accessed 27 July 2022. https://doi.org/10.1080/01930826.2010.488993.

Rawson, J., Davis, M. A., Harding J. and Miller, C. (2013) 'Virtual reference at a global university: An analysis of patron and question type'. *Journal of Library and Information Services in Distance Learning*, 7 (1–2), 93–7. Accessed 27 July 2022. https://doi.org/10.1080/1533290X.2012.705624.

Roberts, S. and Hunter, D. (2011) 'New library, new librarian, new student: Using LibGuides to reach the virtual student'. *Journal of Library & Information Services in Distance Learning*, 5 (1–2), 67–75. Accessed 27 July 2022. https://doi.org/10.1080/1533290X.2011.570552.

Rowland, F. and Rubbert, I. (2001) 'An evaluation of the information needs and practices of part-time and distance-learning students in the context of educational and social change through lifelong learning'. *Journal of Documentation*, 57 (6), 741–62. Accessed 27 July 2022. https://doi.org/10.1108/EUM0000000007105.

SCONUL (Society of College, National and University Libraries) (2019) 'The value of academic libraries'. Accessed 3 March 2020. https://www.sconul.ac.uk/page/the-value-of-academic-libraries.

SCONUL (Society of College, National and University Libraries) (2001) 'Access for Distance Leaners: Report of the SCONUL Task Force'. Accessed 3 March 20220. sconul.ac.uk/pubs_stats/pubs/distancelearners_report.doc

Sewell, C. and Kingsley, D. (2017) 'Developing the 21st century academic librarian: The research support ambassador programme'. *New Review of Academic Librarianship*, 23 (2–3), 148–58. Accessed 27 July 2022. https://doi.org/10.1080/13614533.2017.1323766.

Shank, J. D. and Bell, S. (2011) 'Blended librarianship: [Re]envisioning the role of librarian as educator in the digital information age'. *Reference & User Services Quarterly*, 51 (2), 105–10. Accessed 27 July 2022. https://i.slcc.edu/internalaudit/docs/teaching-become-blended-librarianship.pdf.

Sharpe, K. and Norton, C. (2017) 'Examining our past, considering our future: A study of email reference, 2000–2015'. *Internet Reference Services Quarterly*, 22 (4), 133–65. Accessed 27 July 2022. https://doi.org/10.1080/10875301.2018.1455617.

Siddall, G. and Rose, H. (2014) 'Reading lists – time for a reality check? An investigation into the use of reading lists as a pedagogical tool to support the development of information skills amongst Foundation Degree students'. *Library and Information Research*, 38 (118), 52–73. Accessed 27 July 2022. https://doi.org/10.29173/lirg605.

Silver, S. L. and Nickel, L. T. (2005) 'Are online tutorials effective? A comparison of online and classroom library instruction methods'. *Research Strategies*, 20 (4), 389–96. Accessed 27 July 2022. https://doi.org/10.1016/j.resstr.2006.12.012.

SLS (Society of Legal Scholars) (2010) 'A library for the modern law school: A statement of standards for university law library provision in the UK – 2009 revision'. *Legal Information Management*, 10 (2), 132–41. Accessed 29 September 2022. https://www.cambridge.org/

core/journals/legal-information-management/article/abs/library-for-the-modern-law-school-2009-revision/1D9060BC7CCCED808AB614090B449169.

Smith, G. (2011) 'Supporting distance learning students with disabilities'. *SCONUL Focus*, 53, 39–43. Accessed 27 July 2022. https://www.sconul.ac.uk/sites/default/files/documents/12_1.pdf.

Solomou, G., Pierrakeas, C. and Kameas, A. (2015) 'Characterization of educational resources in e-learning systems using an educational metadata profile'. *Journal of Educational Technology & Society*, 18 (4), 246–60.

Stitz, T. and Blundell, S. (2018) 'Evaluating the accessibility of online library guides at an academic library'. *Journal of Accessibility and Design for All*, 8 (1), 33–79. Accessed 27 July 2022. https://dx.doi.org/10.17411/jacces.v8i1.145.

Stokes, P. and Martin, L. (2008) 'Reading lists: A study of tutor and student perceptions, expectations and realities'. *Studies in Higher Education*, 33 (2), 113–25. Accessed 29 September 2022. https://doi.org/10.1080/03075070801915874.

Tait, A. (2000) 'Planning student support for open and distance learning'. *Open Learning*, 15 (3), 287–99. Accessed 27 July 2022. https://doi.org/10.1080/713688410.

Tang, Y. and Tseng, H. (2013) 'Distance learners' self-efficacy and information literacy skills'. *Journal of Academic Librarianship*, 39, 517–21. Accessed 27 July 2022. https://doi.org/10.1016/j.acalib.2013.08.008.

Thompson, H. (2002) 'The library's role in distance education: Survey results from ACRL's 2000 Academic Library Trends and Statistics'. *College & Research Libraries News*, 63 (5), 338–40. Accessed 27 July 2022. https://doi.org/10.5860/crln.63.5.338.

Tury, S. (2014) 'The information-seeking behaviour of distance learners: A case study of the University of London international programmes'. Doctoral thesis, City University, London. Accessed 27 July 2022. https://openaccess.city.ac.uk/id/eprint/19613/.

Unwin, L., Stephens, K. and Bolton, N. (1997) *The Role of the Library in Distance Learning: A study of postgraduate students, course providers and librarians in the UK*. London: British Library Research Series.

Wales, T. (2005) 'Library subject guides: A content management case study at the Open University, UK'. *Program: Electronic Library and Information Systems*, 39 (2), 112–21. Accessed 27 July 2022. https://doi.org/10.1108/00330330510595698.

Section 3
# Researching and evaluating distance education

# Introduction to Section 3
Stephen Brown

The third section of this book principally addresses the interests of academic developers, researchers and evaluators. The first chapter in this section, Chapter 18, focuses on the relationship between academic development, research and practice, policy, strategy or contexts in online and distance education. It explores how these relationships might be made more productive, beginning by suggesting what may usefully be meant by academic development, research and practice in the particular context of distance education. To provide richer accounts of both academic development and research and of the relationships between them and practice, case studies of research and/or development projects are provided and analysed. The chapter concludes by proposing a more productive relationship between academic development, research and practice for distance education, based on the idea of sustained scholarly practice. It further suggests that the idea of sustained scholarly practice could, or indeed should, be extended still further to embrace policy and strategy.

Chapter 19 follows on directly with an examination of the complementary topic of evaluation. Evaluation is considered here as a form of applied research that has a particular intent to understand practice and thereby to facilitate improvement. This chapter is aimed at those currently planning or already undertaking monitoring and evaluation of distance education projects and courses – which, the author suggests, should include anyone planning and running a distance education course or project. The chapter distinguishes between four dimensions of evaluation, firstly by differentiating between a focus on evaluating outcomes and evaluating processes and secondly by further differentiating between monitoring ('how is it working?' and evaluation ('how did it work?'). It introduces a framework of six questions to guide evaluation and monitoring ('who, why, how, what, when and where?')

and shows how these questions can be used to identify and address important issues in distance education evaluation, including:

- the problem of knowing what causes what
- the problem of measurement
- the problem of measuring difference
- the problem of timescale.

The chapter goes on to explore relationships between evaluation and quality assurance and between evaluation and research, outline some practical approaches to evaluation, describe different evaluator roles and illustrate how different levels of evaluation can be applied to distance learning courses and projects. Again, challenges and approaches are reviewed, which are equally applicable to both the micro level of lesson or module evaluation and the macro level of institutional policy and strategy.

# 18
# Academic development, research and practice in online and distance education

David Baume

## Some relationships between academic development, research and practice

What are the main relationships between academic development (here used to mean both educational development and staff and faculty development), research and practice (including policy, strategy and contexts) in online and distance education? And how might these relations be made more productive?

By academic development, usually abbreviated in the rest of this chapter to 'development', I mean activities undertaken to extend and to improve the quality of distance education, including, but going well beyond, course design.

By research, I mean collecting and making sense of information about distance education, and thereby generating a better and data-informed understanding of it and the theories and models behind it.

By practice, I mean the actual design and running of the courses, in the context of (and also sometimes contributing to) policy, strategy and environment.

These questions matter because research, practice and academic development may be undertaken by different people, different organisational units, with different primary goals – in summary, to understand, run, operate and improve online and distance education. Even when they are undertaken by the same people, these activities may be seen and undertaken through different lenses and via different levers.

The next three sections of this chapter, 'Starting from development', 'Starting from research' and 'Starting from practice (and contexts)', sketch development, research and then practice respectively as starting points. Later sections analyse the natures of development and research as applied to the practice of distance education.

To provide richer accounts of both development and research and the relationships between them and practice, short examples of research and/or development projects are provided and analysed. Baume et al. (2002) review the meaning and nature of educational development projects.

The chapter concludes by proposing a more productive relationship between development, research and practice for distance education, based on the idea of sustained scholarly practice. This account could also be extended further to embrace policy and strategy.

This chapter should be of interest and use to those who plan and run online and distance learning courses, who research distance learning, who work to improve the quality of distance education and who manage and lead distance education. It is intended to provoke productive conversations both within and across these groups, leading to more effective and scholarly collaboration and thereby moving more rapidly towards improved online and distance education.

## Starting from development

Most online and distance learning development projects and course development endeavours throw up observations. These observations may in turn lead to both research and development questions, which may be addressed at a systems level as matters of policy and strategy; for example, if university-wide decisions are being made about the nature of the institution's online and distance education programmes and processes. They also need to be addressed in more detail for each individual programme, module and process. These questions will include versions of the following:

- 'What is the best way to design a course?', with further clarification of what 'best' means in the particular context – perhaps 'most effective' or 'most efficient' in terms of use of staff time, both in course production and subsequently in course operation (as explored in Assinder et al., 2010), 'making maximum use of the expertise available' and 'always meeting or exceeding applicable institutional, disciplinary and professional quality standards'. This is not a pure research question, but some research or investigation and critical and creative thinking will be required to answer the question satisfactorily and confidently.

- 'What features will make a course produce the most effective student learning?', this time with attention to local meanings of 'most effective student learning', which may include 'leading to better student performance, better student satisfaction or better graduate employment'. Again, this is not a pure research question. It also needs some investigation and critical and creative thinking to provide sound, satisfactory, usable answers.

These are some of the many ways in which development generates research questions.

## Starting from research

Research into online and distance education, as with many other topics, is often prompted by new theoretical ideas. Research can have a somewhat recursive quality.

The conventional distinction between pure and applied research may be simplistic. It may be more productive to see this as a spectrum – from pure, through potentially or actually applicable and then to applied. These are not just inherent qualities of the research itself. There are corresponding distinctions to be made between the intent of the researcher – whether to do research that is pure or applicable or applied – and the ways in which readers of the published work choose to respond to it across a similar range, from using it to inform their thinking to using it to inform their practice.

Examples include the following:

- A lot is known about the conditions for learning in higher education (HE) (for an overview see, for example, Baume and Scanlon, 2018). An obvious line of research is to explore how what is known about conditions for learning in HE in general applies and/or may be applied, in particular to online and distance education.
- There is great scope for investigating similarities and differences between the impact and experience of face-to-face and online learning – for example, Allen et al. (2002) and Vogel (2015) give good overviews.
- Research may be undertaken on a distance education course, which would be equally applicable to a corresponding face-to-face course – for example, researching assessment by portfolio (Baume and Yorke, 2002; Baume et al., 2004). Distance and in-person education have much in common and much to learn from each other.

Much of this chapter will explore relationships between development, research and practice in online and distance education. These ideas will be illustrated mainly from work conducted by the Centre for Online and Distance Education (CODE) at the University of London (UoL).

## Starting from practice (and contexts)

Both development and research in online and distance education are often prompted by observations about current practice, observing current student learning, attention to the institutional and national contexts and priorities within which courses operate (such as the Great Leap Online prompted in 2020 by the COVID-19 pandemic) and new and emerging learning technologies. An alertness to what is happening (for example, to what seems to be working brilliantly, well, less well, very little or not at all) can generate ideas and opportunities. These ideas and opportunities may be for immediate changes to practice, scarcely needing to be labelled as development projects. They may be for small studies, perhaps to inform the changes to practice (studies that again scarcely need to be designated research projects). They may also be more substantial investigations.

Many course or programme reviews will also raise questions, typically versions of 'What lies behind particular feedback from students?' or 'What led to particular assessment results?' and always 'What shall we do about this?' Investigation may be indicated if quality assurance is to be more than a ritual.

## Development ...

Development, in this chapter, means taking purposeful steps to improve some aspect of the practice of online and distance education. Development here goes beyond the somewhat tired rhetoric of educational change. It additionally requires explicit attention to the direction of change – to what we mean by 'improve'. It requires us to know, say and explain which way is up and then to justify our account of what constitutes improvement. The language of development brings a necessary rigour to discussion of and work on educational change.

At least three main spectra or dimensions of variation can be identified within such development work:

- from ad hoc to scholarly
- from local (module or programme specific) to university wide, and perhaps with wider implications still
- from responsive to anticipatory.

*Ad hoc to scholarly*
Development work should never be undertaken entirely ad hoc, however urgent the need for the work. In Popovic and Baume's (2016) typology of forms of scholarship, we should always aim to undertake development work at least at Level 1, reflecting critically on practice, and Level 2, using the literature. Some issues in moving to their suggested Level 3 of scholarship, research and publication are considered later in this chapter.

Reflecting critically on practice in a development project typically means digging deeper than the initial presentation of the problem – not rejecting the initial account of the problem but going beyond it. This can involve asking the 'why?' behind the 'what?', analysing the situation in detail to identify possible appropriate research and development approaches and reviewing what the literature may have to offer.

An analytic approach, in this case to taking an assessment online, is illustrated in Chapter 12. In this example, the impending need to move a large amount of assessment online first prompted a detailed analysis of the likely issues and approaches to addressing these issues, rather than leaping into solutions. There is always time to stop and think. This was mainly critical analysis rather than research – in other words, Level 1 scholarship.

Showing Level 2 scholarship in action, the literature is used in exemplary fashion in the Digital Educator Project (UoL, 2019) considered later in this chapter, which is informed by a substantial and very thoughtful critical bibliography.

*Local to university wide*
Most CODE development projects are designed to have application across UoL programmes. Several are described later in this chapter and elsewhere in this book. However, whatever else it may achieve, a development project is only effective when it contributes to improving understanding and practice in a particular programme or programmes, as agreed with the project sponsor.

Consultation with and engagement of programme leaders is an integral part of good development practice. As well as the use of project sponsors, the structure of CODE, with fellows from across the university and beyond, facilitates this, as do connections to the University Programme Leaders Forum and to senior university staff and committees.

*Responsive to anticipatory*
The impact of having access to multiple examination sessions on student performance and concerns over contract cheating has generated responsive CODE projects. These research and analyse the issues in considerable detail and make evidence-based recommendations for future practice.

Work on information literacy, by contrast, suggested issues and opportunities that were not great matters of current concern but can (indeed, in the view of the report authors, should) inform future improved practice across the university (Baume and Cappellini, 2019).

A bridge from responsive to anticipatory development projects asks this question of any project: 'What broader applications may this work have across the university, and perhaps beyond?'

Sensitivity to and anticipation of wider application allows the widest possible audience for, and value from, the work.

## ... and research

### Investigation and research

It may be useful to consider a spectrum of approaches to research, from pure through applicable to applied, as suggested earlier in the chapter. This chapter will focus on the applicable and applied parts of this spectrum because that is where much research and investigation in distance education are undertaken. Examples of CODE work in this zone are described and analysed later in this chapter and, again, elsewhere in this book. The research work of other distance learning universities is also accessible (for example, the Institute for Educational Technology at the Open University (OU)).[1]

Ashwin and Trigwell (2004) offer a valuable account of what they call 'investigation' in HE, which includes but is not limited to research. Their work is concerned with investigating staff and education development, but many of the same considerations apply to investigating particular education activities such as online and distance education. They distinguish between three levels of investigation:

- Investigation to inform oneself and one's own personal professional practice – to produce what they call 'personal knowledge'. Personal knowledge is typically verified only by the knowledge producer, but it is still hopefully useful if it is produced in a scholarly way in at least the first two senses of Baume and Popovic's (2016) account of scholarship: being critical and using the literature.
- Investigation to inform a team, department, faculty or institution, to produce what may be called 'local knowledge', verified and then used by the team.
- Investigation intended for a wider audience to produce 'public knowledge'. This activity is what most people would consider to be research, being refereed and published.

Much of the research (what Ashwin and Trigwell would call investigation) undertaken by development units and teams, including CODE, is at their Level 2, which is intended to produce local knowledge – locally produced and validated and intended for local use. This investigation is not of lower quality than research intended to be published. It is different in kind and in its intended local audience and use. This research is judged, not by whether it is suitable for national or international publication, but on the basis of its rigour and scholarship and both its critical reflection on practice and its use of the literature. Above all it is judged on its utility, on the extent and the ways in which it enables the agreed goals of the development project to be successfully achieved, and then known and understood.

Ashwin and Trigwell (2004) usefully advise against the assumption that a personal or local investigation, however well undertaken, automatically has within it the makings of a publishable article or chapter. It can be hard for academics, researching to support a development project, to accept this. We bring a natural wish to publish and to share more widely. CODE addresses this by identifying whether any larger issues and research questions are compatible with the development project and identifying any opportunities for wider publication from the start of the project. Of course, in development work, aimed to address local issues and needs, issues of confidentiality sometimes make this wider publication impossible or constrain it. Sometimes, too, the time and cost that would be involved in researching and writing a publishable article are simply not available.

These forms of scholarship go beyond the scholarship of teaching and learning (see as a useful introduction, University of Edinburgh, 2017). They constitute a wider scholarship of all the major practices involved in successful, high-quality online and distance education – including academic development (see, for example, Baume and Popovic, 2016; see also the *International Journal for Academic Development*[2]).

## Dissemination of development and research

Development projects usually result in project reports – data, advice, guidance about policy or practice to the person or group who commissioned the work or perhaps a particular course team. Where possible and appropriate, these (or versions of them) are also published on the CODE website, linked from a short news item that summarises the work and helps busy academics to decide whether they should read the full report.

The results of research are output through the conventional channels of academic publishing and presentation – papers, chapters and conference and webinar presentations.

## Examples

The examples in this chapter are about relationships between development, research and practice. They describe work carried out in CODE.[3]

### Student learning hours and learning strategies

Stephen Brown and David Baume

**The source of the project**

The Director of Education, Innovation and Development at UoL, Sam Brenton, brought an issue to CODE. It was not clear how students were actually using the distance learning materials that the university produces. If the university knew more about this, it could perhaps produce more effective and appropriate learning materials.

After some discussion and negotiation, a CODE project was agreed. The work was undertaken by two principals – CODE fellows (Stephen Brown and David Baume) with two CODE part-time research students, Naraesa Francis and Janet Wong.

This was explicitly both a research (investigation) and a development project. It was intended to generate information and understanding that would in turn be used to produce enhanced guidance for teams writing distance learning courses.

**Conducting the project**

The agreed research questions were as follows:

RQ1. How do student study hours and study patterns compare with programme team expectations?
RQ2. How and why do students engage with different types of content and learning activity?
RQ3. What role does peer interaction play in student learning?

Four programmes of study were chosen to be investigated with the agreement of the programme leaders. The programmes were chosen to be as varied as possible in subject matter and thereby generate results that would have the widest possible applicability across university programmes.

In the event:

- Three research methods were originally agreed: an online survey, the completion by some students of learning diaries, and analysis of data from the virtual learning environment (VLE).
- The online survey was developed, piloted and then run successfully with 645 respondents.
- Only seven learning diaries were completed, although those that were completed generated valuable data.
- To enable a deeper individual understanding, seven online interviews were conducted with students around the world.
- Accessing VLE data proved problematic and was not undertaken.

The online survey questions asked: how much time students spend studying and if they think they spend about the right amount of time studying, about the clarity of study guidance and how closely students follow study guidance and which component of their programmes they use and how helpful they find them.

The learning diary pro forma was designed to provide detailed insights into actual student learning behaviour. It asked students to log their study sessions: when they studied, what components of their courses they studied and what they actually did in each study session.

The interview questions were designed to probe the survey responses and learning diaries. Interviewees were asked about their mode of study, previous study experience and their experience of using different course components, communication channels and support services, including the online library.

The VLE study would have analysed:

- what guidance programmes gave students on how much time to spend and how to allocate their time
- how much time students were spending on VLE activities.

The learning diaries were used to obtain some of these data.
In retrospect we might also have asked students:

- how many modules they were currently studying, to help us make sense of study time data
- how much prior experience they had of distance learning (we asked this in the interviews)

- whether they were studying independently or in one of UoL's 120 recognised teaching centres around the world.

**Conclusions of the research**

- For the most part, students report following the study advice given.
- Student self-reported study behaviours ranging from highly effective to very poor learning strategies.
- There are problems with student workload. Students report that the amount of work they feel they need to do in order to study the course satisfactorily exceeds both the study time recommended by programme teams and the amount of time that students feel they have available.
- Overall, we see here a strong preference for content over learning activities and for individual activities over collaborative activities.
- The four programmes covered by this study are satisfactory, or more than satisfactory, for students who are experienced, sophisticated learners.
- For less mature learners there is a need to design future courses in ways that engage them more actively and strategically in the process of learning and in a learning community.

**Suggestions for programme teams**

- Reduce the amount of material to be studied to enable students to complete the work within the recommended time and to facilitate deeper approaches to learning.
- Explain the nature of learning as an active process of knowledge construction, with reference to the use of learning outcomes, learning activities and appropriate collaboration between participants.
- Use intended learning outcomes and examination questions to demonstrate how successful performance requires learning behaviour that extends beyond memorisation to include reflection, analysis, synthesis, presentation and discussion.
- Ensure that all stated learning outcomes are matched to appropriate learning activities and assessment tasks.
- Ensure that the contribution of all individual learning activities to intended learning outcomes and the benefits of such activities are clearly described.

- Ensure that content is always associated with learning activities that go beyond memorisation and recall.
- Explicitly include the development and enhancement of learning strategies and skills in module learning outcomes and ensure that modules include activities designed to help learners to progress and monitor their own skill development.
- Ensure that students engage more with peer interaction by addressing the design of collaborative activities with respect to clearly demonstrable and beneficial learning outcomes, allocation of group members, moderation of behaviour, timeliness of responses and the functionality of the VLE platform.
- Given the substantial differences in responses between courses, they should base their course planning on data from the course in this study that is most similar to the one they are designing, rather than working from the overall preferences reported here.

**Reflections on this example**

- In CODE terms this was a large research and development project, taking in total a few tens of person days over two years or so.
- It started with questions based on a senior manager's growing realisation of a gap in institutional knowledge – about how and why distance learning students were actually allocating their time and effort. Answers to these questions could clearly have implications for the design and operation of courses.
- The contribution of the part-time CODE research students was highly valued: they brought fresh ideas and original perspectives as well as undertaking some of the interviews and analysis.
- Changed circumstances (not least of which was the effect of the outbreak of the COVID-19 pandemic worldwide on student learning opportunities and behaviour) and fresh thinking required modifications to the original plan.
- An early draft report was shared with the client, who suggested which issues deserved particular attention, to reflect both changing university priorities and the feasibility of implementing the various recommendations. In making these changes, the findings and the analysis to date were respected.
- The suggested items for consideration by the programme team are explicitly informed by this research.

This work was undertaken as a discrete piece of research and development. The work included obtaining internal approval for the study methods and engaging the support of key gatekeepers (programme leaders and Student Affairs), as well as identifying the research questions, devising the survey instruments, finding productive ways to analyse the data and drawing implications for practice (see Brown and Baume, 2020).

Were it to be judged worthwhile, the study could be replicated on an appropriate scale as part of regular quality assurance processes, taking only a few full days each time. An issue to be faced in such work is the possible need for sensitivity in respect of findings. A published paper based on this work is available (Brown and Baume, 2022).

## Literacies

David Baume

### The source of the project

In earlier work on information literacy (Baume and Cappellini, 2019) we had become increasingly aware of the many kinds of literacies being discussed in HE, including media literacy, digital literacy, copyright literacy, numerical literacy (numeracy), assessment literacy, careers literacy (employability), library literacy, cultural literacy, other academic literacies, research literacy, visual literacy, disability literacy (disability awareness), environmental literacy (environmental awareness) and a range of subject literacies, including psychological literacy.

I wondered what these various literacies have in common and whether and how they might be conceptualised, treated, incorporated into policy and strategy and taught, learned and assessed.

### Conducting the project

I contacted colleagues in the university with an interest in some of these literacies, and suggested we explore the matter further.

A very small, five-full-day project was developed. Each participant wrote a short paper on 'their' literacy. We spent half a day discussing these and considering the questions suggested above about literacies. A short paper was produced summarising our findings and thoughts (Baume, 2020). A presentation to a CODE (then the Centre for Distance Learning) conference generated lively discussion.

### Tentative conclusions

- Literacies generally describe capabilities; things that students and graduates can or should be able to do, or in some cases simply be aware of.
- Literacies may describe more than capabilities and awareness. They may describe qualities, predispositions, fundamentals of behaviour, guiding values and principles, even elements of academic or professional identity; things that students and graduates actually do and think about, as well as simply can do and think about.
- Other than the disciplinary literacies, these literacies can be conceptualised, treated, taught, learned and assessed to some extent generically, without close reference to particular academic disciplines and professions.
- They can also be conceptualised as important elements of the practice of particular disciplines and professions.
- Some of them are directly and explicitly supported by universities across disciplines or professions – most obviously information or library literacy, employability or careers literacy and digital literacy.

### Reflections on this example

Looking forward, the concept of literacies may offer a useful way to address and rebalance an increasingly problematic relationship between knowledge and practice; more specifically, what may be the overvaluing of knowledge and the undervaluing of the ability to critique and use knowledge. This issue is explored further in Chapter 8.

This example was no more (or less) than an academic seminar in which colleagues with a shared interest devoted a few hours to writing, thinking and discussing a topic of common interest. It has led to further thought and may in due course lead to publication.

It does not have huge and immediate implications for the practice of distance education, but new ways of thinking about and talking about distance education may have currently unforeseeable consequences. It is also an important part of the academic life, especially in these straitened times, to do a little 'blue sky' work. An article has been published (Baume, 2022).

## Predicting student success and increasing student retention

Ormond Simpson

### The source of the project

Ideas for projects can arise in unexpected ways. Some years ago, an OU colleague dropped a thick document on my desk as he was passing. 'Maybe this might interest you?' he said. It was a copy of a thesis by one of his colleagues, Ruth Woodman, who was studying for an MSc in statistics. The title was 'Investigation of factors that influence student retention and success rate on open university courses in the East Anglia region'.

The word 'retention' caught my eye. I had long been interested ('obsessed' was a word some colleagues used) by student dropout in OU. OU graduation rates at that time were around 40 per cent. If we knew more about factors influencing retention, maybe we could do more about dropout?

The thesis was about student progression from Level 1 OU courses to Level 2 and beyond. The main factors influencing that progression were, unsurprisingly, students' performance on their previous OU courses. But most OU dropout occurs among new students, where the factors were likely to be different. I asked Ruth if she could apply her method to new student dropout. She could. How far could we predict which students were most likely to drop out? Ruth's new formula could attach a '% Predicted Probability of Success' (% PPS) to each of the 3,000 or so new students entering the OU in the East Anglia region that year. The % PPS depended on a number of factors – most importantly their previous educational qualification, chosen course, sex and age.

The predictions ranged from around a 9 per cent probability of success – typically for a young new student with a low level of previous qualifications studying maths, science or technology – to an 83 per cent probability of success, typically for an older woman with a high level of previous qualifications studying an arts course. The predictions turned out to be very accurate (Simpson, 2006).

How might the university use this formula and these data?

### Conducting the project

Could we devise and then trial an intervention to increase student retention and success? But first, what kind of an intervention?

We knew that new student dropout in the OU was very heavily front-loaded. Many new students left at the point where they received their course material and often before they had any contact with a tutor. We wondered if a proactive and personal contact at that point might have some effect on their subsequent progress. Our experiment was a very simple one. We made a short phone call before course start to each member of our experimental group but made no such contact with the control group. The calls were short but welcoming, encouraging and friendly and, above all, motivational. We followed up the results at the end of the year.

Next, how do we find out if the intervention worked?

A randomised controlled trial is the gold standard for measuring the effects of any intervention. Large numbers of subjects are needed, which we had. And the % PPS distribution data gave us a ready way to assemble experimental and control groups that had very similar average % PPS and were of reasonable size to analyse.

### Conclusions of the research and later work

Over the four years of the trial, the experimental group had a greater retention by the end of the course than the control group, by an average of around 5 percentage points (Simpson, 2006). I was surprised and delighted that such a modest early intervention could have such a significant long-term result. We compared the cost of the phone calls with the extra income to OU generated by increased retention. The return on investment was around 200 per cent (Simpson, 2008). I don't have an explanation for the effect, although I note a comment on a similar motivational project that also involved a modest intervention: 'the effects are far beyond what you might expect from the simplicity of the interventions' (Dweck, 1999). Perhaps effective interventions are generally prompt, personal and positive.

This project was mainstreamed into OU practice as 'Proactive Motivational Support (PaMS)'. Briefing materials were produced in booklets and on video and training carried out in some regions of the university.

An OU project is still running – the 'Module Pass Rates Model'. This uses a predictive formula to calculate what the pass rate on an OU module should be, given the predictive characteristics of the students entering it. Leaders of modules that substantially depart negatively from the predictions of the formula are requested to examine the reasons for this departure. Also, tutors access the student data to help them guide students (see, for example, Rientes, 2020).

We ran an early proactive motivational trial at CODE for UoL's distance learning programmes. This used emails instead of phone calls. It also raised retention, this time by around 2 per cent. It was also cost effective (Inkelaar and Simpson, 2015). (Chapter 14 describes continuing work by UoL to increase student retention informed by this work.) Further work on this is reported in Simpson (2012).

**Reflections on relations between development and research and practice in this project**

The work was prompted by my lingering concern about student retention on distance learning programmes, a concern I had not been able to address satisfactorily. A colleague, knowing of my interest, showed me some unpublished research that they thought might be relevant, which it was. The author of the research was willing to try to apply her method in this new area. This application was successful – we had a way to predict student retention. Now, could we influence that retention? I devised a very simple form of intervention that might work. We trialled (that is, implemented and then researched the effectiveness of) this method, with positive results. We published this research and development work and the results were applied more widely.

Factors contributing to the success of this piece of development and research included my membership of an academic community that knew about my interests, the willingness of a member of my wider academic community to try a new application of her research approach, an educational setting that supported me in testing my ideas, some combination of skill and luck leading to positive results and publication, leading to wider dissemination and take-up.

### Digital Educator Project

Jon Gregson, Marco Gillies, Christine Thuranira-McKeever, Tony Sheehan and Jonathan San Diego

#### The source of the project

The idea for the project came from Jonathan Thomas, Associate Director of Learning Solutions at UoL. There is a fast-increasing number of educational technologies. What are and will be the training needs of academics in relation to these technologies? Through CODE procedures, this generated a project proposal and an invitation to tender.

#### Conducting the project

The project focused on the needs of digital educators currently working within the programmes of UoL. However, the intention was that the findings would be of interest and value to a wider audience. The project had four consecutive stages, all conducted in 2018:

- Stage 1: Using available research, the significant likely developments in educational technology in the medium term (two to five years) for the HE distance learning sector were outlined. This included identifying and exploring 'big ticket'

technology disruptors, pedagogic shifts and cultural and business challenges. This stage comprised a literature review, split into five major themes: new technologies, teaching tools, learner practices, sector trends and broader industry trends.
- Stage 2: We used 'foresight' research tools to identify drivers of change. We then worked with educators to develop scenarios for use of digital technologies in education and assessed their implications for the digital educator. Each scenario addressed the possible impact of technical and pedagogic innovations on the role of the educator.
- Stage 3: Focusing on specific technological functions and pedagogic innovations, we assessed the readiness of current academics involved as digital educators in distance education design and delivery to adapt to these innovations. The survey to do this was informed by the learning from the first two stages. The survey questions explored awareness, the importance attributed to different innovations and willingness to adapt.
- Stage 4: Finally, drawing on the learning from the first three stages, we undertook further engagement with academic stakeholders from within the UoL member institutions. At a final workshop, ideas were developed for a potential skills development roadmap for the academics involved in distance education, to ensure that academics are prepared to be the digital educators of the future.

**Conclusions of the research**

Following the initial two stages, the research focused on five technology areas: mobile technology, social media, learning analytics, artificial intelligence and augmented/virtual reality.

The research process identified four main factors that should inform a skill development roadmap for the academic 'digital educator':

- major trends in educational technology becoming available and how these can shape design and delivery of distance education
- the context in which students are living and studying and, in particular, how this enhances or constrains their access to technology and their ability to respond to innovative pedagogical approaches

- the current awareness, usage and willingness of academics to adapt to using innovative pedagogical models and digital technologies when delivering distance education
- the varied opportunities for using new pedagogical and digital technology-enhanced approaches within different subjects, taking account of what technologies and approaches are already being used.

The idea also emerges in the study that the roles of academics and/or librarians include knowledge curators as well as teachers. Both roles need excellent digital literacy skills.

From a skills development perspective, the study suggests that digital educators need additional guidance to support their adoption of technology. Digital learning remains in a development stage in many institutions, with some educators overwhelmed by the scale and complexity of the offer.

The adoption of new technology within the sector is variable and the most appropriate skills needs for digital educators at a particular point depend on:

- overall technology maturity (is the technology ready for adoption?)
- individual readiness (is the educator aware and ready to adopt a given technology?)
- institutional readiness (is the institution willing to support a given technology?)

The kind of skills development needed depend on the alignment of technology maturity, digital educator readiness and institutional readiness.

Three clusters of guidance are therefore needed, which support digital educators in evaluating, experimenting and embedding good practice:

- **awareness**, which requires building knowledge about the nature and capabilities of particular technologies with a view to encouraging initial small-scale evaluations within institutions
- reviewing **examples** of technology application, where a technology has already been successfully applied in some contexts, with a view to considering larger-scale experiments within institutions

- understanding good practices in the **application** of a (now well-established) particular technology for learning.

### Recommendations for programme teams

The major recommendation from the study was the need to develop subject-specific skill development roadmaps. These should be based upon needs analysis that addresses context, subject theme, the digital educator's role and the teaching and learning experience that would be desirable for the particular subject. The roadmaps relate current understanding of use of particular technologies against those that are variously established in their use, have low uptake despite current availability, have the potential to support as-yet unexplored pedagogic innovation and are emerging.

Further recommendations focused on the need to provide awareness training for those with budget and decision-making authority regarding the state of maturity and potential of current and emerging technologies. The final training plan also needs to reflect on assessment of institutional readiness and support (including financial investment).

### Reflections on this example

The study generated further interest to apply the findings through action research focused on a particular course. The Digital Educator Phase 2 project is underway, working with the BSc in computer science run by Goldsmiths College. This includes digital educators in the UK and at international teaching centres who support an online version of the course. The intention is to contrast the findings from this study with a humanities degree course such as psychology.

The role of digital educators globally is becoming increasingly important, especially as institutions respond to the COVID-19 pandemic by moving their courses online. This project has therefore been very timely, as the success of online learning will depend greatly on the quality of both learning design and tutor capabilities.

The second phase of the project is also highlighting the importance of the policy context and the choice of learning environment use, as, irrespective of the skills the digital educator may acquire, these factors can constrain or enable the levels of innovation possible for the digital educator (see Gillies et al., 2019).

> **Relations between development and research in this project**
>
> In some ways this has been a classic research and development project. Thinking about coming trends and their implications for practice suggested a research question. A literature review and a questionnaire survey were undertaken. Implications were drawn for future practice and are being implemented in a follow-up study. The work has also generated considerable thought and conversation.

## Sustained scholarly practice

A conventional account of the relationship between research and development describes development as the implementation of the results of research. But this is only part of the story, for development and research in HE in general and in distance education more particularly.

The examples variously show the following:

- In the work on student learning hours, a question arising from reflection on practice, leading to an investigation, leading in turn to conclusions and implications for development, for future practice within the institution and to a publication.
- In the work on literacies, an observation drawn from several literatures leading to a review of the wider literature, involving a range of experts and some tentative implications for further research and, possibly, for thinking and practice – also, a publication.
- In the work on student completion and retention, a particular concern derived from the analysis of data from practice over the years, encountering a methodology for analysing practice, prompting an experimental innovation in practice that was undertaken, researched and published for a wider audience and put into practice.
- The Digital Educator Project, as noted, was a more conventional research and development project. It started with a research question that has implications for future practice.

More case studies might well generate further accounts of relationships between development and research. What can we see so far?

### Before research ...

Before research, there are research questions. These arise from two main types of sources.

Some research questions arise from consideration of the literature and of prior research. This prior research may be in the particular field of study – here, online and distance education or some particular subset thereof – or in some more or less closely related field of study (perhaps, face-to-face teaching and learning, assessment, learning psychology, sociology of education, educational management, educational policy and strategy, philosophy of education, uses of technology in teaching and learning or any or all of the subjects taught and studied and researched in HE) and perhaps more widely still.

Other research questions arise from observation of, review of, critical reflection on, theorising about, practice, asking questions including 'what happened?', 'why did it happen?', 'what did it mean?', 'are there any implications for future practice?' and any number of other productive questions.

## Before development ...

Before development, and acting as prompts for development, there are usually issues, difficulties, priorities, requirements, opportunities, bright ideas (perhaps drawn from the literature), 'what ifs?' and, as above, research observations of, reviews of and critical reflections on practice. Again, questions include 'what happened?', 'why did it happen?', 'what did it mean?' and 'are there any implications for future practice?'

## An interim account of relations between development, research and practice

Some of the prompts for development and for research seem to be very similar: essentially, data or observations and questions.

I had expected to end this chapter with, as sketched above, a slightly more elaborate account of relations between research and academic development in distance learning, going beyond simply 'development is the implementation of the research', perhaps including evaluating or researching the implementation and the effects on student learning of developments and of changes to policy and practice – perhaps a kind of development sandwich: development between two slices of research.

But we can go further.

## Towards a more integrated account

We can bring in and work with three sets of ideas.

First, we can use Ashwin and Trigwell's (2004) useful terminology of 'investigation' rather than 'research'. To recall, their account of investigation has three components or levels: the intentions to generate (i) personal, and then (ii) local, knowledge (personally and locally generated and validated) before we get to (iii) publishable research. The prompts for personal and local investigation and for development are even more similar to each other than are the prompts for research and development, usually being more personal and local, whether prompted by an observation on practice or by an idea from the literature.

Next, we can use Popovic and Baume's account (2016), elaborated on a little in Baume (2016). This describes the first two stages of scholarly activity as: firstly, reflecting on and investigating current practice; secondly, applying ideas from the literature, before we get to Ashwin and Trigwell's model; the third stage, refereed academic publication. Again, a (scholarly) enquiry or exploration may start with observation or investigation of practice or with ideas from the literature.

The third set of ideas is about development. This chapter has explicitly made a distinction between, on the one hand, projects intended to enhance some aspects of the design and operation of distance learning courses and, on the other hand, the practice of designing and running the courses. This distinction is not necessarily the distinction between course design and course operation. Course design can be a routine, although of course highly skilled, process, just as course operation can be. Or course design can be undertaken or considered as a project. Similarly, course operation can be undertaken mainly as a routine activity or mainly as a continuing voyage of discovery. The distinction being made here is rather between a project – something exceptional and distinct, with defined goals and defined start and finish points – and something that is more routine, regular and operational. There is no value judgement as between project and operation. Both are necessary and both have to be done well.

With that clarified, it is also useful to explore the relationship between development projects and the regular business of course design and operation, just as it was with the relationship between development and research. Again, through this lens, we find the operation of courses throwing up questions, issues, observations, problems, opportunities, some at least of which can provide the opportunity, indeed the requirement, for investigation, change or for a development project, whether small or large. These questions, opportunities and requirements may only be relevant to the course where the issue was identified, or they may have much broader implications, often pointing to changes to practice and perhaps also policy, strategy and understanding.

## Taking a stance: sustained scholarly practice

What does all this tell us about a productive relationship between academic development, research or investigation, policy and practice?

We may perhaps characterise this productive relationship as a stance to be taken. I shall characterise that stance as a sustained, alert, open, consistently enquiring, investigative, scholarly, research, evidence and theory-informed attitude or approach towards practice and the further improvement of practice – always seeking to find and to make sense, not just to 'do', and informed by ideas from the widest range of sources.

Academic development, research and practice may productively meet in what we may call sustained scholarly practice.

Research is not just what we do to understand and improve practice. Development, the improvement of practice and capability, is not just the application of research. The relationship between development and research or investigation should be much more intimate and more sustained than that. Rather, the relationship should be continuous, integrated, mutually testing, interrogating, informing and reinforcing. This really would be quality enhancement.

This may sound rather daunting and it certainly is demanding. Specifically, it demands that we never again 'just do'. Rather, while we 'do', we keep on asking questions and at least consider using new ideas and approaches.

But there are reasons for optimism.

Firstly, the great majority of those who teach in UK HE (in late 2021, around 150,000) have, in gaining accreditation against the UK Professional Standards Framework (Advance HE, 2020), shown that they:

- have, and can apply to their practice, knowledge of how students learn, both generally and within their subject or disciplinary areas
- as a value informing their practice, use evidence-informed approaches and the outcomes from research, scholarship and continuing professional development.

So at least some of the necessary knowledge, and the commitment to a scholarly approach, are widely in place.

Secondly, this sustained scholarly practice doesn't all have to be done by one person. It can be done best by the whole team investigating and having scholarly conversations about practice, working together and bringing together their various capabilities and enthusiasms.

Thirdly, educational knowledge and expertise and the commitment to scholarship are not confined to academic staff in universities. They are part of the professional expertise of people working in many other HE roles besides, most obviously, management, administration, student support and learning development, library and information systems and learning technology. All of their contributions are essential and available for effective and improving online and distance education.

## Notes

1  See https://iet.open.ac.uk/.
2  See https://www.tandfonline.com/journals/rija.
3  More such reports can be found at: https://www.london.ac.uk/centre-online-distance-education/what-we-do/our-projects.

## References

Advance HE (2020) 'UK Professional Standards Framework'. Accessed 22 November 2020. https://www.advance-he.ac.uk/guidance/teaching-and-learning/ukpsf.

Allen, M., Bourhis, J., Burrell, N. and Mabry, E. (2002) 'Comparing student satisfaction with distance education to traditional classrooms in higher education: A meta-analysis'. *American Journal of Distance Education*, 16 (2), 83–97.

Ashwin, P. and Trigwell, K. (2004) 'Investigating educational development'. In D. Baume and P. Kahn (eds), *Enhancing Academic Development* (1st edn). Abingdon: Routledge, 117–31.

Assinder, S., Baume, D. and Bates, I. (2010) 'Focussing on student learning to guide the use of staff time'. *Innovations in Education and Teaching International*, 47 (4), 357–67.

Baume, C., Martin, P. and Yorke, M. (2002) *Managing Educational Development Projects: Effective management for maximum impact*. London: Kogan Page.

Baume, D. (2016) 'Scholarship in action'. *Innovations in Education and Teaching International*, 54 (2), 111–16.

Baume, D. (2020) 'Some notes on literacies'. University of London Centre for Online and Distance Education. Accessed 19 November 2020. https://london.ac.uk/sites/default/files/cde/cde-some-notes-on-literacies.pdf.

Baume, D. (2022) 'Literacies, fluencies and academic practices'. Educational Developments, 23 (3), 24–8, Accessed 13 December 2022. https://www.dropbox.com/s/pzt0gwha04je5rb/Ed%20Devs%2023.3.pdf?dl=0.

Baume, D. and Cappellini, B. (2019) 'Preparing University of London students for living and working in the world: The development of information literacy'. University of London Centre for Online and Distance Education. Accessed 9 November 2020. https://london.ac.uk/sites/default/files/leaflets/cde-Information-literacy-final-report.pdf.

Baume, D. and Popovic, C. (2016) *Advancing Practice in Academic Development* (1st edn). Abingdon: Routledge.

Baume, D. and Scanlon, E. (2018) 'What the research says about how and why learning happens'. In R. Luckin (ed.), *Enhancing Learning and Teaching with Technology: What the research says* (1st edn). London: UCL IOE Press, 2–13.

Baume, D. and Yorke, M. (2002) 'The reliability of assessment by portfolio on a course to develop and accredit teachers in higher education'. *Studies in Higher Education*, 27 (1), 7–25.

Baume, D., Yorke, M. and Coffey, M. (2004) 'What is happening when we assess, and how can we use our understanding of this to improve assessment?' *Assessment & Evaluation in Higher Education*, 29 (4), 451–77.

Brown, S. and Baume, D. (2020) 'Student Learning Hours and Learning Strategies Project: Final report'. University of London Centre for Online and Distance Education, 30 December. Accessed 16 June 2021. https://london.ac.uk/sites/default/files/cde/cde-slh-final-report-d8.pdf.

Brown, S. and Baume, D. (2022) '"Not another group activity!" Student attitudes to individual and collaborative learning activities, and some implications for distance learning course design and operation'. *Innovations in Education and Teaching International*, 14 April. Accessed 28 July 2022. https://doi.org/10.1080/14703297.2022.2062424.

Dweck, C. S. (1999) *Self-Theories: Their role in motivation, personality, and development*. Philadelphia: Taylor & Francis.

Gillies, M., Gregson, J., San Diego, J., Sheehan, T. and Thuranira-McKeever, C. (2019) 'Digital Educator Project: Final report'. University of London Centre for Online and Distance Education, April. Accessed 17 December 2021. https://london.ac.uk/sites/default/files/cde/Digital-Educator-Final.pdf.

Inkelaar, T. and Simpson, O. (2015) 'Challenging the "distance education deficit" through "motivational emails"'. *Open Learning*, 30 (2), 152–63. Accessed 28 July 2022. https://doi.org/10.1080/02680513.2015.1055718.

Popovic, C. and Baume, D. (2016) 'Introduction: Some issues in academic development'. In D. Baume and C. Popovic (eds), *Advancing Practice in Academic Development*. London: Routledge, 1–16.

Rientes, B. (2020) 'Using learning analytics to support learners and teachers at the Open University'. Kent.ac.uk. Accessed 29 July 2022. https://www.slideshare.net/BartRienties/using-learning-analytics-to-support-learners-and-teachers-at-the-open-university.

Simpson, O. (2006) 'Predicting student success'. *Open Learning*, 21 (2), 125–38.

Simpson, O. (2008) 'Cost benefits of student retention policies and practices'. In W. J. Bramble and S. Panda (eds), *Economics of Distance and Online Learning*. Abingdon: Routledge, 162–78.

Simpson, O. (2012) *Supporting Students for Success in Online and Distance Education*. New York: Routledge.

University of Edinburgh (2017) 'What is the scholarship of teaching and learning (SoTL)? Accessed 27 January 2022. https://www.ed.ac.uk/institute-academic-development/learning-teaching/staff/sotl.

UoL (University of London) (2019) 'Digital Educator Project final report'. University of London Centre for Online and Distance Education. Accessed 28 July 2022. https://www.london.ac.uk/sites/default/files/cde/Digital-Educator-Final.pdf.

Vogel, M. (2015) 'Online learning and the no significant difference phenomenon', UCL Digital Education Team blog, 20 August. Accessed 3 October 2020. https://blogs.ucl.ac.uk/digital-education/2015/08/20/online-learning-and-the-no-significant-difference-phenomenon/.

# 19
# Monitoring and evaluating online and distance education
David Baume

**Focus on outcomes ...**

We monitor and evaluate online and distance education, just as we monitor and evaluate anything, above all, in order to answer these questions:

'How is it working? – the monitoring question.
'How did it work?' – the evaluation question.

'How' is included in each question to encourage us to add richness, depth and detail to what may otherwise be spurious, unhelpful binary judgements. 'How?' is also a somewhat research-related question (see Chapter 18), aiding us in our search for understanding as well as judgement and steering us through the blurry interface between evaluation and research, considered in more detail later in this chapter.[1]

If we were discussing assessment rather than evaluation, monitoring would be formative assessment and evaluation would be summative assessment. (We should note that this is a UK-based account. The terms 'evaluation' and 'assessment' swap meanings as they cross the Atlantic.)

I will discuss monitoring and evaluation in detail in this chapter using one, other or both of these 'how' questions as ultimate reference points. Before we get into any detail, however, Bamber (2008: 107) offers a valuable overview, stressing the need to undertake 'theory-informed, contextualised evaluations involving a structured approach'. I shall try to make the advice in this chapter live up to each element of Bamber's counsel. Stefani (2009) also provides a useful overview of educational evaluation.

I suggest six clusters of evaluation questions. The six clusters do not form a linear sequence, other than when required by the restrictions of printed text. The order of presentation here may be the most useful in planning monitoring and evaluation.

Effective monitoring and evaluation are crucial to the health of current and future online and distance learning projects or courses. If you are active in online and distance learning, you are most likely to be planning or undertaking some monitoring and evaluation. You may therefore find it helpful to make notes on your answers to these questions and any other questions that your resulting answers may raise.

The ideas and practices in this chapter should help you undertake thorough monitoring and evaluation. Where time and resources are restricted, you will need to make informed selections from this broad set of ideas and practices. If you need to make a case for a budget for monitoring and evaluation, you could refer to the financial and reputational costs of repeated mistakes and continued inefficiencies.

On terminology, I shall refer to 'whatever it is that is being monitored or evaluated' throughout the chapter. I shall use the convenient if not yet familiar term: 'evaluand'. Also, 'evaluation' should also sometimes be taken to include 'monitoring'.

## ... and focus on processes

A focus on processes, by contrast with outcomes, asks whether the evaluand is being undertaken properly (the monitoring question) or has been undertaken properly (the evaluation question). That is, how far have the relevant procedures been followed; the relevant conditions met; the relevant norms, values and regulations ethical standards followed; the relevant research knowledge and scholarship applied to design and operation?

The monitoring and evaluation of processes can involve some judgement. However, the monitoring and evaluation of processes is often more a matter of constructing and using checklists and standards than is the monitoring of outcomes. I shall not say any more about the monitoring and evaluation of processes in this chapter. But please keep in mind this strand of monitoring and evaluation.

# Six clusters of useful questions about monitoring and evaluation of outcomes

## Who?

This can be both an individual and an institutional/organisational 'who'.

- Who owns the evaluation?
- Who decides what is to be monitored or evaluated?
- Who decides how the monitoring or evaluation is to be conducted?
- Who wants to know? Who is asking the questions?
- Who decides the goals, the outcomes or the criteria against which the course or project is to be judged?
- More broadly, who are the stakeholders in the evaluand? Who has an interest?
- Who, if anyone, currently holds the information? Who knows the answers to the questions that the monitor or the evaluator will ask? This question is not intended to imply that the answers to all the evaluators' questions are lying around waiting to be picked up. Evaluation also surfaces tacit knowledge and finds new knowledge. But evaluation does make use of existing knowledge.
- Who will variously seek out, obtain, collate, analyse and interpret the information discovered and draw conclusions, understandings and implications for action from it? These functions do not all need to be undertaken by the same person.
- Beyond the originally identified stakeholders, who else may be interested in the outcomes of the monitoring and evaluation?
- Who ensures that the quality cycle is taken to completion, that the loop is closed, from specification of the goals of whatever is being evaluated, through the planning and implementation of monitoring and evaluation, to the implementation of what was learned from the monitoring and evaluation? If the results of the evaluation are not used, learning has been ignored and effort has been wasted.

## Why?

Beyond the need to see whether or not it has worked/is working, why do we want to monitor or evaluate? Possible reasons include the following:

- for accountability, to show that what was done, achieved and/or produced matches what was intended or promised

- to understand or make sense of the evaluand
- to build on new understandings achieved, or previous understandings confirmed, and thereby make it possible to improve practice (these first three reasons are adapted from Chelimsky, 1997)
- to increase capability and capacity in monitoring and evaluations (this last one is from Baume, 2003).

The results of monitoring can be used to inform and suggest changes to the broad direction or fine detail of the current development project or course. For example, information about the effectiveness of particular activities in an online or distance learning course can be used to inform the design of future activities, probably in subsequent modules, or at module review time.

The results of the final evaluation, by contrast, are most likely to be used in the design of future courses and processes to improve them.

## What?

What is to be monitored or evaluated? What is the evaluand? In this chapter, a distinction will be made between two broad kinds of online and distance learning-related evaluands:

- projects to develop and redevelop courses and methods, perhaps also policies and strategies. These projects often include staff development in online and distance learning capabilities. They are also often partly or wholly e-learning projects
- the operation of online and distance learning courses.

What is the evaluand intended to do, produce or achieve? What are its intended activities, outcomes(s) and/or output(s)? What information will be sought?

We should also look back to the first and second questions under 'who?' – 'who owns the evaluation?' and 'who decides what is to be monitored or evaluated?' and ask:

What criteria will the owners of the evaluation apply to judge the results of the evaluation? Knowing this can help us design the evaluation.

## How?

- How and by what processes will the other questions in this list be answered?

- How will the monitoring and evaluation be planned, conducted and reported? Expertise, cost, availability, timing and ethics will all have to be addressed in planning the evaluation.

## When?

Monitoring and evaluation are typically distinguished by when they are done:

- monitoring is undertaken during the project or course
- evaluation is carried out at the end, hopefully informed by the monitoring.

However, there is a good case for integrating monitoring with evaluation. Both involve the collection and analysis of data, the search for understanding, and the intention to improve, albeit on different timescales, as discussed in the section 'Why?' Monitoring and evaluation can both be started at the very beginning of the project to ensure that relevant data are collected from the start. Indeed, there is a useful role for the evaluator in project planning, most obviously in ensuring that the project outcomes are indeed capable of being evaluated and are more than vague, if worthy, aspirations.

Monitoring and evaluation are most usefully seen as ends of a spectrum of activities, rather than as binary alternatives.

## Where?

This question, in its strict geographic meaning, has become less important, as communication and the sharing of information have become easier. However, it may still be important to note the physical locations in which any actual activities were undertaken.

Additionally, it may be helpful to note the media or channels through which the work is done – the online, digital, forms of 'where' – for example, Zoom, Moodle or the university's online library.

It is also useful to expand the meaning of 'where' to encompass the various contexts of the work. These contexts include discipline, module or programme, department, institution, professional body, quality systems and any other relevant contextual factors, always including institutional priorities, politics and the norms, beliefs, practices and values of the individuals and groups involved.

Using these six clusters of questions

In the rest of this chapter, I shall not constantly refer to these six clusters of questions. Rather, I hope that as you read, test and explore how you can apply some of the ideas in this chapter to your own monitoring and evaluation practice, you will find it useful to refer back to them and answer them.

## Some issues in evaluating online and distance learning

### Evaluating what, exactly?

'Evaluating' a course may sound like a straightforward proposition, but a course is designed and run in contexts and settings. What happens if we pull back and work with, for example, a wider view of the stages of a student's engagement with the distance learning programme in the university? Goals for 11 stages of engagement can be suggested. The attainment of each of the sets of goals can be evaluated. Table 19.1 is adapted and then summarised from Baume (2010). It provides a basis for evaluating a wider view of a distance learning course. As well as being useful in its own right, this example is also intended to show how our choice of perspective can help us decide exactly what is to be evaluated and how the evaluand can variously be subdivided into sections or placed in its wider contexts. The stakeholders in the evaluation and the clients for the evaluation are likely to influence the perspective and what we do and do not include in the evaluation.

### Goals and their achievement: problems and solutions

Focusing on online and distance learning development projects, a development project's goals may be specified in terms of:

- what the project intends to *do*; in terms of its activities – for example, 'We shall plan and run this distance learning course'
- what it intends to *produce*; its outputs – for example, 'We shall devise six hours of appropriate online student learning activities in every ten hours of study, of which two hours will involve collaboration with other students'

Table 19.1  Goals for 11 stages of engagement. Adapted from Baume (2010).

|   | Step | Goals/outcomes for this step |
|---|------|------------------------------|
| 1 | **Discovery (by the student of the programme and institution)** | Most or all potential students are reached by accurate and appropriate information.<br>This information communicates to each potential student what the institution wants to communicate to them.<br>The information tells the student at least some of what they want and need to know, leading in some cases to … |
| 2 | **Enquiry and advice** | … students making any necessary further enquiries or requests for information, advice and guidance.<br>These enquiries or requests receive swift, accurate, clear and helpful responses. On the basis of these responses, the student makes a well-informed and personally, academically and professionally appropriate decision whether or not to apply for a place. |
| 3 | **Application, response and admission decisions** | |
| 4 | **Enrolment and induction** | |
| 5 | **Study** | All of the elements listed below meet the emerging needs of students, and the standards of the institution and of the discipline or profession for which the students are preparing:<br><br>• students' study schedule<br>• the structure, aims and intended learning outcomes of the programme<br>• the online learning activities that they undertake and questions that they answer, both alone and as a member of a face-to-face and online learning community<br>• the reading that they do<br>• the other learning resources available to them<br>• the ways in which they prepare for assessment.<br><br>Students undertake study set for, or negotiated with, them to the best of their abilities. |

*(continued)*

*(continued)*

|   | Step | Goals/outcomes for this step |
|---|---|---|
| 6 | Information and support | Students have ready access at all stages of their studies to the information that they need. Students feel, accurately, that they are part of a supportive social and academic network of fellow students, teachers and other professionals, and that they are developing both personally and professionally in desired ways. |
| 7 | Feedback | Students submit work for feedback according to the schedule provided or negotiated. With each piece of work that they submit, they include their own critique of the work. They receive feedback on their work within the specified schedule, from tutor and from peers. They find that the feedback:<br><br>• confirms what they are doing well<br>• is constructively critical of areas in which they have done less well<br>• makes helpful suggestions about the content of the work that they submitted for feedback and, more generally, about their approach to research, writing, referencing and other important features of their work.<br><br>The students use this feedback to guide their future studies, further assignments, and their preparation for, and performance, in summative assessments. |
| 8 | Assessment | Students have an opportunity to demonstrate attainment and receive marks, grades and/or academic credit for their achievements. Students are rarely surprised by their assessment results, because they have become good judges of their own attainment. |
| 9 | Re-assessment and re-enrolment | Students who have not passed, or not achieved high enough marks to enable them to study what they wish to study next year, are offered prompt and helpful advice on their options, and perhaps the opportunity to be reassessed. Students' experience of the re-enrolment process is prompt, efficient and painless. |

|    | Step | Goals/outcomes for this step |
|----|------|------------------------------|
| 10 | **Graduation** | Students receive acknowledgement of their graduation and have the opportunity to celebrate their graduation. |
| 11 | **Alumni-hood** | To the extent that they wish, students:<br>• associate with some of their former fellow students<br>• take an active interest in the development of the institution<br>• receive news from the institution that matches their current and evolving interests. |

- what it is intended to *achieve*; these effects we may call its outcomes – for example, typically for a distance learning course, 'The students will achieve, and will value achieving, the intended learning outcomes of the course – that is, they will be able to do these things to these standards ...'

Activities and outputs are therefore easy to describe and quantify, however easy or difficult they are to do and produce. Activities and outputs are also easy to establish as goals, as suggested in the short examples given.

However, we undertake activities and deliver products that will have effects on the practices and perhaps also on the knowledge, understanding and world view of immediate colleagues, students, whole departments or even whole institutions. We undertake development projects to improve the quality of our courses and systems. Such outcomes are harder to define and measure than activities and outputs – though never impossible.

Above all, we write courses to support and prompt students to work and learn, and thereby to achieve course learning outcomes. (For advice on writing programme learning outcomes see, for example, Baume, 2009.)

What difficulties may we find in taking an outcomes-based approach to online and distance-learning development projects and in planning online and distance learning courses? And how can these difficulties be tackled?

*The problem of knowing what causes what*

We certainly do not know as much as we would like to know about what actions lead to what outcomes. The chains and nets of influence may be long, complex and slow.

In creating a course, we typically plan a sequence of student learning activities, provide students with access to a range of learning resources, help students to work with each other and provide feedback and guidance. We hope the students will undertake these activities (although, see the example 'Student learning hours and learning strategies' in Chapter 18 of this book for a caution) and use these resources to support their learning. Even with a maximum of data coming from our virtual learning environment (VLE), we cannot be sure exactly what the various things that students are doing mean. There are several links in the chain from what we do and create to what our students do and learn. You may find it useful to map these links out for a course that you know. This will not take long. It would be valuable to compare your intended links to the links your students actually make.

With a development project, these chains and nets may lead from the project team to partner organisations or academic and/or technical departments, those who form policy and manage, to those who design, validate and teach courses and otherwise work with students to – at last – achieve the intended outcomes, which would usually be the students' learning. Again, it is worth mapping out these various intended chains or nets of communication within a project, identifying the most important as foci for evaluation. This typically only takes a few minutes and is useful to compare your plans with subsequent reality.

Some of the things that we most securely know about the conditions for student learning are synthesised in Baume and Scanlon (2018) and summarised in Chapter 8 of this book. If these ideas are being implemented in a course, we have grounds for hope (although of course not certainty) that some good learning will be happening. Evaluation does not have to go right back to basics every time. We can, with caution, apply what we already know.

For example, we know that people are more likely to change their practice when a variety of factors – policies, examples of good practice, theoretical and evidential bases for the change (Ho, 1998), encouragement and support from valued peer groups and leaders – all pull in broadly the same direction. Even such relatively basic understandings of why people may change their practice can guide our actions towards the attainment of project outcomes and are likely to be partial indicators, even partial predictors, of success.

## *The problem of measurement*

It is relatively simple to measure the success of a course – by studying student attainment, as evidenced through marks or grades earned.

Measuring the effectiveness of development projects can be harder. But we have to do this, otherwise how can we demonstrate the value of our work? How can we identify and work towards good, evaluable, determinable, outcomes and then determine how far, and how, these have been achieved?

Firstly, we need to determine the particular differences that we want to make. This works as well for development projects as for the design of courses. For example, in what particular ways do we want our students to be different and to have different capabilities or qualities? We can define this *for* our students; where possible, it is better to define them *with* our students. We should usually be able to link goals for development projects back to improvements in student learning.

Secondly, we should ask and answer the questions: 'How shall we know if we have succeeded?', 'What evidence will show success?' We should go beyond this, and seek to understand, as well as determine, success.

Still at the planning stage, we should then iterate between the suggested intended outcome and ways to measure and determine its attainment, until we have an outcome that we value and whose attainment we can determine.

As we monitor and evaluate, we should also look out for serendipitous outcomes and celebrate the positive ones, as well as learning from the negative ones. But, unless the proposed outcomes of our work are at least to some extent determinable, with or without numbers, our work is little more than an act of faith. Bamber (2020) offers a well-researched and balanced view of the power and the limitations of numerical data in such evaluations.

## *The problem of measuring difference*

In order to establish that a difference has been made it is necessary to know how things were before. A baseline study is an important early preparation for evaluation of whatever the project or course intends to change.

Such a baseline study brings benefits beyond establishing a baseline from which to measure difference. It requires a clarification of what the venture intends to change and of what the baselines will be about. It begins a conversation and thus helps to form productive relationships with stakeholder groups in the early stages of the work.

A baseline study – whether of how things are before the start of a development project or of students' capabilities before they embark on a course of study – also provides a rehearsal or early pilot of the questions and methods that will be used in later formative and then summative evaluations.

### The problem of timescale

The ultimate intended outcomes may not be achieved and become determinable until after the end of a development project. For example, an online or distance learning development project may involve proposing and making changes to practice in a course that may be months or even a couple of years away from first presentation. The longer-term effects of the innovation on student learning may not be able to be evaluated until further years have passed.

One approach is to use proxies for the actual outcome. The proxies need to be measurable or determinable within the timescale available. They also need to be as plausible as possible and as close as possible to the intended outcomes. For example, Rust (1998) found that action plans expressed at the end of a well-run staff development workshop serve as a partially successful predictor that the planned actions will actually be undertaken. This result also makes a strong case for action plans at the end of a module or course as a plausible if partial proxy for action after the end of the course.

The section 'Four levels of evaluation applied to distance learning courses' on Kirkpatrick's evaluation methods suggests another kind of plausible proxy – in summary, students doing tasks during the course that have some similarities to the kinds of things they will do in employment or future study. Irrespective of evaluation considerations, such authentic tasks are good things for students to be doing (see Chapter 8 and its emphasis on planning student activities).

Another approach is to decouple the evaluation schedule from the development project or the course schedule. In other words, push back the evaluation to a time when it can be conducted properly and when it can actually measure what it is intended to measure – that is, the real intended outcomes. For example, if one of our goals is that students will be able to use ideas and capabilities from the course in future employment, then that's what we will have to wait to evaluate, determine and measure. The tendency for evaluation to end with the end of the development project and for course evaluations to be conducted at the end of the semester or the academic year may lead us to distort and truncate our outcomes and/or our evaluation processes to match the timescale available for the completion of evaluation. This is understandable but unhelpful.

A third approach is to break the evaluation into parallel shorter sections. Instead of trying to track cause and effect through all the chains or nets described, it is possible to look at single links. Did the work with senior managers lead to new curriculum policy? As a parallel investigation, perhaps using published data, have other curriculum policies led to the intended changes in curriculum? Again, perhaps using published data, have other such curriculum changes led to demonstrable changes in student capabilities? This form of parallel, research-informed evaluation gives earlier but less accurate data. However, this may be more useful than a long multi-link evaluation plan that can never be undertaken and where, even if it were to be attempted, the passage of time and the intervention of other changes may make tracking from original causes to final effects similarly inaccurate.

## Evaluation and quality assurance

Quality assurance (QA) standards, systems and processes provide an important part of the frame within which monitoring and evaluation are undertaken. Monitoring and evaluation are important approaches to ensuring quality, particularly when quality has been adequately defined, as is not always the case.

However, QA should not fully define the evaluation frame. QA is partly a political process, expressing educational political priorities, which priorities may be nationally political, institutional and/or disciplinary or professional.

We must accept and work with the politics, of course, but not be confined by them. We should also bring our academic capabilities and values to the definition of goals and to the monitoring and evaluation of their attainment. Some of the political dimensions of educational evaluation are explored by Bamber and Anderson (2012).

## Evaluation and research

Chapter 18 of this book considers a difficulty in publishing reports on development and research projects. In summary, the difficulty is a possible clash between the obligation on the researcher to publish a thorough account of what was done and discovered and possible issues of confidentiality or reputational difficulties to the client, the institution or organisation that sponsored the development or research.

Evaluation and research have much in common – above all, the intention to achieve an evidence-based understanding of what is being studied that can be used to bring about improvement. However, evaluations can run into the same difficulty, in whatever scholarly a way they are undertaken. This difficulty is client confidentiality. It can sometimes be overcome with careful negotiation, but not always.

## Can we evaluate our own work?

If the intended outcomes are clear and reasonably determinable, the data collected properly and the judgements clearly rooted in the evidence, then, yes, we can evaluate our own work. However, there may be problems with credibility. We may be able to make a good case for the quality of our self-evaluation. However, an additional outside view is usually a good idea, perhaps using the external examiner model referred to in the section on evaluator roles.

## Some approaches to evaluation

### Types of approaches

Al-Alwani (2014) offers a useful typology of approaches to evaluation of e-learning that is also more widely applicable:

- Case study evaluations. These may be descriptive rather than strictly evaluative, but case studies or stories can provide a useful starting point and evidence for an evaluation, as discussed in 'Richer approaches'.
- Comparative evaluations. These can be descriptive and/or analytical, but they add value by relating the evaluand to other, comparable, projects, processes or programmes.
- Performance evaluations. These typically take the form of outcome-based evaluations, which are the major subject of this chapter.
- Benchmarking evaluations. These may be seen as a form of comparative evaluation, with the additional idea that one of the comparators is accepted as a benchmark or ideal.

### Richer approaches

The idea of evaluation suggests a rational process of data collection and judgement. This section offers a wider range of evaluation roles to consider.

This chapter mostly offers a rationalist/positivist approach to monitoring and evaluation, with an emphasis on explicit outcomes and their attainment. Radically different, though complementary, approaches have been proposed and used.

The illuminative approach that Parlett and Hamilton (1972) propose and Miller and Parlett (1974: 2) illustrate aims 'to explore, describe, analyse, elucidate and portray – in other words to illuminate – the practices and processes of teaching and learning, broadly defined, as they occur in their national settings ...'.

> The illuminative approach ... [is] ... problem centred ..., practitioner-oriented ..., cross-disciplinary ..., methodologically eclectic ..., and heuristically organised, progressively focussing and refining the areas of inquiry as the study unfolds. (Miller and Parlett, 1974: 2)

This illuminative approach can give a vivid account of the evaluand. It does not shrink from judgement, but it brings us a richer, possibly more complete and more accurate picture than does a coolly rational, purely data-centric approach.

Stake (2002) advocates 'above all, evaluation is the discernment of the good' and calls for evaluation to be holistic, thoughtful and experiential. It should find and tell the evaluand's story, asking 'what's happening here?' Stake calls this 'responsive evaluation'.

This can give an even richer picture than the illuminative approach described. Also, the emphasis on finding the good is welcome in a world often concerned with finding the faults.

Still concentrating on the good, Ludema et al. (2000) propose this prompt for an evaluation:

> Think of a time in your entire experience of this [here, course or development project] when you have felt most excited, most engaged and most alive. What were the forces and factors that made it a great experience? What was it about you, others and your organisation that made this a peak experience for you? (Ludema et al., 2000: n.p.)

The authors call this 'appreciative enquiry'. 'Celebratory enquiry' would also have worked well as a name.

As with Stake's (2002) responsive approach, this is methodologically more sophisticated than it may look. Many evaluation approaches, especially those that make extensive use of numbers, focus on means and standard deviations. The truly dreadful, or those high peaks that Ludema et al. (2000) ask us to seek out and then celebrate, may well be dismissed as outliers. Ludema et al. advise us instead to treat the peaks as the best that can be achieved. This is valid because we know that they have been achieved. Rather than dismissing them as outliers, we should make sense of them and of how and why these peaks were attained. Then, over time, we should make those peaks into goals and targets and work to level up.

These are positive approaches to evaluation and hence to goal setting and planning. The results of evaluation should provide a basis for setting the next round of goals. These methods may work equally well for projects intended to improve some aspect of practice and for the courses themselves. These approaches also chime well with one of the conditions for good student learning explored in Chapter 8: describe and expect high standards.

None of these approaches does the entire job of evaluation, but they do have important contributions to make as we seek to give a full account and make a full evaluation – always with the intention to understand and thereby to improve. To numbers, marks and scales they add other valid kinds of data – words, pictures and stories (Brew, 2011).

## Evaluator roles

The evaluator can take a number of roles or characters, including (synthesised from Baume 2008; Cousin, 2001):

- **Judge**, who makes pronouncements on the worth and attainments of the evaluand
- **External examiner**, who samples self-evaluations and makes suggestions on evaluation process and on judgements
- **Evaluation consultant**, who advises on evaluation process
- **Evaluation capacity builder**, who provides training and development for the staff of the venture on evaluation
- **Trusted outsider or critical friend**
- **Research collaborator**, accepting that evaluation and research have many similarities of purpose, method and report
- **Detective**, who investigates and seeks truths
- **Developer**, concerned to produce usable data and concerned that those data are then used for improvement
- **Fool or Joker**, who is playful, seeking to illuminate, is fond of paradox and confusion, occasionally spiteful
- **Mafia don**, the 'heavy' who offers protection from outside forces, but at a price
- **Anorak**, who wants to collect all the data they can possibly find
- **Scientist**, who wants to check what the Anorak has collected, and then theorise about it.

These are of course all parodies. However, as both an evaluator and evaluand over the years, I have seen most of them, and been several of them, perhaps more of them than I know.

This list could provide an entertaining as well as a valuable basis for a negotiation with a possible evaluator. You will probably want a combination of several of these roles and absolutely not want others.

## Some practices for evaluating online and distance learning

### Four levels of evaluation applied to distance learning courses

Kirkpatrick and Kirkpatrick (2016) suggest four levels of evaluation (here called K1–4). Originally developed for evaluating training, the Kirkpatrick model is adapted here to evaluating online and distance learning at all scales, from programme through module, week or block of study, through to particular learning activities or particular learning resources.

*K1: Participants' immediate reactions to the particular evaluand*
These immediate responses are often obtained through some form of 'happy sheet', whether on paper or online.

Happy sheets have their uses and their limitations. It is not of primary importance that students are happy – it is important that they are learning. However, at the most local level, quick initial reactions can have value.

What do you ask students about? Hygiene factors – room temperature, safety, the quality of the coffee and their online equivalents. Ask about new things about the course; aspects of the course in which you do not have complete confidence. Ask about things that you can do something about it, or things that others can do something about. Ask about things that you think may be important. (Alongside asking for a 1–5 ranking on the item, you can also ask for a 1–5 ranking on the importance of each item.)

Rather than saving up all the questions for a large mid-semester or end-of-semester survey, why not ask one or two appropriate questions every week or two? This will give you more rapid feedback. This process will also help your students to feel that they are being heard, or at least listened to. If you are able to act on what they tell you, then do so, and tell them how you have used their feedback. If you cannot, then it's good to tell your students why not.

But immediate reactions are immediate. They are also probably about likes rather than learning. They may enable us to reduce sources of irritation in future development events and processes, in future presentations of the course (indeed, next week, if we have so much flexibility). But, if we have not succeeded in persuading our students of the value of an innovation, we may get a negative initial response. If we are confident in the innovation, we should try harder to help students see its value, as quickly as possible. I am not a fan of the statement, 'You may hate it now, but you will thank me years later.' I have heard this used as a defence for bad teaching and as an excuse for not improving teaching. We should do better than that.

*K2: What students have learned from the evaluand*
Such data should already be available in the VLE, where you should be able to see students' answers to questions and see what they learned (if the questions are asked appropriately). Depending on how the course runs, you may give them feedback on what they learned.

However, student responses are also feedback to you, on some combination of the effectiveness of the learning activities and resources and of the ways in which students engaged with these.

*K3: How and how far students have later used what they have learned*
Because he was concerned with training, mainly in commercial settings, Kirkpatrick was interested in how people used what they learned at work. If your students are both studying and working, then this is a legitimate line of enquiry with them – how have they used at work what they learned with you? Of course, that is not entirely the responsibility of teacher or students – whatever they have learned and however keen they are to apply it, their work circumstances can make it easy, difficult or impossible to use what they have learned.

If your students are in a work setting relevant to their studies, there are at least three ways to deal with this as you evaluate your teaching:

- K3.1: You could ask your students to tell you how they *would* apply in their work setting what they have learned, when circumstances allowed. This is obviously not as good as them showing how they *did* apply their learning to practice, but it is much better than nothing and a plausible proxy.
- K3.2: Irrespective of K3.1, if their work circumstances change during the course, they can then show you how they do apply their learning in practice in their new or changed work setting.

- K3.3: Another option is to take the longer view. You could decide that you have to identify the effects of students' learning on their subsequent professional careers and so undertake follow-up studies a year or more after graduation. Such longitudinal studies obviously require patience, but they can be very powerful and very informative.

If your students are not also in work settings, where they could apply what they are learning, the first approach can be modified a little:

- K3.1: You could ask your students to tell you how they would or could apply, in some plausible work or future study setting, what they have learned, when circumstances allow. This is obviously not as good as them applying their learning to practice, but it is much better than nothing; again, a plausible proxy.

Alternatively, you could use the approach described in K3.3 – taking a longer view.

The K3 question can probably be asked at all levels from the immediate, the single learning activity, through to blocks of study, modules and indeed programmes. Your analysis of student learning at K2 will show you their immediate learning. Their work or planning on a bigger assignment later in the course will show you how they have gone to the next stage, a version of K3, and used, or planned to use, what they have learned. Again, you can give feedback to them on their learning, but their work also provides feedback, monitoring and evaluation data to you and your course.

*K4: Impact of what has been learned on the organisation*
K4 in the Kirkpatrick model asks about the impact of students' use of what they have learned on the effectiveness of their organisation. Ultimately, it measures return on investment in training. Such data are most unlikely to be accessible, but you may be able to find, again, proxies for this – accounts of the impact of their use of what they learned.

## Embrace the fact that goals may change

I have (tacitly) treated goals or outcomes as fixed. However, they change; because we learn (change) and because the world changes. 'Keep things under review' is a tired phrase but we need to do it. Reflective evidence- and imagination-informed changes are symptoms of life, of continued attention in a project or to a course. Note what is changing in the world of the project or the course, negotiate the necessary changes to project or course goals and work with the changed versions.

## Negotiating and negotiated evaluation

The first outcome of a negotiation about evaluation should be an evaluation plan or contract. This would identify the agreed purpose or purposes of the evaluation, perhaps using the four-part typology of purposes – to account, to understand, to improve and to increase evaluation capability – offered earlier. The evaluation plan would also describe evaluation methods, reporting and the resources to be applied to the evaluation. It would include:

- an agreement about who will provide and verify which data and when. The evaluator needs to agree how data about the deliverables delivered will be collected and audited and to what standard of proof. This would support the 'accounting' function
- agreement on quality measures or descriptions for activities and outputs, again supporting 'accounting'
- an agreed process for SMARTening project goals. This refers to the goals being Specific, Measurable, Appropriate or Attainable, Realistic or Relevant and Testable or Time-bound. Other variants of SMART are also used. This process is concerned with 'improving' and also with making proper 'accounting' possible.

So, the evaluation plan can be negotiated and agreed. What about the evaluation itself? Can the evaluation itself be a negotiation?

Negotiation implies conversation, exchanges of information and of interpretations and the collaborative development and testing of evolving models and conceptions. Is this realistic? Surely the evaluator reports and is then finished?

The evaluation is much more likely to be accepted and embraced when the evaluation has been discussed, negotiated and agreed as far as possible. The negotiated evaluation is much less likely to contain errors of fact or interpretation. It is therefore much less likely to be pounced on by the evaluand and used to assault the credibility of the evaluation and the evaluator, should the evaluand so wish, for example, because the evaluation elsewhere contains well-founded criticisms. This can happen.

Conversation and negotiation are fundamental to evaluation for improvement. Beyond that, negotiation and debate are fundamental to the whole academic enterprise and process, of which evaluating to understand and to improve is a part.

Should everything in the evaluation be agreed between evaluator and evaluand? As far as possible, but, ultimately, probably not everything. A good evaluation process provides opportunities for the owners of the evaluand to comment on the evaluation process and on drafts of the reports and judgements that the evaluator makes. Finally, the evaluator must evaluate and report.

It is vital that the responsibility for, the authorship of, the final evaluation report is clear.

## Using what is already available

VLEs collect large amounts of data about what use students are making of the VLE. At a minimum, the VLE will probably log how much time students spend on particular pages and perhaps which online activities they undertake.

Unless they are undertaking an activity based in the VLE, we do not know exactly what students are doing as they look at a page. They could be reading, writing or indeed eating or sleeping. However, we know which page is open and we could build on what we know by asking students, as part of a monitoring and evaluation process, what they were actually doing while they were on that page. An example of this approach, using a learning diary or interviews, is described in the example on 'Student learning hours and learning strategies' in Chapter 18.

If the evaluation is concerned with assessment, then, with appropriate safeguards, anonymised data on student performance and assessment can be used (see, for example, Baume and Yorke, 2002).

QA and student surveys also generate information that may aid evaluation. Such data should be approached and used with the same rigour and scholarship that we bring to the evaluation data that evaluators produce. Some relationships between monitoring, evaluation and QA were explored earlier in this chapter.

We have largely presented evaluation as a systematic, rational process: questions first, data and answers later. This short account of using VLE and other data also suggests a different approach; starting from the other end, from found data. It suggests that we can also monitor and evaluate by looking for information that is already out there and see what suggestions, ideas and possibilities, even questions, these found data may suggest.

One reservation about a formal, outcomes-based, question-based evaluation is that we only get answers to the questions that we ask.

Starting from somewhere else – in this case, from found data – can suggest fresh, sometimes productive, questions, lines of enquiry and evaluation.

We have another reservation about tidiness. Beyond these frameworks and structures there will always be additional needs for particular evaluation data. For example, in 2021 the Centre for Online and Distance Education ran a large course for tutors in a national distance learning university. We were aware, from an interim evaluation and weekly monitoring meetings, that the tutors would have liked more of certain items. Looking to a future rerun of the course, we knew that it would not be possible to provide everything that they asked for. So, we asked them to prioritise the main items they had requested. Evaluation is feeding into needs analysis here. A local adaptation is made to the evaluation process to reflect particular circumstances and the needs of the owners of the evaluand.

## Continuing to learn and using what is learned

Monitoring and evaluation are undertaken with the primary intentions of discovering whether something – here, a distance learning development project or a distance learning course or programme – is working or has worked and also how. It is also important to ensure that specified procedures have been followed, standards met, values and ethics respected and so on.

The first job is always to work out what it would mean for a project or course to be working or to have worked. The meaning of 'success', 'quality' or 'effectiveness', whatever the current and local language is, needs to be resolved long before monitoring and evaluation start. This needs to be resolved at the very earliest stages of project or course planning. Sometimes help is available, for example, in the form of institutional performance indicators. It is very easy just to plunge in and start measuring things. A clear, evaluable account of purpose is essential.

We evaluate in order to be accountable; to show that resources have been properly expended, in pursuit of the university's financial goals as well as its educational mission. But we also evaluate with the intent, first to understand our own practice and then to use our new understanding to drive further improvements to our practice and to the learning of our students. These relations are explored further in Chapter 18 of this book. The responsibilities and mission of a university as an organisation and the goals and values of its staff meet together: in the act of evaluation, in the planning that must precede evaluation and in the use made of the results of the evaluation.

Some of the ideas and practices described in this chapter can be seen in action in Chapter 7.

Monitoring and evaluation usefully replace opinion with information. A note of caution: this replacement of opinions with information is not always welcomed.

A measure of the quality of an evaluation is the use that the institution or other owner of what was evaluated makes of the evaluation process and report.

A measure of the quality of an institution is how enthusiastically it seeks out, welcomes and makes use of sound evaluations of its work.

## Note

1   Some of this chapter is adapted from Baume (2003, 2008).

## References

Al-Alwani, A. (2014) 'Evaluation criterion for quality assessment of e-learning content'. *E-Learning and Digital Media*, 11 (6), 532–42.

Bamber, R. (ed.) (2020) *Our Days Are Numbered: Metrics, managerialism, and academic development* (1st edn). London: Staff and Educational Development Association.

Bamber, V. (2008) 'Evaluating lecturer development programmes: Received wisdom or self-knowledge?' *International Journal for Academic Development*, 13 (2), 107–16.

Bamber, V. and Anderson, S. (2012) 'Evaluating learning and teaching: Institutional needs and individual practices'. *International Journal for Academic Development*, 17 (1), 5–18.

Baume, D. (2003) 'Monitoring and evaluating staff and educational development'. In P. Kahn and D. Baume (eds), *A Guide to Staff and Educational Development* (1st edn). Abingdon: Routledge, 76–95.

Baume, D. (2008) 'A toolkit for evaluating educational development ventures'. *Educational Developments*, 9 (4), 1–7. Accessed 30 July 2022. https://www.seda.ac.uk/resources/files/publications_109_Educational%20Dev%209.4.pdf.

Baume, D. (2009) 'Writing and using good learning outcomes'. Leeds Metropolitan University. Accessed 30 July 2022. http://eprints.leedsbeckett.ac.uk/2837/.

Baume, D. (2010) 'How can we do more with less? "Ideal university"'. *Educational Developments*, 11 (4), 8–10. Accessed 30 July 2022. https://www.seda.ac.uk/wp-content/uploads/2020/09/Educational-Developments-11.4.pdf.

Baume, D. and Scanlon, E. (2018) 'What the research says about how and why learning happens'. In R. Luckin (ed.), *Enhancing Learning and Teaching with Technology: What the research says* (1st edn). London: UCL IOE Press, 2–13.

Baume, D. and Yorke, M. (2002) 'The reliability of assessment by portfolio on a course to develop and accredit teachers in higher education'. *Studies in Higher Education*, 27 (1), 7–25.

Brew, A. (2011) 'Foreword'. In L. Stefani (ed.), *Evaluating the Effectiveness of Academic Development Practice* (1st edn). London: Taylor & Francis, ix.

Chelimsky, E. (1997) 'Thoughts for a new evaluation society'. *Evaluation*, 3 (1), 97–109.

Cousin, G. (2001) 'Less is more: Evaluating educational development projects'. Paper presented at Staff and Educational Development Association Conference, 20–21 November.

Ho, A. (1998) 'A conceptual change staff development programme: Effects as perceived by the participants'. *International Journal for Academic Development*, 3 (1), 24–38.

Kirkpatrick, J. and Kirkpatrick, W. (2016) *Kirkpatrick's Four Levels of Training Evaluation*. Alexandria, VA: ATD Press.

Ludema, J. D., Cooperrider, D. L. and Barrett, F. J. (2000) 'Appreciative enquiry: The power of the unconditional positive question'. In P. Reason and H. Bradbury (eds), *Handbook of Action Research: Participative inquiry and practice*. London: SAGE. Accessed 6 October 2022. https://calhoun.nps.edu/bitstream/handle/10945/40458/Barrett_Appreciative_Inquiry_2001.pdf?sequence=1&isAllowed=y.

Miller, C. M. L. and Parlett, M. (1974) *Up to the Mark*. London: SRHE.

Parlett, M. and Hamilton, D. (1972) *Evaluation as Illumination*. Edinburgh: Centre for Research in the Educational Sciences, University of Edinburgh.

Rust, C. (1998) 'The impact of educational development workshops on teachers' practice'. *International Journal for Academic Development*, 3 (1), 72–80.

Stake, R. (2002) 'Evaluating education'. Coventry University workshop handout, 9 April.

Stefani, L. (2009) *Evaluating the Effectiveness of Academic Development Practice* (1st edn). London: Taylor and Francis.

# 20
# Designing the future
Stephen Brown

> The future is already here – it's just not evenly distributed.
> W. Gibson

The preceding chapters of this book have examined a wide range of aspects of online and distance education and associated issues, questions, methods and models. In this final chapter we return to the idea that these are no longer the exclusive domain of a few niche distance education institutions. Even before the COVID-19 pandemic there were clear signs that distance education approaches were becoming absorbed into the mainstream of higher education (HE) practice. However, in most cases they were used to supplement the on-campus learning experience, not replace it. The Great Leap Online of 2020–1 showed how core teacher–learner and learner–learner transactions normally reserved for on-campus, in-person learning can be managed remotely, online, albeit with variable quality and hence success. The big questions therefore are what path should HE take in the wake of the pandemic and how should we prepare for the next big disruptor that will surely come along? Should we return to 'business as normal' or can what we know about distance education help us to do better?

This final chapter does not attempt to predict a specific future for online and distance education because that will take many forms. Instead, it reviews the trajectory of distance education, from its mid-nineteenth-century origins to the present day, identifying significant trends. Building on these trends and on recent events, it proposes some conjectural scenarios to explore how different kinds of institutions may evolve and what they might mean for the people who engage with them as learners, teachers, support staff and managers. These scenarios are not forecasts, but tools to help you consider for yourself what you know, or strongly expect, will change in your discipline and in your institution's educational provision over the next few years and how you will adapt your educational practice to meet these changes. The chapter concludes by considering what we have learned from the COVID-19 pandemic-forced pivot to online and distance education and how we can use it to inform our choices about the future in such uncertain times.

## What kind of future do we want?

The main context for considering the future of online and distance education has to be, quite simply, the future of the world. This is not just about what is possible, but what kind of future, or futures, we want and what role online and distance education might play in bringing them about.

The United Nations Sustainable Development Goal (SDG) 4, 'Quality Education', acknowledges that education enables upward socioeconomic mobility and is a key to escaping poverty.[1] Extrapolating past trends into the future, a burgeoning global population, combined with calls for greater equality and access by non-traditional learners, seem likely to create ever-increasing demand for HE. Reflecting these challenges, global participation in HE has steadily increased in recent decades (UNESCO, 2018). However, by 2025, the world's population will have doubled in the space of 75 years (Barber and Rizvi, 2013: 6). How far might education needs be met using traditional face-to-face teaching methods under these circumstances? Can we really build enough campuses, recruit and train enough lecturers, create enough new courses, install enough equipment and do it all fast enough to keep up with demand? What will it mean for the role of university lecturers if their numbers increase massively? Could the expectation of a universal mix of research and teaching be sustained? After all, there is only so much research funding to go round and even prestigious research-led institutions rely to some extent on student fee income. The implication seems to be a rise in the number of teaching-only roles and, possibly, institutions.

However, as university tuition fees spiral upwards, how likely is it that learners will continue to be willing to incur what in many cases will be a lifetime debt to pay their way through college? (Belshaw, 2021). Also, is a degree what students still want? In many parts of the world, both 'developed' and 'developing', a university degree is no longer a reliable passport to a well-paid, secure career. How will HE institutions (HEIs) respond if learners increasingly seek out educational opportunities and qualifications elsewhere? Could it mean there is a need for fewer teachers and even fewer universities? Or different types?

These questions have all been prompted by changes in the HE landscape in recent years, commented on in myriad newspaper articles, journal papers and blogs. Much of this change will continue to accelerate, in the short and medium term at least. Driving, managing and coping well with these exponential changes will all make growing demands on our capabilities. Even a full tank of learning will not power our current graduates for their 50 or so years of work – if it ever did. We all need continuing education, or, more precisely, continuing learning, closely tailored to our individual circumstances and needs, including at times and places of our own choosing (insofar as location matters any more). Distance education, which we may redefine as education not requiring physical travel, will be essential, irrespective of its particular format or where it comes from.

## Trajectories

Although the history of distance education in HE dates back to the mid-nineteenth century it has not been a significant part of mainstream HE provision around the world (with the exception of a dozen or so dedicated distance teaching universities).[2] While some universities could point to a small number of distance courses offered alongside their on-campus provision, most institutions have tended to rely heavily on traditional face-to-face methods for most of their undergraduate and postgraduate teaching. In 2015–16 in the USA, for example, although 29.7 per cent of all HE students took at least one distance course, just under half of these students (14.3 per cent of total enrolments) took exclusively distance courses while the other half (15.4 per cent) took a combination of distance and non-distance courses. Almost half of the distance education students were concentrated in just 5 per cent of the institutions, while the top 47 institutions, which represent only 1 per cent of the total, enrolled nearly a quarter or 23 per cent (1,385,307) of all distance students (Allen and Seaman, 2017). Similarly, in the UK, prior to March 2020, the majority of HE course provision was non-distance (Maguire et al., 2020).

Nevertheless, distance learning enrolments have been creeping up at traditional universities. The 2015–16 figures from the same source indicate a 3.9 per cent increase on the previous year in students taking distance courses.

Growth in availability and take-up of distance education was facilitated by the invention of the internet in the late twentieth century, the subsequent deployment of internet-enabled learning management systems (LMSs) or virtual learning environments (VLEs) by institutions and the increased availability and affordability of internet-enabled devices such as mobile telephones and tablet computers. Such developments stimulated an increase in the use of digital technology to distribute course content to learners and, increasingly, to provide learners with ways to interact with that content; for example, through online discussion forums, multiple-choice self-assessment questions, collaborative exercises, simulations, video-recorded lectures, case studies and so on.

These developments were encouraged by governments that saw in online and distance education a means to increase capacity to meet widening participation goals without the accompanying costs and timescales of building more campuses and training more academics. Between 2000 and 2014, the number of students in HEIs more than doubled from 100 million to 207 million worldwide. In the same period, the global HE gross enrolment ratio increased from 19 per cent to 34 per cent (of the five-year age group immediately following secondary school graduation, typically ages 19 to 23) (Allen and Seaman, 2017).

In the UK, there has been a succession of government and non-governmental organisation funding initiatives to explore and embed the use of technology-enhanced learning in HE (for example, TLTP, TQEF, CETLs, Jisc Curriculum Design and Delivery programmes[3]) culminating most recently in the Department for Education (2019) strategy of 'Realising the Potential of Technology in Education'. Similar initiatives have been pursued by the EU through its Framework and Horizon 2020 programmes and elsewhere,[4] prompting some observers to suggest that 'e-education is getting traction in almost all parts of the world and is here to stay worldwide' (Palvia et al., 2018: 8).

The net result of this has been that, while attendance on campus was mandatory for most students until the COVID-19 pandemic, growth in adoption of online technology to enhance on-campus learning (so-called blended learning) has blurred the distinction between 'traditional' and 'distance' learning. On-campus students have increasingly been able to watch recorded lectures from their study bedrooms, read course materials online, test themselves with online self-assessment questions, talk to their tutors and peers online and download and submit assessments and receive feedback via the LMS (Maguire et al., 2020).

Another factor leading to blurring of the boundaries between traditional campus-based and distance courses has been the explosive growth in open educational resources (OER) and massive open online courses (MOOCs) driven by the private sector. In 2008, Stephen Downes and George Siemens created the first MOOC to exploit the interactive potential of internet tools to provide a collaborative, learner-driven learning environment.[5] Open educational practice and collaborative learning were central features. Although only 25 students attended the course on the campus of the University of Manitoba, a further 2,300 from around the world participated online. The potential for large-scale global audiences was spotted by a number of entrepreneurs and, as noted in Chapter 16, there has been rapid growth in more conventional teacher-led and content-based MOOCs. By 2021, there were estimated to be 19,400 MOOCs offered worldwide to 220 million students by over 950 universities (Shah, 2021).[6]

Although developed by commercial enterprises, many of the major MOOC providers have roots in academic institutions, including Harvard, Stanford and MIT and, as the popularity of MOOCs grew, many more universities entered into commercial partnerships with MOOC providers to co-develop and co-endorse courses.

As commercial MOOC providers and universities alike searched for ways to realise a return on their investments, the characteristics of MOOCs changed from the initial stand-alone, non-credit-bearing, non-assessed free model that challenged traditional institutions, to something more like a traditional university course, with fees charged for optional assessments, course completion certificates and transferable credits. Major MOOC providers have offered accreditation through micro-credentials, nanodegrees (Udacity), specialisation programmes (Coursera) or even academic credit transfers to shorten the time and cost of a university degree (FutureLearn). Some institutions have also incorporated MOOCs into their degree programmes or co-developed whole degree-level courses with MOOC providers and some MOOC providers have set up their own online degree courses (Johnson, 2018). By early 2022 Coursera offered a total of 38 bachelor's, master's and postgraduate degrees; according to its CEO Jeff Maggioncalda: 'Students want the flexibility to learn online, and universities are responding by scaling online degree programs using partners like Coursera to meet demand' (Schwartz, 2022).

So, ironically, a model originally expected to disrupt traditional institutions and methods has helped to accelerate the breakdown of distinctions and barriers between mainstream and distance education and has been absorbed by the institutions it was intended to replace.

By the start of 2020, these trends seemed set to continue into the foreseeable future with differences between traditional on-campus and distance education becoming so blurred that some commentators were suggesting that in most institutional contexts it was no longer useful to talk about 'distance education' as such because it was all just 'education' (Hurst, 2001).[7] Internet-enabled, technology-enhanced learning seemed likely to continue to supplement the on-campus student experience, with the notable exception of examinations, which most institutions, regulators, professional bodies and employers agreed could not really be conducted online for reasons of security and academic integrity. Except for the small number of specifically designated distance education institutions, distance education was destined to become just one of many currents running through the mainstream of HE. Then COVID-19 happened.

## Mainstreaming distance education

The impact of the COVID-19 pandemic on the provision and take-up of distance education is hard to overestimate. During the pandemic, global registrations on MOOCs increased significantly (ET Staff, 2021). In early 2020, the pandemic prompted most teaching institutions around the world to move the majority, if not all, of their teaching and assessment activities online very quickly.

The University of London (UoL) is a good example of the scale of this challenge, even for an institution with a considerable history of distance education. UoL has around 50,000 students studying at a distance across 180 countries in 23 different time zones. Paper-based examinations are normally conducted at over 600 verified examination centres worldwide. In January 2020, there were approximately 110,000 exams scheduled and paid for,[8] just as the global network of examination centres was being closed because of lockdown measures. As described in Chapter 12, UoL had only three months in which to design and implement alternative (essentially online) arrangements. The scale of the UoL pivot to online was larger than most, but other institutions faced similar challenges. A 2020 Jisc survey of UK HE students revealed that 81 per cent found themselves unexpectedly studying wholly online (Jisc, 2021).

Not surprisingly, compromises were made by many in the rush to move online. In a survey of US and Canadian institutions, nearly half of respondents said they lowered their expectations for the amount of work students would be able to do (48 per cent), made it easier for students to achieve a pass on their courses (47 per cent) and dropped some of the assignments or exams (46 per cent) (Lederman, 2020). Again, not surprisingly, reactions to the wholesale transfer into distance learning were mixed. Many of the US and Canadian survey respondents expressed anxiety about the rush to remote learning. In the UK, *The Guardian* newspaper reported on the unpreparedness of many UK universities for this sudden and massive shift (Batty and Hall, 2020). Durham University in particular was a focus for opposition from staff and students to plans to move all their courses online (Hall and Batty, 2020). However, Durham was not alone. A 2020 Pearson/Wonkhe survey of HE undergraduate and postgraduate students in England and Wales during lockdown revealed that only around two-thirds of respondents found their online teaching intellectually stimulating, slightly more than half felt that they had had sufficient teaching and learning to adequately prepare for course assessments and only one third said they had regular indicators about how they were performing on the course (Pearson and Wonkhe, 2021).

We could ask: 'What is going on here? How acceptable is it for one third of students to not find their courses intellectually stimulating? Would we normally be comfortable with half our students feeling that they had not been adequately prepared for course assessments, or two thirds not knowing how well they are performing on the course?' (Brown, 2021).

However, in the UK at least, '68% of students rated the quality of online digital learning on their course as "best imaginable", "excellent" or "good" and 62% of them also rated the support they received for online learning equally highly' according to the Jisc 2020 survey of student digital experiences (Jisc, 2021). So, while the pandemic continues to play out, the picture is definitely neither consistent nor clear cut. As noted in Chapter 2, it is clear that student experience is highly diverse and mediated by the extent to which institutions had existing systems for distance learning and by the skills and experience of individual lecturers.

If you are fortunate enough to be reading this book after the pandemic has passed, you may be thinking that these issues were all just a flash in the pan and not something we have to worry about any longer. But COVID-19 was only the latest in a series of recent, highly disruptive virus-based pandemics. SARS and MERS were the most recent precursors and there will be others to follow.[9] If not a virus, then other equally threatening scenarios such as global financial crises, social inequality, political instability and disruptive climate events will require robust responses. For example, in 2005, Southern University, New Orleans, rapidly converted to e-learning after Hurricanes Rita and Katerina caused havoc on campus. In 2011, after an earthquake destroyed the University of Canterbury at Christchurch, New Zealand, online learning was deployed by the university to restart its operations. In 2016, when the University of Camerino, Italy, was similarly destroyed by an earthquake, it too switched to online learning in just one month (Dhawan, 2020). At the time of writing, following the invasion of Ukraine by Russia in 2022, the possibility of employing online distance education to help support HE in Ukraine is being discussed by an international group of universities.

So even if the threat is not specifically COVID-19, education systems and institutions need to develop strong resilience to meet the future risk of major potential disruptors of some kind because if we return to mostly face-to-face teaching every time the latest disrupter has passed, when the next one comes along we shall have to go through the same massive exercise to get everything back online. It makes more sense to build on what has been achieved each time round, learn from the experience and create a new 'normal' that allows us to adapt more flexibly to changing circumstances (Kim, 2020).

The new normal has to work in a more challenging economic context of pandemic-induced massive national deficits, corporate debt and unemployment (Wallace-Stephens and Morgante, 2020). Public and possibly even private funding for HE is likely to be in short supply for the foreseeable future. On top of that, the lucrative market for international students is likely to contract significantly, partly because of funding issues and partly because of reluctance on the part of potential students to travel. (In 2020, the UK was edging towards having the highest rate of COVID-19-related deaths in the world, which did not make it an attractive destination.)

As we have seen, 'normal' was changing anyway. By 2020, many university courses were already a blend of online and face to face and decision makers in many universities were already exploring ways to generate a better return on investment from campus-based digital technologies by expanding beyond the physical limitations of university campuses, in order to increase revenue from student fees (especially from high-fee-paying international students) (Morris, 2020). COVID-19 accelerated the process of blurring the distinction between traditional face-to-face and online distance education but did not fundamentally change the direction of travel.

## Where to from here?

We began by warning that this chapter does not attempt to predict a specific future for distance education. Distance education is part of a larger web of intersecting and overlapping technical, economic, political, social, cultural and environmental systems and the interactions between them are too complex for reliable predictions about how the outcomes of those interactions will affect distance education as a whole. However, that does not mean that we cannot think about possible futures and plan for them on a more manageable scale.

> Those universities that fail to adapt and reimagine themselves as digital organisations may see their appeal diminish and their business come under pressure as students opt for models that suit their lifestyle and preferred way of learning. The signs are that universities are modernising and working hard to make the transition. Those that are bold and rethink their pedagogy, rather than replicate their traditional teaching patterns in the virtual world, can travel faster and, perhaps, further. (Maguire et al., 2020)

Neither should we underestimate the scale of change required. If distance education is to become more embedded and central to institutional missions, then this implies large-scale, institution-wide changes to infrastructure, ways of working, products and services.

> Universities and colleges will not be able to make the necessary shift from the present to the future without taking a whole-institution, strategic approach. If, as seems likely, the future will involve both face-to-face and digital teaching and learning as well as approaches which blend the two, then the effects on the institution will be profound. University teachers will need training that is practical, continuous and inspirational, and teaching and learning materials will need to be constantly reviewed and updated. Capital programmes will need to ensure digital infrastructure is sufficiently prioritised. Libraries, which in many cases have already been wonderfully transformed, will need further transformation, as will all the many and varied learning spaces universities have invested in. All this means vice-chancellors, leadership teams and governing councils need to be at the forefront of thinking through what the digital revolution means and then act accordingly. (Barber, 2020)

Strategies are unlikely to be the same everywhere or even stay the same in any given place as institutions flex to meet changing circumstances. We can think of the potential solution space as a continuum from completely distance education to completely traditional face-to-face education. Some

UK institutions such as the Open University (OU) and UoL are clearly at one extreme. However, very few are likely to revert to completely face-to-face education because distance education ideas and methods have already infiltrated most campuses. The new normal is likely to be a blend of online and face to face, with the added complication of having to manage both modes simultaneously, at least some of the time: so-called hybrid learning, where part of a class may be studying online while the remainder are physically present in class. The tutor(s) of course may be present either way.

Some conjectural scenarios can help us to explore what this might mean in practical terms. As you read the following descriptions of imaginary institutions, you may find it useful to consider: how similar they are to your own, how much of what is depicted here is desirable and why that is the case and what would need to be added, changed or taken away at your own institution to achieve a similar outcome.

## University College Blended

Our first imaginary institution is University College Blended (UCB). Blended learning comprises a blend of face-to-face, on-campus learning activities and complementary online activities (Jisc, 2020). Faculties at UCB mostly operate a spectrum of blended models ranging from 'business as usual' through to the 'flipped classroom'. Under 'business as usual', face to face takes primacy and the online elements are supplementary, so lectures are still delivered live in lecture theatres, but they are also recorded and students can watch the recordings and access lecture notes online. Assessments are still sometimes handed in on paper or performed live, but formative feedback is provided online and progress records can be accessed via the VLE to check marks.

At the other end of the blended spectrum, the 'flipped classroom' model (Abeysekera and Dawson, 2015) switches the traditional mix of in-class and out-of-class activities around so that content delivery such as lectures takes place online while face-to-face time in class is reserved for more discursive, exploratory and creative activities that entail actively engaging with peers to debate, experiment and synthesise. Assessments are mostly submitted digitally via the VLE, but examinations are still conducted in person in on-campus examinations using handwritten paper scripts. Students can access books and journals via the library on campus plus some online journals and supplementary course readings uploaded to the VLE. All the students registered at UCB are expected to attend campus at least some of the time; it is not possible to obtain a UCB degree without doing so.

## Hybrid University

Our second conjectural scenario, Hybrid University (HU) enrols both on-campus and online students so, unlike UCB, some HU students do graduate without ever attending physically. As with UCB, different faculties implement this model in different ways. Some, like UoL, run separate courses for on-campus and online students, but most run the two modes simultaneously within the same course. Therefore, tutors manage learning activities for which some of the students are physically present together in the same room, while others are connected remotely, at a distance. Sometimes the tutors also connect with the class from off campus over the internet. HU assessments and examinations are conducted online only. Remote students are examined online, while on-campus students attend their online exam sessions on campus but have the option to take them remotely. The on-campus library is well stocked with books and journals and basic library materials that are likely to be required for courses are also available online through the VLE.

## University of HiFlex

The University of HiFlex (UoH) employs a mix of blended and hybrid models that varies in response to changing circumstances. Thus, while it has a significant amount of on-campus learning activities like UCB, particularly in practical subjects such as medicine and art and design, it also offers online learning to students at a distance, like HU. It can also switch its on-campus students into online learning when required. For example, if the campus has to be closed during exam time, medical students can still take their practical examinations online, demonstrating their suturing skills by performing on a banana in front of a video camera and their diagnostic skills by observing and commenting on the characteristics presented by a remote patient, again via a video link. Similarly, art and design undergraduates can demonstrate their life drawing skills from home by drawing a live model who is on an internet camera in a studio on campus and uploading their finished drawings to the VLE as scans or photographs. UoH also has a particular interest in offering degree programmes in parts of Africa where electricity and internet connections can be unreliable. It has developed print and mobile phone-based versions of its courses that can be deployed when circumstances require. The mobile phones can be charged from solar panels and can be used to upload and download material when a signal is available, minimising the cost of being online and the risk of signal dropout. As with HU, UoH exams can be taken on campus or online and, additionally, at approved examination centres in remote locations where online exams would be difficult to manage securely because of connectivity issues. As with HU, the UoH on-campus library is well stocked with books and journals and all library materials likely to be required for courses are also available online through the VLE.

### MOOC Institute for Training Ltd

Our final fictitious scenario is the MOOC Institute for Training (MIT Ltd), a limited company that offers courses in popular vocational fields such as computer sciences and business studies. It also offers loans at commercial rates to prospective students to cover fees.

MIT Ltd programmes operate on the 'bush taxi' principle, which is that the programme starts when enough students have enrolled. Therefore, there are no fixed start and end dates and the most popular programmes start several times a year. All MIT Ltd assessments and examinations are conducted online. MIT Ltd courses are supported by an online library that offers different tiers of access for different fee levels. There is a clear progression ladder from micro-credentials for small chunks of learning through to individual course credits that can be built up to certificates and diplomas, and even undergraduate degrees (Debiais-Sainton, 2020). Certificate, diploma and degree programmes are built around freely available MOOCs from other providers. Academic credits are freely transferable between MIT Ltd and other like-minded learning providers through personal, portable learning portfolios and credit records maintained independently by the learners themselves via third-party providers (Ark, 2020). MIT Ltd offers a range of add-on features to suit the needs and/or pockets of its students. These include tuition, learning support, learning resources, formative assessment, examinations and award certificates and transcripts. A key difference between MIT Ltd and the other institutions described here is that MIT Ltd does not have matriculation requirements governing access to its courses. Access is controlled solely by ability to pay course fees.

MIT Ltd is a purely online enterprise with only administrative headquarters. Faculty staff are employed on individual, annually renewed part-time teaching contracts and they provide their services at a distance. Some are highly experienced and high-ranking scholars recruited to provide star-quality lectures, rather like TED Talk speakers, but most are early-career lecturers seeking to boost their CVs and their income. On the one hand, MIT Ltd does not have to bear the cost of developing core course materials, maintaining physical teaching facilities and support services and employing full-time faculty staff, so course fees are lower than those for more traditional university courses. On the other hand, MIT Ltd has to generate a profit for its shareholders and this is a challenging marketplace.[10] Therefore, fees are not as low as might otherwise be expected and, while fees for core components are low, the various add-on features required by many students for a degree do add up to a significant amount each year.

It may be that you recognise in these four imaginary institutions some aspects of your own context, or you may be contemplating introducing some of these elements yourself or anticipating their introduction by others and wonder how they might pan out. So having described a range of different possible institutional futures, let us now consider the implications of these different approaches for students, teaching staff and support services.

## Students

Students at UCB enjoy the traditional benefits of the on-campus university experience: access to tutors, to laboratories and workshops, field trips, plenty of opportunities for social interaction, sports and other leisure activities both on and off campus. They also face the usual challenges of trying to fit all this around working to pay their way through college. Most college and undergraduate students work part time to pay fees and living expenses, even in a wealthy country like the USA (St. Amour, 2019). Spending enough time in the labs and workshops, which are heavily subscribed, and getting to see their personal tutor face to face can also be a challenge because tutor groups are so large and faculty academics are so busy with research, publications, income generation, routine course administration, periodic reviews, strategy development and departmental reorganisations.

Students in faculties that have adopted the 'flipped classroom' approach have more freedom to organise their studies around their extracurricular commitments because attendance on campus is required less often. When the COVID-19 pandemic caused the campus to be locked down, UCB students found most of their face-to-face learning activities replaced by a blend of online lecture notes and one-way video lectures. Additionally, the UCB faculty organised some two-way webinars and online discussion forums. All examinations were hurriedly moved online. Students were generally not very satisfied with the quality of these activities. The lecture notes and video lectures were not very interesting and did not help them to understand their subjects as much as they wished. The more interactive sessions did not work very well because not many people participated and the conversations were too unstructured and focused on social chat. Students from flipped classroom faculties reported greater satisfaction with their online learning experiences, except where they no longer had access to practical facilities. Both groups complained about curtailment of social and extracurricular activities and lack of access to the university library and even access to the university VLE was not as reliable as it needed to be because the servers were overloaded at times. Examinations were a particular challenge as UCB students had no experience of being examined online.

The demographics of HU students vary in relation to their chosen mode of study. On-campus HU students tend to conform to the traditional 18–21-year-old undergraduate profile, for example, whereas the remote students tend to be older, in employment or at least in the job market and many have family or caring commitments. Irrespective of their study modes, HU students generally have more advanced online communication and collaboration skills than their UCB peers because they have more experience of working in simultaneous on-campus/online groups and of working with remote tutors. Consequently, when COVID-19 hit the campus they were better able to adapt to working exclusively online. Remote HU students reported improvements in their learning experiences as tutors seemed to be spending a lot more time online and so were more available and responsive than before. Both groups found access to library resources more challenging as the online library was quickly overwhelmed by demand. Limited site licences for access to items were quickly used up and the range of material available was much narrower than on-campus students were used to. Online examinations did not cause concern for most HU students because they were already a familiar feature of HU life.

Like HU, UoH tends to attract different types of students to its face-to-face and distance education programmes. Again, distance education students tend to be older, in employment or at least in the job market and many have family and caring commitments. They have less time for social interaction and tend to be much more focused on study and exam performance. On-campus students reported that the COVID-19-induced pivot to fully online learning presented few problems apart from grumbles about loss of social and sporting facilities. These students are used to a richly varied diet of online and offline learning activities and support. Remote UoH learners were affected differently. In many cases, they found themselves with more time for studying than usual because they were furloughed from their employment at the height of the first wave of

COVID-19. However, this benefit was countered by the possible threat of unemployment at the end of the furlough period.

From a study point of view, the least affected of all were the MIT Ltd students. On the one hand, most MIT Ltd students choose this mode of study because their work and family commitments do not allow them the freedom to attend a university in person. They also tend to have more financial commitments than traditional undergraduates, so are drawn to an institution that offers flexibility and lower fees (Belkin, 2020). On the other hand, they tend to be older, more mature learners, with more sophisticated self-organisation and learning skills than traditional face-to-face learners, so they are better at adapting to change and disruption. Fortunately, their personal learning portfolio allows them to interrupt their studies and to transfer their credits to other learning providers if, for example, they cannot afford to study for a while or need to relocate for a new job.

## Teaching staff

Teaching staff in the more traditional faculties of UCB are wary of using technology to enhance their teaching because their understanding of the technology is limited, they do not entirely trust it to perform reliably and they are not convinced that they can achieve as good results with it. They also enjoy the flexibility and performative aspects of face-to-face teaching. Flipped classroom teaching staff have a more relaxed attitude towards technology, confident that any problems can be ironed out during the regular on-campus sessions. They too enjoy the flexibility and performative aspects of their face-to-face teaching sessions. They tend to be more disciplined in their time management when working online to stop student contact hours spiralling out of control. When COVID-19 hit, the flipped classroom staff were in a better position than their more traditional colleagues, but they still struggled to develop satisfactory alternatives to their face-to-face learning and teaching activities within just a few weeks. While they were used to creating online resources and online asynchronous learning activities, they had far less experience of managing synchronous group learning activities at a distance. Converting examinations to work online was not too problematic as far as setting questions goes, but marking was a major headache because staff were not used to receiving exam scripts as digital files. For teaching staff in the traditional faculties, the requirement to convert to online learning in just a few weeks was a nightmare. Resentment and resistance after the first six months is widespread despite quickly organised training sessions for academic staff on digital skills and the core principles of digital pedagogy led by colleagues with more experience of online learning. Older staff, less technically savvy than many younger colleagues, are particularly unhappy about the apparent reversal of the status hierarchy whereby their years of classroom experience no longer seem to count as much and senior academics used to spending a greater proportion of their time on research resent being drafted in to shore up the online teaching effort during what has been called by some as 'the year of teaching in universities'.

Looking further ahead, there are concerns about the quality of the next year's cohort of freshers. In the UK and many other countries, matriculation examinations had to be cancelled in 2020 because of the need to contain the pandemic by restricting opportunities for people to mix physically. Additionally, many of these students suffered from learning loss occasioned by schools being closed for months at a time (Kernohan, 2021). There is uncertainty about how to gauge the suitability of candidates for university places and unease concerning the capability of first-year courses to accommodate highly variable levels of attainment among new entrants.

At HU, the teaching role is complicated by the requirement to support both on-campus and remote students, especially when remote and local student groups are combined. This requires a good grasp of the affordances of different technologies and of appropriate pedagogical strategies. Consequently, HU teaching staff did not face such a steep upward learning curve as their UCB peers and most of the teaching and assessment was already internet ready. However, for HU academics the pivot to fully online still entailed a lot of extra work to get everything ready in time and some are showing signs of stress.

Staff at UoH are used to flexibility in teaching modes and have already developed a range of alternative learning activities and materials to accommodate different learning contexts. They also have well-developed pedagogical skills and learning technology awareness. They are supported by a well-resourced and high-calibre staff development unit, including specialist learning technologists, several of whom have worked for dedicated distance education universities. The impact of COVID-19 on this group's workload and work practices was therefore much less pronounced than for colleagues in the other universities described here.

Most MIT Ltd tutors are lecturers and academic-related staff recruited from universities on fixed-term, part-time contracts. COVID-19 did not disrupt MIT Ltd but the employment future for MIT Ltd contractors is uncertain. Student fee income may decrease as prospective and current students decide they can no longer afford to study. Alternatively, it may increase as more people decide they need to reskill in order to secure a new job in the post-COVID world. Either way it is a stressful time.

## Support services

As a largely traditional university, UCB has services designed to support mostly on-campus students, notwithstanding some special arrangements to accommodate distance education students. COVID-19 created major problems for the library, IT services, student welfare, careers, registry and examinations as they struggled to increase capacity and change their ways of working almost overnight. Establishing secure and COVID-safe examinations online for large numbers of students learning a wide variety of different subjects was exceptionally challenging. Equally challenging was responding to the sudden increase in demand on staff development services for help and guidance to convert face-to-face teaching to distance education. Capability to meet this demand was very limited because of the novelty of these challenges. Student halls, on-campus catering, the student union and others grappled with the challenges of the almost overnight loss of most of their usual users. Six months into the pandemic, support staff were reporting high levels of stress and staff sickness rates were increasing noticeably.

At HU the support services were better prepared. In particular, the staff development unit had more experience and understanding of developing and supporting technology-enhanced distance education. Staff developers included dedicated learning technologists and educationalists with good support networks through relevant professional associations. Working closely with faculty academics they were able to create a library of short instructional videos for students covering practical subjects such as laboratory and workshop techniques and skills. These demonstrated how these skills and techniques were performed up close and could be replayed as many times as needed. Although this required a significant investment of time, these videos will be available for years to come and will enhance students' understanding and learning experience (Barber, 2020). Library staff were already accustomed to providing resources and support online and registry already had experience of running exams online. If limited capability was the issue for UCB, the main challenge for HU was capacity; that is, scaling up its already capable but necessarily limited core learning support services.

Because of the flexible nature of its provision, UoH already had sufficient spare capacity to cope well with the pivot to online that followed the pandemic. Staff were used to switching between different modes and well supported with appropriate infrastructure and training. The downside of this from an institutional perspective is the high cost of maintaining and running parallel complementary systems below capacity some of the time. For when students are all learning online, laboratories and lecture theatres lie idle and when on-campus study is more popular, servers, bandwidth and so on are underutilised. Either way the return on investment is suboptimal.

Unlike the rest of the organisations described here, MIT Ltd outsources most of its support needs to suppliers, but it has flexible contracts with service-level agreements that can be scaled up and down in response to demand fluctuations, so the impact of the pandemic has been less challenging. Scalable services include server capacity, network bandwidth and 24/7 IT support, examinations, student records and the online library. MIT Ltd student personal learning portfolios and associated academic credit records are owned by individual learners and maintained via cloud-based blockchain servers so MIT Ltd does not have to carry the overhead of maintaining and ensuring the integrity of these records (McGreal, 2021). Staff development is not an issue because ready-skilled teaching staff are hired through an agency. Most MIT Ltd tutors have academic employment contracts in conventional universities that offer staff development.

## How to choose?

Although these scenarios are imaginary, they are informed by actual events at real universities in recent times, so some aspects of what they depict are already with us. As the quote at the beginning of this chapter noted, 'The future is already here – it's just not evenly distributed' (Gibson, 2003). So, while it is unlikely that any single institution matches any of the four scenarios described here precisely, it is quite possible that your own institution demonstrates some elements of them already and other elements may be feasibly within reach. Such elements could provide the foundations for future change to bring your institution more into alignment with one of these scenarios or a combination of them. So how might we decide which combination of elements to choose and why? The following principles offer some guidance.

### Student needs and capabilities

The scenarios in this chapter highlight huge variation in student needs for on-campus and off-campus services and learning experiences. There is also considerable variation in student capabilities in terms of study skills, technical skills and communication and collaboration skills (Brown et al., 2020). Such variations are likely to be exaggerated by the impact of the pandemic or other disruptors to learning opportunities for students newly entering HE, resulting in the need for HEIs to gauge and respond to wide variations in learning loss among new students (Dickinson, 2021). Failure to respond adequately to these challenges is likely to have an adverse effect on student retention and progression rates and institutional revenue and rankings. Dialogue with students and co-opting students as co-developers could be useful strategies for ensuring continued market relevance.

> When the pandemic first hit and the rapid shift to digital teaching and learning took place, inevitably it was experienced as a stop gap, a temporary provision, not as good as what it replaced but hopefully good enough to get through a crisis. For the future, that way of thinking will no longer be good enough. We need to see the opportunity, as many universities are doing, to enhance the student experience of teaching and learning and to take it to a whole new level. This means continuous dialogue with students and an openness to new ideas.
> (Barber, 2020)

Positive moves in this direction have been made in the UK. In the Jisc 2020 Student Digital Experience Survey a third (36 per cent) agreed they were given the chance to be involved in decisions about online learning during 2020 (Jisc, 2021).

## Access

Access to distance education is necessarily mediated via technologies of some kind. Technology has always been an important aspect of distance education from print and radio through to the internet, with some notable flops along the way (remember interactive video discs anyone?). The COVID-19 pandemic highlighted the ever-present issue in distance education of inequalities of access, sometimes dubbed the 'digital divide' or what the UK Office for Students more recently dubbed 'digital poverty' (Barber, 2020). Some students have greater access to computers and internet bandwidth and support because of their financial wealth.

Similarly, some institutions, regions, countries and even entire continents are advantaged or disadvantaged in this way. Electricity supplies are so erratic and internet and mobile phone network coverage is so patchy in some places that online learning is difficult. In such contexts older, apparently obsolete, technologies can still play a useful role in levelling access (Leary and Berge, 2007). Access is not just an issue in developing countries. In the 2020 Jisc survey of digital learning experience of UK HE students a large proportion of students (62 per cent) experienced problems with poor Wi-Fi connections, regardless of where they did their online learning and over a quarter (29 per cent) reported problems accessing online platforms and services (Jisc, 2020).

### Variety

Universities tend not to operate monocultures because there is usually a need for a 'requisite variety' (Ashby, 1952: 229) or diversity of responses across courses and faculties that necessitates a spectrum of positions. Professional accrediting bodies may have different requirements. Employers tend to have differing expectations about requisite knowledge and skills – even about the kinds of qualifications they are looking for and ways of achieving them. The ability to offer a spectrum of blended learning types and a ladder of qualifications seems likely to be important.

### Flexibility

If variety is a range of potential responses, then flexibility is the ability to switch between them. Circumstances change. For example, during the COVID-19 pandemic there were fluctuating local lockdown arrangements in different parts of the UK and in other countries, with the possibility of full national lockdowns being reimposed at short notice. In order to be resilient to change, institutions need to be able to adapt quickly to sudden disruptions, such as switching to online exams quickly if exam centres are inaccessible.

### Institutional capability

The positions adopted by institutions will depend on their level of expertise and/or organisational ability to enhance and deploy that expertise. As we have seen, the availability of in-house distance education design and delivery skills can make a big difference during the pivot to online learning at scale. Institutions with a track record of successful distance education had a head start over those with less experience when COVID-19 lockdowns began and they achieved more satisfactory results in students' eyes. HEIs lacking sufficient capability in some areas may choose to disaggregate services and outsource some to specialist suppliers.

## Capacity

Capacity is a measure of ability to deploy in-house capabilities at scale. Where only small pockets of expertise exist, ways need to be found to expand these. It helps to align online education strategy with on-campus blended learning delivery to ensure resource deployment is optimised. Investment in skills and buy-in from staff are essential because if staff feel unsure about new ways of working or undervalued then support for change can be half-hearted or even defensive (Brown, 2014). While partnerships with private companies and online platform providers can be used to increase capacity quickly, they require detailed thought to ensure financial commitments are scalable. For example, institutions that had already outsourced critical infrastructure such as online programme management systems found themselves at a commercial and logistical disadvantage during the pandemic when it was necessary to increase distance education capacity rapidly. Similarly, plans for commercialising online teaching materials for online education need to be considered carefully to ensure they do not divert resources away from core business (Morris, 2020).

These six principles offer some guidance on what to look out for, but getting there can be difficult, even with a clear vision of where the goal lies, because at the scale of institutional or system-wide innovation it usually involves cultural change. In Chapter 7, we saw how stakeholder attitudes towards distance learning are significant for its implementation and that culture and practice can change rapidly when participants see the point of or value in a new way of working.

Cultural change has been identified as necessary to overcome barriers to successful implementation of distance education (Chen, 2009; Maguire et al., 2020; Marshall, 2010). It is harder to effect than technical innovation because it involves winning over the hearts and minds of the stakeholders, in this case principally staff and students, although employers, funding bodies and professional standards organisations will be important too. It is relatively easy to make executive decisions about new ways of doing things and to design technical and logistical systems and processes that deliver these new things. However, if the hearts as well as the minds of those who have to implement these systems are not fully engaged, then the result is just as likely to be resistance to change and the emergence of unofficial workarounds (Brown, 2013).

Successful innovation depends on the ability of management to create a culture of trust, creativity and collaboration built upon a supportive administrative and technical infrastructure. For example, the response by staff and students at Durham University to COVID-19-induced changes and elsewhere to large-scale change in HE more generally is evidence that while top-down strategic design implementation has its advantages in terms of clarity of purpose, focused resource allocation and performance monitoring, it can run into resistance if stakeholders do not feel engaged or do not trust the motives behind the changes. Participants can feel aggrieved about lack of involvement in goal setting and may not believe that the proposed solutions meet their needs if they have not been consulted adequately.

On the other hand, bottom-up initiatives led by experimental implementers are often ignored by the rest of the institution, regardless of their merits, simply because they were 'not invented here'. Hearts and minds are best won through institution-wide collective negotiation and agreement of goals and participation in the development of strategies that offer explicit and widely understood benefits for all the stakeholders. However, comprehensive stakeholder engagement can generate unexpected ideas, which again makes it important to be able to embrace variety and flexibility (Brown, 2014).

## Conclusion

This final chapter has argued that distance education is already mainstream in some parts of HE, notwithstanding variations in individual practices. In the future, it seems likely to become even more widespread and central to institutional missions, but it is not going to be the same everywhere or even stay the same in any given place. Individual institutions will need to evolve their own optimal strategy, considering the learners, the staff, their own capabilities, capacity and access. It is worth remembering fundamental lessons from recent events (TeachOnlineCA, 2020):

- technology cannot replace all the work of a teacher
- engagement is as important as content
- design matters
- what the learner does between classes is at least as important as what they do in class
- we have to rethink assessment.

Formal education and training will continue to have a role here. Structured programmes will still be needed, with expert tutors and facilitators of learning, backed by carefully curated learning resources and accelerated by skilfully designed learning activities and processes. Perhaps in some cases, they will lead to qualifications, micro-credentials or accumulate into larger qualifications, but much learning will be informal. As noted in Chapter 16, if content is free (for example, via OER and MOOCs) and alternative micro-credential accreditation routes proliferate, then institutions may need to find a new focus on the quality of teaching, effective pedagogy and strong support systems. In this case, support for learning will blur with coaching, mentoring, consulting or collaborative work and the technologies employed may become almost invisible. Although the history of distance education can be thought of in terms of successive waves of technologies – print, radio, television, telephones, computers and the internet – it has also been about the evolution of understanding ideas about, and attitudes towards, learning and teaching. It is tempting to end with an inspirational, high-tech account of futures for distance education, embracing blockchain, cloud computing, Web 3.0, virtual and augmented reality, analytics-informed and artificial intelligence-boosted learning. Each of these elements is already coming into play. Well implemented, they will each make a vivid and vigorous contribution to the improvement of online and distance education. Doubtless, many others beyond these are even now flickering into life on innovators' screens around the world. However, technology does not stand still for long enough and innovation is too unpredictable for reliable forecasting.[11]

So, technology speculation is not where we are going to end with this book. We began by asking questions about the kind of world we wish to have in the future, not the kinds of technology. Therefore, it seems appropriate to return to the United Nations SDG 4 of 'Quality Education' for all and ask how this might be achieved. Clearly, equity of access and opportunity will be important. Current socioeconomic disparities must be addressed. The social contract between learners and learning facilitators must also be upheld. There is no moral justification for racking up student debt in exchange for qualifications of doubtful value in a rapidly changing world. Distance education, with its ability to provide continuing learning when and where we need it, closely tailored to our individual circumstances and needs, is not the answer on its own but it is part of the answer.

## Acknowledgements

The COVID-19 pandemic demonstrated very clearly how interconnected our planet is and just how much we can achieve through collaboration. In writing this chapter, I have drawn on ideas expressed by colleagues, writers, researchers and practitioners in the field of distance education and online learning over many months, including fellows of the Centre for Online and Distance Education (CODE) at the UoL,[12] and many others from the worldwide online learning and distance education community of practice too numerous to list. I am indebted to them all for their generous suggestions and criticisms, which have helped to shape and enhance the chapter; to my fellow editors for their unstinting efforts to improve the text; in particular, Dr David Baume. I also thank Julian Bream at the Bloomsbury Learning Exchange for facilitating a series of fascinating online brainstorming sessions that simultaneously explored ideas about distance education futures while demonstrating innovative ways of using online tools for collaboration. Any remaining errors or misjudgements are solely mine.

## Notes

1. See https://www.un.org/sustainabledevelopment/education/.
2. When the UoL started offering degrees and examinations by distance in 1865, the requirement of attendance at an approved institution was dispensed with in favour of accepting as candidates anyone passing the London Matriculation examination, no matter where they were registered. Until the establishment of the Council for National Academic Awards in 1964 and the OU five years later, UoL offered the only pathway, anywhere in the world, to obtaining a degree without attending a university.
3. Teaching and Learning Technology Programme: http://www.ariadne.ac.uk/issue/4/tltp/; Teaching Quality Enhancement Fund: https://dera.ioe.ac.uk//5996/; Centres for Excellence in Teaching and Learning: https://www.cemp.ac.uk/about/cetls.php; Jisc: https://www.jisc.ac.uk/rd/projects/curriculum-design.
4. https://www.bmbwf.gv.at/en/Topics/Research/Research-in-the-EU/EU-Framework-Programmes.html.
5. A brief history of MOOCs: https://www.mcgill.ca/maut/news-current-affairs/moocs/history.
6. Excluding China. Chinese MOOC platforms surged in both course numbers and enrolments due to the 2020 pandemic. In early 2022, 24 Chinese MOOC platforms offered over 69,000 MOOCs in Chinese, around twice as many as in 2020 (Ma, 2022).
7. The UoL Centre for Distance Education (CDE) changed its name in 2022 to the Centre for Online and Distance Education (CODE) to reflect these changes.
8. The majority of UoL distance education students pay a separate fee for the exam.
9. https://www.who.int/health-topics/severe-acute-respiratory-syndrome#tab=tab_1; https://www.who.int/health-topics/middle-east-respiratory-syndrome-coronavirus-mers#tab=tab_1.
10. Coursera's revenue grew to $415.3 million in 2021, a 41 per cent increase from the year before, but net losses more than doubled to $145.2 million as the company increased spending on research and development as well as sales and marketing (Schwartz, 2022). In 2022 FutureLearn was showing a loss of £16.1 million against revenue of £11.3 million (Clark, 2022).
11. In September 1933 Ernest Rutherford suggested that the idea of looking for a source of power in the transformation of atoms was 'moonshine'. Two weeks later, after reading an article summarising Rutherford's speech, physicist Leo Szilard went for a walk, during which he conceived the idea of a nuclear chain reaction that could release energy, thus opening the door to the nuclear age (Rhodes, 1986).
12. https://www.london.ac.uk/centre-online-distance-education/who-we-are/our-fellows.

# References

Abeysekera, L. and Dawson, P. (2015) 'Motivation and cognitive load in the flipped classroom: Definition, rationale and a call for research'. *Higher Education Research and Development*, 34 (1) 1–14. Accessed 31 July 2022. https://doi.org/10.1080/07294360.2014.934336.

Allen, I. E. and Seaman, J. (2017) 'Digital learning compass: Distance education enrollment report 2017'. Babson Survey Research Group. Accessed 31 July 2022. https://onlinelearningsurvey.com/reports/digtiallearningcompassenrollment2017.pdf.

Ark, T. V. (2020) 'How portable learning records will unlock education and employment opportunities'. *Getting Smart*, 9 January. Accessed 31 July 2022. https://www.gettingsmart.com/2021/01/how-portable-learning-records-will-unlock-education-and-employment-opportunities/.

Ashby, W. R. (1952) *Design for a Brain*. London: Chapman & Hall.

Barber, M. (2020) 'Digital teaching and learning: The opportunity'. Office for Students blog, 30 October. Accessed 31 July 2022. https://www.officeforstudents.org.uk/news-blog-and-events/blog/digital-teaching-and-learning-the-opportunity/.

Barber, M. and Rizvi, S. (2013) 'The incomplete guide to delivering learning outcomes'. Pearson. Accessed 31 July 2022. https://assets.pearsoncanadaschool.com/asset_mgr/current/20194/the-incomplete-guide.pdf.

Batty, D. and Hall, R. (2020) 'No campus lectures and shut student bars: UK universities' £1bn struggle to move online'. *The Guardian*, 25 April. Accessed 31 July 2022. https://www.theguardian.com/education/2020/apr/25/degrees-of-separation-can-universities-adapt-in-the-rush-to-online-learning.

Belkin, D. (2020) 'Is this the end of college as we know it?' *The Wall Street Journal*, 12 November. Accessed 31 July 2022. https://www-wsj-com.cdn.ampproject.org/c/s/www.wsj.com/amp/articles/is-this-the-end-of-college-as-we-know-it-11605196909.

Belshaw, D. (2021) 'The (monetary) value of a university education during a pandemic'. Open Thinkering blog, 15 January. Accessed 31 July 2022. https://dougbelshaw.com/blog/2021/01/15/university-value/.

Brown, S. (2013) 'Large-scale innovation and change in UK higher education'. *Research in Learning Technology*, 21 (2), 171–83. Accessed 31 July 2022. https://doi.org/10.3402/rlt.v21i0.22316.

Brown, S. (2014) 'You can't always get what you want: Change management in higher education'. *Campus-Wide Information Systems*, 31 (4), 208–16.

Brown, S. (2021) 'Are we nearly there yet? Getting the basics right for effective online learning'. Wonkhe blog, 8 February. Accessed 31 July 2022. https://wonkhe.com/blogs/are-we-nearly-there-yet-getting-the-basics-right-for-effective-online-learning/.

Brown, S., Baume, D., Francis, N. and Wong, J. (2020) 'Student learning hours and learning strategies project: Final report'. UoL CDE, 30 December. Accessed 31 July 2022. https://london.ac.uk/sites/default/files/cde/cde-slh-final-report-d8.pdf.

Chen, B. (2009) 'Barriers to adoption of technology-mediated distance education in higher-education institutions'. *Quarterly Review of Distance Education*, 10 (4), 333–8. Accessed 31 July 2022. https://eric.ed.gov/?id=EJ889336.

Clark, D. (2022) 'FutureLearn may not be a going concern'. Donald Clark Plan B blog, 29 July. Accessed 31 July 2022. http://donaldclarkplanb.blogspot.com/2022/07/futurelearn-may-not-be-going-concern.html.

Debiais-Sainton, V. (2020) 'European approach to micro-credentials'. Paper presented at MICROBOL conference, 31 August. Accessed 31 July 2022. https://microcredentials.eu/wp-content/uploads/sites/20/2020/08/V.-DebiaisSainton-Microbol.pdf.

Department for Education (2019) 'Realising the potential of technology in education'. Policy paper, 3 April. Accessed 31 July 2022. https://www.gov.uk/government/publications/realising-the-potential-of-technology-in-education.

Dhawan, S. (2020) 'Online learning: A panacea in the time of COVID-19 crisis'. *Journal of Educational Technology Systems*, 49 (1), 5–22. Accessed 31 July 2022. https://doi.org/10.1177/0047239520934018.

Dickinson, J. (2021) 'Don't we need a long hot summer of learning?' Wonkhe, 26 January. https://wonkhe.com/wonk-corner/dont-we-need-a-long-hot-summer-of-learning/.

ET Staff (2021) 'COVID-19 drives considerable growth in demand for MOOCs'. Education Technology, 20 January. Accessed 31 July 2022. https://edtechnology.co.uk/international/covid-19-drives-considerable-growth-in-demand-for-moocs/.

Gibson, W. (2003) '"The future is already here – it's just not evenly distributed": *The Economist*, 4 December. *Cities & Health*, 4 (2), 152. Accessed 31 July 2022. https://doi.org/10.1080/23748834.2020.1807704.

Hall, R. and Batty, D. (2020) 'Durham University retracts controversial plan to provide online-only degrees'. *The Guardian*, 25 April. Accessed 31 July 2022. https://www.theguardian.com/education/2020/apr/25/durham-university-retracts-controversial-plan-to-provide-online-only-degrees.

Hurst, F. (2001) 'The death of distance learning'. *Educause Quarterly*, 3, 58–60. Accessed 31 July 2022. https://er.educause.edu/-/media/files/articles/2001/9/eqm0138.pdf?la=en&hash=AEC66239713D92568FA1F1517785C88A1BD365D1.

Jisc (2020) 'Developing blended learning approaches'. Quick guide, 10 July. Accessed 31 July 2022. https://www.jisc.ac.uk/guides/creating-blended-learning-content.

Jisc (2021) 'Student Digital Experience Insights Survey 2020/21: Findings from UK higher education (pulse 1: October–December 2020)', March. Accessed 31 July 2022. https://repository.jisc.ac.uk/8318/1/DEI-P1-HE-student-briefing-2021-FINAL.pdf.

Johnson, S. (2018) 'In move towards more online degrees, Coursera introduces its first bachelor's'. *Distance Learning in Higher Ed*, 5 March. Accessed 31 July 2022. https://www.edsurge.com/news/2018-03-05-in-move-towards-more-online-degrees-coursera-introduces-its-first-bachelor-s.

Kernohan, D. (2021) 'How on earth do we run 2021 admissions now?' Wonkhe, 6 January. Accessed 31 July 2022. https://wonkhe.com/blogs/how-on-earth-do-we-run-2021-admissions-now/.

Kim, J. (2020) '4 reasons why every course should be designed as an online course'. *Inside Higher Ed* blog, 3 November. Accessed 31 July 2022. https://www.insidehighered.com/blogs/learning-innovation/4-reasons-why-every-course-should-be-designed-online-course.

Leary, J. and Berge, Z. L. (2007) 'Successful distance education programs in sub-Saharan Africa'. *Turkish Online Journal of Distance Education*, 8 (2), 136–45. Accessed 31 July 2022. https://www.researchgate.net/publication/26457918_Successful_distance_education_programs_in_Sub-Saharan_Africa.

Lederman, D. (2020) 'How teaching changed in the (forced) shift to remote'. *Inside Higher Education*, 22 April. Accessed 31 July 2022. https://www.insidehighered.com/digital-learning/article/2020/04/22/how-professors-changed-their-teaching-springs-shift-remote.

Ma, R. (2022) 'Massive list of Chinese language MOOC platforms in 2022'. *Class Central: The Report*, 19 January. Accessed 31 July 2022. https://www.classcentral.com/report/chinese-mooc-platforms/.

McGreal, R. (2021) 'How blockchain could help the world meet the UN's global goals in higher education'. *The Conversation*, 19 January. Accessed 31 July 2022. https://theconversation.com/how-blockchain-could-help-the-world-meet-the-uns-global-goals-in-higher-education-152885.

Maguire, D., Dale, M. and Pauli, M. (2020) 'Learning and teaching reimagined: A new dawn for higher education?' Jisc, November. Accessed 31 July 2022. https://repository.jisc.ac.uk/8150/1/learning-and-teaching-reimagined-a-new-dawn-for-higher-education.pdf.

Marshall, S. (2010) 'Change, technology and higher education: Are universities capable of organisational change?' *ALT-J, Research in Learning Technology*, 18 (3), 179–92. Accessed 31 July 2022. https://journal.alt.ac.uk/index.php/rlt/article/view/886.

Morris, N. (2020) 'Scaling up online education? More haste less speed'. Higher Education Policy Institute blog, 29 April. Accessed 31 July 2022. https://www.hepi.ac.uk/2020/04/29/scaling-up-online-education-more-haste-less-speed/.

Palvia, S., Aeron, P., Gupta, P., Mahapatra, D., Parida, R., Rosner, R. and Sindhi, S. (2018) 'Online education: Worldwide status, challenges, trends, and implications'. *Journal of Global Information Technology Management*, 21 (4), 233–41. Accessed 31 July 2022. https://doi.org/10.1080/1097198X.2018.1542262.

Pearson and Wonkhe (2021) 'Students' experiences of study during COVID-19 and hopes for future learning and teaching', February. Accessed 31 July 2022. https://wonkhe.com/wp-content/wonkhe-uploads/2021/02/Wonkhe-Pearson-expectation-gap-II-Feb-2021.pdf.

Rhodes, R. (1986) *The Making of the Atomic Bomb*. New York: Simon & Schuster.

Schwartz, N. (2022) 'Coursera bets on degrees: A small but growing part of the business'. Higher Ed Dive brief, 11 February. Accessed 31 July 2022. https://www.highereddive.com/news/coursera-bets-on-degrees-a-small-but-growing-part-of-the-business/618758/.

Shah, D. (2021) 'By the numbers: MOOCs in 2021'. *Class Central: The Report*, 1 December. Accessed 31 July 2022. https://www.class-central.com/report/mooc-stats-2021/.

St. Amour, M. (2019) 'Working college students'. *Inside Higher Ed*. Accessed 31 July 2022. https://www.insidehighered.com/news/2019/11/18/most-college-students-work-and-thats-both-good-and-bad.

TeachOnlineCA (2020) 'Five key lessons learned from faculty and instructors moving their courses online as a result of the COVID-19 pandemic'. ContactNorth/Nord, 22 April. Accessed 21 July 2022.https://teachonline.ca/tools-trends/five-key-lessons-learned-faculty-and-instructors-moving-their-courses-online-result-covid-19.

UNESCO (United Nations Educational, Scientific and Cultural Organization) (2018) 'Data for the Sustainable Development Goals'. Education stats database. Accessed 31 July 2022. http://uis.unesco.org.

Wallace-Stephens, F. and Morgante, E. (2020) *Who Is at Risk? Work and automation in the time of COVID-19*. London: RSA.

# Index

Page numbers in **bold** refer to tables and boxes; page numbers in *italics* refer to figures; 'n' after a page number indicates the endnote number.

Abubakar, Abdulrasheed, 119, 120, 122, 124
academic development, research and practice, 355, 357–8
   academic development/development, 357, 358–9, 360–2
   CODE, 360, 361, 362, 363, 364, 367, 369, 372, 373
   course design, 357, 358, 379
   development and practice, 360, 361
   development and research, 358–9, 377
   development and research, dissemination of, 363
   Digital Educator Project, UoL (example), 361, **373–7**, 377
   Literacies (example), **368–70**, 377
   policy and strategy, 355, 358, 376, 379
   practice, 357, 360
   predicting student success and increasing student retention (example), **370–3**, 377
   productive relationship between development, research and practice, 355, 358, 380–1
   relationships between academic development, research and practice, 357–63, 377–8
   research, 357, 359–60, 362–3
   research and practice, 359
   student learning hours and learning strategies (example), **364–8**, 377, 392, 403
   sustained scholarly practice, 355, 358, 377–81
ACCA (Association of Chartered Certified Accountants), 102, 106, 187
access to education, 7
   barriers to, 26, 29, 230, 309
   costs of education, 230, 235
   digital era, 29
   distance education, 19, 20–1, 227, 229–30, 234, 425
   equity of access, 7, 429
   future of distance education, 425–6
   HE, 19–20
   inequality, 28, 32, 230, 425, 429
   lifelong learning, 49
   Nigeria: barriers to education, 18, 123, 129
   online education, 230
   synchronous/asynchronous interaction, 236
   technology and, 26, 230, 235, 425–6
   UK, 426
   UoL accessibility, xxvii, 229, 230
   VLEs, 236
   *see also* digital divide; disabilities, students with; inclusion; widening participation
Advance HE (formerly HEA—Higher Education Academy): embedding employability, 64, *65*, 66, 67–8, 81
AGCAS (Association of Graduate Careers Advisory Services, UK), 76
AI (artificial intelligence), 40, 45, 265
   employability and, 69, 78, 80
   marketing digital education, 55, 61
   matching students with university's offer, 54
   MOOCs and, 184
Al-Alwani, A., 396
Amrane-Cooper, Linda, xxxi–xxxiii, 211–26
analytic data
   big data analytics, 61
   learning analytics, 15, 31, 61
   marketing digital education, 61
Anderson, S., 395
Anglia Ruskin University (UK), 71
Anstead, Edward, 195–210
Applegate, L. M., 113
Artess, J., 67, 81–2, 84
Arulmani, G., 72
Arum, R. and Roksa, J., 261
Ashwin, P. and Trigwell, K., 362–3, 378–9
assessments, 15, 17, 31
   as conservative area, 195, 207
   content and its memorisation, 146
   distressed students during assessments, 270
   evaluation as summative assessment, 383
   future of distance education, 416–24 *passim*

HE, 195, 412
ipsative assessment, 87, 136, 254–5, 262–3, 274
learning outcomes as basis for, 148
monitoring as formative assessment, 383
retention: assessment and feedback, 254–5, 261–2, 274–5
rigour and fairness of, 207, 208
summative assessment, 211–12, 262
technologies and, 226
traditional assessment, 195, 197, 199, 207
UoL, xxv, 20, 107, 211–12, 412
*see also* digital assessment; feedback; online assessment: UoL case study, 135, 211, 212
Assinder, S., 113, 143, 358
assistive technologies, 167
disabilities, students with, 227, 232, 237–8, 241, 243, 246, 247, 339
*see also* technologies
Australia
1992 Disability Discrimination Act, 238
employability, 67, 68, 78, 79, 85
Swinburne University, 79
University of Queensland, 78
automated assessment/autograding, 134, 200, 201, 202–4, 205, 208
benefit of autograding, 204, 206–7
grading software, 203–4
limitations, 208
MCQ test, 202–3
simulation, 203
*see also* digital assessment
automation, 37, 69, 204
automated feedback, 206, 207, 208
course design, 140
*see also* automated assessment/autograding

Bamber, V., 383–4, 393, 395
Bandura, A., 169, 171
Barber, M., 96, 415, 425
Bates, A. W., 189
Baume, David, 118–30, 139–66, 211–26, 357–82, 383–406
Bengtson, J. A. and Coleman, J., 337, 338, 339
Biddix, J. P., 27
Biggs, J., 148
Birkbeck College (UK), 197, 198, 199, **305, 306**
Blackboard, 168
Blackboard Collaborate, 198, 265
Blackboard Learn, 237
Blackmore, P., 81
BLE (Bloomsbury Learning Exchange, UK), 196, 197, 199, **306–8**
blended learning, 1, 6, 8, 10, 100, 145, 195, 410, 414
advantages, 1–2
course design, 145
COVID-19 pandemic, 95
disabilities, students with, 232
future of distance education, 415, 416, 417, 426
HE, 21
MOOCs, 27
retention, 232

UCB (University College Blended), 416, 419–20, 421–2, 423
UoL, xxvi, xxviii, 100
US, 409
*see also* dual mode
Bloom, B. S., 204
taxonomy, 151, **152**, 153, 156
British Library: Early Music Online, **301–3**
Brooke, C., 346
Brown, C., 29
Brown, M., 23
Brown, Stephen, 1–12, 15–18, 118–30, 133–7, 355–6, **364–8**, 407–33
Bulathwela, S., 311
Burgstahler, S., 232, 245
Burns, M., 189
Butcher, J. and Rose-Adams, J., 82

Caddell, M., 25, 74, **75**
Cambridge University Library (UK), 346
CampusBird, 60
Canada
Canadian Association of College and University Libraries, 327
University of Manitoba, 411
Cannell, Pete, 19–34, 74, **75**, 293–319
Canvas, 168
capital (human, social, psychological capital), 70–1
Cappellini, Benedetta, 49–63
Catts, R. and Lau, J., 346
CBI (Confederation of British Industry), 39, 67
CC licences (Creative Commons), 246, 285, 306, 307, 315
OER and, 295–6, 304
Chaney, B. H., 58
Charlton, Nicholas, 227–52
Chew, Lynsie, 187–94
China, 430n6
Chow, A. S. and Croxton, R. A., 341
CIPD (Chartered Institute of Personnel and Development), 41
Clifton, G., 26–7
CNAA (Council for National Academic Awards), xxv, 8, 430n2
CODE (Centre for Online and Distance Education, UoL), xxiii, xxxi–xxxiii, 59, 404
academic development, research and practice, 360, 361, 362, 363, 364, 367, 369, 372, 373
aims, xxxi, 59
CDE (Centre for Distance Education), xxxi–xxxii, 11n1, 213, 267, 430n7
CODE fellows, xxxii, 3
function, xxxii
Nigeria, 18, 119, 124, 125, 126, 128–9
Teaching and Research Awards, xxxii
Virtual Campus Project, xxxi
*see also* UoL
Commonwealth of Learning, 28, 299
Conole, G., 28–9
Conolly, Daniel, 230, 231
constructivism, 6, 45, 181–2, 189, 199
copyright, 279, 282, 294

INDEX 435

CLA (Copyright Licensing Agency), 332
OER, 296, 308, 315
online library, 331–2, 345, 347
course design, 133, 139, 163–4
   ABC course design approach, 150–1
   academic development, research and practice, 357, 358, 379
   blended learning, 145
   Bloom's taxonomy, 151, **152**, 153, 156
   challenges, 26–7, 142–3, 156
   digital education, 51
   disabilities, students with, 244, 245–6
   distance and face-to-face learning, 140–3, 145
   essentials for an effective distance learning course, 139–40
   evaluation and, 386, 391, 392
   feedback to students, 140, 142, 144, 155, 156, 161, 164
   Global Blindness MOOC: learner-centred design approach, 280–3
   inclusion, 227, 233
   inflexibility of distance learning platforms, 140
   interactive social learning, 170, 171, 184
   knowledge and capability, 148–9
   learner–learner interactions, 170
   learning: effectiveness, 155
   learning: principles for 155–61
   learning activities, 143, 144, 146, 148, 150, 156, 158–60, 164
   MOOCs, 200
   online library, 347
   outcomes-based course design for distance learning, 148, 150, 163
   pedagogy and, 133, 140–2, 143, 145–55, 164
   problems with language and reality, 143–5
   as sequencing of content, 145–6
   social isolation and, 168
   staff and, 143
   staff development for distance education, 133, 161–3
   starting with questions, 153–5
   synchronous/asynchronous interaction, 141–2, 144, 164
   technology, 164
   transformation in, 133, 164
   UDL approach, 164
   VLEs, 142–3, 144, 146–7, 156, 159, 164
course design: core team, 140
   academics/lecturers, 140, 146–7, 164
   learning designers, 9, 133, 146, 147, 164, 283
   learning technologists, 9, 133, 140, 146, 147, 164
   library-librarians/information specialists, 140, 164
   productive relationship between team members, 147, 163
Coursera, 103, 111, 200, 204, 312, 411, 430n10
COVID-19 pandemic, 2, 43, 311, 376
   blended learning, 95
   digital/online assessment, 3, 135, 211, 212, 412–13

distance education, xxviii, 1, 2, 95, 142, 412–13
distance education: strategic models, 101
employability, 79
future of distance education and, 412–13, 414, 419–23, 425, 425, 426, 428, 429
Great Leap Online, 1, 3, 7, 118, 142, 360, 407, 412–13, 425
HEIs, 101
LMSs, 168
MOOCs, 412, 430n6
Nigeria, 121, 122
OEP, 311, 316
online library, 321
UK, 414, 422
UoL, xxvi, 212, 412
Cox, G. and Trotter, H., 315–16
Cronin, C., 300

Dalrymple, R., 67, 84
Daniel, J., 20, 21
data protection, 269, 331, 332, 347
Davis, L., 40
Davis, Michael, xxiii–xxix, 95–117
decolonisation, xxv, 42, 44, 149, 231
Dickens, Charles, *All the Year Round* (magazine), 229–30
digital assessment, 3, 98, 134, 195–6, 207–9
   BLE, 196, 197
   blurred boundaries: traditional and non-credit-bearing online assessments, 200–1
   COVID-19 pandemic, 412
   credit-bearing distance learning programmes, 134, 195
   distance education, 195, 196–9
   emerging good practices in assessment at scale, 200–7
   enhanced functional approach, 196, 198, 199
   e-tivities, 199
   feedback, 197, 198
   formative assessment, 196, 197, 198, 199, 201, 208, 418
   formative peer review, 201–2
   functional approach, 196, 197, 198, 199
   gamification/Sleuth, 204–7, 208
   innovative approach, 196, 198–9
   MOOCs, 134, 196, 200–1, 202, 204, 208
   peer assessment, 72, 134, 175, 198, 200, 201, 208–9
   self-assessment, 170, 198, 200, 208, 209
   summative assessment, 196, 197, 198, 201, 202, 208, 261–2
   synchronous tools, 198
   UoL Federation, 134, 195
   VLEs, 197, 198, 202
   *see also* assessments; automated assessment/autograding; feedback; online assessment: UoL case study
digital divide, 28–9, 38, 425
   access to internet, 27, 135, 230, 235, 236, 254, 255, 286
   bridging the digital divide, 35
   digital learning, 16, 18
   disabilities, students with, 235, 236

Nigeria, 18, 123
social divides and, 230
*see also* access to education
digital era
  barriers to accessing education, 29
  digital capabilities, 69, 88, 300
  digital literacy skills, 29, 284, 345, 375
  digital natives, 29, 38
  digitisation, 69, 98, 100, 302
  ownership of mobile digital devices, 26
digital learning, 16, 35–6, 45–6
  antecedents, 45
  approaches to, 43–4
  benefits, 40
  contemporary education environment: context, 37–40
  definition, 36–7, 40–1
  distance education, 41–2
  HE and, 36, 38–9, 45–6
  relationships between digital, online and distance education, 16, 35–6, 37, 41, 42–4
  technological advances, 37, 45
  translation: design, development and delivery of courseware, 42
  working together, 43
digital poverty, 38, 425
disabilities, 135
  ableism, 230
  definitions, 228–9, 239
  medical/deficit model, 228, 231, 233
  social model, 228–9
  *see also* disabilities, students with; inclusion
disabilities, students with, 135, 227–8, 247–8
  accessibility needs, 228–9
  accessible teaching and learning content, 235–8
  assistive technologies, 227, 232, 237–8, 241, 243, 246, 247, 339
  blended learning, 232
  content accessibility: non-technical solutions to, 235–6
  course design, 244, 245–6
  CRPD, 238
  digital divide, 235, 236
  discrimination, 239
  distance learning, 230, **234–5**
  education policies, 237–8, 242
  EU, 241, 333
  example, **234–5**
  global university, access in, 229, 236–7
  good practice examples, 246–7
  HE, 230, 233, 239–40, 241–4, 247
  hidden disabilities, **234–5**, 236, 333
  improving inclusivity, 241–7
  improving inclusivity and accessibility of existing courses, 244–5
  legislation, 229, 231, 238–41, 333
  online learning, 232
  online library, 333, 334, 339, 348
  'self-advocacy' model, 231
  self-disclosure, 231–2
  software, 228, 237
  technology, 232, 235, 236–7
  UDL, 232, 245
  UDL, Ministry of Education, New Zealand, 247
  UK, 238–9
  universities: common issues, 241–4
  University of Auckland, New Zealand, 247
  University of Edinburgh, 247
  UoL, 135, 230, 231, 232, 238, 246, 247
  US, 333
  VLEs, 237, 246
  WCAG, 237, 240–1
  *see also* disabilities; inclusion
distance education
  access to, 19, 20–1, 227, 229–30, 234, 425
  administration and assessment as essential to, xxiii
  advantages, 2, 6, 25, 97, 99, 102, 429
  analogue components, 35
  authenticity and legitimacy, xxvii
  bad reputation/stigma, xxviii, 1, 6–7, 20, 124, 129, 141
  challenges, xxvii–xxviii, xxix, 4–5, 31, 139, 156
  competition, 54
  correspondence/correspondence education, 20, 26, 41, 54, 168
  costs, 97, 99, 112–13, 235
  COVID-19 pandemic, xxviii, 1, 2, 95, 142, 412–13
  criticism of, 253
  definition, 4, 6, 8
  developing world, 97
  disintermediation, 115
  effectiveness, 6–8, 142
  failure, 100
  flexibility, 2, 52, 115, 144, 253, 411
  funding, 112, 113
  HE, 45, 49, 407, 409, 412–14, 428
  HEIs, 17, 95
  history of, xxiii–xxviii, xxix, 3, 6, 8, 10, 19–20, 41, 54, 100, 168, 409–10, 429
  inclusion and, 227, 229–32, 242
  internet and, 10, 410
  key elements, 4
  mid-nineteenth century origins, 10, 19–20, 41, 168, 409
  open/distance learning distinction, 7
  power structures: reinforcing prevailing power structures, 42
  relationships between digital, online and distance education, 16, 35–6, 37, 41, 42–4
  as resource intensive, xxviii
  success, 100, 116
  technology and, 4, 5, 6, 22, 26, 32, 45, 100, 112, 410, 425, 429
  teleconferencing, 26
  trends, 10
  worldwide adoption of, 410, 411
  *see also* blended learning; ODE; ODL; online education; open education; OU; UoL
distance education: strategic models, 17–18, 95–6, 114–16
  business models, 96, 102, 110, 111, 112, 113, 114, 116
  COVID-19 pandemic, 101

INDEX 437

drivers underlying institutional adoption of distance learning, 97, 102
e-business models, 112, 113
e-learning as strategic, 100–1, **101**
examples, **106–10, 114–15**
'experimental implementers', 101–2, 428
external actors, 18, 114
HEIs, 96–116
institutional drivers, **98**
needs and expectations of distance learning stakeholders, 96, 103–10
online provision: funding/monetising, 96, 112–13, 115–16
OU, UK, 111
relationship to other educational provision, 100–3
resources: providers and bundling, 96, 110–12, 116
senior managers, 103
'strategic design implementers', 101, 102
strategic importance of distance learning HEIs, 96–100, 114
UoL, 102–3, **106–10**, 111, **114–15**
value chain, 18, 96, 99, 111–12, 115
*see also* stakeholders
distance learners, 15–16, 19–20, 31–2, 413
assessments, 15, 31, 270
challenges faced by, 25, 187, 188–9
characteristics, 22–3, 41
emotions, 23
engagement, 19
examples, **23–5**, 27
identities, 22
learning analytics, 15, 31
motivations for distance education, 22, 25, 30, 73–4, 82, 88, 97, 114
online identity, 254
personal factors, 19, 20, 22–3, 25, 30, 255
social isolation/loneliness, 134, 168, 182, 184, 185, 187, 188, 189
student learning hours and learning strategies (project), **364–8**, 377, 392, 403
student support, 30, 32
technology, impact of, 26–9
transitions, 16, 31
understanding distance learners, 15, 16, 17, 19, 68
variety of, 19, 51, 323
*see also* dropout; peer-related issues; retention
distance/traditional education comparison, 22–3
advantages, 6, 36
attrition rates, 182
balance between upfront investment and operating costs, 112–13
blurred distinction, 1, 2, 143, 410–12, 414
challenges, 31
costs, 112–13
differences, 2, 4, 36, 60, 100, 112–13, 140–1, 146–7, 182, 253
dropout, 30, 168
effectiveness, 7
flexibility, 22, 60, 236
human aspects of learning, 54–5

linear/non-linear journeys, 25
pedagogy, 140–1
retention, 253
similarities, 6, 54–5, 162
student retention, 60
teaching methods, 146–7
technology, 100
Dolmage, J. T., 230
Donald, W. E., 82
Downes, Stephen, 411
Dron, J. and Ostashewski, N., 189
dropout (distance learners), 30, 168, 182, 189
attrition, 30, 31, 182, 187, 188, 193
blended learning, 232
distance/traditional education comparison, 30, 168
MOOCs, 30
online education, 232
OU, 370–1
*see also* retention
dual mode, 20, 123
*see also* blended learning
Durham University (UK), 413, 428
Dweck, C. S., 372

education
costs, 230, 235, 294, 408, 410
educational affordances, 5–6, 37
educational technology, 26, 373, 375
social mobility and, 42, 408
technologies and, 5, 311
*see also* distance education; online education; open education; TNE; traditional education
education policies
academic development, research and practice, 355, 358, 376, 379
developing digital skills, 39
disabilities, students with, 237–8, 242
policy and strategy, 8, 10, 118–19, 355, 356, 358, 378
Educause Learning Initiative, 39–40
edX, 111, 200
Edyburn, D. L., 232
Egesah, O. B. and Wahome, M. N., 325, 345
employability, 17, 64–5, 349
Advance HE (HEA): embedding employability framework, 64, *65*, 66, 67–8, 81
AI and, 69, 78, 80
appropriate model for distance education, 73–4, 88
business placements, 272, 273
Career Planning Micro-Module, 73
co-curricular methods, 74, 76, 77, 81, 82, 84–6
conclusions and recommendations, 65, 88–9
COVID-19 pandemic, 79
curricular methods, 17, 74, 76, 86–7
definitions, 64, 65–74
distance students' intended career transitions and employability needs, **75**
DOTS Model, 72
employability learning, 17, 64, 74, 84, 86, 87, 88

employability skills, 17, 66–72, **75**, 78, 83–4, 87
ESE, 70–1
extracurricular methods, 74, 77, 81, 82, 84–6
factors linked to, 66
internships, 272–3
measuring and evaluating employability impact, 17, 64–5, 79, 84–7
models of, 17, 66–74, 82
Nigeria, 121
part-time and distance students, 73–4, 80, 82
'positioning' models, 66, 70–2
'possessive' models, 66–70, 83
'processual' models, 66, 72–3, 83
self-employment, 70
senior management commitment, 17, 81, 88
technological skills, 69
understanding distance students' needs, 17, 88
virtual careers fairs, 78
WEF, 69–70
WIL, 68, 78–9
employability: HE specific cases
Anglia Ruskin University, UK, 71
Australia, 67, 68, 78, 79, 85
OU, UK, 67–8, 78, 80
Universidade Aberta, Portugal, 84
University of Birmingham, UK, 79
University of Central Lancashire, UK, 72
University of Maine, US, 68–9
University of Southampton, UK, 71
UoL, UK, 71–2, 73, 74, 78, 271–4
employability development: approaches in HE, 64, 74–84, 88–9
acceptance and engagement, 82–4
principles and strategic priorities, 81–2
remote delivery of activities, 78–9
resource considerations, 79–81
typical activities, 77–8
'e-tivities', 45, 199
EU
Framework and Horizon 2020, 410
project for open-source educational gaming, **314**
Web Accessibility Directive, 241, 333
European Association of Distance Teaching Universities: 2019 MOONLITE Hague Declaration, 310
evaluation (monitoring and evaluating online/distance education), 355, 384, 405
'appreciative enquiry' approach, 397–8
benchmarking evaluations, 396
case-study evaluations, 396
changing goals, 401–2
comparative evaluations, 396
continuing to learn and using what is learned, 404–5
course design and, 386, 391, 392
evaluands, 386
evaluation, reasons for, 404
evaluation and quality assurance, 395, 403
evaluation and research, 395–6
evaluation as summative assessment, 383

evaluator roles, 398–9
goals, 388, 391, 398
goals for 11 stages of engagement, 388, **389–91**
illuminative approach, 397
K1–4 (four levels of evaluation), 394, 399–401
monitoring/evaluating distinction, 383, 387
monitoring as formative assessment, 383
negotiating and negotiated evaluation, 402–3
outcomes-based evaluations, 383–4, 396, 401, 403–4
performance evaluations, 396
problem of knowing what causes what, 391–2
problem of measurement, 392–3
problem of measuring difference, 393–4
problem of timescale, 394–5
processes-based evaluations, 384
rationalist/positivist approach, 396
responsive approach, 397
self-evaluation, 396
SMARTening project goals, 402
using what is already available, 403–4
VLEs, 392, 400, 403
'who, why, how, what, when and where?', 355–6, 384, 385–8
examinations, *see* assessments

Facebook, 24, 27, 142, 171, 174, 178
Fawns, T., 43
feedback (to students), 2, 6
automated feedback, 206, 207, 208
corrective and critical feedback, 256
course design, 140, 142, 144, 155, 156, 161, 164
digital assessment, 197, 198
effective feedback, 256
formative feedback, 133, 167, 198, 199, 256, 416
ipsative feedback, 261
longitudinal approach to, 256–7
MOOCS, 57
OU, UK, 161
peer feedback, 133, 140, 161, 198
peer review, 201–2, 254, 257
retention: assessment and feedback, 254–5, 261–2, 274–5
UoL, 161
*see also* digital assessment
flexible learning, 8, 39, 53, 97, 123, 270
Flickr, 304
Fourth Industrial Revolution, 37, 272
Fragaszy, D. M. and Perry, S., 175
Francis, Naraesa, 364
Fung, D.: *Connected Curriculum*, 44
FutureLearn, 111, 200, 312, 411, 430n10
future of distance education, 10, 60, 32, 407–8, 428–9
access to distance education, 425–6
assessments/examinations, 416–24 *passim*
blended learning, 415, 416, 417, 426
capacity, 427
changes required, 415

conjectural scenarios, 10, 407–8, 416–28
COVID-19 pandemic experience, 412–13, 414, 419–23, 425, 425, 426, 428, 429
disruptive events and distance education, 413–14
distance education as mainstreaming in HE, 407, 412–14, 428
flexibility, 426, 428
Global Blindness MOOC, 290
HU (Hybrid University), 417, 420, 422, 423
importance of distance education, 409
innovation, 427–8, 429
institutional capability, 426–7
MIT Ltd (MOOC Institute for Training), 418–19, 421, 422–3, 424
MOOCs, 411
stakeholders, 427, 428
students, 419–21
student's needs and capabilities, 424–5
support services, 423–4
teaching staff, 421–3
UCB (University College Blended), 416, 419–20, 421–2, 423
UoH (University of HiFlex), 417–18, 420–1, 422, 423–4
variety, 426, 428
VLEs, 416, 417, 418, 420
worldwide adoption of distance education, 410, 411

gaming, 79, 167, 171
digital assessment and gamification/Sleuth, 204–7, 208
EU project for open-source educational gaming, **314**
marketing digital education and gamification, 61
*see also* technologies
Gannon, K., 36
Gerstein, J., 189
Gibson, W., 407, 424
Gillies, Marco, 195–210, **373–7**
Global Blindness MOOC (MOOC for public health), 136, 277–8, 289–90
challenges, 136, 277
collaborators, 280, 283–4, 290
course team, 279, 282, 290
efficiency, 136, 277
equity, 136, 277, 278, 279, 290
evaluation, 284–9
evaluation methodology: limitations, 289
getting started, 278–85
ICEH/LSHTM, 278, 282, 284, 290
impact, 286–7, **288–9**, 290
learner-centred design approach, 280–3
lessons learned, 277–8
MOOC production, 283
OER, 278
quality, 136, 277, 278, 279, *280*, 284–5, 290
stakeholders, 280, **281**, 283–4, 290
steering group, 279, 280, 283
target learners, 280, **281**
training cascade, 278, 283–4, 287–8, 290
users' goals and needs, **281**
ways forward, 290

globalisation
corporate globalisation, 54
HE, 49
global north: distance education, 37, 42
global south
digital divide, 28
distance education, 37, 42
HE, demand for, 28, 32
mobile digital devices, 26, 37
open universities, 21
Goldsmiths College (UK), 202, 204, 302, 376
Gonnet, Sarah, 227–52
Google, 54, 287
Google Maps, 304
Google Play, 269
Google searches, 320, 323, 336
Gourlay, L., 36
Gregson, Jon, **373–7**
*Guardian* (UK), 413

Hammond, M., 171
hardware, 111, 237
Harris, Joanne, 253–76
Hatzipanagos, Stylianos, 211–26
Havemann, Leo, 195–210, 293–319
HE (higher education), 408–9
access to, 19–20
assessments, 195, 412
blended learning, 21
costs, 408
demand for, 28, 32, 118, 119–22, 408, 410
digital learning, 36, 38–9, 45–6
disabilities, students with, 230, 233, 239–40, 241–4, 247
distance education, 45, 49, 409
distance education as mainstreaming in HE, 407, 412–14, 428
exceptionalism and ableism, 230
globalisation of, 49
global south, 28, 32
HE programmes/vocational programmes distinction, 58
inclusion, 135, 229
OEP, 297, 299, 301, 316
open education, 293–4, 308
purpose, 38
traditional education, 409
UK, 409, 410, 426
UoL, xxiv–xxvii, 41
US, 409
value proposition of, 50
*see also* employability; HEIs; Nigeria
HEA (Higher Education Academy) *see* Advance HE
health-related issues
mental health, 269–70
promoting well-being, 268–71
self-help bibliography, 270
TalkCampus app, 269
*see also* Global Blindness MOOC
HEFCE (Higher Education Funding Council for England), xxxi
HEIs (HE institutions), 17, 37, 59, 410
competitive marketing, 59–60
COVID-19 pandemic, 101
distance education, 17, 95

440   ONLINE AND DISTANCE EDUCATION FOR A CONNECTED WORLD

drivers/reasons underlying the adoption of distance learning, 97, **98**
funding sources, 113
online library, 325, 327, 333
*see also* distance education: strategic models; HE
Hersh, M. and Mouroutsou, S., 230
Hipwell, J., 140
Holmes, L., 66
Hooley, T. and Grant, K., 74
Huang, Q., 30
Hughes, Gwyneth, 211–26, 253–76
Hyams, Beatrice, 227–52

Icarus simulation tool, 134, 187–8
awards, 193
benefits, 190–1, 193
challenges associated with online learning programmes, 134
Icarus design, 188
Icarus design rationale, 188–9
impact, 190–3, **192**
limitations of the study, 193–4
MPAcc, 187–94
inclusion
course design and pedagogy, 227, 233
distance education and, 227, 229–32, 242
equitable access to materials, 227
HE, 135, 229
inclusive education, 233, 242, 334
marketing digital education and inclusiveness, 16, 49, 50
multiculturalism and, 233
online education, 230
stakeholders and, 242–4
UoL, 229, 230, 232, 243, 246
*see also* disabilities, students with
India, 312
Ingelbrecht, N. and Lowendahl, J.-M., 265
interactive social learning, 133–4, 167–8, 184–5
asynchronous online forum: key features to maximise learner participation in, 171, **172–3**
concepts in social learning and examples, 176–7, **177–81**
course design, 170, 171, 184
examples, **176**, **177–81**, **182–4**
individual and group learning through social interaction and societal impact, 175
interactions in education, 170
learning communities: fostering of, 133, 167, 181–2, **182–4**, 185
LMSs, 167, 168, 170–1, 182
low cost, 167
online social interactions and learning, 170–4
participatory approaches, 168, 171
as resource intensive, 134, 167
scaffolded structure for learning, 133, 167, 168, 183
student-centred learning, 133, 170
synchronous/asynchronous interaction, 171

VLEs, 167
*see also* social learning
internet
access to, 27, 135, 230, 235, 236, 254, 255, 286
distance education, 10, 410
LMSs, 168
mobile devices, 37
MOOC model, 21
online education, 5
*see also* digital divide
Ireland: Dublin Core Metadata Initiative, 338
Ish-Horowicz, Shoshi, 227–52, 320–52
Italy: University of Camerino, 414

Jackson, N. J., 189
Jacoby, J., 341
JAWS (Job Access with Speech), 228, 237
Jefferson, Thomas, 293
Jegede, Olugbemiro, 122–3
Jisc, 2, 235–6, 271, 301, 412, 413, 425, 426
Johnstone, Danielle, 227–52
Jorre de St Jorre, T., 83
Jorum repository, 301, 317n7

Kahu, E., 23, 254, 255
Katan, Simon, 195–210
Kazakoff-Lane, C., 345
Kirkpatrick, J. and Kirkpatrick, W., 394, 399–401
Kirschner, P. A., 5
Kop, R., 29
Kromidha, Endrit, 49–63
Kuhlthau, C. C., 346

Latchem, C. and Jung, I., 189
Laurillard, D., 5
Conversational Framework, 43, 44
Lave, J. and Wenger, E., 181–2
Lea, M. R. and Jones, S., 29
learning
cognitive apprenticeship theory, 171
constructivist theories, 6, 45, 181–2, 189, 199
effectiveness, 155
learning design, 16, 27, 30–1, 32
learning preferences/preferred learning styles, 158, 164
learning theories, 6, 169
as more complex than accumulation of content and knowledge, 148
personal interest learning, 235
principles for 155–61
scaffolded structure, 133, 167, 168, 183, 282, 320
*see also* digital learning; interactive social learning; ODL; social learning; UDL
learning activities, 6, 50, 51, 100
course design, 143, 144, 146, 148, 150, 156, 158–60, 164
employability, 73, 74
learning communities, 184
concept, 181–2
distance learning communities, 182

INDEX **441**

fostering learning communities, 133, 167, 181–2, **182–4**, 185
peer support and collaborations, 167, 182
Lebowitz, G., 328
legislation
   disabilities, students with, 229, 231, 238–41, 333
   online library, 331, 333, 347
Lewis, R. and Spencer, D., 7–8
libraries, 137, 320
   Alexandria library, 320
   course design and librarians/information specialists, 140, 164
   law libraries, 327
   librarians, 140, 164, 344, 375
   online library/traditional library comparison, 137, 320, 321, 325, 328, 331, 337
   UK, 327
   value of academic libraries, 326
   *see also* online library
lifelong learning, 39, 50, 66, 83, 87, 97, 299
   access to 49
   key competencies for, 67
   online library, 345, 349
   open education, 308, 309
Literacies (project), **368–70**, 377
Liu, T. C., 171
LMSs (learning management systems), 2, 144, 167–8, 410
   challenges, 170
   interactive social learning, 167, 168, 170–1, 182
   internet-based platform, 168
   learning strategies of learners, 174–5
   plagiarism detection software, 175
   social learning, 169, 170
LSE (London School of Economics, UK), 301
LSHTM (London School of Hygiene and Tropical Medicine, UK), 197, 198
   Global Blindness MOOC, 278, 282, 284, 290
   ICEH (Centre for Eye Health), 278
Ludema, J. D., 397–8

Macfarlane-Dick, D., 161
Macintyre, R., 29
McLoughlin, C., 233
McMillan, D. W. and Chavis, D. M., 181
Maggioncalda, Jeff, 411
Maguire, D., 415
Makerere University, Uganda, 37–8
Malaysia, 312
Mallon, M. N., 324, 336, 343, 344, 345
Mandela, Nelson, 42
Maniati, Diana, 227–52
Marginson, S., 230
marketing digital education, 16, 49–50, 59–62
   AI, 55, 61
   big data analytics, 61
   challenges, 60
   customer mindset, 51–3, 58
   failing in, 49
   finding the right students and being easy to find, 50, 53–5
   gamification, 61

inclusiveness, 16, 49, 50
learning as enjoyable experience, 50
marketing management, 50–1
'mobile-first' approach, 60–1
MOOCs, 52–3, 57
paid referrals, 56
peer-to-peer model of marketing and learning, 55–7
product mindset, 51
redefining marketing for distance learning programmes, 50–3
sales mindset, 51
students as ambassadors of programmes, 16, 50, 56–7, 105
team and technology behind the process, 50, 57–9
technology, role of, 58–9, 60
UoL, 53, 58, 59, 60
value proposition of distance education courses, 49, 50
Mason, G., 84
May, H. and Bridger, K., 241–2
Miller, C. M. L. and Parlett, M., 397
Milligan, C. and Littlejohn, A., 25
Mitchell, R. K., 103
mobile learning, 8, 37
mobile phone/devices, 61, 194, 321, 410
   capabilities of, 37
   developing countries, 61
   distance education, 26, 27, 37–8
   marketing digital education: 'mobile-first' approach, 60–1
   smart devices, 26, 45
   ubiquity, 26, 27, 37, 60
Molleman, L., 174
Molloy, E. and Boud, D., 256
monitoring and evaluating online/distance education *see* evaluation
MOOC for public health, *see* Global Blindness MOOC
MOOCs (massive open online courses), 21, 25, 144, 411
   AI and, 184
   beginnings, 411
   blended learning, 27
   China, 430n6
   'cMOOCs', 299–300, 309
   course design, 200
   COVID-19 pandemic, 412, 430n6
   credit-bearing programmes, 201, 312, 411
   critique of, 196
   as different from distance education, 196
   digital assessment, 134, 196, 200–1, 202, 204, 208
   disadvantages, 29, 99
   dropout from, 30
   'EMPLOY101x', 78
   'Enhance Your Career and Employability Skills', 71–2, 78
   feedback, 57
   internet, 21
   low-cost access, 277
   marketing digital education, 52–3, 57
   MIT Ltd (MOOC Institute for Training), 418–19, 421, 422–3, 424
   'Nanodegrees', 312, 411

online library, 342–3, 345
open education, 297, 309–10, 312
  rise of, 31–2, 99, 196, 411
  role and value of, 99
  sustainability of MOOC business models, 312
  synchronous/asynchronous interaction, 309
  University of Manitoba, Canada, 411
  worldwide adoption of, 411
Moodle, 168, 237, 306, 387
Moore, M. G., 4, 170
Moriña, A., 231
Morris, S. E. and Grimes, M., 340
Mosley, N., 43
Moyo, L. M., 338
MPAcc programme (professional accountancy), 187–94
multiculturalism, 233

Nakamura, L., 233
New Zealand
  UDL, Ministry of Education, 247
  University of Auckland, 247
  University of Canterbury, 413–14
Nicol, D., 161, 257
Nigeria, 18, 96, 102, 118–19
  annual conference/symposium, 125–6
  barriers to education, 18, 123, 129
  Boko Haram, 121
  changing culture and practice, 129–30
  CODE, 18, 119, 124, 125, 126, 129
  COVID-19 pandemic, 121, 122
  demand for education, 119–22
  digital divide, 18, 123
  employability, 121
  enlarging existing/building more universities, 122–3
  Federal Ministry of Education, 119
  HE, 118
  HE aspirations, 119–20
  HE: challenges, 120–2
  HE: future options, 122–3
  National Open University, 123
  National Teachers Institute, 123
  NOUN (National Open University of Nigeria), 123
  NPE (National Policy on Education), 119, 121, 123
  NUC (National Universities Commission), 18, 119, 120, 123, 124, 125, 126, 129
  NUC/CODE programme of work to date: impact of, 128–9
  NUC/UoL: MoU, 124–5
  ODL, 118, 119, 123, 129
  ODL: capacity building for, 123–8
  political instability, 121
  'Rasheed Revitalisation Plan', 119–20
  RIDE conferences, 125
  tertiary education, 119, 120
  University of the Air (Ahmadu Bello University), 123
  University of Ibadan, 124
  University of Lagos, 123
  UoL and, 124–9
  workshops in London, 124, 125
  workshops in Nigeria, 126–8, 129

ODE (open and distance education), 293–4
  see also open education
ODL (online distance learning), 38
  Africa, 124
  see also distance education; Nigeria; online education
OECD (Organisation for Economic Co-operation and Development), 313
OEP (open educational practices), 137, 293, 295, 411
  adoption of, 314–16
  affordability and business models, 311–13
  challenges, 300, 308–14, 316
  cMOOCs, 299–300, 309
  COVID-19 pandemic, 311, 316
  definitions, 298, 300
  evolution of, 296–300
  HE, 297, 299, 301, 316
  networked participatory scholarship, 297
  OEP and OER in practice, 300–8
  OEP/OER relationship, 136–7, 296–8, 300, 314
  quality, 310–11
  skills gap, 313–14
  special interest groups, 297
  widening access, 308–10
  see also OER; open education
OER (open educational resources), 21, 28, 294, 411
  '5 Rs', 298
  adoption of, 314–16
  benefits, 313
  Birkbeck College, **305**
  BLE, **306–8**
  CC licences and, 295–6, 304
  challenges, 316
  cMOOCs, 300
  copyright, 296, 308, 315
  definition 295
  EU project for open-source educational gaming, **314**
  Global Blindness MOOC, 278
  Google Maps, 304
  LSE, 301
  OECD on, 313
  OEP and OER in practice, 300–8
  OEP/OER relationship, 136–7, 296–8, 300, 314
  OER Africa, 299
  OER/open access publications overlap, 295–6
  OER repositories, 300–1, **301–3**, 303
  OERu, 21
  open source software, 293, 296
  OU, UK, 28, 303
  quality, 310–11, 313
  SOAS, **305**
  UCL, 301, 303, **304**, **305**
  UNESCO, 295
  UoL, 301, **301–3**, **304–8**
  Wikimedia Commons, 303–4
  see also OEP; open education

Okebukola, Peter, 122
Oliver, B., 66, 83
online assessment, *see* digital assessment
online assessment: UoL case study, 134–5, 207, 211, 226, 361
   CDE, 213
   COVID-19 pandemic, 135, 211, 212, 412–13
   digitally proctored (invigilated) examinations, 213, 226
   move to online assessment, 207, 211, 212–13
   move to online assessment: evaluation, 213–14, *214*
   move to online assessment: evaluation of academic integrity, **221**
   move to online assessment: evaluation of academic sentiment, **222–5**
   move to online assessment: operational issues evaluation, 213
   move to online assessment: student behaviours evaluation, 213, **215–16**
   move to online assessment: student outcomes evaluation, 213
   move to online assessment: student sentiment evaluation, 213, **216–20**
   technology and assessment, 226
   VLE: examination paper, 213
   *see also* assessments; digital assessment
*Online and Distance Education for a Connected World*, xxiii, xxix, xxxi, 2, 3
   aim, 8–9
   approaches, 9
   case studies, 10, 18
   'Doing distance education', 9, 133–7
   pathways through, 8–10
   'Planning distance education', 9, 15–18
   'Researching and evaluating distance education', 9–10, 355–6
   target audiences, 9, 10
online education
   access to education, 230
   challenges, 187, 188–9
   COVID-induced 'Great Leap Online', 1, 3, 7, 118, 142, 360, 407, 412–13, 425
   definition, 8
   disabilities, students with, 232
   disruptive events and, 413–14
   inclusion, 230
   internet, 5
   MOOC model, 21
   opposition from staff and students, 413
   overlap between online and distance education, 168
   quality of, 413
   relationships between digital, online and distance education, 16, 35–6, 37, 41, 42–4
   UoL, xxiii, xxvi, xxviii
   *see also* distance education; ODL
online forums, 24, 26, 161,
   retention and discussion forum activities, 254, 256, 260, 261
online library, 137, 140, 320–1, 347–9
   accessibility, 323, 325, 329, 333–5, 338, 347–8

back-up from local physical libraries, 335
beginnings of, 321
challenges, 322, 325, 330, 333
chats and text messages, 324, 341–2, 348
collection development, 331
copyright/licensing, 331–2, 345, 347
course design, 347
COVID-19 pandemic, 321
data protection, 331, 332, 347
definition, 321–2, 347
developing an online library, 325, 329–44
disabilities, students with, 333, 334, 339, 348
discoverability, 329, 335–43, 348
discovery services, 336–8
distance learners' information-seeking behaviour, 323, 324, 325, 348
distance learners' needs, 322–5, 329, 330–1, 335, 346
equity principle, 326, 328, 348
guidance and help, 340–2
HEIs, 325, 327, 333
information literacy skills, 322–3, 331, 340, 346–7, 349
law libraries, 327
legislation, 331, 333, 347
librarians, 330, 338, 343, 344–7, 348
metadata, 338, 348
MOOCs, 342–3, 345
online library/traditional library comparison, 137, 320, 321, 325, 328, 331, 337
procurement service, 334, 339
provision, 326–32
recommendations, 324, 332, 334, 337, 348
self-help bibliography, 270
sign-on authentication system, 324, 348
synchronous interaction, 341, 342, 343, 346
training, 342–4, 348
universal design, 338–9, 348
WCAG, 333, 338, 339
web-scale discovery services, 336–7
*see also* libraries
online library: specific universities and countries
   Cambridge University Library, UK, 346
   Canada, 327
   OU, UK, 137, 321, 323, 327, 333–4, 340, 341, 347
   UK, 327, 346
   University of Sunderland, UK, 346–7
   UoL, 137, 321, 323, 324, 328–9, 336, 337, 338, 347
   UoL: 'Ask-A-Librarian' live chat service, 324, 341–2
   US, 326–7, 337, 338–9, 345
open education, 136–7, 293–5
   definition, 7–8
   HE, 293–4, 308
   MOOCs, 297, 309–10, 312
   ODE, 293–4
   'open'/'closed' education dichotomy, 136, 137, 294–5
   open/distance learning distinction, 7
   open education movement, 298, 308

open pedagogy, 310
promise and drivers, 298–9
widening participation, 295
*see also* OEP; OER
Open Education Research Hub, 299
open universities, 21, 99, 295, 313
financial considerations, 295
global south, 21
'mega university', 21
retention and success, 30
specialist open universities, 21
*see also* OU
Osborne, R., 87
OU (Open University, UK), xxiii, 5, 8
associate lecturers, 161
distance education: strategic models, 111
dropout, 370–1
employability, 67–8, 78, 80
establishment of, xxv, 8, 20, 41, 430n2
feedback, 161
impact, 21
OER repositories, 28, 303
online library, 137, 321, 323, 327, 333–4, 340, 341, 347
Online Talent Connect, 78
opening up access to HE, 20–1
OpenLearn and OpenLearnCreate sites, 28, 303
partner institutions, 111
retention, 370–2
success, 6

Parkinson, Alan, 187–94
Parlett, M. and Hamilton, D., 397
Parnell, S., 326, 328
Parsley, Sally, 277–92, 293–319
part-time distance learning, 28, 346
2018 Guidance from the Government's Office for Students, 28
employability, 73–4, 80, 82
Patel, Daksha, 277–92, 293–319
Pearson Global Learner Survey, 69
pedagogy, 4, 429
course design and, 133, 140–2, 143, 145–55, 164
distance/traditional education comparison, 140–1
inclusion: course design and pedagogy, 227, 233
open pedagogy, 310
planning of pedagogy, 145
post-web fusion pedagogy, 314
peer-related issues
collaboration, 6, 133, 160, 167, 182
formative peer review, 201–2
learning communities and, 167, 182
peer assessment, 72, 134, 175, 198, 200, 201, 208–9
peer feedback, 133, 140, 161, 198
peer review, 201–2, 254, 257
peer support, 15, 31, 80, 133, 167, 182, 199, 268
peer-to-peer model of marketing and learning, 55–7
retention and peer review activities, 254, 257, 260–1, 274, 275

Pereyaslavska, K., 334
Perryman, L. A. and De Los Arcos, B., 299
persistence (distance learners), 83, 135
key factors for, 254, 256, 268
recommendations for improving persistence, 274–5
retention/persistence distinction, 253
*see also* retention
Peters, O., 22, 26
Philpott, Matthew, 118–30, 320–52
plagiarism, 60, 160, 177, 183, 205, 222, 224, 225, 308
learning through copying/plagiarism distinction, 175
plagiarism detection software, 175
Popovic, C. and Baume, D., 361, 362, 379
Portugal: Universidade Aberta, 84
Powell, Philip, 95–117

Quality Assurance Agency, 327–8

Rappa, M., 110
retention (distance learners), 19, 29, 30–1, 60, 135–6, 253–5, 349, 425
blended learning, 232
causes of achievement disparity, 255
enabling retention online, approaches to, 135–6, 254
Icarus simulation tool, 193
innovations in promoting retention, 135, 257–8, 261
MPAcc programme, 193
online education, 232
open universities, 30
OU, 370–2
predicting student success and increasing student retention (project), **370–3**, 377
recommendations for improving retention, 136, 182, 255, 274–5
retention/persistence distinction, 253
social isolation and, 184
student engagement, 253–4, 274
students' personal factors and, 255, 274
VLEs, 255
*see also* dropout; persistence; retention: promoting academic engagement; retention: providing social integration/sense of belonging
retention: promoting academic engagement, 135–6, 254, 255–7
assessment and feedback, 254–5, 261–2, 274–5
discussion forum activities, 254, 256, 260, 261
information on last date of access and student self-tracking, 254, 256
online tutor guidance and feedback, 256–7
peer review activities, 254, 257, 260–1, 274, 275
UoL, study of retention at, 254–5, 257–63, **259, 260**
*see also* retention
retention: providing social integration/sense of belonging, 136, 254, 255, 275
embedding the student experience, 264
employability, 271–4

INDEX 445

enhanced digital provision: social media, 264–5
enhancing digital provision: student blog and My Digital project, 265–6
improving student satisfaction, 266–7
onboarding, 255, 263, 273, 275
pastoral support, 267, 275
promoting opportunities to the stakeholder community, 268
promoting well-being, 268–71
UoL, student induction and support case study, 263–74
*see also* retention
Robbins, L.: 1963 Robbins Report, 38
Roberts, S. and Hunter, D., 347
Rofe, J. Simon, 35–48
  IR Model of Intellectual Reflection, 44–5
Rowland, F. and Rubbert, I., 346
Rowntree, Derek, 8
Russell, Thomas, 7
Rust, C., 394
Rutherford, Ernest, 430n11
RVC (Royal Veterinary College, UK), **176**, **182-3**, 197, 198

Sabherwal, S., **288–9**, 290
Sadler, D., 157
Saki, 168
Salmon, Gilly, 38
  'e-tivities', 45, 199
  Five-Stage Model, 45
San Diego, Jonathan, **373–7**
Scanlon, E., 155, 392
SCONUL (Society of College, National and University Libraries), 326
  2001 'Access for distance learners: Report of the SCONUL task force', 327
Scotland, 27
  University of Edinburgh, 247
Sheehan, Tony, **373–7**
Sherman, Sarah, 195–210, 227–52
Siemens, George, 411
Silva-Fletcher, Ayona, 167–86
Simmons, Howard, 328
Simpson, Ormond, 232, **370–3**
Sims, J., 100–1
Singh, G. and Hardaker, G., 100
Skype, 24, 198, 228, 343
smart devices, 26, 45
Snapchat, 171
SOAS (School of Oriental and African Studies, UK), 197, 198, 199, **305**
social learning
  definition, 169
  group learning, 169
  LMSs, 169, 170
  social learning and learning strategies, 174–5
  social learning theory, 169, 171, 174–5
  social media, 41
  *see also* interactive social learning
social media, 26, 54
  digital education and, 27
  enhanced digital provision, 264–5
  social learning, 41

software, 69, 110–11, 170, 228
  access to, 29
  disabilities, students with, 228, 237
  grading software, 203–4
  open source software, 293, 296
  plagiarism detection software, 175
  software markets, 111
Solomou, G., 338
South Africa, 29
Speight, S., 83
Sri Lanka, **176**, 219, 270
Stacey, P., 313
Stake, R., 397
stakeholders
  distance education stakeholders, 103, 427
  future of distance education, 427, 428
  Global Blindness MOOC, 280, **281**, 283–4, 290
  inclusion and, 242–4
  needs and expectations of distance education stakeholders, 96, 103–10
  retention and promoting opportunities to the stakeholder community, 268
  Stakeholder Salience Model, *104*, 104–5
  stakeholder salience theory, 103–4
  types of, 104–5
  UoL, 103, **106–10**
Stefani, L., 384
Stevenson, J., 233
Stiasny, Mary, xxiii–xxix, 95–117
Stitz, T. and Blundell, S., 333, 338–9
Stone, C., 31
Street, H., 30–1
Stroud, Joanna, 195–210
students, *see* disabilities, students with; distance learners
Sutherland, G., 229
synchronous/asynchronous interaction, 2, 6, 26, 36, 78
  access to education, 236
  'asynchronous contact', 142
  asynchronous online forum: key features to maximise learner participation in, 171, **172–3**
  course design, 141–2, 144, 164
  digital assessment: synchronous tools, 198
  interactive social learning, 171
  MOOCs, 309
  online library: synchronous interaction, 341, 342, 343, 346
Szilard, Leo, 430n11

Tait, Alan, 3, 30, 211–26
Tang, Y. and Tseng, H., 322
technologies
  access to education and, 26, 230, 235, 425–6
  assessment and, 226
  course design, 164
  digital learning, 37, 45
  disabilities, students with, 232, 235, 236–7
  disruptive technologies, xxvii, 116
  distance education and, 4, 5, 6, 22, 26, 32, 45, 100, 112, 410, 425, 429
  distance learners and, 26–9
  education, technologies used in, 5, 311

educational technology, 26, 373, 375
marketing digital education, 58–9, 60
mobile and social networking technologies, 167, 171, 173
multimedia technologies, 167, 171
*see also* assistive technologies; gaming; internet; mobile phone/devices; virtual reality
Terras, K., 242
tertiary education, 97, 119, 120, 230, 238
Third Wave Digital, 60
Thomas, Jonathan, 373
Thuranira-McKeever, Christine, 167–86, **373–7**
Timmers, P., 110
Tinto, V., 182, 254
TNE (transnational education), xxvi
regulation, xxix, 108
traditional education (face-to-face)
advantages, 6
assessments, 195, 197, 199, 207
disadvantages, 22
as dominant paradigm, 22
face to face interaction, 4, 22
UK, 409
US, 409
*see also* distance/traditional education comparison
transactional distance, 4, 299
Tury, Sandra, 320–52
Twitter, 171

UCL (University College London, UK)
accessibility materials, 246
digital assessment, 187, 197, 199
OER, 301, 303, **304**, **305**
teaching translation through editing Wikipedia, **305**
Udacity, 111, 312, 411
UDL (Universal Design for Learning), 164, 180, 232, 245
UDL, Ministry of Education, New Zealand, 247
UK (United Kingdom)
1998 Human Rights Act, 238
2010 Equality Act, 238–9
2019 'University Mental Health Charter', 269
2019 Department for Education: 'Realising the Potential of Technology in Education', 410
access to education, 426
COVID-19 pandemic, 414, 422
CRPD, 238
disabilities, students with, 238–9
HE, 409, 410, 426
online library, 327, 346–7
use of technology-enhanced learning in HE, 410
Ukraine, 414
UN (United Nations)
CRPD (UN Convention on the Rights of Persons with Disabilities), 238
SDGs (Sustainable Development Goals), 35, 136, 277, 299, 408, 429

UNESCO (UN Educational, Scientific and Cultural Organization), 295
University of Birmingham (UK), 79
University of Central Lancashire (UK), 72
University of Southampton (UK), 71
University of Sunderland (UK), 346–7
Unwin, L., 328
UoL (University of London, UK)
1849 Supplemental Charter, xxiv
accessibility, xxvii, 229, 230
assessments, xxv, 20, 107, 211–12, 412
blended learning, xxvi, xxviii, 100
challenges, xxvii–xxviii
Chatbot, 265–6
competition, xxvii–xxviii
COVID-19 pandemic, xxvi, 212, 412
cross subsidy, xxvii, 98
customer mindset, 53
Digital Educator Project, 361, **373–7**, 377
disabilities, students with, 135, 230, 231, 232, 238, 246, 247
distance education, xxiii, 59, 95
distance education, history of, xxiii–xxviii, xxix, 3, 6, 8, 20
distance education: strategic models, 102–3, **106–10**, 111, **114–15**
Distance Education Resource Centre, xxxi
drivers underlying the adoption of distance learning, 98
educational decolonisation, xxv
employability, 71–2, 73, 74, 78, 271–4
'external degree' model, 20, 41
feedback, 161
female students in, 229, 232
HE, xxiv–xxvii, 41
history of, xxiv–xxv, 41, 99, 141, 430n2
inclusion, 229, 232, 243
Inclusive Practice Panel, 230, 246
Inclusive Practice Policy, 243
Independent Guided Study Scheme, xxvi
'learn.london', 266
marketing digital education, 53, 58, 59, 60
Nigeria and, 124–9
OER, 301, 301–3, **304–8**
online education, xxiii, xxvi, xxviii
online library, 137, 321, 323, 324, 328–9, 336, 337, 338, 347
online library: 'Ask-A-Librarian' live chat service, 324, 341–2
openness, 8
partner institutions, xxv, xxxii–xxxiii, 53, 58, 59, 102–3, 111
Postgraduate Certificate in Learning and Teaching in Higher Education, 257–8
prices, 115
regulation role, **106–10**
reputation, xxviii, 124
research and conferences, xxxii–xxxiii, 3, 307
retention study, 254–5, 257–63, **259**, **260**
RTCs (Recognised Teaching Centres), xxvi, 161
Senate House Library, 337
stakeholders, 103, **106–10**
Student Experience Steering Group, 270
Student Experience Team, 125, 264, 265

INDEX  **447**

student induction and support case study, 263–74
teaching/examination historical dichotomy, xxiii, xxiv
technology, xxviii
UoL colleges, 53, 59
UoL Federation, xxiii, xxv, xxvii, xxxi, 134, 195
*UoL Graduation Alumni*, 193
as wartime university, xxiv
well-being promotion, 268–71
widening participation, 304
worldwide provision, xxiii, xxv–xxvi, 3, 327, 412
*see also* CODE; online assessment: UoL case study
US (United States)
  1990 Disabilities Act, 238
  ACRL (Association of College and Research Libraries, US), 326–7, 345
  blended learning, 409
  disabilities, students with, 333
  HE, 409
  Kansas State University Library, 337, 338
  online library, 326–7, 337, 338–9, 345
  Southern University, New Orleans, 413
  University of Maine, 68–9
UUK (Universities UK), 39

Verdinelli, S. and Kutner, D., 232
virtual reality, 167, 171, 429
  virtual classroom, 168, 182
  *see also* VLEs
VLEs (virtual learning environments), 167, 184, 266, 410
  access to education, 236
  course design, 142–3, 144, 146–7, 156, 159, 164

digital assessment, 197, 198, 202
disabilities, students with, 237, 246
evaluation, 392, 400, 403
future of distance education, 416, 417, 418, 420
online assessment: UoL case study, 213
retention, 255
Voce, Julie, 19–34

*Wall Street Journal*, 54
WCAG (Web Content Accessibility Guidelines), 237, 240–1, 333, 338, 339
Web 2.0, 5–6
Web 3.0, 429
WEF (World Economic Forum), 69–70
Weller, M., 31
Wellman, B., 182
Wells, H. G., xxvi
Westheimer, J. and Kahne, J., 181
WhatsApp, 157, 171, 228
widening participation, 16, 26, 27, 28–9, 31, 295, 410
  Global Blindness MOOC, 290
  UoL, 304
WIL (work-integrated learning), 68, 78–9
Winter, David, 64–94
Wong, Janet, 364
Woodman, Ruth, 370

Yorke, M., 66
YouTube, 297, 304

Zawacki-Richter, O. and Anderson, T., 31
Zoom, 24, 387